A HISTORY OF
PASTORAL CARE
IN AMERICA

A HISTORY OF PASTORAL CARE IN AMERICA

From Salvation to Self-Realization

E. Brooks Holifield

Abingdon Press
Nashville

A History of Pastoral Care in America:
From Salvation to Self-Realization

Copyright © 1983 by Abingdon Press

Second Printing 1984

All rights reserved.

Library of Congress Cataloging in Publication Data

HOLIFIELD, E. BROOKS.
  A history of pastoral care in America.
  Includes bibliographical references and index.
  1. Pastoral theology—United States—History.
  2. Pastoral counseling—United States—History.
  3. Pastoral theology—Protestant churches—History.
  4. Protestant churches—Doctrinal and controversial works.
  I. Title.
  BV4006.H64   1983   253'.0973   83-3730

ISBN 0-687-17249-7

MANUFACTURED BY THE PARTHENON PRESS AT
NASHVILLE, TENNESSEE, UNITED STATES OF AMERICA

To Rex, Wenonah, and Kerrie

and

In memory of Susie
and my father

Contents

A HISTORY OF
PASTORAL CARE
IN AMERICA

Preface

This book, on one level, is a history of Protestant pastoral counseling in America. It examines the "private" side of clerical activity as a mirror to the broader pattern of change in American religion. On another level, it is a history of the relationships among theology, psychology, and the changing social and economic patterns in America throughout the past four centuries. On still another, the book is a history, in narrow scope, of Protestant ministry in the United States. It looks at one continuing clerical activity—one normally hidden from public view—and attempts to use it as a measure of change within the Protestant mainstream. The thesis of the book is contained in the subtitle: A long look at the private conversations of pastors and their parishioners reveals the movement from an ideal of otherworldly salvation to an implicit ethic of self-realization in American Protestantism.

I do not presume to discuss the diverse ways in which ordinary Protestant pastors have actually counseled men and women in distress. I have, rather, examined a changing ideal. I have looked at the ways casuists, pastoral theologians, and pastoral psychologists (the terminology shifts from era to era) have advised the clergy to conduct themselves in their private interchange with parishioners seeking counsel. In uncovering that history, I was impressed by the way it reveals changing attitudes toward the "self" in American religion. The story proceeds from an ideal of self-denial to one of self-love, from self-love to self-culture, from self-culture to self-mastery, from self-mastery to self-realization within a trustworthy culture, and finally to a later form of self-realization counterposed against cultural mores and social institutions. By following that movement toward an ideal of self-realization, one gains a better understanding of Protestantism's part in the formation of what Philip Rieff has called a therapeutic culture.

It has become common within Protestantism to distinguish between pastoral counseling and pastoral care. The latter term often designates the whole range of clerical activity aimed at guiding and sustaining a congregation; the former specifies a more narrowly defined relationship between a pastor and a person in need. I find such a distinction useful, and though I believe a history of pastoral counseling can illumine changing notions of care, I do not claim to have written a comprehensive history of pastoral care in Protestantism. I should add, however, that the modern "pastoral care" movement was, for a brief period, singularly preoccupied with counseling. That preoccupation has now diminished.

My narrative comes to its conclusion at the end of the 1960s. More than one of the manuscript's early readers have expressed dissatisfaction with my decision to stop at that point, but I have resisted their admonitions. I would argue that my primary contribution as a historian (if it turns out to be a contribution) is to interpret the background out of which the more recent discussions have emerged. And I would also argue that the end of that decade did mark a turning point; the subsequent period saw an unfolding and development of positions adumbrated at that time—particularly the positions discussed in the final chapter and concluding statement. Hence the terminus at the close of the 1960s has, I think a certain appropriateness.

A grant from the National Endowment for the Humanities in 1976–1977 provided an opportunity to begin my research. For that financial support I am grateful, as I am also for aid of other kinds from friends and colleagues. The editors of *Theology Today* permitted me to use, in chapter 6, a portion of my article on "Ethical Assumptions of Clinical Pastoral Education" (*Theology Today* 36 [April 1979]: 30-44). Lee Rotch typed most of the manuscript (several times). Dean Jim Waits provided time for writing and reflection. The librarians at the Pitts Theological Library at Emory University provided continuing assistance. And my colleagues and students at Emory University's Candler School of Theology offered both support and criticism. I am especially grateful to Rod Hunter, Chuck Gerkin, Steve Tipton, Gene Tucker, John Patton, Linda Schearing, David Hackett, Valarie Morris, and my colleagues in the Historical Studies Department of Emory's Division of Religion. I did not always follow their advice, but I invariably profited from it.

And I am grateful, above all, to Vicky, Erin, and Ryan.

1

Theological Traditions

The Christian clergy have been a talkative lot. But for almost twenty centuries they have spent more time listening to people than preaching to them, and from the beginning they discovered that it was hard to listen, but even harder to respond appropriately to what they were hearing. As early as the second century, they began to write letters and treatises instructing one another about spiritual direction and consolation, repentance and discipline, grief and growth. They designated their task as the "cure of souls," and so voluminous were their prescriptions that by the seventeenth century it was difficult to find an original cure for a wounded spirit. In 1647 an English clergyman, Thomas Fuller, published his suggestions about *The Cause and Cure of a Wounded Conscience*. As if to apologize for adding yet another book to overcrowded clerical libraries, he recorded an imaginary dialogue between an older sage physician of the soul and a theological student who rebuked his mentor for his lack of originality: "But, Sir, I expected some rare inventions from you, for curing wounded consciences: whereas all your receipts hitherto are old, stale, usuall, common, and ordinary; there is nothing new in any of them."[1] During the next three centuries, an expanding company of ministers, who came eventually to be known as pastoral theologians, would spend their lives in search of "receipts" with something new in them. And nowhere would they pursue that quest more assiduously than in America.

They brought to their task conflicting traditions, clashing temperaments, disparate methods of "pastoral conversation," and differing views of theology. Indeed, to trace the changing styles of "pastoral care" in America is to tell a story of transformations in theology, psychology, and society. To overhear the pastors as they offer private counsel is to learn something about the history of the ministry as a social institution. And if one listens throughout a period of three centuries, one can trace a massive shift in clerical consciousness—a transition from salvation to self-fulfillment—which reveals some of the forces that helped to ensure "the triumph of the therapeutic" in American culture.[2]

In the beginning was theology. However much the pastoral theologians of every era have drawn upon prevailing psychological wisdom, or adapted themselves to prevailing social conventions, or rebelled against them, they have always understood themselves to be theologians. And the theological issues that divided them in the past have continually reappeared in new guises in each period of pastoral care, from the second century to the twentieth. Each of the four main patterns of Christian pastoral care in early America—Roman Catholic, Lutheran, Anglican, Reformed—reflected a distinctive theological heritage, though all shared some common assumptions. The years have dulled some of the confessional differences, but the older debates, like the shared assumptions, have never fully disappeared. We begin, then, with theology, with notions of sin and spiritual development that have, in one form or another, stood in the background of three centuries of pastoral care in America.

16

Sin

By the second century, the church had developed
standard methods of private guidance and public penance.
By the sixth, Celtic writers in Ireland were producing a
flow of Penitential Books that would alter the tone and
method of both penance and guidance. The twelfth century
saw the full development of a sacramental theory of
priestly absolution, and by 1215 the Fourth Lateran
Council declared it necessary that every adult confess at
least once a year to the local priest. The Catholic moral
theologians of the sixteenth century completed the process
by elaborating a complex body of *casuistry*—the application of general principles to particular cases—which
promised to solve every spiritual dilemma that anyone
could imagine. And that entire history then found
expression in America in the labors of parish priests and
missionaries, from Florida to California.[3]

The Protestant Reformers rejected much of that Roman
tradition, but they developed their own traditional
patterns. The American Puritans were Reformed theologians whose "answering methods" echoed with the
accents of Calvinist piety and theology. The German
Lutheran pastors whose methods of spiritual care prevailed in early American Lutheranism were Pietists who
bore the imprint of the introspective theology taught at the
University of Halle in Germany in the seventeenth and
eighteenth centuries. And the moderate Anglicans who
occupied most of the southern churches in the colonies
exemplified a form of ministerial practice that had
gradually developed after 1534 to fit the emerging parish
system in England. Tradition, written and unwritten,
helped define the diversity in the cure of souls.

In all four traditions the clerical counselors envisioned
the cure of souls primarily as a remedy for sin. Despite the
vast scope of pastoral counsel, which could vary in its
concerns from the safety of the state to the scruples of the
tidy conscience, the aim was always to allay the doubts
resulting from sinfulness, or to temper the passions

17

disordered by sinfulness, or to correct the vision clouded by sinfulness. The aim was to overcome sinful temptations and undermine sinful resolves, to arouse the conscience against sin and to calm anxieties about sin. But though convinced that sin was the problem, the clergy could reach no unanimous conclusions as to an appropriate remedy, for they shared no consensus as to the nature of sin. This absence of theological consensus was manifested in the diversity of their methods of counsel.

The Roman Catholic clergy believed, in accord with the canons of the Council of Trent (1545–1563), that sin was both an inherited condition and a range of specifiable concrete acts, both a status and a series of transgressions. But since baptism, in their view, had removed the "original sin" and its guilt, the main task of the spiritual physician was to remedy the "actual" sins committed when the will freely consented to an inward inclination toward evil. For purposes of spiritual care, the Catholic clergy defined *sins* as discrete acts of transgression. The theologians enumerated the transgressions and classified them: some were sins of commission, others of omission; some were formal—deliberate violations of the divine law—while others, merely material, were either involuntary or otherwise excusable; some were mortal, separating the sinner from God's grace, while others, merely venial, were not so drastic in their results.[4]

Of course, to concentrate pastoral attention on actual sins was not to equate transgression only with public, visible acts. *The Catechism of the Council of Trent,* completed in 1564 to "instruct pastors and such as have the care of souls," cautioned that sins of desire or sins "buried in the darkest secrecy" often inflicted the deepest wounds on the soul. But even a secret evil was an act of consent, a movement across a forbidden boundary, a violation of a natural or revealed law. For the spiritual counselor, convinced that baptism had removed the stain of original sin, the sins that mattered were transgressions.[5]

To eradicate the evil, the Roman Catholic spiritual physicians had at their disposal the sacraments of the

Church, including the power to judge sins, forgive them, and prescribe salutary penalties. The process required that each penitent give a detailed accounting of morally sinful transgressions. When the Council of Trent published its manual for pastors, it insisted that Christians reveal to the priest "each and every" mortal sin. "To confess our sins," said the commission that prepared the catechism, "we must recollect them." Only after that recitation of sins—by a parishioner who evidenced a spirit of contrition, candor, and acts of satisfaction—could the priest offer comfort with the formula of forgiveness: *Ego absolve te* ("I absolve thee").[6]

Since the physician of the soul conceived of sin primarily as transgression, each act, each intention, each circumstance assumed special importance, and European Catholic theologians produced one manual after another for confessors who sought the latest methods for evoking detailed confessions and selecting the proper penalties from a complicated catalog of options. Those methods prevailed even in the provinces and the wildernesses of America. Jesuit missionaries wrote of their efforts to explain the intricacies of penance to the Hurons who knelt contritely and declared their sins one after the other, while English priests in Maryland wrote of repeated, often futile "counsel" with their people. Absolution was no easy matter—for either the penitent or the priest.[7]

When Martin Luther, in 1520, published his criticisms of Roman Catholic pastoral care, he acknowledged "some truth" in the teaching that a contrite heart could be "attained by the enumeration and contemplation" of sins, but he had already begun to think less about particular sins and more about sin as a condition of faithlessness that could find expression even in praiseworthy acts. Sin, for Luther, was an incapacity to trust God; it was exhibited most clearly in self-righteousness—the good deed that was done in an effort to secure existence, the brittle pride that protected a false sense of security, the anxious and self-serving presumption that defended a fragile self-glorification, the frightened and irresistible impulse to

19

trust "created things" rather than the Creator of all things. The serious "sin" with which the pastor dealt, then, was self-centered faithlessness, not particular transgressions.[8]

Luther believed Christians should acknowledge their sinfulness. The Lutheran Pietists of the seventeenth century believed they should feel it. Convinced that an emotional experience of "rebirth" marked the true Christian, the Pietists subtly revised Luther's notion of sin by including ethical selfishness and spiritual "deadness," or "dryness," as part of their definition of *faithlessness*. Pietists in America—such as Henry Melchior Muhlenberg in Pennsylvania—practiced a method of "soul analysis," taught at the University of Halle, which uncovered "signs" of sinfulness in feelings of spiritual deadness.[9]

While the pietistic Lutherans, like the Roman Catholics, encouraged confession, public and private, they sought not the enumeration of sins, but the feeling of repentance, especially in the communal confession at the Lord's Supper, before which they made an effort to speak with each communicant. In those and other private conversations with the sick or dying, the melancholy or indifferent, and the anxious or inquiring—they typically began by inducing a feeling of despair, with the goal of evoking a change of heart, an alteration of the emotions, that could issue in rebirth. Muhlenberg used the method often, as when, for instance, he counseled a woman suffering from consumption. He started the conversation by urging her "to reveal the inward condition and state of her heart." Had she ever felt worthless? lost? faint? spiritually withered? powerless? dark? Such feelings of despair, he thought, could serve as a sign that the Word had begun to live in her heart. Only after he had posed the standard questions about her feelings of despair did Muhlenberg ask her if she had "experienced" Jesus as life, joy, and bliss. "Fairly so of late," she answered, "but not as completely" as she wished.[10] By leading her through a series of negative feelings before he asked about her faith, Muhlenberg exhibited in practice the Lutheran Pietist notion of sinfulness. To find signs of despair was to recognize the

20

potential for health, and to induce the emotional apprehension of an arid faithlessness was to take the first step in the cure of the soul.

The mainline clergy of the Church of England were not, on the whole, quite so interested in feelings. Neither did they have much interest in a precise analysis of sin. The Thirty-Nine Articles of Religion (1563)—the main Anglican creedal statement—asserted, with the Protestant Reformers, that the infection of original sin remained within every person, including every Christian, and that even noble deeds were sinful if they did not spring from the gift of a true and lively faith. With such assertions Luther would have fully agreed. But the Articles tempered that depiction of sin by emphasizing the possibility of gradual growth in a soul enabled by "prevenient grace" to "have a good will," and by accenting the usefulness of "good works" as evidence of saving faith. Anglican theologians therefore developed some conflicting notions of sinfulness. The classical English writers, especially Richard Hooker, believed that sin was a condition of separation from a holy Creator. Such seventeenth-century successors as Jeremy Taylor introduced a notion of "holy living," in which once again, sin became primarily transgression.[11]

In practice, though, both the earlier and the later Anglican writers, at least those who felt obliged to defend the English parish system against Roman Catholic and Puritan critics, moved toward another understanding of sin. They bemoaned a disruption of cosmic order that could result in the disobedience of disorderly souls to the rightful authorities in Church and State. Sin, for them, was a willful breaching of civil peace and religious unity. The threat—and the memory—of public chaos pushed the Anglicans toward a notion of sin as "disorder."[12]

This image of sin helped define Anglican pastoral care. The distinguishing mark of such works as George Herbert's *Country Parson* (1652), Gilbert Burnet's *Discourse of the Pastoral Care* (1713), and Edmund Gibson's *Directions Given to the Clergy* (1724) was their assumption that pastoral responsibility extended to every detail of life within the geographical parish. "The Country Parson," wrote Herbert, "desires to be all to his parish, and not only a pastor, but a lawyer also, and a physician." The ideal pastor exhorted, judged, comforted, and catechized to ensure that "all things be done decently and in order," including the seemingly trivial things of ordinary social life. If sin was disorder, its remedy required a comprehensive ordering of public and private life. The "casuistry" of Anglicanism—its modifying of general rules to fit particular "cases of conscience"—provided not only guidelines for the pastor in private confession but also examples of answers to every kind of personal and social question. The confessional, even when modified to accord with Anglican theology, lost its primacy in pastoral care. In a disordered world, the pastor's "place" was every place within the parish.[13]

The fourth tradition of theology and pastoral care—the Reformed tradition—drew upon still another conception of sinfulness. The Reformed patriarch John Calvin had agreed with Luther that unfaithfulness was the "root" of the fall into sin, but he had added that "disobedience was the beginning of the fall."[14] By the seventeenth century, the theologians who disseminated Reformed ideas within the Church of England were preaching that disobedience to God—or idolatry, as they often preferred to say—was the heart of sinfulness. William Perkins expressed the idea positively when he insisted that "the ground of the nine later commandments is the first. 'Thou shalt have no other gods before me.'" Richard Sibbes expressed the same idea in its negative form: "The breach of the First Commandment is the ground of the breach of all the rest."[15] Idolatry was the refusal to observe God's law, and the Puritan theologians, especially, believed that the Bible minutely defined unlawful acts—from murder to sabbath-breaking—thus specifying, as it were, the content of the disobedience. But on a deeper level, idolatry was a determination of the heart, a misdirected consent to one or another evil master, whether a Satanic power or an inordinate passion. Any act could be sinful if it flowed from a rebellious will.

22

The theme of idolatry informed the Puritan pastoral ideal. The Puritan pastor, especially in the seventeenth century, became a specialist in the cure of the idolatrous heart. He analyzed motives, evaluated feelings, sought to discern hidden intentions and to direct inward consent. He therefore had to master the "varieties of grave experienced counsels, which may serve as precious remedies (wisely applied) for many evils, and holy directions for the good government of the Christian life." To learn those remedies and directions, the ministers read "case divinity"—or Protestant casuistry—which provided examples and rules for "untying and explaining diligently Cases of Conscience (as they are called)."[16]

The turn to casuistry among the Puritans occurred when it was becoming clear to almost everyone that Queen Elizabeth had succeeded in smashing the crusade to transform the Church of England according to Continental Reformed ideals. Puritan Reformers' failure at parliamentary maneuvering convinced some pastors that reform must begin in the local congregations; indeed, in the hearts of individual English Christians. By 1630, one Puritan minister, William Ames, had acknowledged that the single-minded effort of the Reformers to "purge the floors of the Church" had allowed a "grievous spiritual plague" to overwhelm parish congregations. Therefore he and others resolved to concentrate on pulpit oratory and innovative pastoral methods for diagnosing spiritual pride and temptation.[17] Without abandoning their aspirations to be architects of a new ecclesiastical order, the frustrated Reformers labored increasingly as physicians of the soul. In part, then, the turn to casuistry reflected the temporary failure of reform and the desire to recoup any losses by moving to the deeper plane of personal change.

The interest in casuistry also resulted, however, from a theological problem. When John Calvin claimed that God, through an eternal decree, foreordained eternal life for some and eternal damnation for others, he believed himself to be propounding a comforting doctrine. It removed the anxiety inherent in the struggle to earn salvation through meritorious activity. Calvin intended to direct the believer's attention away from introspective self-concern and toward Jesus Christ; to provide no occasion for constant spiritual pulse-taking. What Calvin experienced as liberation, though, could appear as terrifying ambiguity, and it frightened even Christians who accepted his doctrines. They yearned to be "undoubtedly sure" of their salvation.[18]

For both political and theological reasons, therefore, Puritan casuists turned their attention to the intricacies of inward piety. Their writings were essays in the doctrine of assurance, explaining how indifferent or anxious souls could obtain a "pacified conscience" as a sign of assurance that they would be saved. These English Puritan writers also were replying to Roman Catholic critics who complained that their reliance on "faith alone" produced a moral vacuum; so their casuistic writings, like those of their opponents within the Church of England, expatiated on the ethics of government and economics as well as on the imperative of private piety and morality. But the Puritan casuists became especially useful for ministers who wished to teach their people how to obtain "sound evidence of a good estate."[19]

The chief theoretician of the new Puritan pastoral care was William Perkins, a Cambridge divine who himself reportedly "dyed in the conflict of a troubled conscience."[20] Perkins's *Discourse of Conscience* in 1596 marked the emergence of the new interest. Three years later Richard Greenham, a Puritan preacher at Dry Drayton near Cambridge, published his *Godly Instructions for the Due Examination and Direction of All Men*, which was followed by other detailed handbooks by Perkins and William Ames. By 1656, when Richard Baxter exhorted the clergy to devote more of their time to personal conversations, he could assume the existence of a comprehensive literature teaching the pastor how to converse with individuals about spiritual matters. By that time, in fact, there were complaints that it was almost impossible to find a new remedy for wounded consciences. Everything had already been said.[21]

A typology that isolates four distinctive motifs in Christian views of sin and pastoral care can do little more than mark the flexible boundaries between traditions that obviously had much in common. The four traditions—Roman Catholic, Lutheran, moderate Anglican, and Puritan—agreed in stating the problem, but differed in defining it and specifying methods for alleviating it. The theological differences were often subtle—matters of emphasis and nuance—but they clearly suggested differences in pastoral practice. The four patterns of religious language, which defined sin as status and transgression, as faithlessness, as disorder, and as idolatrous disobedience, had manifest parallels in four distinct understandings of the cure of souls.

Spiritual Development

Tradition was not merely a source of division. The four dominant traditions also brought to American religion the common theme of spiritual development. Whatever their views of sin and their pastoral techniques, the pastors agreed that the cure of souls was a process marked by development through specifiable stages or levels. A pastor's task was to help the pilgrim ascend through a hierarchy of stages—from dull and insensitive depravity to holiness. During the Reformation, Martin Luther had condemned Catholic developmental language; he had wished to describe the Christian as both a thoroughgoing sinner and a forgiven saint. By the seventeenth century, though, even Lutheran Pietists were attracted to the image of spiritual growth. Hence American pastors agreed that to designate the problem as one of "sin" was not to despair of a solution. If sin were one side of the pastoral equation, salvation was the other, and salvation was obtained through a process of development. The process was defined differently in each of the four traditions, and the differing definitions occasioned many of the theological debates of

25

the seventeenth and early eighteenth centuries. In retrospect, though, the agreement seems as important as the disagreement. Within American churches, the cure of souls was almost universally defined by the metaphor of spiritual growth.

Roman Catholic theologians depicted the Christian pilgrimage as a gradual development that was approximate to "salvation in ascending stages." In adults the Catholic writers discerned a movement initiated by the gentle promptings of divine grace, which led from recognition of sin to faithful belief, from belief to hope, from hope to love for God, from love for God to penitence, from penitence to the forgiveness of sins and inward renewal, and from renewal to a richer life in faith, "advancing from virtue to virtue," increasing in faith, hope, and charity. And from beginning to end, the sacraments nurtured the process and rectified lapses.[22]

The metaphors of development persisted even among the Protestant Reformers who abandoned or reinterpreted the older medieval theology. Luther rejected the imagery, but Lutheran Pietists were eventually describing a change from a state of nature to a state of grace, accompanied by inner struggle and leading to growth in faith, wisdom, and piety. They spoke of a rebirth that encompassed both faith and the gift of a "new nature"; and then they spoke further of the process of striving for perfection.[23] The Anglicans included in their Thirty-Nine Articles the description of a transition in which faith was strengthened and grace "increased."[24] Unlike Luther, both the Pietists and the Anglican Reformers emphasized a process that produced inward change in the faithful. They hoped for increasing control over such passions as anger, lust, pride, and fear, and for expanding capacities of love and compassion. For them the Christian life moved through stages of development toward a higher goal of holiness.

The Puritan theologians, especially, defined the process in great detail. In the sixteenth century, William Perkins outlined ten levels of religious growth. The pilgrim's progress often began, he said, with some outward or

26

inward "cross" that exposed the self's insufficiency. That burden usually led to a second stage, an awareness of "law"—the rigor of God's demand. Such an awareness opened the way to a third and higher level: a recognition of the power of sin. And the result of that transition was yet a fourth stage, defined as a "legal fear" or an intimation that damnation was possible.

The first four levels were but "works of preparation," and only a special gift of grace could lead to the fifth stage of religious growth—namely, a serious consideration of the promise of salvation. Contemplation of that promise opened the way to the sixth level, in which the convert began to feel the first "sparks of faith" that accompanied divine pardon. The budding faith led, however, to a dangerous seventh level: a travail of doubt and despair. At that level it was particularly important for the minister to be able to recognize such despair as a normal prelude to "assurance," which constituted the eighth level of the Christian ascent. And the able counselor, trained in casuistry, could have predicted further struggles during a ninth stage, a period of "evangelical sorrow" in which sin became grievous to the saintly person purely because it was sin. In the final stage, though, God provided the Christian with the grace of heartfelt, voluntary, joyful obedience. But even then the process continued: The Puritan theologians liked to speak of "sanctification" as a process that goes on for a lifetime.[25]

Pious New Englanders, especially, wanted to learn how to map their progress, and the Puritan pastors became masters of introspection, cartographers of the inner life, adept at recognizing the signs of salvation. The classic works of early New England theology were essays in what a later generation would call the psychology of conversion. Thomas Shepard, a pastor in Cambridge, Massachusetts, exhibited the standard pattern of New England theology in his *Sound Believer: A Treatise of Evangelical Conversion*, when he tried to "mark out" the "Spirit's work in the conversion of a sinner" by explaining the measures and

27

degrees of conviction (the knowledge of sin), compunction (the "sense" of sin), humiliation, faith, pardon, reconciliation with God, and sanctification. In the Bay Colony, ministers expected their people to be able to describe their movement through the stages, and during the early seventeenth century, a public "relation" of conversion was a normal requirement for church membership.[26]

One Joseph Champney of Malden, Massachusetts, in his public narration of conversion, exhibited the self-knowledge that pastoral care was expected to produce. First, he said, had come his "conviction." The Lord had "discovered" his sin in his failure to honor his parents; he had rebelled against them and against God. Then came compunction and humiliation. Oppressed by his sense of unworthiness, he had yearned for annihilation. But Champney heard one of the ministers say that the Lord took delight in those who sought him while they were young, and he then began to consider the promise of salvation. He decided to "seek a part in God through Christ."

Champney could not, however, part with his lust and ease until God had "stirred" his heart with the initial sparks of faith, whereupon he became increasingly aware of his sinfulness. His "temptations" grew so strong that he despaired, until the Lord "visited" him with the assuring thought that God would save those who could not save themselves. The new awareness was "exceeding precious and sweet," yet it led to struggles: "I had more discovery of sin and temptations were strong against me." Champney thereupon decided that no others were so evil as he—but the Lord again helped him "to seek him," and a sermon soon "encouraged" him. That happy event led to still other discouragements, but Champney was finally able to say that he was "following after" the Lord.[27] William Perkins would have been pleased. Champney's experiences repeatedly illustrated the very stages that Perkins had elaborated so carefully.

Champney's doubts never disappeared, and his minister

would have worried if they had. The Puritan physicians of the soul believed that even the saints would be assaulted with doubt and temptations. The faithful struggled for assurance of salvation, but they knew—for their ministers had told them—that the assurance would be imperfect. Hence the process of dying and rising continued anew each day, and pastoral counsel could be required at any time.[28]

Denominational differences within the Reformed tradition could affect expectations about pastoral duties. Most Congregationalists wanted their pastors to be experts in the interpretation of inner spiritual experience; some Presbyterians were more interested in the pastor's capacities to evaluate the doctrinal beliefs and public behavior of parishioners. But in each denomination, the preacher had to know something about the intricacies of inwardness. By a process of minute psychological analysis, the pastors uncovered the subtle transitions within each level of a continuing ascent—the stages within stages and the distinctions within distinctions. They could map each turn of the soul as it traveled to the heavenly city, and they taught Joseph Champney and others like him to interpret the fears and temptations that stood in the way. In so doing, they helped to ensure that the images of spiritual growth and development would work themselves deeply into the language of American piety.

Theologians argued for years about the fine points of the progression, for almost every Christian group in America held to some such religious psychology. Even in the nineteenth century, Methodists and Presbyterians were still quarreling about the proper "order of salvation."[29] An expectation of religious growth, as well as a sensitivity to sin, marked the religious traditions that stood in the background of early American pastoral care.

My discussion of such themes as sin and spiritual growth could well be supplemented with additional doctrinal topics. One might point to differences, for example, in the doctrine of the Church: the Catholic doctrine of the Church as the body of Christ, an extension of the Incarnation, could be related to a notion of sacramental priesthood; the Lutheran conception of the Church as the Community of the Word could illumine early Lutheran pastoral activity; the Anglican sense of the Church as a comprehensive national congregation, with the power to decree rites and ceremonies, could clarify the liturgical dimensions of Anglican pastoral care; and the Reformed insistence on a disciplined community could lead into a discussion of the pastor's duty to admonish the wayward. Clearly, the range of theological differences and corresponding pastoral activities was more extensive than an introductory chapter can suggest. To enumerate pastoral tasks—spiritual guidance, preaching, consolation, admonition, counsel, marriage, confirmation, ethical judgment, and a host of others—would be to repeat the encyclopedic detail already available in John T. McNeill's *History of the Cure of Souls.* My purpose is more modest: to suggest a relationship between patterns of pastoral care and the two theological issues that would, with others, reappear in various forms in every period of American church history.

Though we have begun with theology, this is not to suggest that the history of pastoral activity corresponded simply to changing theological conceptions. It is the interweaving of theology with other fields of learning, such as psychology and ethics, and the interconnection of pastoral activity with changes in culture and society that reveal the complexity of the cure of souls in the mainstream of the American churches. Pastoral theology was never a self-contained intellectual system, but rather a complex of inherited ideas and images subject to continued modification in changing social and intellectual settings. The manuals that encoded the conventions of pastoral activity were never products merely of ecclesiastical tradition or scriptural injunction, but rather a reflection of both the churches' communal memory and the ministers' sensitivity to the surrounding society. The history of the pastoral care is, on the whole, a glance at the activities of an educated elite among the clergy, and even then, it is of necessity a simplification of an enormously complicated reality. Yet the story is revealing. The changing forms of private conversation offer a distinctive insight into the public contours of the Protestant mainstream, in a country that once considered itself the last great hope of Protestant ideals.

2

Counsel in a Hierarchical World

Throughout the first two decades of the seventeenth century, Mistress Joan Drake of Esher in Surrey, England, underwent agony of soul, in fear that she had sinned against the Holy Ghost and therefore faced certain damnation. A host of visiting ministers attempted to relieve her suffering by overpowering her arguments. All of them failed, some miserably. She once tried to hit one of England's best-known preachers with a piece of her bedstead while he was praying for her. But in 1618 Thomas Hooker became the rector of St. George's church in Esher, and he, fresh from the university with a "new answering method," soon elicited from Joan Drake an ecstatic testimony of religious conversion. The success enhanced his reputation. "Indeed," wrote one admirer, "he now had no superior, and scarce any equal, for the skill of treating a troubled soul."[1]

Thomas Hooker's conversations with Joan Drake inevitably mirrored the cultural and intellectual assumptions that most men and women in England and America accepted without serious question. They embodied an unspoken agreement between pastors and their parishioners about the nature of the self, the society, and the vast world beyond both. Hooker's labors occurred, in short, within a hierarchical world. Seventeenth-century pastors in England and its colonies carried into every pastoral conversation a shared agreement about the hierarchical ordering of reality. They lived within a hierarchical society, argued about the fine points of a hierarchical psychology, worshiped in churches that, even in New England, bore the marks of hierarchical organization, and believed fervently in a hierarchy of cosmic powers and principalities. Their world was one of levels, stages, ranks, and gradations. Gentlemen stood above commoners, men above women, saints above sinners, and angels and demons above earthly mortals; reason was higher than passion, revelation higher than reason, and the supernatural superior to the natural. In their theories about society, their thinking about the church, their commonplaces about the self, and their theology, the colonial physicians of the soul could agree that there was a continual interplay between the higher and lower levels of a hierarchy.

Joan Drake of Esher

When Thomas Hooker journeyed to Esher to assume the care of Joan Drake's soul, he brought to the task his era's most recent and innovative methods, and the narrative that relates his struggle with her despair provides a detailed case study of seventeenth-century pastoral care. Hooker sailed to New England during the Puritan migration of the 1630s, and there he achieved an almost legendary reputation for his "singular ability" to resolve difficult cases of conscience. In his Hartford, Connecticut, congregation he set aside one day each week for pastoral conversations with "all sorts of persons," who, it was said, eventually numbered in the thousands.[2] With his visitors, Hooker employed the techniques of pastoral care taught in the English universities and the American colonial colleges. Far more than he would have wished to acknowledge, though, he also carried into his conversations a body of cultural wisdom shared with Roman Catholic priests and Lutheran Pietists. To begin with the cure of Joan Drake's soul, therefore, is not only to glimpse a Puritan tradition that stimulated the first outpouring of American writings on the cure of souls but also to overhear a private conversation that echoed with the public conventions of seventeenth-century society.

Joan Drake was a woman of lovely brown complexion and jovial constitution who had submitted dutifully to the injunction of her parents that she marry the man of their choice. The unpleasant duty "stuck close unto her," and following the birth of her first child she began to suffer from headaches, stomach pains, sadness, and discontent. She became convinced that she was undone, damned, and without hope of mercy. When she began to deride the local ministers, her family decided she needed expert care, so they sought the services of John Dod, the rector of Fawsley, Northamptonshire. Famed for his pastoral skills, Dod had often invited the perplexed to his dinner table or paced with them across the floor of his parish church. Joan Drake's family felt that he was the "only fit person" to diagnose or treat her malady.[3]

Dod agreed to come, and one of Mrs. Drake's spiritual advisers recognized immediately that the family had chosen the right man when the devil compelled the woman to lock herself in her room the moment Dod appeared. Dod promptly settled in for a long siege against the devil: He moved into the manor house. But Joan Drake told him that she had no affection for her family and friends and no love for God, that she was therefore doomed, and that she would permit no prayers or fasts on her behalf. She also swung at Dod with a piece of her bedstead; she swallowed pins; and she attempted, ominously, to steal knives from the dinner table.

Dod made no progress until the day Mrs. Drake angrily told him to leave and he replied with matching anger. She felt immediate remorse and "opened her whole heart sincerely," so that Dod could easily identify and classify the "temptations" that were causing her despondency. She reported three such temptations: She had committed the unpardonable sin against the Holy Spirit, she knew herself to be damned, and she felt inclined to seek empty pleasure as compensation for her sorrow.

Having succeeded in persuading her to be specific, Dod immediately "fell flatly upon the businesse, how to beat down and convince her erroneous opinions wherein she was so settled." He used a passage from the Letter to the Hebrews to convince her that she could not have sinned against the Holy Spirit: Because she had never partaken of the Spirit, she was not "qualified" to commit the unpardonable sin. Mrs. Drake conceded the point but still claimed to know that she was destined for reprobation. He then used a passage from Deuteronomy to convince her that the devil, who alone would have revealed such distressing news to her, could not know the decree of God. Again she finally agreed with Dod's argument, but then fell back on her third temptation and insisted that her evil temper and inclinations revealed her true state. So Dod turned to the second chapter of Micah to persuade her to employ the "means of grace"—prayer, meditation, and reading and hearing the Word—with the hope that diligence might issue in salvation. But he had reached the limit of his success, for Mrs. Drake, while conceding the point, confessed that she had "no power" to follow his advice. And when Dod departed to give her time for reflection, Satan once again had his way. She suffered a relapse.[4]

The case was a challenge to the clergy, and visiting experts were determined to resolve it. Archbishop John Usher, the Primate of Ireland, spoke to her of Christ's mercy, but to no avail. John Forbes tried to dispute "toughly" with her, but he too made little headway. Dod returned and resumed his conversations, but with mixed results.

Finally, three years after he had entered the house and Joan Drake had first locked her door, Dod persuaded

Thomas Hooker to try his "new answering method."
Hooker brought no drastic innovation. He began in the
usual fashion, testing her spirit in order "to finde her
disposition," with no effort to "enforce any thing upon
her." He then introduced the usual array of scriptural
passages as the major premises of arguments designed
to convince Mrs. Drake of his interpretation of her case.

Hooker's arguments differed slightly from Dod's.
Rather than urging Joan Drake to exert herself or telling
her that she was not as evil as she thought, Hooker told
her that her very distress signified that she was chosen.
He turned her attention to biblical passages suggesting
that "hard trials" were "incident upon Gods best
beloved people." When she wondered why repentance
was necessary, Hooker assured her that God did not
invariably set such a condition and that, in any case, her
desire to repent was itself "a kind of repentance."
Hooker's strategy was to convince the woman that her
inner resistance and despairing thoughts could be
interpreted as signs of a broken heart. And since he
believed that the "breaking" of the heart was a prelude
to spiritual health, Hooker could advise his client that
her weakness was, in fact, her strength.

The advice proved to be salutary. After Hooker
departed, she gradually improved, and by the time Dod
returned she had already begun to feel the bliss in which
she ended her days. In recording *The Wonderful History,
Case, and Cure of Mrs. Joan Drake,* her friend Jasper
Heartwell noted that her final conversations were
"heavenly, rationall."[5]

Because the conversations that had brought her to the
point of conversion juxtaposed an insistent rationality and
a highly literal supernaturalism, the case of Joan Drake
exemplifies a style of pastoral care characteristic of the
age. In only one respect does it misrepresent seventeenth-
century Protestant practice. When Richard Baxter published *The Reformed Pastor* in 1656, he assured his readers
that the minister was the "counselor for their souls," just
as a lawyer was the counselor for their estates and a

physician for their bodies. But when Baxter urged ministers to expend their energies in pastoral nurture, he assumed that preaching was still the primary means of analyzing "cases of conscience." He assumed, as well, that regular catechetical exercises, with the systematic instruction of families, would reduce the need for such extended measures as it was necessary for Dod and Hooker to employ with Joan Drake. He believed, in short, that the word *pastoral* referred not merely to private conversation and counsel but also to public preaching, the administration of sacraments, guidance in public prayer, and work with families. The main part of pastoral care was teaching and guidance: The pastor opened the Word and works of God. Baxter imposed only one limiting restriction; he did insist that the conversion of infidels was not "pastoral" work, for the pastor was the overseer of persons already within the Church. His task was to glorify God through the traditional range of healing, sustaining, guiding, and reconciling activities that characterized work in a local congregation. Pastoral conversation was normally embedded in a corporate ideal; the context was the Church.[6]

It would be misleading, then, to identify seventeenth-century pastoral care with private counsel. But in their conversations with troubled persons, seventeenth-century pastors did reveal the convictions and attitudes that governed all their pastoral activity. Every private encounter embodied the assumptions taken for granted in the wider public domain. Thus all the colonial pastors would have agreed that the struggle for Joan Drake's soul was a conflict with supernatural powers. They would have described the entire range of their activities in hierarchical imagery: They were creatures dealing with higher forces. For us, Hooker's engagement with Joan Drake can serve as a mirror, showing a world only dimly remembered.

Hierarchy: Reason and the Supernatural

The hierarchical suppositions of the era bestowed on pastoral care a certain homogeneity that united Puritans,

37

Anglicans, Lutherans, and Roman Catholics. They envisioned reality as a vast chain of being that stretched from the heavenly throne of God to the lowest material object. At the summit of the Real was God—uncreated, unchanging, eternal. At the summit of the created order were the angelic hierarchies, numbering in the thousands of thousands, dwelling in celestial spheres, yet able also to appear on the earth, which did indeed seem bedeviled by fallen angels—demons and wicked spirits under the command of Satan, the highest of the fallen. A little lower than the angels stood men and women, sharing with the angels a rational nature, and with the world of lower animals the faculties of sensation, memory, and passion. Humanity occupied a middle position in the created order. Each person, in fact, was a little world, a microcosm, composed of all the higher and lower capacities and elements. The hierarchical ladder then ascended beneath the human realm to include the varied levels and classes of animals, the ranks of vegetative life (an elm was nobler than a weed), and the ranked orders of inanimate objects and elements (in which water was nobler than earth, air superior to water, and fire higher than air).[7]

The clergyman, a counselor responsible for the cure of souls, was charged with the duty of understanding and interpreting the upper level of the hierarchy—the activity of God and the acts of supernatural beings. Since the ministers and their parishioners occupied a lower level, however, they were forced to master the supernatural by using their mere natural capacities of logical analysis. While a special intuitive understanding—and thus a superhuman capacity—marks the angel, clergy and other mortals must derive their ideas laboriously through discursive reason, building one conclusion upon another. Natural human understanding required logic, even when it was assisted by a divine revelation in Scripture. In a hierarchical world, there was no choice but to attack even supernatural ills with the weaponry of natural logic.

The clergy were specialists in the supernatural. They envisioned the cure of souls as a combat with Satan and his hosts; their pastoral methods were weapons in a warfare to force the enemy from his stronghold.[8] They could assume command in that battle because they were stewards of mysteries that transcended the reach of most other people. Of course, they had to resolve a lot of mundane problems, as well. They instructed their people about oaths and vows, quarrels and vices, health and riches, clothing and recreation, alms and relief, and an array of other ethical and political questions. But the minister cared first for the conscience, a natural power with a unique capacity for giving "supernatural" testimony. Such a faculty was especially susceptible to subversion by the forces of evil, but it was also the route of access to the sacred. For that reason, the cure of souls always impinged on the region of the supernatural.[9]

The clergy were not the only specialists in supernatural mysteries. They complained of competition from "wizards and soothsayers" who used charms, love magic, fortune-telling, divination, and astrology to solve any problem. When pretenders claimed to have special access to supernatural beings, the clergy accused them of blas-phemy and of implying that "God hath provided a salve for every sore." Soothsayers taught the hopeful how to win wealth and influence people—and did so without requir-ing any radical transformation of the client. The clerical cure of souls was more rigorous: The preachers imposed a duty of self-scrutiny and launched into pastoral conversa-tions designed to break the defenses of the "stony heart" and overcome "secret unwillingness." The clergy viewed a venture into the supernatural as a risk and a threat that required the humbling of the self. They despised the soothsayers who made it seem easy.[10]

The preachers did not lack confidence in their own knowledge of the hierarchy of created powers, including "all the Powers of Darkness." Increase Mather's *Cases of Conscience*, written during the witchcraft hysteria in New England, explained in detail the behavior of witches and wizards. When Samuel Willard of Boston wrote his *Compleat Body of Divinity*, published posthumously in

39

1726, he even included descriptions of the angels who made their abode in the "third heaven." But despite the appearance of overweening self-confidence, the ministers accepted their charge with trembling, knowing that an error in judgment could mean eternal damnation for an unsuspecting soul. It was no casual matter to trifle with the supernatural. Thomas Clap, in New England, warned his fellow counselors that if any person for whom they had responsibility chanced to perish, the offending minister who had "the care and charge" of that soul would bear the blame, unless he could give "a fair account." For that reason, "supernatural Assistance" was necessary. Both courage and divine aid were needed to beat down "the Kingdom of Satan."[11]

When we dwell on the supernaturalist preconceptions of pastoral care in the seventeenth century, however, we investigate only one side of the relationship between reason and the supernatural. The acts of supernatural beings could pose seemingly insuperable problems, but the clergy believed firmly in rational methods of cure for spiritual maladies, and in their attempts to penetrate the mysteries of the higher realm, they explored the limits of a pastoral logic.

That logic fit into a certain hierarchical pattern explicit in the ministers' theology when they talked about the relationship between reason and revelation. On the first page of his *Compleat Body of Divinity*, Samuel Willard wrote that "the great thing which all rational and immortal creatures have to be mostly inquisitive about is happiness," and for Willard that quest for happiness presupposed two levels of theology: a "natural" level and a "revealed" one. Natural theology, grounded in a rational analysis of human experience and the created world, concerned itself with happiness; revealed theology, derived from the Bible, concerned itself with salvation. And just as salvation was the apex of happiness, so revelation was the fulfillment of reason. Revelation, then, was "above" reason, though never contrary to it.[12]

The theologians thought about the relationship between reason and revelation in three ways. First they felt that reason approximated revelation, carrying the mind step by step to the boundaries of the higher revealed truth. Reason found in the human spirit a yearning for an infinite good that would satisfy the soul; it recognized that no created reality provided lasting satisfaction; it could prove that a transcendent and infinite Good was real; it could then uncover the moral order—the law of human nature— to which one must conform in order to live in accord with the infinite Good. Reason could also show that human beings, as sinful creatures, did not naturally possess the good for which they yearned. Hence reason pointed beyond itself and beyond the natural order to a higher order revealed in Scripture. The theologians believed, second, that reason could validate revelation; that there were rational proofs for the truth and authority of biblical teachings. And third, reason interpreted revelation, showing again and again exactly how it fulfilled our natural knowledge.[13]

The seventeenth-century interpreters of Scripture always assumed that reason and revelation were complementary. Some of the theologians, for example, argued that both reason and revelation pointed toward a "covenantal" theology. Reason alone could discover in human nature a moral order imposing its demands on men and women. A rational interpretation of Scripture could then show that such a moral order reflected a "covenant of works," a set of demands that God had issued to Adam in the Garden of Eden. But the Bible also revealed a second covenant, hidden from the unassisted reason—a "covenant of grace," a decision by God to be merciful even when the human race failed to obey the covenant of works. The two covenants corresponded in precisely the same way reason corresponded to revelation: The one complemented the other.[14]

Their sense of a mutually complementary relationship between reason and revelation encouraged the pastors in their conviction that natural logic could unravel super-natural mysteries. Samuel Willard's pastoral labors, for instance, exhibited the same logic as his systematic theology. Just as reason could approximate revelation, so rational pastoral methods could uncover mysteries of both divine and demonic activity. Willard studied Protestant casuistry at Harvard before he began, in 1663, to serve a small church in Groton, Massachusetts, where he soon became known as "an Excellent Casuist." "When any Cases of Conscience came under his thought," wrote a friend much later, Willard "deliberated maturely on all Circumstances, and laid the Whole by the unerring Rule, and with great Judgment determined agreably."[15] His deliberations at Groton were not always as mature as the description suggested, but they did embody the rational suppositions characteristic of seventeenth-century pastoral activity.

One day in October 1671, for instance, one of Willard's parishioners, Elizabeth Knapp, suddenly clutched her legs and throat and cried out in pain. For days she wept, laughed, gestured absurdly, cast herself at the fire, confessed sins, suffered hallucinations, fell into fits, confessed to a compact with the devil, denied any compact with the devil, skipped about the house, roared, yelled, barked like a dog, bleated like a calf, and stared vacantly into space. Her family summoned Willard, who began inquiry and analysis, prayer and conversation, diagnosis and prescription.

He sought to elicit her own explanations of her plight. When she admitted to consorting with the devil, yet without sealing a covenant with him, she suddenly found her tongue drawn into a semicircle against the roof of her mouth. Willard continued to press for answers. When she could speak again, she told the pastor that now she was a child of God. Willard remained wary, suspecting that the claim was a presumptuous blasphemy "put into her mouth by the adversary." She admitted that she had lied, and Willard pressed for more holes in her story. Even when she finally acknowledged that she had agreed to seven years of diabolical servitude, but now was ready to repent, Willard did not abandon his caution. He noted that she had not bewailed her betrayal as a sin. When she did so, he invited her to give a "more methodical relation," but he warned her that he would believe only what he had good grounds to accept. And indeed, her new relation of events failed to convince him. Willard assured her that "if she would make use of me and more privately relate any weighty and serious case of conscience," he would tender all the help he could. But he would not accept her story. He remained baffled and would offer no diagnosis.

When her fits resumed, the family again called Willard. But this time his arrival brought forth from Elizabeth Knapp a low masculine voice which accused the minister of being "a great rogue" and of telling the people "a company of lies." Willard dealt directly with the voice. Beginning to debate with it, he said, "Satan, thou art a liar and a deceiver, and God will vindicate His own truth one day." But the voice again accused him of being a rogue. "Through God's grace," said Willard, "I hate thee." "But you had better love me," the voice replied. And so continued the repartee until onlookers in the house also began to talk back to the voice. Since Willard thought they might not be up to a conversation with the devil, he quickly called for prayer, in which he proceeded despite the protests of the demonic sound.

For days Willard visited the household, exhorting, praying, observing, asking questions, reasoning with Elizabeth Knapp, and debating the voice. He was always alert to contradictions. He was also aware of the expectation that he should explain as well as cure Elizabeth Knapp's maladies, and his private observations in his journal revealed something of his methods of explanation. His reasoning was an appeal to both logical and empirical evidence. He noticed that the very strength of her fits was "beyond the force of dissimulation." He observed that the convulsions did not seem to waste her body or her strength; she gained weight and regained her "natural strength" between fits. He noted that when the voice spoke he could perceive no motion in her mouth or tongue and that her throat swelled as much as the size of a fist. In short, Willard recorded symptoms, drew inferences, and sought causal connections.

He suspected that the fits were diabolical, but he finally confessed bewilderment. Unable to determine whether Elizabeth Knapp had covenanted with Satan, he decided to suspend judgment "and willingly leave it to the censure of those that are more learned, aged, and judicious." "She is the object of pity," he said, and he called on the townsfolk to be compassionate. But his method had failed him. The supernatural was too elusive.[16]

On the surface, there might seem to be little similarity between Willard's conversations with Elizabeth Knapp and Thomas Hooker's treatment of Joan Drake, but both ministers shared the same assumptions. In both conversations they made explicit reference to "cases of conscience"—the language of Protestant casuistry. In both conversations the pastoral procedure was to combine inquiry and argument. Willard assumed that the devil would have "used many arguments" with Elizabeth Knapp, and he felt obliged to offer counterarguments. It was her persistent "contradictions"—her incapacity to respond to argument as Joan Drake had—which convinced him that her case was "unanswerable": "Her declarations have been so contradictory, one to another," he said, "that we know not what to make to them."[17] In both conversations, moreover, the pastors used one technical term that provides a special clue for understanding their procedures. The word was *method*. Thomas Hooker had a "new answering method," and Samuel Willard pressed for a more "methodical relation." In the use of that term, they revealed their confidence that natural logic could resolve supernatural dilemmas.

In describing the work of the minister, Hooker and Willard used a term with a long history and a precise philosophical meaning. In 1556 the French logician Petrus Ramus had issued a book titled *Dialecticae Libri Duo*, in which he tried, by simplifying Aristotle, to reform the study of logic. Ramus proposed that logicians begin their work by finding words that best described the world, and then classifying those terms—which he called arguments—according to ordered rubrics. In the ordering, the logician would usually think in dichotomies, trying to discern two (sometimes three) specific and concrete terms implicit within each more general term. Each of the two more concrete terms would then be subdivided into two others even more concrete, until every logical notion was clearly understandable.

Having analyzed each term in that way, the logical thinker could then combine the words into self-evident propositions or, if necessary, into more complicated chains of reasoning. The Ramists assumed that proper analyses and skillful combining of the right words would reveal the truth. To describe the combining of the words into propositions—statements that could be described as true or false—they used the word *method*.[18]

Examples are abundant. In the sixteenth century, William Perkins had illustrated the usefulness of the method for the pastor charged with the cure of "distresse of minde." Such a distress, he observed, in a typical Ramist dichotomy, was of two degrees: fear of condemnation and despair of salvation. Each form of distress, moreover, arose from temptations that were, naturally for a Ramist, also of two kinds: temptations of trial, which tested and proved constancy in faith, and temptations of seducement, which enticed the unwary to fall into evil. Temptations of trial were themselves twofold: they could be struggles with a wrathful God or afflictions designed by God to test faith. Temptations of seducement were of three kinds: blasphemous temptations proceeded directly from the devil; another kind arose from sins; and the third kind emerged from a corrupted imagination.[19]

By adroit questioning, the pastor could use such a method of analysis to discern the religious state of a distressed parishioner. He could assure a worried gentleman that his spiritual pain was, say, an outward affliction

of trial producing a fear of condemnation, not a blasphemous temptation producing despair. Presumably the
sufferer would take comfort in learning that he was merely
fearful rather than despairing. And the diagnosis permitted the pastor to discern a fitting solution. The casuistry
textbooks were medical primers for surgery on the soul;
they classified and analyzed ailments of the spirit. In his
examination of Joan Drake's temptations, Thomas Hooker
apparently concluded that she suffered from something
much like a despair of salvation produced by a temptation
of seducement arising out of either faithlessness or a
corrupted imagination. He responded accordingly. Samuel
Willard's bafflement in dealing with Elizabeth Knapp
came from his growing awareness that the contradictions
in her reports—and the irrationality in her behavior—
were so pronounced as to hinder any logical conclusions on
his part. She could not provide a sufficiently "methodical"—
or rational—explanation.[20]

Perkins' descriptions, and the procedures used by
Hooker and Willard, assumed that pastoral analysis would
help reason maintain its proper rule and order.[21] The same
assumption governed the application of the "remedie" to
the soul's distress. Perkins recommended that the minister
first ask questions that could unearth "causes"; a second
series of questions might then reveal "effects." Was there a
desire to repent? A godly sorrow for sin? A determination
to forsake sinfulness? A love for the children of God? At the
conclusion of such a period of questioning, the minister
could respond with syllogistic arguments. In a session
with someone like Joan Drake, who was fearful of
condemnation, the syllogism would consist of two premises and a conclusion: The first premise could be any
appropriate passage from the Bible; the second, a
testimony from the distressed conscience. The conclusion
followed irresistibly: "He that hath an unfained desire to
repent and beleeve, hath remission of sinnes, and life
everlasting: but thou has an earnest desire to repent and
beleeve in Christ. Therefore remission of sinnes and life
everlasting is thine."[22] The questioning and the logic did

not always produce the desired results, but the clergy believed that their method usually was trustworthy, precisely because it was reasonable.

When, in 1643, William Ames published his text on *Conscience with the Power and Cases Thereof*—a choice example of Protestant casuistry that was still being used in Yale College and other American schools in the mid-eighteenth century—he consistently followed a Ramist pattern of thinking in dichotomies. In dealing with a "scrupulous" or excessively fearful conscience, for example, he observed that scruples arose when someone was reflecting on past actions, or planning future ones. On either occasion, scruples might appear for one of two reasons: God either wished to punish the conscience, or he wished to test it. In either case, the minister might choose to remove the scruples by one of two methods: by arguing against any scruples "which reason can take away by due tryall of the grounds of them," or by attacking them "as it were by *violence*," urging the troubled parishioner to suppress them, to refuse "to think or consider of them."[23] Thus a Ramist way of thinking made deep inroads into one tradition of American pastoral care. Ames even organized the topics of his casuistry in a series of dichotomies: he provided instructions about inferiors and superiors, husbands and wives, parents and children, masters and servants, ministers and flocks, magistrates and subjects, and other pairings. A certain pattern of logic shaped the way pastoral problems were viewed; a certain habit of thought shaped the very formation of the issues.

The pastors could trust a logical method because it was so widespread. The process of logical analysis used in pastoral care was identical with the procedure often used in law, physics, mathematics, and medicine.[24] The casuists liked to dwell on the analogies between the cure of the soul and the healing of the body. Just as the physician could alter the flow of blood by cutting a vein, so could the pastor redirect grief from worldly cares to higher ends. Just as surgeons brought swellings to a head by applying plasters to draw the corruption, so the minister should strive to reduce a general grief to particular instances.[25] But medicine could serve as a model mainly because physicians shared with the clergy a method of universal application. The learned professions were united in their allegiance to logic. Not all were Ramists, but all presumed to be logicians. To be a healer—whether of the body or of the soul—was to be, above all, a logical thinker.

In a cosmos populated by creatures of varied rank and power, from inanimate objects to supernatural beings, the cure of souls required a knowledge of both the visible and the invisible worlds. Seventeenth-century pastors labored with one hand grasping a casuistic handbook and the other holding a mirror to a supernatural world that they could see but dimly. They dealt with higher and lower powers. In either case, they depended on reason and logic. In a hierarchical universe, reason was a bridge between one world and another.

A Social Hierarchy

The clergy envisioned the cosmos as a vast hierarchical chain of being, in which revelation and reason guided their negotiations with the higher powers. They also viewed society as a hierarchy, in which they themselves stood among the higher powers. And in both their pastoral practice and their psychological theory, they exhibited the social assumptions of their time. They defined the self as if it were a troubled monarchy, and they performed their pastoral duties as members of a clerical aristocracy. Most ministers viewed society as a series of ranks and orders, and their theories of pastoral care reflected both their social perceptions and their social location.

American colonists came from a European society that had located its inhabitants in pyramids of kings, queens, barons, viscounts, earls, marquises, dukes, squires, knights, baronets, gentlemen, ladies, merchants, yeomen, artisans, laborers, and servants. The people near the top had stayed in England and Germany and Scotland; they had no reason to seek betterment in America. The colonial social structure was therefore derived from the middle range of the European, especially the English hierarchy, supplemented by indentured servants and African slaves. But the colonists still thought in the social categories of an ordered European culture. Those ways of thinking were hard to abandon, even when the colonies began to move away from their original hierarchies of inherited status to those of wealth and achievement.

The early ministers preached, prayed, and counseled amidst pervasive reminders of social ranking. Governor John Winthrop's sermon to the Massachusetts Bay settlers in 1630 gave classic expression to a social consensus: "God almightie in his most holy and wise providence hath soe disposed of the Condicion of mankinde," said Winthrop, "as in all times some must be rich some poore, some highe and eminent in power and dignitie; others meane and in subjeccion."[26] This attitude prevailed in social institutions and practices from Massachusetts to Virginia. A few of the colonies—Maryland, the Carolinas, New Netherland—were even begun as feudal societies, complete with patroonships, manors, baronies, and levies. The feudal dream soon faded, and all the American colonies became havens for small landowners and merchants. But even such colonists of the middling sort clung to the older hierarchical values.

Despite the relative equality of colonial society—in comparison with, say, England—the economy was fashioned so as to remind people continually that somebody towered above them and somebody else languished beneath them. The towns of New England apportioned farmland according to the "rank and quality" of the farmers who sought it (sometimes granting ministers a special place near the top of their lists). The officials of Virginia distributed plantation land according to the number of servants the planter brought to the colony, and after the second generation the grand families achieved both social and political eminence. And in all the colonies the customs of land distribution and inheritance ensured that most young people would remain in many ways dependent on older family members long after they had begun to assume adult responsibilities.[27]

The ranking was confirmed by colonial manners. Persons of every rank had their appropriate titles and designations, ranging from "goodman" and "goodwife" for the yeomen farmers and other common folk to Esquire for some of the councilors. (In calling the African slaves by their first names only, the white colonists therefore assigned them a place entirely outside the social world.) The titles of "gentleman" and "lady" connoted a diffuse social superiority accorded civil officers, the owners of large estates, or the highly educated. The oral forms of address for the genteel were Mistress and Master, so that even a chance encounter on the street could be a reminder of social location.[28]

Titles were not the only yardstick of rank. In New England, in a procedure known as Dooming the Seats, the churches assigned their members to pews according to rank, dignity, age, and wealth. Each Sabbath day offered a display of local hierarchy. So did each ceremony at Harvard College, where members of every entering class were "placed" in their proper social order. And several colonies passed laws to ensure that even daily apparel would mirror the ordering of society. The Massachusetts General Court, like other courts, expressed its "utter detestation that men and women of meane condition should take upon themselves the garb of gentlemen, by wearing gold or silver, lace or buttons, or points at their knees" or other adornment reserved for "persons of greater estates, or more liberal education." Virginia, like other colonies, administered legal punishment "accordinge to the qualitie of the person offendinge." Virginians even disapproved when an inconsequential merchant presumed to challenge a gentleman to a horse race.[29]

Looking back at his childhood in early eighteenth-century Virginia, an Episcopal rector named Devereux Jarratt recalled his sensitivity to the social distinctions:

We were accustomed to look upon what were called *gentle folks*, as beings of a superior order. For my part I was quite shy of *them*, and kept off at a humble distance. A *periwig*, in those days, was a distinguishing badge of *gentle-folk*—and when I saw a man riding the road, near our house, with a wig on, it would so alarm my fears, and give me such a disagreeable feeling, that, I dare say, I would run off, as for my life. Such ideas of the difference between *gentle* and *simple*, were, I believe, universal among all of my rank and age.[30]

Colonial ministers, then, had to deal not only with higher and lower cosmic powers but also with higher and lower persons.

The clergy had no objection to such ideas. They believed that "the All-Wise God" had ordained all the "Orders of Superiority and Inferiority among men, and required an Honour to be paid accordingly." Samuel Willard in Boston insisted that "due Distances" should be "maintained between Superiors and Inferiors." The social ranking, said William Hubbard of Ipswich, mirrored the order in "the goodly fabrick of the world." The beauty and strength of society required that persons be disposed into different stations. "It is not then the result of time or chance, that some are mounted on horseback, while others are left to travell on foot." From New England to Carolina, the clergy defended the distinction between the gentility and the multitude, the "vulgar herd." In colonial Philadelphia, even the Quakers, once despised for their egalitarian heresies, eventually extolled in their Yearly Meeting "the true honour and obedience due from . . . inferiors to superiors."[31]

Who, then, were the clergy and where did they fit in the social ranking? The answer is complicated. Between 1607 and 1776, more than 4,714 clergymen became settled ministers in the American colonies. Thirty-five percent were Congregationalists, clustered in New England; 25 percent were Episcopalians, congregated in the middle and southern colonies. The clergy of both groups, serving established churches and receiving their salaries from public taxes, clearly stood higher in the society than did the 12 percent of colonial preachers who led Baptist congregations. And there were not a great many ministers outside those three groups; 10 percent of the colonial pastors were Presbyterians; 6 percent came from other Reformed churches; 3 percent were Lutherans; 2 percent, Moravians; and 2 percent, Roman Catholics. The remaining 5 percent were divided among an array of smaller groups— Schwenkfelders, Labadists, Sandemanians, and others— with little claim to eminence in the wider society.[32]

In a land of farmers and merchants who lived mainly in the countryside and villages, far from the oversight of any dukes or barons, the clergy almost automatically occupied a higher place in the social order than did most of their European counterparts. The American social ladder simply had fewer rungs than the European. In colonies with state-supported ecclesiastical establishments, ministers expected deference and complained when they failed to receive it. In early New England they ranked in wealth and status higher than any other group except the magistrates, and when in the 1630s an erratic group of dissenters began "slighting . . . God's faithful Ministers and condemning and crying down them as Nobodies," the courts, with ministerial backing, silenced and banished the malcontents. By 1646 the Massachusetts General Court passed laws against any expressions of "contempt" for God's messengers. In seventeenth-century Virginia, the clerical financial status was well above that of most landowners (though well below that of larger planters), and although they did endure "public affronts" from a few unsympathetic governors and aristocrats, the ministers could count on the state for protection against "disparagement." As early as 1610 the laws of the colony required Virginians to hold preachers in "all reverent regard," and while they sometimes complained of mistreatment, they held a secure position. Devereux Jarratt recalled that "people in the lower walks of life" in Virginia had not been "accustomed to converse with [Anglican] clergymen, whom they supposed to stand in the rank of gentlemen, and above the company and conversation of plebeians." Outside Virginia and New England, local conditions variously affected clerical reputations, but most ministers seem to have flourished socially and economically wherever they lived.[33]

The primary reason for this high clerical standing was undoubtedly the assumption that the clergy were "ambassadors" of God, "shepherds" of the Lord, or "priests" with special access to the sacred. It was not difficult for John Cotton in New England to establish that the "key of authority of rule" in a church belonged especially to the ministerial elders who "labor in the word and doctrine," for that kind of labor was indeed special. There were even claims that those people who harbored "prejudices against Ministers" had been seduced by the devil, which seemed plausible precisely because the minister was so obviously the Watchman of God.[34]

Yet there were other grounds for clerical elevation. Most of the clergy, after all, were educated men, and their university training gave them an immediate claim to the status of gentlemen. Ninety percent of the 1,000 preachers in colonial Massachusetts were college graduates, and in the seventeenth century, 50 percent of Harvard's graduates became ministers. At least 60 percent—and probably 80 percent or more—of the 489 Anglican ministers in colonial Virginia had received college training; the Virginia Company, from the beginning, had taken great pride in the "sufficiencie of learninge" of the ministers they supplied for the colony. The governor of Maryland was "amazed" in 1714 when he found some "illiterate men . . . in holy orders." The ministry was a learned calling; only a few "hot-gospelers," Quakers, and other eccentrics questioned that. Throughout the colonies, the clergy embodied a link to the universities of Oxford and Cambridge, Heidelberg and Halle, Glasgow and Edinburgh, Basel and Jena, Leyden and Upsala, Marburg and Erlangen, and Seville and Dublin, as well as the new American colleges. It was by virtue of their education that the colonial clergy were addressed as Master—a title that confirmed their social position alongside other professionals within the gentility.[35]

The close association of ministers and magistrates further confirmed clerical eminence. The pastors served as advisers and arbitrators for colonial governors, preached election sermons to colonial legislatures, and in the southern colonies, performed civil functions. Public duties could even overlap pastoral activity, the most vivid example being the custom of conducting public pastoral interviews with criminals about to be executed. The clergy sought to elicit a public confession from the "wretch" in the gibbet. They often succeeded. "Your discourse fits me for my death," said one condemned criminal to the preacher at his side. "I beg you to do what you can for me," said another. In their discourses with the condemned, often recorded in great detail by onlookers, the clergy served as physicians of the soul and symbols of public order at the same time.[36]

And finally, patterns and symbols of family life elevated the clergy. In almost every region in New England, merchants, magistrates, and ministers formed a single interrelated family. In Virginia, continuous intermarriage among the aristocracy created "one great tangled cousinry," and James Blair, who married into the powerful Harrison family, assured the Bishop of London in 1724 that the clergy were able to "match to very good advantage with the Gentlemen's daughters of the Country." Equally important, though, was the symbolic value of the clerical role in a patriarchal society: The clergy manifestly derived a subtle authority through their identity as "fathers." "We must have the *Bowels of Parents* in us, be ready to listen to the Complaints and pity the infirmities of our People, to *Nourish* and *Cherish* them as a *Father doth his Children*," wrote a New Englander in 1726. Images from family life profoundly influenced the way early Americans understood themselves, shaping even their conception of such institutions as churches, jails, and lodgings for the poor. When ministers, in accord with ancient tradition, assumed the name and the role of "father," they appropriated a powerful social symbol.[37]

It should be added that colonial Americans never fully

agreed on the role of the father. In some families the paternal ideal was to maintain unbending authority by breaking the will of children, guarding against excessive display and affection, suppressing feelings of anger or pride, and teaching self-denial. Other parents tried not so much to break as to bend and control the will of their children in order to produce voluntary obedience. They combined affection with clear expectations of dutiful obligation, so that the young would learn self-control, industriousness, and respect. And in still other families, the parents wished neither to break nor to bend the will, but rather preferred that their children fulfill and express themselves. These parents usually punished their off-spring with a few well-placed blows, satisfying parental justice without implanting many seeds of guilt, accepted as natural any childish displays of anger, fostered budding ambition, and smiled at youthful pride.[38] Such divergent images of parental and fatherly roles were reflected in conflicting styles of pastoral care. But regardless of the minister's preferred style of "fatherly" guidance, the linking of the pastoral with the paternal immeasurably enhanced clerical standing in a patriarchal society.

The combination of a sacred office, education, social eminence, esoteric knowledge, and familial relationships imparted a distinctive tone to clerical discussion of the cure of souls. The casuistic handbooks, written mainly in England but widely read in America, urged the clergy to exercise irrefutable authority. During pastoral conversations, they warned, the distressed soul should never be allowed to "rest upon his own judgment." Unless the perplexed submitted themselves to "men of wisdom"— the pastors—and accepted their advice, they would "remain uncomforted."[39]

Ministers warned each other against haughty or magisterial behavior. They insisted that a good pastor would bear with the peevishness and rashness, the disordered affections, of the distressed. A good minister would "put on him (as it were) their persons, beeing affected with their miseries, and touched with compassion of their sorrowes."

Clerical authority did not preclude genuine sympathy. But there was no question about the authority: The minister undertook a pastoral conversation not as an equal but as an expert with high social standing. When Samuel Sewall's daughter Betty became dejected after reading a mournful sermon, Sewall and his wife did not feel themselves competent to offer comfort or advice, though Sewall was an educated judge who presided over a Boston court. Instead they sent immediately for the pastor, Samuel Willard, who closely questioned Betty Sewall before he announced that she was "confused." Willard displayed no magisterial behavior. He even confided that he, too, had once been confused. But the Sewall family had called for his services with the alacrity that would later mark a call to the family physician. Willard came to the household bearing an aura of authority conferred by a society that valued his learning, respected his knowledge of supernatural powers, and by calling him Master, accorded him the standing of social gentility.[40]

The hierarchical ordering of society, then, pervaded the tone of pastoral counsel, informing a consensus about the proper bearing and authority of the pastor, helping to define the meaning of clerical authority, and shaping lay expectations about clerical duties. In a stratified patriarchal society, the pastoral role naturally seemed to require an authoritative paternal bearing. The tone of private conversation dimly reflected the ordering of public institutions.

A Hierarchical Soul

The social order informed not only the demeanor of the minister but the very definition of the soul. The language of social experience—a vocabulary related to rulers and masters and servants—overflowed into the language of psychology. The clerical writers found that both their cosmology and their sociology seemed to translate easily into their discourses about will and understanding and passions. The social world seemed to reappear within the depths of the soul; political and social institutions seemed to have their counterparts within the inner life.

In describing the soul, the ministers thought in hierarchical patterns. Whether Catholic or Protestant, they drew on a medieval and scholastic tradition that depicted the soul as a gradation of higher and lower powers. They studied commentaries on Aristotle, revisions of Plato, and criticisms of the Stoics. Protestants read Aquinas and Augustine as attentively as did Catholics. And they also pored over the textbooks of such sixteenth- and seventeenth-century Christian philosophers and dogmaticians as Franco Burgersdyck, Bartholomaeus Keckermann, Theophilus Golius, and Gisbert Voetius—men whose names were revered in the colonial colleges well into the early eighteenth century. The authorities disagreed on matters large and small, but all took for granted the hierarchical ordering of the person.[41]

Moreover, the ministers thought of the soul's inward hierarchy in straightforward political and social metaphors. Some faculties, they thought, were "superior," others "inferior." Some were properly "rulers," with "commanding power," rightly invested with the capacity to govern. Others were "imperious," attempting always to usurp the position of their betters. The ministers spoke not merely of the will or the understanding or the passions; they described one faculty as the Queen or Prince, another as the Councillor, still others as servants. The soul was an "Empire" with royalty and attendants. It was, in other words, a mirror reflection of the political and social hierarchy. The vocabulary of clerical psychology resonated with the social experience of the clerical psychologists.[42]

A good number of seventeenth-century ministers, especially among the Puritan clergy, conceived of the inward life as a violent civil war, provoked by a rebellion of "self." In the clerical vocabulary, the word *self* could mean simply "the very person, consisting of the soul and the body"—the natural or personal self. Or it could mean "this person considered in its capacity of earthly comforts, and in relation to the present blessings of the world." This, said

57

Richard Baxter, could be called "earthly self (yet in an innocent sense)." But usually the word *self* connoted willful egocentricity. *Self* meant *self-centeredness.* "The very names of Self and Own," wrote Baxter, "should sound in a watchful Christian's ears as very terrible, wakening words, that are next to the names of sin and satan."[43] The clergy filled their sermons with a panoply of negative references to the "self": They complained of self-love, self-exaltation, self-affection, self-credit, self-conceitedness, self-will, self-fullness, self-honor, self-imagination, self-safety, self-sufficiency, self-interest, and any number of similar selfish maladies.[44] *Self* was primarily a religious term, not a neutral philosophical designation. "Selfhood" was primarily a condition to be overcome, not a possibility to be realized. "Is not SELF the great idol which the whole world of unsanctified men doth worship?" asked Baxter. The goal of the Christian was therefore self-emptiness, self-trial, and self-denial—anything to conquer the "infection of self." The ministers acknowledged that *self* also could be taken to mean "a person in his sanctified state; which is spiritual self," and hence did not invariably have a pejorative weight.[45] But in the lexicon of the theologians, the word usually suggested rebelliousness and overweening self-assertion, and it almost always occurred in the setting of religious rhetoric, not philosophical analysis.

The word *soul* had different connotations. The soul was a "spiritual substance" which derived its identity from a unique divine creative act. It was the gift of the Creator, the handiwork of God, and hence it was good. The soul, moreover, was the core of human identity. Its nature was "constant" over time. Being created immediately by God rather than by means of natural generation, the soul was not subject to any natural law of generation and corruption (though a "person," as a union of soul and body, stood subject to both). Hence the clerical psychologists did not bother much with the problem of "personal identity" that so troubled theorists after the publication in 1694 of the second edition of John Locke's *Essay Concerning Human Understanding.*[46]

58

The Lockean treatise offered a revealing contrast to the prevailing clerical psychology. First, Locke used the term *self* not to designate a religious disposition, but to demarcate a problem in the philosophy of mind. Second, he did worry about the problem of personal identity, and doing so, he identified the self with a distinctive human capacity. Locke's self derived its identity from the capacity of an individual consciousness to be aware of its own past and to anticipate its future:

> For since consciousness always accompanied thinking, and it is that which makes every one to be what he calls self, and thereby distinguishes himself from all other thinking things, in this alone consists personal identity, i.e., the sameness of a rational being: and as far as this consciousness can be extended backwards to any past action or thought, as far reaches the identity of that person; it is the same self now it was then.[47]

Each person was conscious of being the same self over time, and that consciousness, enduring throughout a lifetime despite all the changes in the person's body and thoughts, constituted personal identity—indeed, constituted "what we call self."[48] Locke also accepted the reality of a soul, or spiritual substance; he simply insisted that personal identity, selfhood, consisted not in the continuation of that substance but in the continuity of a single consciousness throughout a lifetime. Implicit in the Lockean notion of selfhood were intimations of autonomy and individualism, which could clearly dissolve the chain of being in a hierarchical cosmos. In that sense, it can be said that the seventeenth-century clergy lived in a world of souls, not of selves. Or at least they tried.

Souls, like societies, were hierarchical. The clergy thought of a person, in fact, as being a microcosm—not merely of a stratified society but also of the hierarchical universe. The human body, they believed, participated in and represented the lower levels of the cosmos, the world of material objects. The "vegetative soul," or ability to

59

grow, marked each person's kinship with the world of plants. The "locomotive soul," or capacity to move, exhibited a point of commonality with the stars. The "sensitive soul," or capacity to perceive, think, remember, and feel, represented the proximity between human and animal life. And finally the "rational soul," or power of knowing, judging, and choosing, demonstrated the likeness between human beings and angels. A person was a hierarchy of powers, and each ascending stage integrated the lower stages into a higher unity. The highest was reason.[49]

The clergy did not insist that each capacity was a separate soul. "Whether they have so many distinct Souls in them, as they have Kinds of Life, or whether they perform all these Functions by one and the same Soul, let Philosophers dispute," wrote Samuel Willard. Ministers usually referred simply to the various activities of the singular soul. They also did not intend to denigrate the lower levels of the psychological hierarchy. But because each higher stage both trascended and integrated the lower, the "Life of Reason," perched atop the biological ladder, rightfully assumed command and "Government" over the other powers. By nature, men and women were supposed to be rational.[50] Yet the psychological order, like the cosmic and social orders, was forced to withstand rebellions from the lower depths, and it was the task of the clergy to clarify and defend the proper ordering. This task led them to sustained reflection on three broad issues.

The first was the relation between the soul and the body. Composed of the four elements, earth, air, fire, and water, the body was the lowest level of personal life. But the clergy did not disdain the body; it was, they thought, "Essential and Integral" as the seat not only of motion and sense but of reason itself.[51] It became a problem only when physical desires overwhelmed rational restraint or when physical maladies engendered spiritual stress. The body could rebel against the fragile imperium of reason, and a successful rebellion was often signaled by the onset of "melancholy." Impressed by the medical writings of the second-century Greek physician Claudius Galenus, a few English authors in the sixteenth century began to popularize a distinction between the true afflictions of conscience and a melancholy that occurred when gross elements in the blood settled in the spleen and created "vapours" that pressed upward to the brain, causing it "without external occasion to forge monstrous fictions." Even as Robert Burton was writing his rambling and detailed *Anatomy of Melancholy* (1621), the clerical casuists were begining to caution spiritual advisers that such problems as scrupulosity might well be rooted, as William Ames explained, in "Melancholy, or some such like constitution of body." And they sometimes warned that melancholia could not be cured by comforting words or persuasive arguments. The cure for melancholy—when there was a cure—was not introspection, but action. An active life might be the only way to preserve spiritual equilibrium when the body rebelled against the soul.[52]

Reason normally maintained its hegemony, though, by using its two faculties of understanding and will. Both were remarkable powers. The understanding was not to be confused with the senses, or with the imagination (which merely received sensory images), or with the "cogitation" (which ordered and arranged those images, whether in perceptions or in dreams), or with the memory. Understanding was distinguished, rather, by its capacity to form judgments about truth. The will was not to be confused with emotions or desires. It was distinguished by its capacity to cooperate with the understanding and to use the affections as its instruments, or handmaids, to set the body in motion in the pursuit of happiness. The distinctive activities of willing and understanding constituted the "Reasonable Soul." All else, however important, was subordinate.[53]

At least all else was supposed to be subordinate. In practice, clerical casuists did not assume that the rule of reason was unchallengeable. The "cogitation," they noted, was prone to reflect not only on the images provided by the sense and imagination but also on the motions of the

"Heart." The resulting movement of the soul was termed an *affection*. And affections were powerful, even when they retained their proper subordination to the higher faculties.

The second broad issue in the clerical psychology, therefore, was the relationship between the reason and the affections. In theory, the mind should have no serious difficulty in maintaining its control. "The eye or mind of a man sits like a coachman, and guides the headstrong affections," wrote Thomas Shepard of Cambridge. And he also believed that when God truly illumined the understanding of the godly, their affections flowed forth unerringly in hope and love toward Christ. Compelled to contend with a motley array of religious enthusiasts in the Bay Colony, Shepard developed a lasting suspicion of unenlightened affections. "I never liked violent affections and pangs," he wrote, "but only such as were dropped in by light." He was by no means averse to reminding his congregation that hypocrites could have "mighty strong affections" in religious matters. But he had no intention of depreciating the role of affections in religion: When Christ presents himself to the godly, "the mind sees, the affections make after him, will fastens on him."[54]

Since the created order was good, the affections shared in that original goodness. And since the created order was redeemable, the affections, too, could be redeemed. But the clerical psychologist must assume disorder—sinfulness—as a premise. Adam's willful rebellion had unleashed the lower powers against the higher, threatening the rule of the rational nature. The "exorbitant" power conferred on the affections by the fall into sinfulness gave them a "crooked bias," causing them to move "in a wrong way, and on wrong objects," said Samuel Willard. And Thomas Shepard added that in a fallen world the affections could engage the mind in a contest of mutual destruction: "The heart makes the eyes blind, and the mind makes the heart fat." Indeed, if the mind were darkened, the affections could lead the soul headlong into "falls and deviations in crooked ways." With the connivance of a fallen mind, perverse affections could continually disrupt the soul's internal equilibrium.[55]

A great portion of pastoral care therefore consisted of conversations with people who had fallen prey to the unchecked power of the "sensitive soul" and its unruly affections. One consistent goal of the physician of the soul was to assist the forces of rationality to maintain internal order. Control of the affections did not mean their suppression; the clergy would have considered the utter destruction of the impassioned life as simply another distortion. But the ministers grieved about disordered passions. One commented that some affections, like anger, always seem to have something evil within them: The "wrathful man," he said, is like a "hideous monster" with his "eyes burning, his lips fumbling, his face pale, his teeth gnashing, his mouth foaming, and other parts of his body trembling and shaking." And colonial parishioners were far more inclined than later stereotypes might suggest to give way to sexual passions, angry aggression, and other "distempers" of affection. Both in New England and in Virginia, the clergy found themselves repeatedly compelled to discipline their members for outbursts of ungovernable affections.[56] To write about the fitting relationship between the mind and the affections was to explore the hidden dynamics of both social order and Christian piety.

Such reflections about harmonies between higher and lower powers of the soul produced a continuing debate about yet a third issue: the relation of the will to the understanding. No other theoretical issue in psychology so occupied colonial writers; no other issue better illustrates the tendency of the clergy to use political and social metaphors to unravel the intricacies of psychology.

Some American ministers were "intellectualists," who argued that the will always obeys the dictate of the understanding. Norman Fiering has unearthed notebooks and commencement theses at seventeenth-century Harvard in which students pondered the claim that "the understanding shows to the will, [what] is to be embraced and [what] to be rejected: then the will desireth and governeth [those] inferiour faculties, to wit, the sensitive and locomotive appetite . . . for as the understanding judgeth, so the will desireth." For the colonial intellectualists, the understanding functioned, in Stoic fashion, as the ruler of the soul; the will invariably followed its command. Men and women always chose what they judged to be good; they willed in accordance with their understanding of their situation.[57]

A second group of clergy preferred a voluntarist doctrine which accorded the will both autonomy and self-direction. The Jesuit followers of the Spaniards Luis de Molina and Francisco Suarez defended a "liberty of indifference," in which the essence of free choice was the will's capacity to move independently toward its object without waiting for the prior judgment of the intellect. In effect, they contended that the will possessed its own cognitive capacities, its own distinctive way of comprehending a situation, and it could therefore act independently. Indeed, the will not only had the power to direct the attention of the understanding toward one or another object, but the ability to defy the intellect's judgment. Men and women could choose what they knew to be unwise; they could refuse what they knew to be good.[58]

Most of the well-known colonial Protestant theologians, however, adopted what Fiering has called a pietistic voluntarism, which emphasized the will's dependence on divine grace but insisted that in the inner economy of the fallen soul, the volition commanded a power that could ignore or even dominate the understanding. The will was the Prince, the understanding merely a "grave Counsellor," but the entire kingdom of the soul stood powerless before the corrupting might of sin. Thomas Hooker argued that the understanding was especially powerless before the combined might of corrupted will and affection:

> For reason and understanding are the underlings as it were of inferior and lower ranck, and can but as servants and attendants offer and propound to the will and affections; what they see and conceive may be most convenient, and the wretched waywardness of our hearts, will either snub or

silence them . . . damp and pervert the light of judgment, tel reason she is a fool and is deceived.[59]

In such a view the will was a Queen, or as Samuel Willard put it, the "supream Faculty"; the understanding was merely a strategist devising means to accomplish the will's ends. But without divine aid, the Queen inevitably chose selfish and self-destructive ends, and the servant devised evil means. The Pietist theologians were technically voluntarists in their psychology, but they had no illusions about the extent of willpower.[60]

To advance a voluntaristic psychology was not to reject the "rational" methods of the pastoral casuist. It was merely to suggest that the task of the pastor was to persuade as well as interpret; and it was a way of understanding the soul's frequently intractable resistance to even the best-framed arguments. To propose a hierarchical concept of the soul, moreover, was not to envision a static, compartmentalized self. The conception functioned more often as a means of comprehending internal conflict, rebellion, and on occasion, chaos. But the clergy did not think of conflict as the ideal. Reliance on hierarchical imagery also implied a quest for order, for internal equilibrium. Their theories could offer both an explanation for Joan Drake's distress and a hope for the resolution of her dilemma; both a clarification of Elizabeth Knapp's struggle with demonic powers and the possibility that even she could find peace.

Conclusion

American pastoral care traditions are rooted in an ancient introspective piety which demands that Christian clergy possess a knowledge of the inner world. It would not be outrageous to suggest that the extraordinary preoccupation with psychology in twentieth-century America owes something to the heritage of experiential piety; that America became a nation of psychologists in part because it had once been a land of Pietists. In the mid-seventeenth century, Thomas Hooker instructed his people in the intricacies of "meditation." The practice of meditation, he said, was a way to send our thoughts "afar off," to revive a "fresh apprehension of things done long before," bringing to mind "such things which were happily quite out of memory, and gone." By "recounting and recalling our corruptions to mind, by serious meditation," he said, we "sew them all up together." But meditation dealt with the present as well as with the past: It was "the coasting of the mind and imagination into every crevis and corner," where it "pryes into every particular, takes a special view of the borders and confines of any corruption or condition that comes to be scanned," and "takes into consideration all the secret conveyances, cunning contrivements, all bordering circumstances that attend the thing." When admiration for such a form of meditation becomes deeply embedded in a culture, it enjoys a remarkable tenure, despite changes in the way it may be described and understood. American culture still bears the marks of repeated efforts by a multitude of Christian clergy to "map out the dayly course of a mans conversation and disposition."[61]

The aim of the clergy's introspective cartography was to explore the ravages of sin and elevate hopes for spiritual growth. In the seventeenth century, sin—whether viewed as transgression, faithlessness, disorder, or disobedience—suggested defiance of a supernatural hierarchical order. Spiritual growth meant a process of "sanctification," empowered by supernatural grace, which created in the soul a capacity to obey and honor the highest-ranking of all hierarchical beings. And the sense of hierarchy brought a certain unity to the pastoral function. A certain way of thinking, a particular habit of thought, seemed to make sense of the world, whether public or private, visible or invisible. In dealing with cosmic forces, social structures, or dynamics of the soul, the minister could identify an underlying continuity; all shared a hierarchical ordering.

66

3

The Understanding and the Affections

In 1727 the Reverend Ebenezer Parkman of West-
borough, Massachusetts, made a hurried visit to the home
of one Lieutenant Forbush, whose wife, dying, feared that
she lacked "the truth of grace." Although he proceeded in
time-honored paths, he felt no need to confine himself
"strictly to any method," because he already knew—or so
he thought—the "greatest weight" in each case. When Mrs.
Forbush told him that her approaching death struck fear in
her, Parkman immediately began to "enquire into the
grounds of her fears," interspersing brief homilies on
repentance, obedience, and love to God and the godly.

"Don't you find in you such a love to God as has made
you both repent of sin and obey His commands from a
desire of His glory?" he asked. "Do you love the disciples
of Christ, those that you think bear the image of God
unfeignedly?"

"I hope really that I do," she replied, with exactly the
mixture of trust and humility that Parkman was seeking
to find. He had been so confident that Mrs. Forbush could
give the proper answers that he had neglected to dismiss

her relatives. Suddenly old Thomas Forbush, a member of the family, interrupted with a laconic but impassioned rebuke: "Sir," he said, "we are grown folks."

The interruption created consternation. Parkman was completely taken aback by the old man's "passionate manner." The ailing woman quickly assured the company that the pastor had proceeded "much to her comfort and benefit." But when Forbush complained that Parkman had erred in probing matters that to others seemed self-evident, the minister attempted to explain and defend his style of counseling, claiming that "the most pious, and the most judicious ministers" would surely approve his methods. True, he said, he well knew that Mrs. Forbush was a woman of conspicuous and genuine piety. For that reason he had not deigned to "rake into all the particulars of her past conversation in the world," even though her answers to such questions would have been "instructing" to the anxious family. True, he said, he and Mrs. Forbush had reviewed the minutiae of piety "numberless times" in the past; his critic merely had failed to grasp the extraordinary import of his questions. Parkman had been serving as a tutor and guide to the invisible world.

"I have been endeavoring," he said, "to assist this person in preparing actually to give up her account to the great judge." And though she may have answered the questions many times before, he felt obliged to lead her in this last review, lest she make the slightest mistake when she delivered her testimony. Parkman was the expert in the mysteries of the supernatural world, and Mrs. Forbush was his pupil. "We act most wisely to look all over as carefully as possible to find out whatever escapes or flaws there may be, since it can never be done [here]after throughout Eternity, and Eternity depends upon this account."

In testing whether her "heart" was truly gracious, he added, he had merely asked the familiar and traditional questions about obedience and love to the godly. But old Forbush remained unconvinced. He would not want

68

Parkman, he said, "to ask him such sorts of questions."

"No, Mr. Forbush," said Parkman, "I'm afraid that you would not care that I should deal feelingly with your soul."

The minister felt "inwardly grieved" that his challenger should display such "ignorance and passions." The interruption unnerved him, and he brooded over it for hours. The only explanation that he could offer as he lay awake that night was that the suddenness of the summons to Mrs. Forbush's bedside had prevented his usual address to heaven before such ministrations. "It was twelve when I got home. . . . I went to bed but could not sleep for a long time. I beseeched God to quicken me hereby in my work, and make me more diligent to accomplish myself lest I meet with worse trials than this."[1]

The difference between Thomas Hooker's earlier success with Joan Drake and Ebenezer Parkman's disastrous encounter with the Forbush family should not be exaggerated, for the two conferences bespoke the continuity in the cure of souls during the seventeenth and eighteenth centuries. Hooker and Parkman shared the same assumptions about hierarchical authority, took for granted the same supernatural setting for pastoral care, and employed similar forms of rational "method" in their work. Yet many of the themes that would dominate eighteenth-century debates over pastoral care also appeared in Parkman's account: caution and comfort, ministerial bearing and authority, the ambivalent attitudes toward "passion" and feeling, and the relationship between doctrinal understanding and the "heart." Eighteenth-century pastors maintained the hierarchical vision of the society and the soul. But some of them began to wonder whether the acknowledged higher powers, in the soul, in the church, or even in the state, could—or should—preserve their hegemony.

The Psychology of Awakening

On September 14, 1740, the English evangelist George Whitefield arrived at Newport, Rhode Island. He preached at 10:00 the next morning and then proceeded to travel from one end of the colonies to the other, addressing vast crowds, inspiring clerical imitators, evoking bitter contention, eliciting massive waves of conversion, and unleashing passions that would not subside for years. He and his fellow revivalists drew their adherents from every social class, from New England to Georgia. Whatever its deeper causes, the Awakening consisted of an outburst of religious oratory, with saints enlivened and sinners converted. It was a response to a configuration of biblical texts, ideas, images, and metaphors that defined and redefined religious experience. And it was also the source of one schism after another.

The revivalists and their opponents argued about itinerant preachers, censorious preachers, unconverted preachers, lay preachers, and separatist preachers. They debated about the rights of churches, the purity of churches, the membership of churches, and the relationships between churches. They quarreled about the doctrine of conversion, the means of conversion, the assurance of conversion, and the criteria for conversion. And they disagreed, too, about the cure of souls.[2]

Because of the Awakening, the cure of souls became a topic of pressing concern from New Hampshire to Georgia. Religious revivals kept the ministers busy with a stream of distraught and anxious inquirers seeking someone who could interpret their thoughts and feelings. William Cooper at Brattle Street Church in Boston reported that more people came to him during a week of the revival than during the previous twenty-four years of his ministry. In an early revival in Windsor, Connecticut, Timothy Edwards counseled as many as thirty people a day. The Awakening was a marathon of religious conversation as well as a display of pulpit oratory.[3]

Some came to pastors simply with "deep Soul-concern." Some felt "encouraged" or claimed they had been "set at liberty." Others brought reports of "melancholy," or "exceeding Terror," or "self-loathing." Many told their pastors of visions and trances, or sensations of quivering or warmth or weight. Others came with feelings of unworthiness and despair—some weeping, a few threatening suicide. Some had their minds "fixed upon some particular wicked practice" that had inexorably damned them. Many were sure that "they differ[ed] from all others" in the enormity of their hidden thoughts. The worriers could prove inconsolable; the exuberant might be superficially optimistic in merely "hoping" that "they were got under Convictions." But in whatever condition they came, the flow of souls reminded one minister of a tattered caravan: "Thus they wander about from mountain to hill, seeking rest and finding none." And the clergy could not agree on their opinions of those spiritual wanderers.[4]

"The central conflict of the Awakening," writes a twentieth-century historian, "was . . . not theological but one of opposing theories of human psychology."[5] This observation is insightful; it is, at the same time, peculiarly misleading, especially if one understands it to suggest a clear dichotomy between voluntarists and intellectualists or between an outmoded scholastic psychology and a modern one, or to imply that theology was tangential to the real psychological issues. In the first place, the theological context of any clerical assertion about psychology profoundly affected the interpretation of the psychological claims. Conflicting notions of sinfulness and spiritual growth altered the force of even the most technical psychological assertions. In the second place, the antagonists had far more in common than any such dichotomy might suggest. Yet they did disagree about the relative importance of the understanding and the affections, and though the differences were more subtle than the heated rhetoric of the 1740s implies, they established issues that would trouble clerical psychologists for more than half a century.

The clergy during the Awakening did not offer dispassionate analyses of human psychology. They were embroiled in a mighty struggle about conversion, and almost everything they wrote about psychology had some bearing on their theological feints and thrusts at one another. They

71

were making attempts to understand what was happening in the revival, or making proposals about what should be happening. They were also, one should add, continuing an old tradition in American religious thought. In the opening decade of the century, Solomon Stoddard, the pastor in Northampton, Massachusetts, boasted that "the World has had but little distinct understanding about the work of Conversion, until some latter Divines at Boston: [John] Norton, [Thomas] Hooker, and [Thomas] Shephard, and some others have held forth light; there was great darkness about the way of conversion."[6] The New England clergy, at least, believed that one of their special callings was to enlighten the world about conversion. The clashes during the Awakening represented, in part, their efforts to fulfill that vocation.

The Awakening divided many of the colonial clergy into factions of New Lights, who supported the revival, and Old Lights, who viewed it as a distasteful time, when "multitudes were seriously, soberly and solemnly out of their wits."[7] The dominant figure in the New Light army was Jonathan Edwards, pastor at Northampton, grandson of Stoddard, and the most perceptive student of religious psychology in eighteenth-century America. The symbolic leader of the Old Lights was Charles Chauncy, a pastor in Boston, and the most prolific and determined critic of religious "enthusiasm" in the colonies. The two men did indeed disagree profoundly about psychology, and about much else besides. But to speak as if the colonies had fragmented into intellectualist and voluntarist factions, or even as if everyone took sides with either the Old Light or the New Light faction, is to ignore, first, the wide spectrum of opinion in the middle, and second, the even wider range of issues on which opponents agreed.

The clergy did not abandon the older hierarchical ways of thinking about the soul. They continued to believe that some faculties were higher, others lower; or that some were deeper within the core of the soul; or that some were more central to religious experience. Their hierarchical presuppositions prompted some of the most intense

72

disagreements, but it was these shared assumptions that made their disagreements about the value of the faculties so resistant to resolution.

Everyone continued to believe that the soul was higher than the body. After all, Edwards said, the body was propagated by parents, the soul created directly by God. Everyone continued to worry about the bodily incursions that produced "melancholy" in the soul. Edwards described his sense of helplessness in the face of melancholy when his uncle, Joseph Hawley, fell into that bodily "distemper." The devil took advantage of Hawley's condition, said Edwards, and drove him into despairing thoughts and sleeplessness. Nothing anyone could do seemed to help. Hawley was "in a great measure past a capacity of receiving advice, or being reasoned with." Despairing of salvation, he knew only one solution. On a Sabbath morning, he "laid violent hands to his life, by cutting his own throat." Shortly thereafter, Edwards advised the clergy that it might be wise to withhold from melancholy sinners the full truth about their spiritual condition, because of their "strange disposition . . . to take things wrong." He finally concluded that the only cure for such a bodily ailment was diversion: "going on steadfastly and diligently in the ordinary course of duty, without . . . leisure to attend to the devil's sophistry." The cure for melancholy, when there was a cure, was not introspection but action. An active life might be the only way to preserve spiritual equilibrium when the body subverted the empire of the soul.[8]

Most of the clergy, from every side, continued to emphasize the older catalogue of faculties, especially the understanding, the will, and the affections. All agreed that the Fall into sinfulness had so disordered human faculties that none could be fully trusted. The Old Lights were terrified of the fallen passions, which they believed to be in need of continual governance and restraint. The revivalists shared that fear. The Presbyterian Gilbert Tennent, who seemed a veritable wild man as he traveled through New Jersey and Pennsylvania denouncing unconverted preachers, insisted throughout his career that unregulated

73

affections were fit more "for Theaters than [for] Churches," and that passions were "good servants" but "bad guides." His chief ally in the Presbyterian Church, Jonathan Dickinson of New Jersey, described the fallen passions as violent and inordinate, and he worried about "animal Affections and Passions" masquerading as gracious exercises. Jonathan Edwards believed that "inferior" affections governed most people and that "false" affections often lurked within religious ecstasy.[9]

The clergy concurred, as well, on the limitations and distortions of the other fallen faculties. The revivalists saw the understanding as being trapped in "brutal Blindness." Their critics agreed that understanding stood in desperate need of "light."[10] The revivalists described the fallen will as obstinate. Their critics agreed that it was rigid and resistant.[11] Hence despite the earnestness of his rhetorical crusade for rationality, even Charles Chauncy did not entertain the thought that a merely "notional" religion—intellectual assent to religious propositions—could serve as a substitute for the faith of "the whole inner man" who had been made a "new creature" by the transformation of all the faculties.[12] And despite the vehemence with which Jonathan Dickinson decried "mere rational Convictions," he never believed that "transient affections" could substitute for the renewal of the "whole soul"—a renewal which began, he added, with the gracious illumination of the understanding.[13]

On the surface, the conflict over psychology might seem to have been merely an extension of the older split between intellectualists and voluntarists, but it was more complex than that. Chauncy did proclaim, of course, that the renewal of the will and affections presupposed prior enlightenment of the understanding. His Cambridge ally Nathanael Appleton told Boston ministers that the Spirit began its saving work by informing the understanding and convincing it of the soul's sinfulness. But that was a standard view, shared by almost everyone. Gilbert Tennent, accused of "seditiously Working on the Passions," replied that the revivalists excited the "lower Passions" only through "the Information of the Understanding." And such a reply was entirely consistent with his theology and his psychological theory: "The blessed God," he said, "treats with men as rational Creatures, by applying to their rational Powers; and therefore whatever Good they get passes through their Understandings, to their Wills and Affections."[14]

Tennent's claim evoked no dissent among the revivalists. Jonathan Dickinson said that the renewal of the will invariably occurred through the "illumination" of the understanding. In conversion, wrote Joseph Sewall of Boston, "the understanding, now savingly enlightened, beholds Jesus Christ, in order of Nature before the Will and Affections are drawn to close with him." William Williams of Hatfield, Massachusetts, thought that any faith which sprang from some "sudden impression upon [the] Affections" would be only temporary, because it was not "rooted and grounded in a good understanding." The gifted Presbyterian artisan of the revival, Samuel Blair, who worked in New Jersey and Pennsylvania, wrote that in conversion, the light of the understanding "determined" the will "so [that] it no longer resists." The understanding, he added, served as "the directive and leading faculty of the Soul, which is to guide and influence the Will and other Affections." And according to Solomon Williams in Massachusetts, "all the Calvinistical ministers" agreed that the Spirit enlightened the understanding, the understanding assented, the judgment approved, and the will chose and trusted Christ. His claim was an overstatement, but few revivalists presumed, at least in theory, to appeal directly to the passions, bypassing, somehow, the understanding. Almost all affirmed the priority of the understanding in the formal structure of the soul.[15]

Jonathan Edwards, though, had his own slant on the intricacies of psychology. Like everyone else, he believed that the religious affections arose from a gracious enlightening of the understanding. But Edwards also thought that the custom of speaking as if the faculties somehow operated one at a time failed to explain what he

75

called sensible knowledge, especially the "sense of the heart" that was awakened by "the supreme beauty . . . of divine things." In sensible, as contrasted to speculative knowledge, the understanding and the will were inseparably united. Sensible knowledge was a form of understanding infused with an inclination, or affection. It was a mode of apprehension that engaged the whole person. All the more did Edwards believe, therefore, that in any spiritual understanding of "divine things," which surely engaged the whole person, there could be no "clear distinction . . . between the faculties of understanding and will, as acting distinctly and separately." Religious affections flowed from a perception of the soul that was at the same time cognitive and conative. Hence for Edwards, it made little sense to talk about the priority of the understanding. Though he was not alone in his idea of the unity of the soul, he had more success than most of his contemporaries in pushing the faculty psychology beyond its own boundaries.[16]

In several ways, Edwards was drawing on the new psychology of John Locke's *Essay Concerning Human Understanding*. First, his notion of a "sense of the heart" presupposed the Lockean distinction between "signs" and "ideas." In a cognitive act that employed signs, the mind abstracted a characteristic of an object and used it to represent the object, in a conceptual shorthand that made thinking easier. By contrast, knowledge by means of ideas was a direct apprehension of an object in its concreteness. When Edwards spoke of a sensible understanding, he had in mind a spiritual apprehension that was analogous to such a direct sensory perception. Second, Edwards' notion of a unique inward spiritual "sensation," wrought by divine grace in the mind of true saints, presupposed the Lockean conception of "simple ideas," elementary sensations (like the sensation of a color). Simple ideas, Edwards observed, arose entirely apart from any "compounding of . . . perceptions or sensations which the mind had before." And he thought that a supernatural spiritual perception— a saintly soul's inward "sense"—was the religious counterpart of "what some metaphysicians call a new simple

76

idea."[17] In such ways did Edwards make use of Locke's new insights, though as often as not, he disagreed with Locke. Moreover, his intention was not to forge a radically new psychological theory but to illustrate and modify the older psychology of his Puritan forebears. His treatises contained far more references to older Reformed divines than to eighteenth-century philosophers. He stood in a theological tradition that had long displayed a fascination with the hidden convolutions of understanding and volition. He was a masterly psychologist, not despite his Puritanism, but because of it.

For all their emphasis on the understanding in conversion, the colonial clergy rarely felt obliged to announce whether the will always followed the last dictate of the understanding, even though the faculty and students at colonial colleges staged grand disputations on the topic. To insist, as both Old and New Light clergy often did, that an operation of the understanding preceded or accompanied the operation of the will was not to claim that the will necessarily acceded to the understanding's view of things. Most clergy on both sides believed that had Adam not fallen, the will would have trotted along behind the understanding like a sheep following a shepherd. But Adam had fallen, and the fall complicated everything for clerical psychologists. The revivalist Jonathan Dickinson came close to the old intellectualist view when he said that the understanding "determines" the choice of the will: "It is impossible for a reasonable Being to do otherwise than *will* what appears to be, in all circumstances, *best* for him and most agreeable and desirable to him." But Dickinson also believed that in the sinful soul, the "vitiated Appetites" join with the "darkned Understanding" in showing the will the "most worthy . . . choice." A pure intellectualist would not have added such a sober qualification. The antirevivalist Charles Chauncy thought that an intellectualist psychology best explained the experience of converts: The Spirit, he wrote, having "removed the Ignorance that was in them, through the blindness of their Mind, he persuades and enables them to

Chuse and Act, according to the Dictates of their enlightned Understanding." But Chauncy also believed that "confusion and disorder" reigned among the fallen faculties, so presumably there could be no assurance that the unenlightened understanding would always draw the unruly will after it.[18]

A clerical assertion about the psychology of the soul in the eighteenth century might refer, then, to human nature before the fall, to the fallen and sinful soul, or to the soul transformed by divine grace. A minister might have advanced an intellectualist position to describe the soul before the fall, a pietistic voluntarism to describe the condition of the fallen soul, and either a voluntarist or an intellectualist account to describe regeneration. Samuel Davies, the New Light missionary to Virginia, felt that in unfallen human nature, the will acted according to the understanding's representations, but that the fall had initiated "Tumults and Broils" between the two faculties, so that the will now "perpetually reluctated and struggled against the Dictates of . . . Reason." The revivalist Samuel Blair believed that in conversion the enlightened understanding would "sweetly overcome" the will, but that in our fallen state "the will often refuses obedience to the understanding's dictates." The theology complicated the psychology—and it also blurred the lines of division between antagonists.[19]

Jonathan Edwards again struck out in his own direction. He did not think it necessary to "enter into a particular disquisition of all points debated on that question, whether the will always follows the last dictate of the understanding." And his notion of the unity of understanding and will in sensible knowledge altered the terms of the question, in any case. To Edwards, it was self-evident that acts of the will had "some connection with the dictates or views of the understanding." He was willing to say that "the soul always wills or chooses that which, in the present view of the mind, considered in the whole of that view, and all that belongs to it, appears most agreeable." In "some sense," therefore, he would admit that "the will always follows the last dictate of the understanding." Indeed, he would go so far as to say that "the will always *is*, as the greatest apparent good, or as what appears most agreeable, is." But in the odd wording of that last sentence, one discerns Edwards' dissent from the intellectualist psychology. He looked on an act of volition as merely a conceptually distinguishable movement in an activity of "the whole faculty of apprehension"; the will followed the understanding's dictates only in the sense that an intellectual judgment was an ingredient within the "compound influence" that moved the will. According to Edwards, the will acted in response to "motives," and a motive was not an isolated "dictate" of the understanding but a complex inducement, grounded both in the unified activity of all the faculties and in the nature of the object that was known and loved. Hence on psychological grounds alone Edwards had difficulties with the intellectualist creed.[20]

He also had some theological questions. A number of English writers had used the intellectualist psychology to argue that "God's operation and assistance" in conversion was "only moral, suggesting ideas to the understanding." In contrast, Edwards believed that God's "physical" operation was necessary for the soul. By *physical*, he did not mean corporeal, but immediate and direct, transforming the entire soul as a unity of understanding and will. By raising questions about the psychology, he was also making a theological point.[21]

Edwards, then, was distinctive, but his distinctiveness cannot serve to mark the dividing lines between Old Lights and New Lights. His criticisms of the current psychological vocabulary would have struck as many revivalists as antirevivalists. It remains true that differing views of psychology did divide the clergy, with consequences for their preaching and also for their habits of private counsel. But their disagreements, which arose from the common habit of thinking in hierarchical patterns, had more to do with their evaluation of faculties than with technical questions about the internal structure of the soul.

The problem was that the ministers affixed differing hierarchies of value to the faculties. In effect, two sets of spatial metaphors, more frequently assumed than expressed, silently guided them. The Old Lights presupposed an image of higher and lower powers. The New Lights drew implicitly on an alternative metaphor: the image of surface and depth. For the antirevivalists, the understanding was higher in value and importance than the affections. For the revivalists, the understanding was only of preliminary importance, and to linger at that level, they thought, was to risk superficiality. For the antirevivalists, the affections were lower in value than the understanding. For the revivalists, the affections were the "deeper" powers. The clergy did not explicitly employ those contrasting tacit metaphors in their arguments with one another—or at least not always. But they were quite consistent in their recourse to the presuppositions implicit in the terms.

No one ventured to say that the religious understanding counted for nothing or that the religious affections were altogether insignificant. It was important to Edwards that renewed affections flow forth in true conversion and also that the mind become "susceptive of the due force of rational arguments for . . . truth." Charles Chauncy not only spoke out for a "religion of the understanding," but he also recognized that "the human passions are capable of serving many valuable purposes in religion . . . always provided that they are kept under the restraints of reason." So we are dealing with differences of emphasis and degree. But matters of nuance have perennially occasioned tumultuous disputations within Christendom, and it did not take long for Old Lights and New Lights to begin shouting.[22]

Chauncy claimed that the revivalists failed to encourage the proper subordination of the passions—indeed, that they fomented insurrection within the soul. How could the revivalist preachers even suggest that the Spirit gave the passions sway over men and women in order to make them Christians? "Would not this be to invert their frame? To place the Dominion in those Powers, which were made to be kept in subjection?" To entrust to affection the guidance of "reasonable beings" was to ensure that "people should run into Disorders." One of the essentials in "the new-forming" of the soul was the restoring of "the Government of a sanctified Understanding." By neglecting that duty, the New Light ministers had opened the way for the devil to prey on countless unwary, deluded, zealous souls "and lead them captive at his Will." Chauncy believed that the affections were low in the natural order of things; he could not imagine that religion would subvert that ordering.[23]

In contrast, Edwards believed that true religion consisted "chiefly in affections"—his reason being that the affections constituted the hidden source of all human action. By 1742, when he published *Some Thoughts Concerning the Present Revival of Religion in New England*, he believed that the critics of the Awakening subscribed to false "philosophical principles." Not only had they sundered the affections from the will but they had also concluded, mistakenly, that affections did not appertain "to the noblest part of the soul." As a result, they had placed their confidence in the illumination of the understanding, and their religion remained superficial: "The informing of the understanding is all vain, any further than it affects the heart; or, which is the same thing, has influence on the affections."[24]

In 1746, when Edwards published his *Treatise Concerning Religious Affections*, he expounded on his favorite metaphor suggesting that the affections embodied the depths of the soul: the metaphor of the "spring." "The affections," he wrote, "not only necessarily belong to human nature, but are a very great part of it." They were, in fact, "the spring of men's actions." Every human activity flowed forth from the spring of affection: "These affections we see to be the springs that set men agoing, in all the affairs of life, and engage them in all their pursuits." All the "motion" of human profit seeking, glory seeking, and pleasure seeking was but the surface rippling of the deeper spring. And as

"God has so constituted human nature, that the affections are very much the spring of men's actions, this also shows, that true religion must consist very much in the affections." Edwards believed that the affections were deep in the order of things; he could not imagine that religions would ignore that ordering.[25]

The other revivalists frequently diverged from Edwards in their analyses of the inner workings of the faculties, but they shared his belief that "doctrinal knowledge" had to "penetrate" to the heart, beneath the level of "mere rational Convictions."[26] With equal assurance, other Old Light clergy shared Chauncy's opinion that an "understanding rightly informed" was far superior to the "raised Affections." Many of the clergy probably staked out a position somewhere in between. We can be assured, though, that most did take some position. Psychological theory had theological consequences, and it had practical implications as well.[27]

Comfort and Caution

The dispute over the evaluation of the faculties had immediate bearing on what the clergy called "the Pastoral Care of . . . Souls." By pastoral care they meant the entire panoply of clerical duties: preaching, administering the sacraments, governing in the congregation, studying in private, and praying in solitude. They also used the term to mean "the private treating of souls, in the great affair of their eternal salvation." A pastor's duty embraced other private ministrations—care of the sick and the grieving, for instance—but the topic of burning interest during the revival, and for years afterward, was "eternal salvation," and the era's debates on pastoral care inexorably returned to that momentous topic.[28]

About one point there was little dissent. Almost everyone assumed that the main pastoral duty in dealing privately with men and women anxious about their salvation was "discernment." As experts in the religious life, the clergy were to offer diagnoses of spiritual states.

82

Thomas Foxcroft of Boston had spoken for most of the later American clergy when, in 1718, he described the duty of the pastor: In healing the conscience, he said, the minister is to *"discern* the true *state* of the Person *distressed*—his natural temper, the nature, cause, degree, symptom, and prognostice of the spiritual disease labour'd under." Throughout the century, most pastors believed that pastoral counsel consisted of making judgments grounded in discernment.[29]

An accurate judgment was the prelude to pastoral advice, and, as ministers had long recognized, guidance of others could be dangerous if it proceeded from careless discernment. "A too hasty conclusion, or a judgment not well founded," wrote Devereux Jarratt, "might be attended with fatal consequences." If in counseling their parishioners the ministers happened to "mistake their State, and misapply Remedies and Directions," said Thomas Clap, "it might prove fatal." There were two tempting errors to be avoided. A pastor counseling someone who suffered "under the beginnings of real conviction" was sometimes prone to offer premature encouragement that led the sinner into "a false and dangerous peace." But the opposite error was equally hazardous. The pastor counseling someone who had been "truly humbled and converted but under spiritual Darkness" needed to guard against exhibiting "the Terrors of the Law" and thereby driving the weak convert "into Despair and . . . Sorrow." Everything depended on accuracy in discerning the state of the soul.[30]

In theory, everyone agreed that the minister who would make "a wise and prudent Use of private Arguings and Warnings" must represent both the gospel and the law but that matters of timing and the recognition of individual differences were all-important in deciding when to offer "comfort" and when to withhold it. "Like a skilful Physician," said Edwards, ministers should "suit [their] Directions, to the various Circumstances of particular Souls." They must adapt their "counsels and Directions to their various Cases," he said. "Not healing those slightly who are wounded in Spirit, lest they be ruined by a false Foundation: Not making the Hearts of those sad whom God would have not have made sad, lest they be discouraged and faint in their minds." Edwards' sentiment was unexceptionable, and the most unyielding Old Light pastor would have repeated it gladly.[31]

Beneath the surface of agreements on strategy, the ministers recognized that pastors, like everyone else, differed in style and temperament. "Some are Boanerges, fitted to delve the Thunders of the Law, and the Curses from Mount Ebal, others are sons of Consolation, fitted to pronounce the Blessings from Mount Gerrizim," wrote the Cambridge Old Light preacher Nathanael Appleton.[32]

> Thus one who looks upon his Neighbour to be in a Fault, or in an Error, apprehends a mild and gentle Management will best Answer the End, for convincing and reclaiming a faulty Brother, and in this way manifests his Love to him. Another thinks that such a gentle Way of treating him would be hurtful to the Man himself, and dangerous to others, and so from the same principles of Love, proceeds in a more severe and rigorous Manner with him.[33]

Charles Chauncy continued his efforts to convince his colleagues that the "diversity" of ministerial gifts was a divine provision for "the amazing difference in the natural make of people"; and he implied that diversity should be expected among those offering private pastoral counsel. But the Awakening seemed to push people in opposite directions.[34]

In part, the problem was theological. The ministers could not, as a group, decide whether the rebirth of a sinner normally required an intense "conviction of sin." The New Light ministers thought it did. "We assert the necessity of preparatory Convictions as God's ordinary way," wrote Samuel Finley, an itinerant revivalist in the middle colonies, "and that they are commonly wrought in the Soul by Means of Preaching the Law and its Terrors." The revivalists did not say that God could save a sinner only by using the law to arouse conviction of sin and misery, but they were not accustomed to seeing God work in any other way. "There must be Self-Despair," declared Finley.[35] Some of the Old Lights, too, believed that there could be no conversion without some degree of "conviction," but they were taken aback by what they saw as a revivalist effort to interpret conviction as meaning agony and terror. Other Old Light pastors denied that "preparatory Convictions" were really necessary; they accused the revivalists of needlessly terrorizing the soul.[36]

Closely related to the question of conviction was a second issue: What was meant by *rebirth*? The New Lights wanted the proud heart broken and the sinfully assertive self suppressed. And they knew that only a crisis, whether sudden or extended, could subdue the prideful will. The crisis was a dissolution of the old defensive self, and such a demise was the necessary condition of any saving change. The Old Lights disagreed. They tended, rather, to see the change as gradual, perhaps painful and laborious, but rarely dramatic, and hardly ever requiring "fears and terrors." The southern Anglican Samuel Quincy insisted that the Spirit of God always issued "gentle" calls and worked on the soul "by way of rational conviction." "We grow into the Christian life," he said, by "insensible Gradations," in which one virtue is slowly added to another. "Grace imitateth nature," said Charles Chauncy, "beginning, usually, with small degrees, and growing up to maturity by leisurely proceeding." The very image of rebirth suggested to him that babes in Christ would undergo a course of "growth and ripeness" by "slow degrees."[37] Both groups, then, believed that the sinner must be born again, but their conflicting images of rebirth seemed to require quite different methods of spiritual obstetrics.

The problem was complicated by the awareness on all sides that rebirth was something of a mystery. The Old Light pastors told everyone who would listen that regeneration was hard to certify and that some fearful souls were already reborn—or on the way—without knowing it. Only a few fortunate Christians would have an inner assurance that they had undergone true regeneration, and people who claimed saintly status were often the most deluded.[38] According to the New Lights, however, it was absurd that one could be reborn without knowing about it; they felt Christians should have a "sensible discovery" of the change. But they recognized that not every crisis was a "true" rebirth—unwarranted confidence could be a sign of pride in disguise. New Light preachers often maintained a wary suspicion of eager souls who "endeavour'd just to get themselves affected by Sermons." Caution was a clerical tradition, especially in New England, where even the clerical patriarchs of the seventeenth century had suffered "internal desertions and uncertainties" about their own salvation. The New Lights lived within that tradition.[39]

Both groups agreed, then, that it was often hard to discern the inner workings of another person's soul. Both agreed that the pastor nevertheless had some responsibility for offering discerning judgments. They could not agree, though, about the criteria for making those judgments. The Old Lights decided that visible behavior was the only ground for a pastoral evaluation. The New Lights preferred to probe beneath visible behavior to the deeper level of the hidden religious inclinations.

To the Old Light clergy, "visible behavior" meant more than respectable deportment. "The principle Mark and Criterion by which to judge of ourselves, or to form a judgment of charity as to others," wrote the Presbyterian John Thomson, was "a Godly and righteous Walk and Conversation." The favorite word of the Old Light clergy may well have been *fruits*. By fruits, not feelings, would one recognize the saintly. And fruits were manifold.[40]

Charles Chauncy was known for his bluntness in private conversations when he called on his parishioners each Monday morning. He did not deny that discernment was a cardinal duty in religious counseling. But he charged that the New Light clergy were forming judgments with undue regard for the transient affections of people and with insufficient attention to "the permanent temper of their Minds discovered in the habitual Conduct of their Lives." Believing that God used "a rational Method" in the conversion of a sinner, Chauncy concluded that in order to "judge the interior state of others," ministers should rely on the "external manifestations" of faith in visible behavior, since these were susceptible to some degree of rational evaluation. Such fruits as unselfishness, long-suffering, meekness, peace, joy, and enduring love exhibited far more clearly than did any crisis or hidden affection the condition of the will and understanding. The pastor was to evaluate manifest understandings and visible behavior, about which there could be a reasonable judgment of charity.[41]

Chauncy spoke for a host of ministers who deplored the "stress on the workings of . . . passions and affections." The faculty at Harvard College thought it silly to claim that everyone reborn of the Spirit would have the "feeling of it." They suspected that the pastors who persisted in probing feelings and inclinations were guilty of "enthusiasm." Alexander Garden, the commissary of the Anglican Church in Charleston, expressed a similar sentiment when he insisted that ministers should help people discover "rational objective Evidence" of their spirituality. Concerned less with introspective anxieties than with life and behavior, the Old Light clergy told any parishioners whom they happened to counsel that the important requirement was simply to "walk in love."[42]

The revivalists were unwilling to grant that a "holy life" provided enough evidence "to judge well of a person's state." They believed that saints possessed evidence of their own state, because the work of grace was "sensible." It was the task of the minister to evaluate that internal evidence. The New Light pastors did not insist on unquestionable assurance and certainty; they did not insist that everyone know "the exact time" of conversion; they did not disregard the evidence of a holy life. But they believed that it was necessary for any clerical judgment to penetrate beneath appearances: "Now, by what Means can we judge well of his state," asked Samuel Finley, "and yet not judge concerning a Work of Grace in the Heart?" The revivalists felt compelled to delve into hidden affections, to talk with people about inward experiences and inexplicable feelings.[43]

How was one to penetrate beneath the surface? The old textbooks in casuistry still proved useful; the clergy studied closely the works of William Perkins, Richard Baxter, and William Ames. But the time was ripe for a new kind of handbook, and the Awakening issued in the most acute and detailed treatise on the cure of souls written in early America. Jonathan Edwards, in *Treatise Concerning Religious Affections,* intended to prove that the revival was a true work of God. In defending the Awakening, though, he filled his book with richly textured descriptions of the religious inclinations. The argument consisted mainly of a detailed outline of the "signs" that ministers (and others) could use in discerning whether the affections had truly been transformed.[44]

Edwards acknowledged that the pastor could not really know "another's heart." He conceded that God's workings were very mysterious and that many people could not recognize "the time of first grace" in themselves. The wisest pastor lacked the ability "to make an open separation between saints and hypocrites" and therefore could judge only "qualifications and experiences," not "persons." But Edwards believed that the minister did need to risk a judgment about a person's orientation toward God and the world.[45]

The main sign of authentic spirituality, he said, was a certain sense of the beauty and excellency of divine things, a new way of "seeing" God and the world. A truly converted person was one whose love for God had been evoked purely by God's own loveliness rather than by any selfish motive. Such a disposition of love would find expression not only in a new depth of understanding and firmness in conviction but also in an inward harmony and balance that would produce quietness of spirit, humility, and tenderness. Edwards was therefore more interested in people's "seeing" than in their willing or knowing; pastoral conversation should be more an aesthetic criticism than a legal judgment. The faithful person would "view nothing as he did before," and the pastor must evaluate that new vision.[46]

From this notion of genuine religion, Edwards derived a variety of practical criteria. Because the new sense of things was an orientation of the whole self, with no sharp distinction between the heart and the head, the minister was not to be unduly impressed by either the fervency of the heart or the acuteness of the understanding. People who evidenced a merely "notional" view of religion had not understood it, but emotional display was no more trustworthy than was intellectual precision. The pastor should be aware, Edwards added, that people preoccupied with the beauty of their own religious experiences had probably gone astray, that those ostentatious in their humility exhibited their spiritual pride, and that anyone who relied on the authority of others had not sensed the beauty of divine holiness. But only by appreciating the religious affections could one discern these and other subtleties of true and false spirituality.[47]

The topic of clerical judgment angered people because of its public consequences: To debate the criteria for pastoral discernment was to discuss the church as a social institution. Gilbert Tennent thought pastors should probe at hidden feelings and underlying intentions; that new converts, before being admitted to the church, should give a "satisfactory Account of their Experiences to those who are the proper Judges of such things." Only a style of pastoral conversation which discovered the wellsprings of piety in the depths of the heart could prepare men and women to offer such an account and to join such a church.[48]

Tennent agreed with Jonathan Edwards that the public accounting of experience should occur under the "direction of *skilful* guides"—namely, ministers. But by the early 1740s a few preachers began to insist that all "the saints certainly know one another . . . by their own inward feelings" and that as a result, ministerial judgments were no more authoritative than those of any true saint among the laity. In reaction against such "enthusiasm," the ministers who disliked all the pastoral probing at "passions and affections" charged that churches were being uncharitable when they required evidence of inward conversion, and presumptuous when they attempted to judge it. Believing that any church would inevitably contain both wheat and tares, they urged pastors to limit themselves to visible evidence and to be generous in their judgments.[49]

The disagreements about criteria of evaluation reflected a difference in pastoral styles. The pastors at one end of the spectrum were criticized for being soft, external, smooth, and lax (they preferred to think of themselves as comforting). The pastors at the other end were accused of being rash and discouraging (they preferred to think of themselves as precise and cautious). They all tried to strike the right balance between precision and consolation. But what seemed comforting to Charles Chauncy appeared deceitful to Jonathan Dickinson, and what seemed precise to Dickinson appeared harsh to Chauncy.

The contrasting styles may have been related to the sometimes broad range of social difference between Old Light and New Light clergy. In New England, at least, the Old Light pastors were more likely than the New Lights to come from middle- and upper-class families in the larger towns and cities and to be the sons of ministers. The New Light clergy were more likely to have been born in small towns or villages, into families of modest social origins, and to have no parental ties to the established clergy.[50] Whatever the social configurations—and there were many exceptions to the pattern—the Old Light clergy manifestly valued a style of pastoral conversation that was less intense and intrusive, more reserved and polite—more in keeping, in fact, with the normal conventions of refined eighteenth-century behavior—than was the New Light ideal of intense pastoral probing, which some of the unawakened colonists found offensive and tasteless.

In any case, the New Light clergy believed that the most

dangerous pastoral temptation was the desire to offer premature comfort to persons under conviction, thereby producing complacency at exactly the wrong moment. The spiritual physician could ill afford to suggest the presence of health in the diseased soul. Comfort and assurance would arrive when the time was right, but the minister dared not substitute soothing words for honest evaluation. The fanatical James Davenport took time from his book burning to excoriate Joseph Noyes of New Haven for trying to comfort a woman who came to him under conviction.[51] And even the moderate New Lights feared that comfort was risky because it mitigated the intensity of a necessary inner struggle.

An untimely or careless word of consolation might bring temporary comfort, but only at great cost, wrote Samuel Blair:

> I was all along very cautious of expressing to people my judgment of the Goodness of their States, excepting where I had pretty clear Evidence from them, of their being savingly changed yet they continued in deep distress, casting off all their Evidences: Sometimes in such cases I have thought it needful to use greater Freedom that way than ordinary, but otherwise, I judged that it could be of little use, and might readily be hurtful.[52]

Blair's religious counsel consisted more often of efforts to "correct and guard against" the "mistakes" of people who valued comfort above truth.

Precise discernment did not denote harshness or abruptness of manner. Edwards urged that ministers be "easy of access . . . open and free, pitiful and compassionate, tender and gentle" to those who approached them, and he encouraged people who were "under religious impressions" to visit him in his study. He became known, in fact, for the "tenderness, kindness, and familiarity" of his discourse: "He was a skillful guide to souls under spiritual difficulties; and was therefore sought unto, not only by his own people, but by many who lived scores of miles off."[53]

And he was delighted when he could offer a positive judgment.

Edwards did receive criticism for offering affirmative interpretations too freely:

> I have been much blamed and censured by many, that I should make it my practice, when I have been satisfied concerning persons' good estate, to signify it to them: which thing has been greatly misrepresented abroad . . . to prejudice the country against the whole affair. But let it be noted that what I have undertaken to judge of has rather been qualifications and declared experiences than persons. Not but that I have thought it my duty as a pastor to assist and instruct persons in applying Scripture rules and characters to their own case (in doing of which I think many greatly need a guide); and have, where I thought the case plain, used freedom in signifying my hope of them to others; but have been far from doing this concerning all that I have had hopes of; and I believe have used much more caution than many have supposed.[54]

But Edwards also worried that unthinking pastors might offer comfort too quickly. He believed that any word of comfort promoting "self-flattery and carelessness" could block the way to the genuine humbling of the heart that a religious crisis should produce. He therefore advised ministers to remind troubled persons that God was "under no manner of obligation" to them. The pastor's first task was to interpret the signs of faith or faithfulness, much as a scholar might interpret a text. Accuracy was far more crucial—and far more loving—than comfort.[55]

It was inevitable that Edwards' caution and restraint when dealing with men and women under conviction would seem excessively severe to ministers who doubted that an agonizing period of conviction was even necessary. New Light ministers sometimes seemed to boast that their judgments alone were properly "severe." "Many people are easily persuaded that a Judgment is rash, if it be severe," wrote Samuel Finley, "but a short Consideration will see, that severity and Rashness widely differ."[56] The

Old Lights did not object in principle to a "severe" judgment, if it were clearly justifiable. But they saw New Light severity as having transgressed the boundaries of both justifiability and justice.

To some of the Old Lights, it seemed that the revivalists had drawn "a Veil over the lovely attribute of Divine Mercy." They did not worry that comforting words would create a false peace. Indeed, they claimed that most of the sober, orthodox souls who sought their advice needed comfort more than cautionary warning. The Anglican pastor Samuel Quincy, laboring in Georgia and South Carolina, expressed dismay that anyone would permit a troubled soul to suffer "great Horrors and Agonies of Mind." It was inconceivable to him that a pastor would encourage "terrors of a guilty conscience." On the contrary, the pastor should try to calm "violent Perturbations of Mind" by explaining that they arose from "natural fears." Pastoral care was a process of "calm Consideration" and persuasion. The danger to be avoided was harsh judgment, which could discourage the soul and cast it into despair. The pastor was to support the soul as it moved through the gradations of spiritual growth, knowing that a fitting life was far superior to a broken will, a word of comfort preferable to scrupulous caution.[57]

Charles Chauncy observed, toward the end of 1741, that in their sermons, some preachers could reach the understanding, some could affect the passions, and some touch the conscience. But still others, he said, possessed the remarkable gift of speaking "comfortably to distressed sinners" in words of "tenderness and compassion." Each style had its merits, Chauncy thought, but he believed that preachers who could comfort were best: "This was the gift of our blessed Savior Jesus Christ." He could not imagine "a more useful gift than this of being able to speak comfortably to distrest sinners. They need the consolations of God."[58] The excellence of consolation, whether from the pulpit or in the privacy of the home, seemed self-evident to the Old Light clergy.

The conflict over pastoral styles was rooted both in

theology and in the conflicting evaluations of the human faculties. Intent on penetrating beneath surface appearances to the affections in the depth of the soul, the revivalists adopted a pastoral style which encouraged saints and sinners to endure a long, wrenching, agonizing period of inner turmoil. Inner chaos seemed to them to provide the clue to understanding the rebirth of the soul. In contrast, the Old Light clergy, confident that the will and the understanding stood highest in the hierarchy of faculties, felt that involuntary and irrational "fears and terrors" were not signs of "God's grace but of satan's Temptations."[59] Rather than encouraging inner turbulence, they strove to exhibit the gospel truths that would quell it.

The debates spread through the Congregational, Presbyterian, and Anglican churches and extended as well into smaller religious groups. Orthodox Lutherans described Lutheran Pietists such as Henry Melchoir Muhlenberg as "too strict" in their pastoral care because of their insistence on probing for feelings of despair. The Pietists, in turn, charged that the leaders of the orthodox remained on the surface when they limited themselves to matters of doctrine and behavior. Roman Catholic clergy were forced to choose between the position of the rigorists, who imposed strict requirements for penance, and the laxists, who often saw confession itself as a sufficient medicinal cure for sin—or from among the doctrines of the "probabilists," who permitted Christians facing moral dilemmas to select and act on the less demanding of two generally acceptable options; the "probabiliorists," who insisted that the stricter option must always be chosen; and the "equiprobabilists," who tried to find a middle course. The Catholic theologian who made the greatest effort to define the mediating position was the eighteenth-century Italian Bishop Alphonsus de Ligouri, whose *Moral Theology* and other writings offered pronouncements on over 4,000 pastoral questions, giving 34,000 citations from 800 authors. It is no surprise that he eventually became the leading authority for

American priests, though his ascendancy did not occur until well after the end of the colonial period.[60]

Among Protestants, the eighteenth-century debates planted some doubts about the hierarchical style of pastoral care. The New England Baptist Isaac Backus concluded that "common people have as good right to judge what *gifts* are edifying and what *experiences* are clear." Ministers had assumed more authority, he said, than judges had in the civil courts. Backus was converted in a field in Connecticut during the Awakening, and he agreed with the revivalistic rigorists who probed and tested the feelings. But he felt that ministers sometimes got in the way of "godly persons" who knew more than the clergy about inward experiences. He himself was ordained in 1748 as pastor in a church that had separated from the Congregational establishment, and he sought and received ordination again when he helped to form a Baptist congregation in Massachusetts. But his most vigorous defense of the "pastoral" authority of the laity came after his ordination. Like a good number of his pietistic brothers and sisters, he had begun to have doubts about some of the older hierarchies.[61]

Toward a New Era

The Awakening created a conflict that lasted throughout the century. For more than fifty years the clergy repeated the old arguments about church membership, conversion, and the faculties. Their psychological vocabulary proved to be remarkably elastic: It reappeared again and again not only in theological squabbles but in ethical treatises, handbooks of rhetoric, manuals of etiquette, and political speeches. Every issue of church and state seemed to require some judgment about the nature and significance of the will, the understanding, or the affections. And whether in piety or in politics, partisans of the understanding repeatedly quarreled with admirers of the affections. The Awakening had popularized a vocabulary that would divide Americans for decades, and only in the light of that tension can one understand the determined quest for balance in pastoral care in the early nineteenth century.

In 1770 the Edwardean theologian Samuel Hopkins of Newport, Rhode Island, rejoiced that Edwards' *Treatise Concerning Religious Affections* had been reprinted and was "spreading far and wide." The disciples of Edwards— who by 1770 were being described by their detractors as New Divinity theologians—hoped that the treatise would remind misguided pastors that sinful actions proceeded from a disordered will, rather than from a darkened understanding and that only the "immediate operation of the Spirit" on the will could redeem the soul. And the Edwardeans continued the tradition of clerical caution. Hopkins would never express more than a hope that his assorted spiritual crises had produced a "saving" change in himself. Many who think they are converted, he said, are really "strangers to true conversion." He once visited a dying woman who was "full of joy and comfort, supposing she had had saving discoveries of Christ." Upon examining her, he decided that she was "deceived," that her comfortable impressions were only "the workings of her imagination." "She was confident," he said, "but I told her my fears. How exposed to the delusions of the devil are ignorant persons! especially those whose understanding is shattered, and their imagination lively by a fever."[62]

The Old Calvinist critics of the Edwardeans replied that regeneration took place when God enlightened the mind "spiritually and savingly to understand." They agreed that sinful actions proceeded from a disordered will, but they added that disorder of the will arose from a prior darkness of the understanding. The Spirit saved the sinful by opening their understandings, not by any "physical" operations on their wills. In their pastoral conversations, therefore, the Old Calvinist ministers encouraged the doubtful to "endeavour and use means to obtain converting grace." "God did not create us for suffering," said Moses Mather in 1770. The implication was that pastoral care should consist mainly of the alleviation of spiritual pain.[63]

The "liberal" clergy—a label that designates mainly the Congregationalists and Anglicans who were soft on original sin and high on good works—believed even more strongly than the Old Calvinists that Christians were "the proper Heirs of Comfort." "In judging of our spiritual state," said Lemuel Briant of Massachusetts in 1749, pastors should look simply to "patient *Continuance* in the ways of Well-do-ing." To do otherwise, he said, was to create unnecessary despair: "The Consequences of depretiating moral Vertue are very injurious to such as are sincere and upright Christians, in robbing them of that divine Comfort that they are the proper heirs of, and filling their Minds with needless Fears and Scruples about their spiritual State."[64]

By 1765 Charles Chauncy had begun to describe redemption as "forming the character" as well as saving the soul; by 1785 he denied the hardline doctrine of original sin and published a theory of universal salvation.[65] For the liberals, virtue and comfort had become the twin foci of the gospel.

Though the century witnessed a continuation and expansion of the older debates, it also witnessed a redefinition of the older terms. No aspect of the conceptual transition was more important than the growing infatuation with the "self." As early as 1679 the Earl of Shaftesbury in England had argued that "self-Affections" were quite useful and admirable, and before long a few English writers were contending—somewhat as Thomas Hobbes had earlier—that the impulse of self-preservation was the bedrock of morality and social order. The Scottish philosopher Francis Hutcheson, who wrote his celebrated *Inquiry into the Original of our Ideas of Beauty and Virtue* (1725) to counter egoistic theories of morality by showing that virtuous actions arose from "an entirely different Principle of Action from Interest or Self-Love," did acknowledge that self-love was not really so bad. Truly moral persons could, with good conscience, he said, exercise benevolence toward themselves. And in 1726, the Bishop of Durham, Joseph Butler, made it positively fashionable for the clergy in England to believe that "self-love and benevolence, virtue and interest, are not to be opposed." He explained that benevolence and self-love "were so perfectly coincident that the greatest satisfactions to ourselves depend on our having benevolence in a due degree; and that self-love is one chief security of our right behavior towards society." After all, said Butler, if we are to love our neighbors as ourselves, we must love ourselves.[66]

Jonathan Edwards could not help worrying about all that self-love. He normally referred to the self only when he talked about self-love, which for him signified mainly "a man's regard to his confined private self, or love to himself with respect to his private interest." Edwards acknowledged that there was a broader sense of the term, in which *self-love* became equivalent to any delight in the pleasing or the beautiful, and he acknowledged as well that even the narrower self-love could promote social order. But for Edwards, as for the earlier Puritans, *self-love* described mainly "private" affections, and for him such "private self-love" was sinful.[67]

By the early 1740s, though, a genial company of good-natured colonial preachers had begun to propose that self-love had its proper place in the Christian life. The liberal Congregationalist pastor in Boston's West Church, Jonathan Mayhew, believed that self-love and "self-enjoyment" would lead naturally to benevolence and charity. In 1746 the liberal Anglican rector in Stratford, Connecticut, Samuel Johnson, explained in his *Ethices Elementa*, the first American text in moral philosophy, that "the Law of Self-Love or Self-Esteem" imposed an obligation "of valuing our selves and our own Interest, and of seeking and pursuing our own Preservation and Well-being or Happiness." Johnson still wrote about self-denial, but with the intent of encouraging "the Mastery of [the] self," which would permit it to "become what [it] ought to be."[68]

The new rhetoric about the self was no monopoly of the liberals. By the 1760s, Old Calvinist theologians were arguing that "a principle of self-love is essential to us, as moral agents," and they urged that ministers appeal to self-love and the desire for happiness as a means of encouraging sinners to "prepare" themselves for saving grace. Distinguishing self-love from selfishness, the Old Calvinists wondered how anyone could doubt that a prudent regard for oneself promoted both morality and piety.[69]

The Edwardeans were appalled. Joseph Bellamy said that the Old Calvinist appeal was "criminal"; Samuel Hopkins worried that even Edwards had conceded too much to the proponents of self-love. Bellamy and Hopkins represented a pietistic reaction against a broad cultural transition from communal to individualistic social ethics. The philosophers who had rationalized the expanding British market economy had used the notion of self-love to justify the pursuit of individual happiness. In contrast, the New Divinity theologians associated self-love with "pride and ambition" in the social order. Samuel Hopkins concluded that self-love of any kind was the core of sinfulness, and he called for an ethic of "disinterested benevolence" devoid of any self-regarding motives. The true saint, he thought, would be so selfless as to accept damnation for the glory of God. For the New Divinity theologians, there was no middle ground between total selfishness and total selflessness. But in the long run their protest failed. The lovable self was here to stay.[70]

These changing views of the self paralleled related reevaluations of the understanding, the will, and the affections. The introduction of the New Learning into American colleges produced no great crisis, but it did initiate a gradual rethinking of the older psychology. The world of Locke and Newton was not hospitable to hierarchical souls.

In 1714 a copy of John Locke's *Essay Concerning Human Understanding* showed up in the famous shipment of books that Jeremiah Dummer sent to Yale College. By the 1720s, the essay was being read in colonial colleges; by the 1750s it was widely used as a primary textbook, and the later popularity of the Scottish revisionists who tried to save

Locke's empiricism by correcting his errors ensured that a distinctively post-Lockean perspective would eventually permeate college and seminary classrooms.[71]

Locke's influence on the educated clergy was general and diffuse. The technical innovations of his epistemology wrought no revolution in the churches; yet Locke established or confirmed some lasting patterns. He made certain that *experience*, however construed, would be an honorable term in American thought. It was telling, moreover, that the classic English-language text in philosophy was, in substance, an essay in psychology. And it was also important that Locke concentrated so single-mindedly on the operation of the understanding. The celebrity of the book helped to confirm a clerical preoccupation with rationality that would endure for more than a century.

The will also attracted its share of attention, especially after Jonathan Edwards published his *Freedom of Will* in 1754. He wrote the book, drawing somewhat on Locke, to show that Calvinist determinism was entirely compatible with moral responsibility. Men and women bore the burden of their inevitable misdeeds, he said, even though they were enmeshed in a chain of causes. They were unable to choose the motives that elicited their acts, but they were free to act (and an act implied consent). They were free to do as they willed. Edwards located freedom in the external act, not in the choice itself. But this freedom was sufficient, he thought, to relieve God of any responsibility for sin. So Edwards attempted to reduce the notion of self-determination to absurdity.[72]

It took a while for anyone to answer, at least in print, but in 1770 James Dana, a minister from Connecticut, observed that Edwards had fallen into verbal confusion when he had said, on the one hand, that motives determined the will, and on the other, that "the will always *is* as the greatest apparent good . . . is" (that is, that the volition and the motive were identical). If the motive were not distinct from the volition, Dana asked, then how could it cause the volition?[73] Theologians wrestled with

the problem without ever resolving it, but their disputations did have one ironic and unintended consequence:
The debate over the will eventually directed their
attention back to the affections.

In 1793 a pastor in Massachusetts, Samuel West, said
that Edwards had erred in identifying the will and the
affections. West believed that there were three faculties of
the mind: perception (or understanding), volition, and
"propension." A propensity was an involuntary affection,
like love or anger, and it was clearly an "effect." But
Edwards had confused propensities with volitions and had
concluded that volitions, too, were effects. The solution,
thought West, was simply to reflect on the difference
between, say, feeling angry at a slight and deciding to seek
revenge. By conflating the will and the affections, Edwards
had blurred such a distinction.[74] The cogency of West's
argument was less important than the tendency it
illustrated—a tendency for the debate over the will to
engender renewed attention to affection as a distinctive
power in the soul. West's book failed to attract much
attention, but other theologians soon began to advance the
same kind of argument with greater effect. A growing
predisposition to defend freedom of the will led not only to
new conceptions of volition but to a new awareness of
affection and sentiment.

Finally, the eighteenth century also witnessed a momentous discussion of the affections quite apart from any
question of their relation to the will. Even before 1700, a
few Puritan clerical psychologists had ventured to locate
the affections in the heart or will, rather than in the lower
sensitive soul. A few philosophers also had taken a second
look at the affections. René Descartes complained that
nothing in the science of the ancients was so defective as
"what they have written on the passions," and he
proceeded to redefine those "passions" as "modes of
awareness" which disposed the soul "to will the things . . .
nature tells us are of concern to us." When the later
Cambridge Platonists, drawing on Descartes, began to
declare that the will and affections could know the

101

"beauty" of God as accurately as could the understanding, or to refer to a "boniform faculty of the Soul" which integrated will, affection, and intellect into a "relish" for the good, then the foundations were in place for what Norman Fiering has described as a virtual revolution: The affections and passions came to be valued as guides to benevolent activity. The Scottish moralist Francis Hutcheson brought the revolution to completion when he elaborated the notion that complex internal "sensations"—such as a "moral sense"—constituted distinctive modes of apprehension which prompted benevolent activity by eliciting the higher affections.[75]

Edwards tried, in his *Nature of True Virtue,* to show that Hutcheson's "moral sense" arose either from self-love or from the merely natural conscience—that it was not the "truly virtuous taste" and "relish" for the beauty of Being that the redeemed could enjoy. But Edwards then proceeded to define *virtue* as a consent of the heart to "being in general," thereby reuniting the idea of moral sentiment with the notion of the gracious affections from which it had developed. Despite Edwards' reservations, moreover, the notion of a moral sense would take hold throughout the entire spectrum of colonial religious and moral thought. The orthodox Presbyterian John Witherspoon taught it at Princeton; the unorthodox President Thomas Jefferson tried to teach it to politicians. It was a long way from the seventeenth-century affections, bubbling up from the sensitive soul, to the eighteenth-century moral sense, venturing forth to apprehend ethical intricacies; but the older psychology laid the foundation for the new ethics. In the land of Protestant Pietism and Lockean empiricism, the moral sense theorists had found a secure home.[76]

The discussions about the understanding, the will, and the affections held manifest practical implications for the practice of the cure of souls—and so did an alteration in the American social hierarchy. The truth is that although the forces of custom and ideological commitment maintained a system of deference and subordination throughout the century, the colonies lacked the material and institutional resources to sustain a stable traditional hierarchy. Few colonists abandoned the old hierarchical images and ideas, but many filled them with new content, and the cultural transitions presented new problems for the physicians of the soul.[77]

Primarily, some colonists became wealthy while others did not. It took only a short time for the colonial economy to produce deepening chasms between the rich and the poor, and despite the abundance of land, the poorer colonists lacked the means to exploit the earth so as to overcome the inequities. The old Protestant Ethic, the doctrine that everyone is called to an earthly task to be pursued diligently, had once justified inherited social inequalities. By the eighteenth century it was being used to justify the systematic, diligent, unostentatious pursuit of wealth, as well as wealth's unequal distribution. The importing of African slaves starkly and viciously symbolized that inequality, and in eighteenth-century cities, lists of poor whites also expanded dramatically. Even in smaller towns the number of vagabonds increased. And as the rich became richer and the poor more numerous, the old social hierarchy assumed a new form. Wealthy colonists viewed themselves as socially estimable, and in a telling gesture, a multitude of prosperous farmers and merchants, who had not the slightest claim to inherited gentility, began to drop such terms as *yeoman* and to designate themselves as *gentleman* and *esquire*. New patterns of deference arose, and the clergy were bound to be affected.[78]

The ministers felt uncomfortable with all the new pretension. They criticized the "exorbitant Reach after Riches, which is becoming the reigning Temper in Persons of all Ranks in our Land"; they disliked it when men and women were "only esteemed according to what they were worth." Not that the clergy were egalitarians: Most continued to believe that there should be "different Orders, with various Subordinations, to answer the Ends of Society." Everyone had been "allotted" a "peculiar station." Wrote Jonathan Edwards in 1755, "There is a beauty of order . . . when the different members of society have all their appointed office, place, and station, according to their several capacities and talents, and every one keeps his place, and continues in his proper business." Even amid the excitement of revolution in 1780, the Reverend Samuel Williams of Massachusetts expressed an enduring clerical consensus when he assured his congregation that Christianity provided security for "those several stations, whether of authority and pre-eminence, or of subordination and dependence, which nature has established." But when men and women attached social distinction to wealth without recognizing other capacities and talents, when they fought for position and elaborated new criteria of success and still claimed to be located precisely in their rightful "place," then the clerical portrait of social beauty seemed skewed.[79]

It was revealing, though, that when the newly ascendant ladies and gentlemen of the American provinces tried to learn their way around in elevated society, they found the way to refinement marked with many of the same signposts that once had pointed the way to piety. One mark of refinement, it seemed, was a proper balance and harmony of the understanding, the will, and the affections, and one clue to some subtle changes in the cure of souls was the proliferation after 1745 of such manuals of etiquette as J. Hamilton Moore's *Young Gentleman and Lady's Monitor . . . Calculated to Eradicate Vulgar Prejudices and Rusticity of Manners: Improve the Understanding: Rectify the Will; Purify the Passions.*[80] American publishers printed and reprinted more than fifty-seven editions of such etiquette books between 1745 and 1800, with instructions on the government of the affections, the cultivation of the understanding, self-control, and the development of "sensibility." In some, Christianity became an adornment of gentility: "Religion," wrote one author, "is rather a matter of sentiment than reasoning," and refined sentiment was the badge of social elevation.[81]

The problem for the clergy was not that they were

drastically falling behind in a race for social status, though some did worry about slippage and complained about the "levelling" of the position of ministerial work to that of mechanics, merchants, and physicians. There were some struggling Anglican missionaries in the middle colonies and some Baptist farmer-preachers of exceedingly modest means in the South, but as a class the clergy were by no means paupers or marginal figures in the society. Their income as a group was usually equal to that of doctors and lawyers—or higher—and they still maintained a strong sense of their importance in the culture.[82]

The problem was that new social distinctions carried conflicting expectations and criteria for ministers. At a time when some people valued education highly, while others did not, and some valued refined manners, while others cared not a whit for them, and some valued learned sermons, while others felt disappointed in them, ministers had to make some adjustments. The preacher who mingled with aristocrats risked the dislike of the common folk, while the poor and humble parson could suffer the disdain of the high and mighty. Inevitably, there were complaints about ministers who paid "a singular deference to the great of their flock," treating them with "more courtesy and respect than they [did] the common part." During the 1780s and 1790s, many Americans decided that they deserved deference from their inferiors, but many of the inferiors decided not to defer to anyone. The clergy were caught in the middle, and one consequence was a series of rhetorical assaults on "ecclesiastical monarchy" and clerical "tyranny" that continued for decades.[83]

To some of the clergy the problem, at least partially, seemed to be one of psychology—maintaining a proper balance among the inner faculties. If only everyone, rich and poor, grand and common, could control the passion for position and the lust for gain, cultivate the understanding and temper the heart, then harmony might prevail. It was not surprising that the clergy so often addressed the problem of social change with a psychological vocabulary. Almost everyone occasionally talked about

105

almost everything in psychological categories. Political speeches during the revolutionary years returned repeatedly to the theme of English "passions" and colonial "affections"—"base passions and vile lusts" in conflict with "the dictates of right reason," and the love of liberty as an inextinguishable passion with self-preservation as an inexpungable instinct.[84] It is no wonder, then, that after the Revolution, historians of the new nation depicted the war as a struggle between reason and "the rudeness of human passions." And during the subsequent debates over the Constitution, political theorists worried that "the passions . . . not the reason, of the public would sit in judgment." By the 1780s, differing evaluations of reason, the moral sense, and the passions tended to divide Republicans and Federalists in much the same way that conflicting appraisals of the understanding and the affections had once divided Old Lights from New Lights.[85]

In view of that intense interest in "human faculties" on the part of preachers and politicans, rhetoricians and polite authors, poets and lawyers, philosophers and physicians, it could not have seemed unusual that in the educated circles of the clergy, the expectation of mastery in "mental philosophy" was soon taken for granted. And it was not surprising that one pressing question for the cure of souls at the beginning of the nineteenth century was the quandary as to the right balance of rationality and sentiment in pastoral conversations. The Awakening had popularized a psychological vocabulary and hence a way of thinking about society, politics, and piety. It was that vocabulary and that way of thinking that would shape the cure of souls in America for half a century.

4

Balance, Gentility, and Self-Culture

In 1850 the Reverend Ichabod Spencer published his
Pastor's Sketches, a manual in which he described his
conversations with "anxious inquirers." In Brooklyn,
Spencer had acquired a reputation as a master of the cure
of souls, and his book sold well: It was reprinted five times
within a year, and 6,000 copies were soon in circulation in
a nation with fewer than 27,000 clergy. His narratives
received admiring attention throughout the century. Yet
Spencer was cautious and even somewhat defensive when
he published a second series of *Pastor's Sketches* in 1853.
Not everyone would approve of his mode of conversation,
he wrote. But he assured his readers that he never had
knowingly uttered a single sentence that would "wound
the feelings." Some expressions might "sound abrupt, and
perhaps *severe*," but surely none could be "found offensive
to refined taste." His goal had simply been "to cause the
truth to be understood."[1] Spencer's defense of his conver-
sational method embodied both a presupposition and a
problem that typified the cure of souls in antebellum
America. The presupposition was that the pastor, in

appealing to the will, would accord proper weight to both rationality and sentiment. The problem was in determining how to insist on "truth" while deferring to refined taste.

The handbooks on pastoral care in the early nineteenth century mirrored the social changes that had transformed a market and agricultural economy into a maturing urban and industrial order. They also reflected a conviction among educated Protestant clergy that Christianity was rational and that psychology was the servant of faith. In trying to balance persuasion, sentiment, and rational argument in pastoral work, the theologians were responding both to the demands of a social setting and to the inner tensions of their intellectual heritage. The result was the ideal of "gentlemanly counsel" that prompted Ichabod Spencer's defense of his pastoral sketches.

Ichabod Spencer

Spencer's friends remembered him as a man of massive frame and commanding presence, with eyes that glared above short gray whiskers. He was known for "great faithfulness, great painstaking, and even great *tact* in his pastoral services." He was also known, though, as a rough and tyrannical personality who was not always a "gentle Shepherd." Usually reserved and reticent in polite conversation, he could display an ironic, satirical wit that made acquaintances uncomfortable. The two sides of his personality displayed some deep tensions in his character. Spencer was a man of "self-scrutinizing spirit"—prone to a "depressed state of mind"—who often complained that he "never was fit for a minister of the gospel." He eventually suffered a series of nervous breakdowns which disrupted his pastorate at a large Presbyterian church in Brooklyn and prevented his acceptance of a position as professor of pastoral theology at what would become the Hartford Seminary Foundation. His struggle to maintain a balance between tactfulness and bluntness was, on one level, the expression of his inner conflict. On another level, however, Spencer represented the two sides of an ambivalence in an urban clerical culture which valued both delicacy of manner and unflinching truthfulness and which sometimes worried that the two could not be easily joined.[2]

Like Thomas Hooker two hundred years earlier, Spencer had developed an "answering method" for dealing with despair, for he believed that "entire despair" was "incompatible with seeking God." When a depressed middle-aged member of his congregation seemed unwilling to reveal to him the state of her "heart," Spencer suspected that something was amiss.

He called on her one day to tell her that her taciturn manner baffled and disturbed him, and she confessed her conviction that her day was "gone by." "I am given over," she said. "The Holy Spirit has left me." In a cold, decided manner, she told him of her utter despair. And since her "day of grace was past," she declared that she wished to discuss the matter no further. But Spencer, even before she finished speaking, had begun to plan how he could "remove her error." He began by asking questions.

How long, he wondered, had she been in this state of mind?

"Eighteen years," she replied.

Had she ever prayed? Not for eighteen years. Did she feel unhappy? She seldom thought of it, she answered, and she "never intended to think of it again."

"Do you believe the heart is deceitful?" Spencer asked her.

"Yes, I *know* it."

"It may be, then, that your wicked heart has deceived *you*, in respect to your day of grace."

"No," she said. "I am not deceived."

But Spencer noticed that his observation had staggered her, so he followed with a demur: "Yes," he said, "you are."

"No. I am not. Nothing can save me now: and I do not wish to have my mind disturbed by any more thought about it."

"Why do you attend church?"

"Only to set a good example. I believe in religion as firmly as you do; and wish my children to be Christians."

"Do you pray for *them*?"

"No: Prayer from me would not be heard."

"Madam," he responded, "you are in error. I know you are. And I can convince you of it. If you will hear me, lend me your mind, and speak frankly to me, and tell me the grounds on which your despair rests, I will convince you that you are entirely deceived. . . . May I come to see you again about it?"

She refused. Spencer again insisted: "Madam, you must! I *cannot* leave you so! I will not! I love you too well to do it. I ask it as a personal favor to myself; and I shall not think you have treated me politely, if you refused it. May I see you a little while to-morrow?"

"I will *see* you," she said, "if you so much desire it."

Spencer thanked her profusely, but he observed to himself that she had seemed "as unmoved as a stone. She did not shed a tear, or heave a sigh." And when he called the next day, he tempered his strategy to her impassive state. He asked for "reasons or evidences" on which her opinion rested. She offered one evidence after another, confirming each with a text of Scripture. But rather than reply immediately, Spencer suddenly decided to leave. He thought that such a tactic might gain him a second audience with her, and he also wanted time to study her case. He had expected, he wrote, to find the "old affair of the 'unpardonable sin' or 'sin against the Holy Ghost,' but . . . found a far more difficult matter."

When he returned, she seemed, as he had feared, reluctant to see him, but he "gave her no time to make any objections." Insisting that she did not need to assent to anything unreasonable he might say, he took up her "evidences" one by one, beginning with the weakest. And within an hour he had disposed of several objections.

"But there are stronger ones left," she said.

"We will attend to them hereafter," Spencer replied.

"But remember, you have found your mistake in respect to *some*; therefore it is possible that you may be mistaken in respect to *others*."

The woman said nothing, he reported, "but evidently her confidence was shaken." For five or six weeks, therefore, Spencer debated with her at least once each week, initially evoking her "intellectual" interest, chipping away at each of her arguments. But toward the end of their sessions, he summarized their conversations, noted that he had not dealt with her final objection, and told her that a successful resolution of that last problem would no doubt convince her that she could transcend despair. Rather than continue the conversation, however, Spencer told her that the decision was now hers. He would return, but only if she *wished* to see him again.

By now Spencer was confident of success, and his ploy worked. The woman replied that her opinion was unchanged, but that she "should like to hear what I had to say about this remaining point, which, (as she truly said) I had avoided so often." Spencer called the next day and took up the last item, "reasoning with her, and asking if she thought me right, from step to step." Finally, "her bosom heaved with emotion, and her whole frame seemed agitated with a new kind of life."

When Spencer asked her if she still had reason to believe "that her day of grace was past," she began to cry, clasped her hands, and paced the room, exclaiming: "I can be saved! I can be saved!"

Spencer said nothing, remained until she became more composed, and then took his leave with a silent bow. Within a few weeks she was a blissful soul.[3]

Social Order

Spencer, in 1850, did not sound strikingly different from Hooker in 1630 or Parkman in 1720, but by the time he wrote *Pastor's Sketches*, a migration from the countryside into towns, cities, and factories had signaled the transition

111

from a self-subsistence agricultural economy, organized around household industries, to a nascent industrial economy built around the factory. The leap from the family-craft system to mercantile and factory capitalism altered even the tone of pastoral conversations in the privacy of Victorian parlors.

In the eighteenth century, Americans had organized their economy in hierarchical patterns. Both on farms and in the small artisan industries, the ideal was the organization of production under personal hierarchies modeled after the family. Farmers and small merchants worked alongside their laborers and usually provided their room and board. Slave owners viewed themselves as paternal supervisors of "their people." In such an economy, both wage earners and slaves stood subject to the immediate discipline of masters, within units of production that resembled large households. The system seemed well-adapted both to an agricultural nation and to the ideals of hierarchy and deference inherited from the past.[4]

By the beginning of the nineteenth century, some of the merchants accumulated enough wealth to establish larger, more impersonal hierarchies of production, in a system known as merchant capitalism. The wealthy shopkeepers had money, access to credit, knowledge of the markets, and the means to store and sell finished products, and they began to absorb the old household craft system into their more complex economic relations with workers, farmers, and planters. Gradually the "master" of the craft system began to disappear, or to become the "contractor" in a system in which merchants hired "journeymen" to do contract work or furnished raw materials to men and women who worked in their own homes. The agricultural economy—whether slave or free—retained the older paternal values, but the rest of the society moved toward an impersonal contractual economy in which workers were no longer dependents in a propertied household but agents of production in a fluid marketplace. A symbol of the change was the exodus of workers from the homes of their employers into their own dwellings—and their own neighborhoods.[5]

The "transportation revolution" after the War of 1812 both expanded and altered merchant capitalism. By 1815 politicians and merchants were excited about turnpikes; by 1830 the steamboat had dramatically reduced the cost in money and time of travel and trade. The building of the Erie Canal in 1825 began yet a new era, which was barely underway when the chartering of the Baltimore and Ohio Railroad in 1828 created even grander dreams. To the poets and storytellers, it seemed that an ugly machine had burst into the American garden, but for the merchants, cheap transportation opened the way to an expansion of commerce and wealth.[6]

The revolution in transportation helped transform merchant capitalism into factory capitalism; the expansion of the Lowell textile mills in Massachusetts in 1813 showed how an enterprising merchant could exploit the new technology to tap larger markets. By the 1820s, the merchants were increasingly organizing production under one roof, turning journeymen into wage earners and masters into foremen. By the 1840s, factory capitalism in the northeast was coming into its own.[7]

The change in the economy produced an increasingly segmented society. It created firm boundaries between the domestic and the economic, as both laborers and merchants began to live in one place and work in another. It established sharper divisions between men and women, as the new organization of trades, crafts, and factories left urban women at home in "domestic" rather than publicly productive roles. It deepened the chasm between slave and free by opening new markets for southern cotton and rice. It intensified the gap between public and private, as the household became not the locus of production but a retreat from the marketplace. It drove a wedge between capital and labor, as capitalists tried to increase productivity and workers formed "unions of the trades" to protect themselves. And it established more visible lines of division between town and country, for the new commerce required urban concentration, produced urban wealth, and exalted urban values.[8]

In 1790 only 200,000 Americans lived in towns and cities with a population larger than 2,500. By 1829 the number exceeded one million. Only about 7 percent of Americans lived in those towns in 1810; by 1860 the figure was 20 percent. In 1776 there were fewer than a dozen cities of 5,000 or more inhabitants; by 1850 there were 147. Whether the changes in the economy produced the urbanization, or the move to the towns made possible the economic change, the new economy and the proliferation of towns proved to be mutually sustaining.[9]

An egalitarian rhetoric echoed throughout the towns and cities, and to recall the Jacksonian era and subsequent years is to conjure up visions of common people (white ones, at least) marching toward abundance. The rhetoric had little relation to urban realities: The age was marked by enormous disparities of wealth and status and by nervous social climbing. The Connecticut theologian Horace Bushnell complained in 1847 about "the lower stratum . . . comprising the vicious, the idle, the unprogressive and thriftless of every sort." The Pennsylvania theologian Philip Schaff complained in 1855 about the opposite end of the spectrum, the "mushroom aristocracy" and its "outward show." "Whether the enormous increase of luxury, and worldly pomp, and splendor, will gradually undermine the Republic, whose proper foundation is the patriarchal style of simplicity and honesty, time must tell." Some ministers thought that a caste system had grown up in America, and a few social critics agreed. "We have our own castes of society," said one observer in 1826, "graduated and divided with as much regard to rank and dignity as the most scrupulous Hindoo maintains."[10]

In America, said Schaff, "Almost every one tries to become a gentleman or a lady; that is, to attain the English ideal of outward and inward intellectual and moral culture, so far as his circumstances and position allow." Nowhere was that yearning for the appearance of gentility more visible than in the cities and towns, whether North or

South. The respectable townsfolk reassured themselves repeatedly—in newspapers, journals, letters, and tracts—that their hometowns were models of enlightenment, refinement, and elegance. The upper classes set themselves apart by living in wealthy enclaves (often at the periphery of the cities), marrying among themselves, joining the same organizations, and looking down on benighted souls from the countryside. "I like the country people very much," wrote a Virginian in 1858. "I think there is much truth and simplicity about them. But then they have not the allurements that we Town People have to contend with."[11]

The notion of urban gentility among the middle classes displayed a peculiar duality. They viewed themselves as enlightened and rational men and women of "mental culture." They boasted of the diffusion of knowledge, and they formed countless organizations to promote it: schools, academies, colleges, lyceums, debating clubs, philosophical societies, museums, and libraries that promised to disseminate "useful knowledge of literature, moral philosophy, natural history, and similar topics. Technical explanation and scientific description became forms of middle-class recreation, as townspeople flocked to hear lectures and buy books on physiology and phrenology; traveling showmen advertised themselves as "professors of chemistry"; local groups created "naturalists' societies" to further "the knowledge of minerals, plants, and other departments of nature"; and the authors of how-to manuals stimulated a national passion for amateur technological problem solving and a fascination with detailed explanations of staircases and sailing ships, precious stones and dyed wool.[12] The popular preoccupation with "science" and technology helped to define the meaning of *rationality* in the antebellum towns.

At the same time, their middle-class culture glowed with sentimentality. It engendered a vast audience for gilt-edged gift books with flowery gold covers and precious titles: *Poetry of the Flowers, The Gift of Affection, Gift of Sentiment, Gift of Flowers,* or *Love's Wreath,* and *Dew Drops*

115

of the Nineteenth Century. The theater was melodramatic; poetry was teary-eyed; popular painters favored romantic nature allegories and nostalgic depictions of quaint characters, distributed in quantity by Currier and Ives; the best-selling novels featured either Gothic melodrama or pious and heart-tugging bathos. When there were objections to the exhibition of Hiram Powers' "Greek Slave," a sculpture of a nude young woman whose head was bowed in pensive reliance on God as she was sold in a Turkish auction, the Unitarian minister Orville Dewey defended her virtue: "The 'Greek Slave,'" he said, "is clothed all over with sentiment, sheltered, protected by it from every profane eye." His defense perfectly captured an urban cultural ideal.[13]

Writers on pastoral topics recognized that the dual expectation of rational utility and soft sentimentality had implications for ministerial behavior. Ministers with "rustic, boorish habits" were likely to be excluded from respectable society, wrote one pastoral theologian. "The necessity for an educated ministry," he added, "was never greater than at the present time." Anxieties were common among fledgling urban pastors, who were sometimes explicitly reminded that they were preaching to "town folks." "I am out of my surroundings," wrote Joel Hawes when he preached his first sermon at Hartford before "judges, governors, doctors, lawyers, merchants, and people in the highest grades of society." Theodore Munger, later a celebrated liberal theologian, wrote to his mother in 1854 that he had preached well at a country church: "But because I succeeded there it is no indication that I should succeed before a city congregation," he said. By the 1840s, the clergy were arranged in strata of ascending social ranks, and the elite occupied the higher town pulpits. The ministry was becoming a "career" in the modern sense, with most ministers expecting to advance upward through several pastorates, moving toward the larger, wealthier, urban congregations. The ministers who succeeded in those pulpits had to exhibit the appearance of learning and also to exemplify, in Ichabod Spencer's words, a religion of "kindness, and good manners, and good taste."[14]

The allure of the towns was evident in the progress of the Second Great Awakening, which not only swept the frontier after 1800 but also assumed the form of an urban revivalism that captured the towns and cities. The movement was aptly symbolized in the *Memoirs* of evangelist Charles G. Finney, who adapted the techniques of unfashionable Methodists and made them fashionable in city churches. Consciously or not, he wrote his *Memoirs* as a chronicle of the urbanization of the revival. When Finney began preaching, in the small villages of western New York, he ridiculed "splendid sermons" intended for a "cultivated congregation," boasting that as a lawyer he knew how to talk to "the people." But when he wrote about his career, the outline charted a movement from the village to the town and city, and from simplicity to sophistication. By the time he reached the chapter on the Rochester revival, he was boasting that his methods attracted "the highest classes of society." By then, it seemed, his lawyerlike sermons were intended not for the common people, but for "all the most intelligent people" who were "in the habit of . . . weighing arguments on both sides." And the evangelists did prosper in the towns. By the 1840s, after Finney had moved on to become professor of didactic, polemic, and pastoral theology at Oberlin, revivalism had won the acceptance of the urban middle class.[15] The triumph of "evangelical" Protestantism within a small-town culture established the setting for the emergence of American "pastoral theology."

Pastoral Theology and Urban Culture

Almost without exception, the proponents of pastoral theology were ministers in town and city churches or teachers in antebellum colleges and seminaries which were attuned to urban expectations. The Americans were following a long European tradition. German pastors had written treatises on pastoral theology throughout the

117

eighteenth century, and Anglican writers in England published no fewer than thirty-six pastoral theology textbooks during the nineteenth, all aimed at transforming the English parson into "a different kind of gentleman."[16] But the American pastoral theologians were responding also to a domestic demand for evangelical gentility in America.

The course of study in early Protestant seminaries reflected the growing importance of pastoral theology. The earliest seminaries normally ordered their curriculum into three or four fields of study, always including some combination of biblical literature, systematic theology, ecclesiastical history, and sacred rhetoric. The earliest teachers of pastoral theology were the rhetoricians, church historians, and systematicians. At Andover, founded in 1808, pastoral theology was a part of church history; at Princeton, founded in 1812, it fell within the scope of ecclesiastical history and church government. But by the time the Harvard Corporation formed its theological faculty in 1819, it seemed useful to plan for a distinctive chair of "Pulpit Eloquence and the Pastoral Theology," which came into being eleven years later. By 1821, Auburn Theological Seminary, a Presbyterian school in New York, had appointed a professor of sacred rhetoric and pastoral theology, and General Theological Seminary, an Episcopal school in New York City, had named a professor of pastoral theology and pulpit eloquence. In 1839, Yale Divinity School made its first full-time appointment in "Practical Theology." But by then some schools were beginning to include pastoral theology within the "systematic" fields. At Princeton in 1840, for instance, Archibald Alexander, who had been professor of didactic and polemical theology became professor of pastoral and polemical theology. It seemed that the subject could be taught almost anywhere within the theology curriculum. The courses consisted mainly of instruction in rhetoric and preaching, but the dual designations in the titles of the professorial chairs (distinguishing sacred rhetoric from pastoral theology) indicated that homiletical guidance did not exhaust the topic. Pastoral training also included the style and bearing of ministers in their more intimate relationships with individuals and small groups and hence embraced such diverse issues as ministerial judgments about religious experiences, methods of private conversation, and clerical etiquette. By no accident, the subject flourished in the seminaries founded by those denominations that laid claim to the urban middle classes—people who were impressed by clerical etiquette—or the fact of its absence.[17]

Not all the early manuals in pastoral theology originated in seminaries, but even a sketchy listing of the most popular American texts locates their authors in an urban setting. In 1813 Ezra Stiles Ely's anecdotal *Visits of Mercy* appeared while he was serving as pastor of the Third Presbyterian Church in Philadelphia. In 1827, Samuel Miller, a teacher at Princeton who had previously been the pastor of the Wall Street Presbyterian Church in New York City, where he was admired for his "cultivated and graceful" bearing, published *Letters on Clerical Manners and Habits*, with instructions on proper decorum in pastoral conversation. The year 1842 saw the appearance of Heman Humphrey's *Thirty-Four Letters to a Son in the Ministry*, written by a Presbyterian minister who was serving his final year as president of Amherst College. Two years later, Enoch Pond, the editor of a Congregationalist journal in Massachusetts (and later a church historian at Bangor Seminary in Maine) released his *Young Pastor's Guide; or, Lectures on Pastoral Duties*, with the intent of helping the preacher construct "polished and finished" sermons and guiding the minister in "more private intercourse with his people." In the same year, Archibald Alexander, who had been the pastor at the Pine Street Presbyterian Church in Philadelphia, published *Thoughts on Religious Experience*, a guide to help pastors discriminate between genuine and spurious "religious feelings"; and in 1849 the Episcopal Bishop of Virginia, William Meade, who lived in Richmond, published the *Lectures on the Pastoral Office* that he had delivered to the seminary students in Alexandria. Ichabod Spencer's *Pastor's Sketches* appeared while he was a pastor in Brooklyn. And on the eve of the Civil War, the pastoral theologians of the urban seminaries were beginning to publish their textbooks—like James Spencer Cannon's *Lectures on Pastoral Theology* (1859), originally delivered as lectures in the Dutch Reformed Seminary in New Brunswick—systematizing the lore and wisdom that was supposed to mark pastors who had received a "better education."[18]

The large popular denominations, the Methodists and the Baptists, did not neglect the topic. The Methodists reprinted *The Preacher's Manual*, written in 1800 by the English Wesleyan Adam Clarke, who had intended to prove that John Wesley had been an early advocate of clerical gentility. They also published an American edition of the *Pastoral Theology* of Swiss theologian Alexander Vinet. And the Baptists had Francis Wayland's *Apostolic Ministry*, in which the president of Brown offered lectures on preaching and "parochial visitation." But even in the churches of the masses "pastoral theology" was, for the most part, a field for urbane clerical gentlemen, not frontier exhorters. The authors wrote largely out of their experiences with the educated and affluent middle classes in the towns, and the tone and content of their manuals reflected that social setting.[19]

The pastoral theologians were sensitive to the advances of other professional groups in the towns. When doctors and lawyers formed local bar associations and medical societies during the 1820s, some of the ministers began to worry that "the other professionals are running before the clergy of the country." The Presbyterian George Howe in South Carolina warned his fellow pastors: "All the professions are advancing. We must at least advance with them, and if possible keep before them, or be despised." Edwards A. Park at Andover lamented that promising young men were turning to other professions because the ministry seemed to demand "a sacrifice of mental excellence." And the pastoral writers were especially troubled by the attitudes of physicians who resented their pastoral conversations with the sick. They alluded often to interprofessional tensions, and at one level, their writings represented an attempt to confirm the professional standing of the clergy.[20]

To be sure, the pastoral manuals were not simply reactions to urban expectations. They were also the products of a revivalist piety which defined the principal work of the clergy as the "conversion of souls" through preaching and individual exhortation, and they were expressions, too, of the "new devotionalism" that had altered the organization of the churches during the Second Great Awakening. The revival spawned an array of Bible classes, Sunday schools, benevolent societies, devotional gatherings, and prayer meetings that brought increasing numbers of people together in small groups. "To give satisfaction" in such a setting, wrote Heman Humphrey, the ministers must know how to conduct "private religious meetings" in which there was free conversation and public confession; how to encourage people to express their opinions about themselves and about others, to reveal their feelings as well as their thoughts, and to speak honestly about difficult matters in a public setting. Enoch Pond assured ministers that they did not need to attend or lead more than three "extra religious meetings" each week, but by 1840 the small groups were among the primary settings for "pastoral" care. Pastoral theology provided guideposts for the new piety.[21]

The growing interest in pastoral theology, then, was not simply a reaction to social and economic change. But the pastoral theologians were nonetheless exceedingly sensitive to the gradations of status and authority in an urban culture. Samuel Miller instructed the clergy to be especially delicate with the wealthy and others of high station who were fastidious in sensibility and accustomed to deference. Other writers reversed the advice and told the clergy that clerical refinement was more in demand by the poor than by the rich. But everyone took note of the class distinctions, even if only to insist that ministers should lay aside any haughtiness in dealing with their own social inferiors.[22]

121

The special interest in the spirituality of women shown by some of the pastoral theologians also grew out of a sensitivity to the social patterns of the towns. The separation of the private and domestic sphere from the public economic order had created a distinctive cultural role for urban women. Unlike their sisters on farms and in the mills, the women of the towns found that the economy had few paid public positions for them. As a result, by the 1840s some were uniting in the first American Feminist revolt; some had accepted the dictates of a cult of domesticity that located the rightful place of women solely in the home; and some were pouring their energies into voluntary societies, especially churches. The statistical evidence is skimpy, but it appears that women greatly outnumbered men in the churches, sometimes by a margin of two to one. On one point, therefore, the pastoral theologians agreed: An adept physician of the soul would need to understand and work with women. Samuel Miller warned the clergy that unless they could win the esteem and confidence of women they would not be "very acceptable or very useful." "The female part of every congregation have, in general," he said, "an influence which, while it cannot be defined, cannot, at the same time, be resisted."[23]

The stereotypes of feminine domesticity, piety, and refinement—stereotypes that could have made sense only on a few southern plantations and in the middle- and upper-class society of towns and cities—helped to define the tone of pastoral care. In the 73 sketches recorded in Ichabod Spencer's two volumes, 46 of the pastoral conversations were with women. The English pastoral theologian John Warnock published a similar volume of case studies in America in 1826; 25 of his 36 interviews took place with women. And those preconceptions about women shaped clerical conceptions of pastoral labor. The clergyman's "delicacy," wrote Samuel Miller, was to be "as scrupulous and pure as that of the most refined lady." Early nineteenth-century pastoral care was designed for an institution filled with women. And since most urban pastors defined those women as creatures delicate and pure, a corresponding delicacy seemed an essential component of the clerical manner.[24]

If one social trend suggested the need for delicacy, another seemed to call for a ministerial bearing that was more decisive than delicate, more magisterial than refined. The growth of towns produced a flood of young men from the countryside, rushing to join the masses of European immigrants who were crowding into cities and towns. During the 1830s, a host of popular writers, including ministers, published one manual after another advising young men how to avoid vice, cultivate manners, and make money. Henry Ward Beecher's *Lectures to Young Men* (1844) sold more than 50,000 copies in twenty years. John Todd's *The Young Man* (1844) sold out its first edition within a year. Horace Mann's *Few Thoughts for a Young Man* (1850) sold 20,000 copies in its first edition. Joel Hawes' *Lectures to Young Men on the Formation of Character* (1826) eventually sold about 90,000 copies.[25]

In the manuals for young males, the phrase "decision of character," connoting purposiveness and inner control, became a slogan for the cultural ideal. After the English essayist John Foster released an American edition of his book *Decision of Character and Other Essays*, the ability to engender "decisiveness of character" became a mark of counseling skill among clergy. One evening each week, Horace Bushnell reserved the study of his Hartford church for conversations with young men. Across town, his rival and critic Joel Hawes invited them to interviews in which he offered instruction in a "manly, business-like style." In such a setting, pastoral theology could not depend simply on delicacy and refinement. Somehow, counseling also must exhibit a tough rationality, a resolute heartiness.[26]

The hallmark of ministerial resolution was a willingness to offer advice. Counseling with young men included the transmission of cultural wisdom, the application of rules and guidelines. A youthful clerk who had heard that Ichabod Spencer could be "stern and severe" sought ministerial guidance about his employer's insistence that he cheat unwary customers. "I was brought up in an obscure place in the country," the boy told Spencer, "and don't know much about the ways of the world." Spencer informed him that he had but one choice—to disobey his superior even at the risk of losing his position. "Go anywhere," he said. "Do anything—dig potatoes—black boots—sweep the streets for a living, sooner than yield for one hour to such temptation." Spencer assured the boy that his dishonest employer would eventually fail in business and that God would surely reward the boy's honesty. Tell your employer, he said, "that you cannot consent to lie for anybody." Moral counseling consisted of the dispensing of such clear-cut advice. The young man sought out Spencer precisely because of his reputation for giving uncompromising admonition. Nineteenth-century Protestants expected their ministers to be demanding even as they were affectionate. The pastor represented authority—and used it without hesitation.[27]

Yet it was a common understanding that ministers in the towns should have a pleasing manner. Ministerial influence, said Enoch Pond, must now be "more that of affection than of stern authority. It must be that of love rather than fear." Clerical success required a certain winsomeness, a balance of refinement and rationality, decisiveness and delicacy. Or as Spencer phrased the issue, ministers must take into account both "truth" and "feelings." There is no evidence that they consistently adopted an "affectionate" tone with women and a decisive "rational" tone with young men. But they associated women with the affections and young men with the will, and they attempted to bring both within the calm governance of the understanding.[28]

In the South, one other portentous social change—the expansion of slavery—created a unique pastoral literature. The ministers who wrote the manuals for the "mission" to the slaves repeated the familiar advice about sentiment and rationality: They felt the need to insist that Blacks had no "defect of mental constitution" and that they therefore needed both instruction and sympathy. The problem was that few white ministers took the time to offer either sympathy or instruction, with the result that "pastoral" care in the slave community became primarily a matter of mutual support among the slaves. The white pastoral theologians tended to be Whigs, who favored the abolition of slavery, but that issue never surfaced in their pastoral writings, although these registered every other quiver of social change. In fact, the turmoil of the abolitionist crusade prompted many Protestant congregations to define themselves as "sanctuaries," centers of devotion secure from the outside world. The pastoral literature accepted that segmentation of religion and society, and moved toward exclusive attention to the inner life. The "pastoral" was beginning to stand in contrast to the "public."[29]

Gentlemanly Counsel

The handbooks on pastoral care advocated one overarching requirement for the pastoral counselor: The physician of souls was to be a gentleman. The ideals of piety and gentility pervaded the private and public writings of the prominent clergy. They appeared in letters, diaries, sermons, tracts, and textbooks of every kind: "A minister is presumed to be a gentleman. He must be not only what might by possibility pass loosely by that designation, but he must always be found in the forerank of gentlemen." Pond added "Christian." Every minister, therefore, must embody piety, dignity, refinement, gentleness, and truthfulness. The list seemed innocuous, but it displayed the familiar cultural duality. On the one hand, as Samuel Miller continued to insist, the clerical gentleman's delicacy should be as refined as a lady's. On the other, there could be no "dissimulation." The truth should be told at all costs. Pastoral theology would show the way.[30]

The pastoral writers agreed, first, that the minister must visit the families of the church with regularity and system, and take careful notes on each conversation. Nobody doubted, however, that preaching was the chief duty of the minister. Textbooks contained far more guidance on the construction of sermons than on the fine points of pastoral visits and even spoke of individual conversations as further occasions for "preaching of the Word of God," though they recognized that formal sermons in the household were no longer acceptable. But Samuel Miller's dictum that "ministers are visiters by profession" would have received almost universal assent.[31]

Even a glance at nineteenth-century clerical biographies suggests that ministers diligently trekked from house to house. Thomas Robbins of Connecticut was one of many who recorded pastoral labors, and they bespeak, at the least, persistence. In November 1805, Robbins devoted eight afternoons and evenings to his visits; he would call on as many as fourteen families a day, often riding all morning and afternoon. In 1810 we find him sometimes spending ten full days each month doing nothing but visiting—talking with a young woman who had "hope," an older man "distressed in mind," a woman who was sick. "I find such visiting laborious," he wrote, "but it is useful. I mean to have them ministerial visits."[32]

A second guideline impressed upon their readers by the pastoral theologians was the need to study human nature, to read the human heart, to catalogue the "variety in the constitution of human minds." To know human nature was to be able to classify persons and their maladies, and in presenting their classifications, the pastoral writers borrowed from the methods of science. Or to be more precise, they borrowed from the prescriptions of Sir Francis Bacon. Most of them would have agreed with the American philosopher of science Samuel Tyler that "the Baconian philosophy is emphatically the philosophy of protestantism." And they used the authority of Bacon to suggest that the traditional evangelical habit of classifying spiritual states was simply the religious counterpart of Baconian induction.[33]

"A thorough acquaintance with the inductive mode of seeking truth is a most important element in the preacher's mental character," proclaimed *The Biblical Repertory and Theological Review* in 1831. By the "inductive mode," the journal was referring to Bacon's experimental method, which began with the observation of discrete facts, then arranged the facts into their proper classes, and only then sought unifying generalizations. Bacon taught, as the Americans read him, "that the whole of philosophy is founded on observation, and is nothing more than a classification of facts and phenomena . . . rising first, from particulars, to classifications of the lowest degree of comprehension, and from these, to those of a higher degree." Such a method promised "power over nature"; it promised pastoral success, as well. In 1830 an anonymous "Baconian Biblist" complained that too many pastors lacked "knowledge of individual cases" and therefore could not give "particular instructions." The pastoral theologians tried to remedy that problem by observing and classifying spiritual states.[34]

Some of the schemes of classification antedated the popularity of Baconianism, but since the surge of interest in mental philosophy in the 1820s, for which Bacon was a patron saint, the pastoral theologians were keenly aware of the "variety in the constitution of human minds . . . diversity in the strength of natural passions, and . . . difference in the temperament of Christians." The exercise of classification therefore became increasingly challenging. Everyone tried it. Some divided the flock according to conventional religious and moral categories: people were religiously ignorant, or degraded, or inquiring, or infidel, or awakened, or pious; and ministers would behave differently with each group. Other writers attempted to distinguish and classify dispositions: melancholy, depression, buoyancy, despondency, remorse, and other similar modes of religious consciousness. Still others classified according to natural temperament: cautious, sanguine, morbid, mercurial. The first task in pastoral care was to discern the proper classification for any particular case.[35]

The pastoral theologians also tried, of course, as their

predecessors had, to classify the stages in the order of salvation. It seemed reasonable that if God had conferred salvation according to a revealed plan, the permutations of inward experience should follow that order. The theologians differed as to the components of the pattern. Some thought that true piety began with a subjective feeling of conviction and guilt, which led to contrition and reformation; then came trust and confidence of faith, accompanied by the experience of conversion, which initiated the process of sanctification. According to other theologians, especially Calvinists, the Christian's religious experience began with regeneration; faith came next, then repentance, and then a gradual sanctification. Each scheme was amenable to meticulous refinement, and even theological allies disagreed on the minutiae, but almost everyone was convinced that religious feelings followed standard patterns susceptible to classification. Lyman Beecher in Connecticut became disenamored with the standard classification, and he tried to persuade pastors to collect data for a new "clinical theology" by studying and publishing "cases of conscience" as if they were cases of law or medicine. But Beecher did not propose that anyone cease trying to classify spiritual experiences. He simply urged a method even more in keeping with the spirit of Baconian induction.[36]

A third note of consensus among pastoral theologians was that the cure of souls required an appeal to the will. The goal was usually to elicit a decision. The counselor was to reach the conscience, form the character, evoke religious conviction, and promote moral behavior, or persuade a person to move beyond melancholy and despair. Enoch Pond believed that people were able to "direct *thoughts* very much at will"; the evidence of that was their capacity to give or withhold attention at their own pleasure. In a properly self-governed person, the will could therefore control even feelings and passions. As a consequence, the "highest science," for some of the pastoral theologians, was the science of "the will."[37] Ichabod Spencer illustrated the practical implications of such a position when he published one of his conversations with a grieving woman in his church.

He began by assuring her that he did not "blame" her for mourning, acknowledging that the will did not have control over an overwhelming passion such as grief: "God will not blame you for it. You cannot avoid it if you would; and you would not if you could." But Spencer soon moved toward an appeal to the will: "I can weep with you," he said, "but God alone can do you any good." And then he began the old process of ministerial interrogation:

"Do you think you are submissive to His will?"

"I'm afraid not, sir. I know His will is right; but I cannot feel reconciled to it as I ought."

"My heart bleeds for you, my dear friend; but . . . you must not murmur; you must not rebel or repine."

The final appeal, then, was to the will. Grief ought to produce faith. "I especially strove," Spencer recalled, "to persuade her to make a just use of her bitter affliction."[38]

The pastoral theologians felt a real impatience with anyone who utterly refused to make a just use of bitter affliction. Heman Humphrey instructed the clergy about what to do when the afflicted frankly rebelled against God. "You do not know what you have done!" he advised them to say. "I am amazed. I am confounded. What have you not done to wear out His patience, and bring down His holy displeasure? . . . You make me shudder."[39]

Finally, the writers of the manuals agreed that pastoral conversation should exhibit a balance of rationality and sentiment. The pastor who wished to move the will had to use both rational analysis and sympathetic silence. Hence the problem of balancing rationality and sentiment came down in practice to a question of words. Should the physician of souls rely on the power of words, or the influence of silence? "The people are accustomed to instruction and persuasion by the earnest speaker," wrote one pastoral theologian. "Reason about it as we may, the fact is as wonderful now as it ever was." And yet everyone recognized, at least in theory, that words could sometimes get in the way. By *rational analysis*, the pastoral writers did not mean ministerial lectures during sessions of religious counsel. Samuel Miller warned against "continued address," which he acknowledged to be "the favorite manner of some." He recommended, instead, "the plan of affable and affectionate interrogation, which will lead the individual, at every step, to disclose the state of his own mind." Such a procedure would allow a minister to avoid both premature comfort and a hasty conclusion: "Lay open every wound to the very bottom, before you attempt to heal it," he advised.[40]

Miller insisted that in their interrogations pastors should not abandon "the technical terms of evangelical religion," despite the advice of some writers. If the terms were dropped, he thought, then "the things intended by them would soon disappear also." A specifically Christian vocabulary was indispensable to the Christian physician of the soul. Language and experience were inseparable: A specific universe of language imposed a structure—an order—on experience. Miller could not accept the notion of any pattern of experience that endured unchanged within varying linguistic contexts. The religious depression of an evangelical Protestant, for example, was quite unlike other forms of depression that might be adequately described by a purely psychological vocabulary. A softer, more genial, more pleasing set of words would alter the meaning of the religious experience.[41]

The sentimental side of the formula found expression not so much in words as in silence. "I have in many instances," wrote one pastoral theologian, "remained silent for a long time, under the most painful consciousness that whatever sympathies I might attempt to offer would come so far short of what the stricken heart needed, as to be offered utterly in vain." Silence was useful as a signal of sympathy, but its final purpose was still to move the will. "Mingling your tears with theirs will touch their hearts," wrote Heman Humphrey, "when the kindest words would but aggravate their distress." The Boston

Unitarian Joseph Stevens Buckminster believed that ministers should rely on their "domestic affections," and therefore in moments of acute distress they should offer merely "the silent pressure of the hand from a heart deeply moved." But those recommendations for sympathetic silence did not signal any disillusionment with theological rationalism or the attempt to move the will. Silence was one side of the pastoral equation; rational analysis was the other. The ideal was so to balance each side as to move the will in whatever direction the pastor thought best.[42]

Insofar as there was intense debate over pastoral methods, the division was not between rationalists and sentimentalists, but between high-church pastors who wanted to restore the older Catholic practice of confession, and low-church clergy, who did not. Especially in the Episcopal Church, a burgeoning high-church party began, early in the century, to call for mandatory private auricular confession as the primary agency of pastoral care. A while later, high-church Lutherans advocated a similar return to private confession, and by the end of the antebellum era Lutheran immigrants were embroiled in debates over confession and clerical absolution. Roman Catholics, in the meantime, were defending the confessional against ludicrous attacks by the Protestant Know-Nothing movement, which viewed the confessional booth as a place of sedition and seduction. But in the evangelical Protestant mainstream, the issue was the proper balance of rationality and sentiment in the appeal to the will. In pursuing that question, the pastoral theologians endeavored to move beyond the conflicts of the eighteenth century and to walk in step with the intellectual fashions of the nineteenth.[43]

The Theological Background

To locate the pastoral discussion about rationality and sentiment exclusively within a revivalist tradition and an urban social setting would be to miss the broader intellectual background which informed every argument.

The pastoral theologians were not simply responding to changes in society. They also were drawing on the intellectual movements that shaped clerical education in the colleges and seminaries—especially rational theology and mental philosophy. The quest for a balance of will, intellect, and sensibility stood near the heart of both theology and psychology in the nineteenth century.

When the physicians of the soul sought theological insight, they seemed at first to face a host of conflicting options: Calvinist, Wesleyan, Lutheran, Unitarian, Roman Catholic, or some variant of one or another. But underlying the diversity was a remarkable theological consensus. Even in their disagreements, most ministers, including those who wrote about the cure of souls, held to a "rational orthodoxy."

A rational orthodox theologian assumed the unity of truth—and most American theologians were apostles of the unity of truth. Hence they proposed a reasonable "natural theology" as the normal proof and prolegomenon of revelation. They assembled time-honored rational arguments for the existence of God, based on the harmony of the natural order, the mutual adaptation of its parts, its complexity, the necessity of a sufficient cause for its existence, and the universality of religious belief. The insights thus garnered constituted a "natural" knowledge of God, independent of a special biblical revelation. Such a natural theology furnished a foundation for the higher revealed theology. It discovered natural analogies to revealed mysteries; it pointed beyond itself to higher truths (the natural theologian, for instance, could discern God's existence, but not God's nature); and it defined the questions for which the Christian revelation supplied the answers. Both natural science and mental philosophy served as apologetic weapons in the armory of Christendom.[44]

The rational orthodox theologians believed, for example, that theology received its "shape and character" from "the philosophy which we adopt of the human mind." It was a common claim, as Asa Burton of Vermont wrote in 1824, that the "foundation of divinity" was knowledge of

132

"the principles and operations of the mind." When James Marsh, president of the University of Vermont, published an American edition of Samuel Taylor Coleridge's *Aids to Reflection* (1829), his introduction stated that theologians could have "no right views of theology" until they also had "right views of the human mind." Though Marsh's particular views of the mind were offensive to many other theologians, few would have disagreed, in principle, with his assertion. When Theodore Munger heard the lectures of the celebrated Nathaniel William Taylor at Yale, he reported that Taylor had "a system of mental philosophy of his own which is unlike any other, and as his system of theology is built upon that he lectures to us a whole term upon it." Nobody doubted that the findings of mental philosophy shaped the doctrine of sin and determined the proper interpretation of regeneration. But that was only the beginning. The rational orthodox theologians insisted that almost all assertions about God rested somehow on analogies derived from the human mind; that the standard arguments for the existence of God presupposed philoso-phical assumptions about the nature of cognition and volition. Even the very idea of God was "borrowed from our previous conception of the human mind, and our own spiritual existence."[45]

The philosophy of mind, then (to choose only one discipline as an example) was an exercise in natural theology. It undergirded the traditional arguments for the existence of God. It determined the meaning of theological assertions. It discerned analogies in the human mind that validated revealed doctrines—the doctrine of the Trinity, for instance. It provided analyses of human existence that corresponded to biblical teachings. It revealed the incom-plete and fragmentary character of natural human knowledge and thus suggested the need for a higher revealed truth. It then defined the terms used in the interpretation of that revelation. "The decision of a single question in psychology," wrote a clerical professor at Amherst College, "may affect a whole system of faith or morals."[46] And the rational orthodox theologians made the

133

same kind of claim about natural science, and metaphysics, and moral philosophy. Right reason, in whatever discipline, moved inexorably toward revealed truth. Natural theology prepared the way for revealed theology.

The typical American theologian also trusted rational argument to produce convincing "evidences" that the Bible was a true revelation. Reason could identify the signs that might be expected to accompany a divine revelation and could verify their authenticity. The evidence, everyone agreed, was addressed to the reason, and courses on the "Evidences of Christianity" became standard requirements in American seminaries and colleges, even in the state schools. Rare indeed was the minister who thought that scriptural revelation contained any mysteries repugnant to "right reason." In "receiving . . . the most mysterious doctrines of revelation," wrote Archibald Alexander, "the ultimate appeal is to reason." The theologians therefore gathered dozens of "external" and "internal" proofs that the Christian Bible was the unique Word of God. In the external arguments, the historical plausibility of the biblical miracles and the seemingly verifiable fulfillment of the biblical prophecies provided evidence for the divine origin of the Bible. The internal arguments advanced the claim that Scripture was uniquely consistent; it was consistent with the highest ethical ideals of the race, and it was consistent with science and philosophy. Such "evidential" arguments presented themselves to human reason, which alone could determine whether the Bible was the authentic Word.[47] Natural theology verified revealed theology.

Finally, the rational orthodox theologians believed that reason interpreted revelation. The interpreter investigated the grammar, the historical context, and the subject matter of the biblical text to uncover the intentions of its authors. And more than once the ministers blatantly interpreted Scripture in accordance with the findings of nineteenth-century science. Relatively modern notions of geological time, for instance, routinely provided interpretive clues for understanding the meaning of the creation narratives in Genesis. Biblical interpretation was the application of reason to the sacred text.[48]

The "rationalism" of mainstream antebellum theology was by no means simply a mark of nascent liberalism. The more unyielding the conservatives' solicitude for the biblical revelation, the more they strove for rational proof and explanation. Both Unitarian liberals and mainstream evangelicals agreed that the rational investigation of the created order—including the inner order of the mind and conscience—would uncover proofs and analogies to demonstrate the reasonableness of Christian teaching. Most American theologians were convinced, said one Methodist, that God had "never enjoined upon man the duty of faith, without first presenting before him a reasonable foundation for the same." Most viewed their discipline as an inductive science which gathered its facts from the Bible, the external world, and the inner consciousness, reaching conclusions that would convince any rational person.[49]

Rational orthodoxy was an extension of seventeenth-century Scholasticism and eighteenth-century British apologetics. It continued the post-Lockean English pre-occupation with the reasonableness of Christianity and the unreasonableness of Deism. Four British writers served as authoritative guides for Americans: Sir Francis Bacon taught them the inductive method of observation and generalization; Bishop Joseph Butler showed them how to find analogies between human experience and divine revelation; Archdeacon William Paley refined the scientific arguments for the existence of God and the evidences for the divine origin of the Scriptures; and the Scottish philosopher Thomas Reid instructed them in using philosophy to defend theology. The result was a theology that found nature filled with pattern and regularity, and therefore with intelligence; that found the Scripture susceptible to validation by the methods of scientists and historians.

In their contention that rational arguments could validate the Bible, though, the theologians also advanced a justification for taking the affections seriously. Their "internal" proofs often consisted of claims that Scripture was consistent not only with all other truths, but also with the yearnings of the heart. The Bible was adapted to human nature, congenial to "all the faculties and propensities," and was especially fitted to search the heart and affect the conscience. Religious conversion therefore provided not only evidence of salvation, but confirmation of the entire Christian revelation. Rather than suppress religious feelings, the theologians insisted that any rational theology would welcome them.[50]

In 1815 William Ellery Channing warned the clergy of Boston not to be so appalled by the "pernicious effects of violent and exclusive appeals to the passions" that they address men and women "as mere creatures of the intellect." He reminded them that "affection is as essential to our nature as thought, [and] that the union of reason and sensibility is the health of the soul."[51] Channing was a Boston Unitarian, but his admonition was a Protestant commonplace. The same pious rationalists who published expositions on the evidences of Christianity also wrote voluminously of warm hearts and raised affections. Drawing on both seventeenth-century Pietism and eighteenth-century romantic sentimentality, they established a theological genre—and a homiletical style—intended to move the heart, or touch the affections, or refine the sensibility.

The outpouring of theological sentimentality proceeded apace with the technological and organizational innovations which encouraged the formation of the great tract societies. Using the Religious Tract Society in London as their model, American churches established regional and denominational societies as early as 1803. By 1814 the New Englanders had constructed both a bustling organization and a rationale for its existence: Religious tracts would not be vehicles for "learned cricitism [or] discussions in polemic theology," but would contain "pithy expressions, lively representations of truth, and pathetic addresses" to "affectionately [direct] the sinner to the

Lamb of God." The theological tract would not be a "plain didactic essay" but an affecting appeal—often using narrative and dialogue—that would cause the reader to "feel" every argument that was adduced.[52]

In 1825, the regional societies merged into an American Tract Society, which flooded the country with theological sentiment. Within two years, it had printed 3,815,000 copies of 200 separate tracts designed to appeal both to the the "lower ranks" and to the "intelligent and discerning"— and also designed to appeal, above all, to the heart. The tract societies often reprinted various formulations of the rational evidences, and the tracts were by no means the sole agencies of theological sentimentality, but they so popularized the appeal to the affections that one can view them as symbolic of an emerging "devotional theology" which counterbalanced pious rationalism with sentimental piety.[53]

The tracts were inexpensive and drab in appearance, but they emulated the style of the popular gilt-edged gift books that graced the parlor tables of Victorian homes. Often decorated with drawings illustrating domestic tranquility, gentle maidens, and pious children, they promoted an unabashed emotionalism designed to elicit soft smiles, gentle tears, and disquieting anxieties. The main interest of devotional theology was conversion, but rather than systematic treatises on the morphology of religious experience, the theologians usually produced dire warnings and heartwarming narratives. They told the stories of *The Dairyman's Daughter, The Blacksmith's Wife*, and *Jonathan Brown the Bargeman*. They offered instructions on "the way to be saved," aids for "self-examination," and exhortations to the unconverted which moved the will with "affecting" topics. No one thought that appeals to the affections conflicted with orthodox rationalism. The rational orthodox theologians and the devotional theologians were the same people. By writing in both modes, they exemplified the ideal balance between the reason and the affections.

In addition to its focus on conversion, devotional theology also helped to popularize a "cult of frailty and mortality" which both continued and altered a tradition of consolation literature that had its roots in ancient pre-Christian western culture. In such tracts as *The Friendly Visit to the House of Mourning* and *The Stricken Bride*, the clergy combined heart-rending depictions of death with exhortations to conversion and resignation. The exemplary death scene represented the ideal of balance: "All was sober—all was serene—all was gentle—all was rational." Believing that sorrow possessed a "weaning, subduing, elevating power" which trained the spirit for "a higher and more permanent state," the devotional theologians called for "the sentiment of . . . resignation." They did not censure the expression of feeling—for even Jesus had wept at the grave of Lazarus—but they did call for an "implicit trust in Providence." In a typical example of consolation literature, Unitarian Henry Bacon wrote of his meditations amid the tombs of Auburn Cemetery, his fascination with the grave of a child ("a sweet spot it was indeed"), his visits with a dying Christian ("a smile of heavenly sweetness beamed through the manifest agony she was enduring, like a sunbeam stealing through the storm-agitated clouds"), his anticipation of the "future state," and his conviction that it was "faith's duty to submit" to "the Heavenly Father's Will."[54]

The same advice appeared in the devotional guidebooks for the sick that became popular in the 1830s. Sickness was a "valuable opportunity for spiritual improvement"; it taught men and women the frailty of life and awakened them to a true sense of their condition and character. It was another occasion for "resignation," "unrepining submission" to God's will, and the selfless performance of duty. The devotional writers insisted repeatedly that sick people had duties—to their families, their attendants, their doctor, and their minister. To denude illness of its duties was to remove it from "the range of discipline, destroy its character, make it no longer the blessing it has claimed to be—the disguised angel—and establish it as a strange neutral ground in the divine economy." Seen in its proper light, sickness had a "soft beauty," showing that "every thorn of trial is hung with a diamond." The devotional theology advanced a difficult and heroic ideal—but the ideal was always bathed in the soft light of sentiment.[55]

One mark of devotional theology was its tendency to interpret religion in terms of domestic affections. A picture that frequently appeared in tract society publications depicted a family scene with mother and children gathered round as father read from pious literature; and the figure of "mother" also became a standard of evangelistic appeals. The interest in family piety paralleled a broader tendency to interpret Jesus as the embodiment of such domestic virtues as patience and gentleness, and the devotional theologians frequently described him as a man of "meek and lovely and gentle spirit" who was "moved by human sympathies." By no accident, the religious songs of the period referred not so much to divine majesty or cosmic order as to the softer feelings of the self. Such songs as "Nearer, My God, to Thee," "Just as I Am," and "I Need Thee Every Hour" outdistanced the older psalms in popularity.[56]

In practice, then, the theology of antebellum America tended to exhibit a certain polarity: The same minister who instructed his congregation about evidential logic on one Sunday was likely the following week to indulge in maudlin descriptions of domestic felicity and sorrow. Some theologians tried to embrace both sides of the polarity in one consistent formula. In 1850 Edwards Amasa Park of Andover wrote an intriguing article on "The Theology of the Intellect and That of the Feelings," attempting to combine the values of dialectical precision and analytical argument with a theological style that was "graceful to the sensibilities." Sentiment and reason, Park said, should influence each other. Images that quickened the heart might well verify theological abstractions. Doctrines that failed to stir the soul, or that overrode even "the most delicate emotion of the tenderest nature," should be judged as deficient. Park never doubted that theology of the reason would maintain its ascendancy: "In all investigations for truth, the intellect must be the authoritative power, employing the sensibilities as indices of right doctrine, but surveying and superintending them from its commanding elevation." The intellect would have the last word, but both styles of theology were "appropriate in their own sphere," and each sphere overlapped the other. Park's essay was criticized from both sides. Charles Hodge at Princeton thought he had sold out to sentiment. Horace Bushnell believed him to be naively rationalistic. But nobody could have accused him of being out of touch with his times. The essay treated one of the dominant issues of antebellum Protestant religious thought. And though a few transcendentalists elevated intuition and feeling above discursive rationality, most ministers held views quite close to those of Edwards Park. They moved back and forth between reason and sentiment with every confidence that the bridge between them held firm.[57]

It is plausible to argue that the style and content of devotional theology—including its dialogues and narratives—influenced the methods of pastoral care quite as much as did the rationalism. Several of the pastoral theologians—Alexander, Pond, Miller, Humphrey, and others—wrote for the American Tract Society, and the imaginary pastoral conversations that filled the tracts followed faithfully the guidelines in the pastoral theology textbooks. In any case, the dialectic of rationality and sentiment in theology formed the intellectual setting for the discussions about the use of persuasion and silence, exhortation and sympathy, in pastoral care. The aim of pastoral care, like the aim of evidential theology, was to convince and persuade. The primary method was interrogation and argument.

The argumentation, though, was not designed simply to convince the intellect and charm the sensibility but was expected to move the will. In an era of evangelicalism, theologians closely studied the workings of the will in conversion and spiritual growth. The result of their reflections was a subtle but momentous transition in Protestant definitions of sin and salvation.

The disputes over the will began with the controversies between Calvinists and Arminians. The designation *Arminian* referred to the theology of Jacobus Arminius, a pastor and professor at Leyden in the sixteenth century who had decided that the "high Calvinism" of the Reformed Scholastics inadvertently depicted God as the author of sin. Arminius proposed that God had decreed to save all believers and that Christ had died for all people, so that sufficient grace was given to all. He believed that faith was the fruit of grace and that the will had no power to believe unless empowered by grace, but he denied that grace was irresistible. The will could resist, he said, and there was therefore no question about where to locate the responsibility for its sinfulness.[58]

By the end of the eighteenth century, the label Arminian was being used to refer to three disparate groups: Anglican traditionalists, liberals, and Wesleyans. Anglican Arminianism was more a mood and temper than a precise set of doctrines; liberal Arminians denied or modified the doctrine of original sin, redefining sin as a personal act and salvation as a process in which the will cooperated with divine grace; the followers of John Wesley believed sin to be inherited but grace ubiquitous—everyone, they thought, was sufficiently empowered by "prevenient grace" to turn from sinfulness to faithfulness and obedience. Common to all three groups, though, was the assertion that freely deciding men and women bore the responsibility for sin. The primary locus of sinfulness was the will.[59]

By the early nineteenth century in America, *Arminian* referred primarily, though not exclusively, to Methodists, who proudly associated themselves with the revolt of Arminius. Against the Calvinists, they claimed that prevenient grace freed every will from bondage. Christ had died for all people, and through grace, all had the capacity (Methodists called it "gracious ability") to believe, repent, and reap the benefit of the Cross. Against the Edwardean Calvinists, they insisted that a volition was an "original cause" and that to speak of "motives" was simply to

141

describe the will in action, "moving" one way or another. By the late 1840s, Methodist clergy were adopting the views of such philosophically inclined theologians as Albert Taylor Bledsoe, who located Edwards' fallacy in his failure to distinguish between the will and the sensibility. His analysis of consciousness suggested to Bledsoe a clear difference between desires, affection, and feelings, on the one hand, and volitions, on the other. To desire rain was not to put forth a volition; to be moved by a pleasant sensation was not to will; to be pleased was not to choose. Edwards' neglect of that difference had produced the absurd result that a volition was simultaneously active and passive. Bledsoe then added that consciousness could, in any case, distinguish mental acts that were "self-active," original, producing causes from other mental experiences that were "necessitated," and that Edwards could not, with his approach, explain the differences in the subjective experiences. Such argumentation carried the Methodists quite a distance from their Wesleyan origins; Wesley had exalted free and universal grace; his nineteenth-century successors talked far more about free will, using a modish philosophical theology to analyze the inner workings of volition.[60]

Generations of American Calvinists rehearsed the Edwardean analysis of motivation in order to prove that the will was powerless to choose the good without the special influence of divine grace, but that the reprobate still were responsible for their decision to capitulate to sinfulness. The Calvinists asserted that Arminian "free will" made human activity seem "unmotivated" and therefore dangerously arbitrary. They also accused the Arminians of forgetting that salvation was a merciful gift. Calvinists insisted that the will was active both in sin and in salvation. In redeeming the elect, God did not disregard their nature as moral agents: God's grace did not automatically *compel* people to accept the offer of salvation—it made them *want* to accept it. And that was sufficient freedom for anyone.[61]

It was not enough, though, for Wesleyans, or for the

influential New England Unitarians, who rather ignored than refuted Edwards. William Ellery Channing simply announced that "consciousness" contradicted Edwards and thereby should restore confidence in "the moral connection between God and his creatures." But in New England, at least, Unitarian dicta seemed more threatening than did Wesleyan argumentation, and it was largely in response to Unitarianism that Nathaniel William Taylor at Yale made an effort to redefine Calvinist doctrines of sin and salvation. Taylor and the other New Haven theologians taught that sin, in a true Calvinist view, consisted in an act of the will, not in a propensity or property of human nature underlying volition. The Taylorites preached that the sinner was able to repent, but unwilling to do so; that sinfulness consisted in actions, not in the imputation of Adam's guilt; and that regeneration was a voluntary change in the elect, undertaken in response to the moral suasion of the Spirit, which presented truth to the mind. Taylor's doctrine did not convince Unitarians or Wesleyans—and many Calvinists found it utterly wrong-headed—but it both symbolized and influenced a popular attitude toward the will in mainline Protestantism.[62]

By the 1830s, Charles G. Finney could tell the crowds at his revivals that "sinners were bound to change their own hearts." Weary of "metaphysical subtleties" about "inability," he assured them that the declarations of the Bible were all in accord with the true philosophy of mind, which taught that the heart was clearly "something over which we have control, something voluntary." If God required obedience, God was "bound in justice to give us *power* to obey"—and Finney saw no need to call that power a "gracious ability." It was a gift of God, but it was entirely "natural." It was, in short, good old willpower.[63]

The combined forces of revivalism, the Wesleyan theology, the New Haven doctrines, and the Unitarian movement were sufficient to move popular American Protestantism gradually toward an understanding of sin as an act rather than a status—as a volitional decision

143

rather than a common condition. John Wesley had defended the doctrine of original sin, but he also had defined sin explicitly as a voluntary transgression of a known law. The New Haven theologians reconceived of depravity as "man's own act," and of sin as the "acts" of moral agents who violated "a known rule of duty." Finney defined sin as a refusal to yield to the influence of the Spirit. Such notions of sin helped to create the moralistic tone of antebellum pastoral care. If sin was an act of the will, then moral exhortation seemed fully fitting.[64]

It was the purpose of pastoral counsel, then, to convince the intellect, appeal to the affections, and persuade the will—and to remain within the boundaries established by refined sensibility. In endeavoring to hold together a commitment to the "truth," an appeal to the will, and a sensitivity to the "feelings," Ichabod Spencer showed himself to be a man of urban culture, but he also displayed the practical implications of a theology deeply indebted to a faculty psychology. The psychology so permeated the theology that it established the boundaries of discourse. At one level, then, it was the explicit theology that guided Spencer's conversations; at another, it was the psychology implicit in the theology. Together, these formed the intellectual context of antebellum pastoral care.

The Psychological Background

When Spencer sought insight into pastoral care by studying the writings of nineteenth-century American psychologists (or "mental philosophers"), he discovered a similar preoccupation with the themes of will, sentiment, and reason. We can be certain that like most educated pastors, Spencer had at least a rudimentary acquaintance with mental philosophy. He was a graduate of Union College in Schenectady during a period when a course in "Intellectual Philosophy" was required for graduation, and he surely would not have been asked to teach pastoral theology at Hartford without such knowledge, for the pastoral theologians believed that all ministers should "be at home in the philosophy of the human intellect." Ezra Stiles Ely wrote a textbook of *Conversations on the Science of the Human Mind;* Enoch Pond wrote journal articles on mental science; and Heman Humphrey edited and published a colleague's mental philosophy lectures. Mental philosophy was a standard resource for the practice of pastoral care.[65]

Most mental philosophers were themselves clergymen who believed that good pastoral work required a knowledge of the faculties and principles of the mind.

> And the profession of a minister is such, it is one part of his study to account for the conduct of mankind. In this way he explains their characters, shows them what they are, and opens to their view the inward springs of action, and the external effects they will produce, so clearly, that persons often think that someone has informed him of their feelings and conduct.[66]

One special virtue of mental philosophy was its capacity to "shed abundant light on some of the practical doctrines of Revelation" that were of interest to pastors.[67]

Pastors obviously needed to know how to appeal to the will. The topic had divided them ever since the Awakening. Did one address the understanding? Or did one arouse the affections? And ever since the publication of Jonathan Edwards' *Freedom of Will* in 1754, pastors had argued also about the assignment of moral and spiritual responsibility. Was it necessary to presuppose a freedom of indifference by which the will could direct its own choices? Or was it sufficient that men and women could do what they willed to do?

The debates over the will stimulated American interest in the divisions of the mind. Edwards—known universally as President Edwards, owing to his brief tenure as the president of the college at Princeton—had usually spoken of a bipartite division of the mind, into the will and the understanding. He had believed that the affections were only the more vigorous inclinations of the will. But his

145

critics—and some of his allies—had continued to refer to the will, the understanding, and the affections as if they were three separate faculties, though only Samuel West had made an issue of this tripartite ordering.

The tendency in popular writing—sermons, polemical treatises, etiquette books, and political speeches—was to distinguish three faculties. The accent on the affections, and on the "moral sense," in Scottish ethical thought provided some hefty theoretical support for that habit. When John Witherspoon's Princeton lectures on moral philosophy were published in 1805, they could announce without explanation that "the faculties of the mind are commonly divided into these three kinds, the understanding, the will, and the affections."[68]

The mental philosophers, however, often repeated an older bipartite formula. John Locke's *Essay* designated will and understanding as "the two great and principal actions of the mind." The Scottish philosopher Thomas Reid, widely read in America, wrote in his *Essays on the Active Powers of the Human Mind* (1788) that "the division of the Faculties of the human mind into Understanding and Will is very ancient, and has been very generally adopted; the former comprehending all our speculative, the latter all our active powers." Reid's successor at Edinburgh, Dugald Stewart, also distinguished simply the "intellectual powers" and the "active moral powers." And when Thomas Upham, a Congregationalist minister, a professor of mental philosophy at Bowdoin, and the most influential antebellum psychologist in America published his *Elements of Intellectual Philosophy* in 1827, he argued for a bipartite division of the mind into "intellectual" and "sentient" powers, the latter including the will, the emotions, and the moral feelings.[69]

By that time, though, tripartite psychology was on its way to triumph. The impetus came in 1824, when Asa Burton, the pastor of a Congregationalist church in Vermont, published *Essays on Some of the First Principles of Metaphysicks, Ethicks, and Theology*. Using methods developed by the Scottish philosophers, he had set out, like

Edwards, to show that Calvinism was compatible with "moral agency." Though he made no reference to James Dana's rebuttal of Edwards, his book was, in substance, an effort to solve the problem that Dana had raised—namely, that by virtually identifying motives and volitions, Edwards had failed to explain how motives could cause volitions. The solution to such a problem, Burton thought, was obvious, once one discovered the difference between the will, and the "heart" or "taste." The taste, comprising affections and passions, was the faculty of feelings and desires, and it was manifestly different from the will. Neither feelings nor desires could be volitions. There was a difference between feeling sad and wanting to be sad; there was a difference between, say, desiring a drink of water and choosing to gratify that desire.[70]

Once one recognized those differences, one had the solution to Dana's problem. Motives were not simply modifications of willing, as Edwards had seemed to suggest. The will acted in response to an inclination of the "taste," or "heart," which was distinct from the will and antecedent to it. It was from within the heart that motives attracted the will one way or another. The will, then, governed the understanding, but the will was only an executive faculty: "It is no more than a servant to the heart, to execute its pleasure." The taste was the true spring of action in the human mind.[71]

By 1834, Thomas Upham was probably the most influential of the American mental philosophers. In that year he supplemented his popular textbook with a *Philosophical and Practical Treatise on the Will,* in which he reversed his earlier views and, acknowledging Burton's work, concluded that one needs to distinguish "intellectual, sentient, and voluntary states of mind." Thereafter, the tripartite formula became a staple of American mental science. A few people did protest against any notion of distinctive faculties. The German Reformed theologian at Mercersburg Seminary, Frederick Rauch, who tried to unite German and American mental philosophy in his *Psychology; or, A View of the Human Soul* (1840), insisted

147

that the mind simply was not a compound of faculties, however they were defined and divided. But most American texts adopted some form of the tripartite scheme, appealing to the authority of Upham, or to that of Immanuel Kant or of the French philosopher Victor Cousin, or more frequently to the authority of their own "consciousness." In their view, sentiment was as deeply rooted in the self as were intellect and volition. Mental philosophers therefore became increasingly occupied with the observation and classification of even the subtlest shadings of sensibility.[72]

In his *Essay Concerning Human Understanding*, John Locke had attended primarily to modes of cognition. He was interested in how the mind knows. His conclusions, though, had opened the door to Hume's skepticism, which had, in turn, drawn the criticism of Thomas Reid and the Scottish "common sense" philosophers, who attempted to refute skepticism by means of a detailed introspective examination of mental activity. Such an investigation, the Scots wrote, was the task of "consciousness," which Reid defined as the faculty of discerning "the operations of our own minds." Reid's philosophical method—appeal to consciousness—became the hallmark of the Scottish philosophy and the heart of American mental science. Reid set an example for Americans when he eventually turned his attention from the narrow epistemological questions, which had dominated his polemic against Hume, to wide-ranging descriptions of all the powers of the mind: perception, sensation, conception, abstraction, judgment, reasoning, taste, volition, instinct, habit, appetite, desire, affection, and moral sensibility.[73]

Both Reid and Dugald Stewart, whose *Elements of the Philosophy of the Human Mind* became a standard text in American colleges, believed themselves to be applying the inductive method of Sir Francis Bacon to the study of the mind. Stewart claimed that Reid's speculations were "conducted . . . in strict conformity to the rules of inductive philosophizing." Reid's great object, he said, had been to follow Baconian guidelines and to "record and classify the phenomena which the operations of the human mind present to those who reflect carefully on the subjects of their consciousness." Both men discovered during their refutations of Hume, whom they considered guilty of failing to recognize "the extraordinary merits of Bacon as a philosopher," that the analysis and classification of the contents of consciousness could reveal important differences among mental activities that previously had been confused with one another. Reid, for instance, thought that Hume, in arguing that our senses give us sure knowledge only of our subjective sensations, had not noticed the distinction, revealed in introspection, between internal sensations and the perceptions of real objects. The sensation of pain from a pinprick, for instance, is quite different from the simultaneous tactile perception of the pin itself. Such discoveries convinced American theologians that "the inductive science of mind," conducted in accord with Baconian precepts, could lead to "progress in every department of truth." They were especially hopeful that it could illuminate "the moral condition of the soul."[74]

The result was almost a century of sustained effort to distinguish and classify mental operations. Defining *consciousness* as the mind's cognizance of its own phenomena (though there were alternative definitions), the mental philosophers sought to discover the minute differences that distinguished sensations and perceptions; or emotions, desires, and volitions; or feelings of revenge, envy, and jealousy. They analyzed distinctions in the ludicrous, the witty, and the burlesque; or in pride, conceit, vanity, and haughtiness; penitence, discontent, sadness, mournfulness, and grief; fear, dread, and horror. They noted the shadings of difference between contentment and cheerfulness; disgust and indignation; surprise and wonder; beauty and sublimity. They distinguished various classifications of love and malevolence. They classified cognitive acts, emotions, volitions, and mental illness. And they even tried to classify dreams that arose from bodily sensations, from previous waking thoughts, or from unexpressed longings. All this they accomplished through the observation and description of mental states in themselves and in others.[75]

Some of their texts reveal an interest in stages and levels of development. Frederick Rauch, whose *Psychology* drew on Hegel, described the stages of childhood, youth, maturity, and old age. Joseph Haven's mental philosophy defined the stages of grief, from shock and violent anguish to the period of "deepest sorrow," governed by laws of association, in which the bereaved recalled the words or gestures of a lost loved one, and finally, to a time when "other plans and duties" could be acknowledged. The psychologists sought the "laws" that governed growth, with the hope of finding "practical benefits," and they advertised the usefulness of such studies for preachers and pastors. The pastor, wrote Nathan Fiske, came in touch with "every variety of character" and must "act upon the mind in every condition of temper, susceptibility, and tendency." Mental philosophy could teach "appropriate counsels" for each stage of natural and spiritual growth.[76]

The value of mental philosophy for the clergy, though, came undoubtedly not so much through specific suggestions about appropriate counsel—for the philosphers had little to say about that—as through a tendency to expand the pastor's vision of the inner world. The critics of mental science found it drab. It was Horace Bushnell's opinion that mental philosophers tried to "make up a true man out of some ten or twenty or forty words in the dictionary." He felt that poets could describe the soul better than could psychologists. But in cataloging the array of human feelings, the philosophers performed something of the function of novelists, however sketchy their depictions. By naming and examining nuances of feeling and thought, they undoubtedly intensified the sensitivity of their readers—including pastors—to the shadings of human experience. Joseph Haven observed in 1857 that "the range and power of the sensibilities" depended "essentially upon the range and vigor of the intellectual powers." He meant only that the activity of the intellect preceded that of the sensibility, but his project as a mental philosopher also

150

presupposed that the intellectual awareness of internality created possibilities for new experience. The multitude of definitions—distinguishing wrath from indignation, anger from chagrin, mirth from cheerfulness—constituted exercises in self-objectification. The naming of internal feelings surely widened the range of subjective experience. In that sense, the move toward an explicit tripartite psychology and the numerous descriptions of affective states helped to form the consciousness of the sentimental era. It made it possible for people to objectify their inner lives to themselves in new ways. It also created more precise concepts for the clergy to use in their dealings with the inner world.[77]

The hope was that awareness would bring equilibrium, promote a harmony of intellect, affection, and volition. But inner harmony did not imply inner equality. The philosophers still thought in hierarchical patterns, and despite their attention to intellect and sensibility, they assumed that the governor of the soul was the will. In order of operation, the intellect assumed priority. "There could be no doubt," wrote Haven, "that the activity of the will is preceded, in all cases, by that of the intellect," and the intellect, he added, then worked on the mind "through the medium of the sensibilities." But the terminus of the process was an act of the will. All the delicate balancing of intellect and sensibility was aimed at making right decisions and performing duties. It was the will, wrote Haven, that secured "the power of a man over himself, to be other and better than he is, and to do what God requires."[78]

Thomas Upham expressed the same idea. "The process of the mind," he wrote, "is from intellection to emotions, and from emotions to desires." He declared that there could be no desire "without the intervention of some emotion," but also that the will was "the culminating point in man's spiritual nature."

It sits the witness and the arbitress over all the rest. It is essential alike to action and accountability, to freedom and

order, to intelligence and virtue. Without this all else is
nothing. It is in reference to this, that all other susceptibili-
ties keep their station, and perform their functions. They
revolve around it as a common centre, attracted by its power,
and controlled by its ascendancy.[79]

In practice, this meant that psychology stood in the service
of ethics. "To know ourselves," said E. S. Ely, "is to be
prepared for profitable exertions, and a cheerful discharge
of duty."[80]

One way to ensure a balance of the faculties was to form
habits. Only the power of habit could consistently subdue
recalcitrant passions, could steadfastly focus the attention, could discipline the will. "No theme of remark is
more common," said Nathan Fiske, "than the power of
habit. . . . It is by the power of habit and by this alone that
the mind has control of its own character and its own
destiny." Fiske's first observation was accurate; his
second, revealing. The accent on balance suggested that
thought, will, and affect should coexist, each sustaining
and yet limiting the others. But the heavy burden placed
on the will threatened to upset the balance. By the same
token, the admiration for habit represented an understandable preference for steadfast dispositions rather than
transient emotional peaks and sporadic exertion. But
habit could also come to mean the stifling of spontaneity.
When combined with the traditional Protestant distrust of
impulse, the yearning for habitual balance governed by
the will could easily become an internal crusade to impose
order upon a recalcitrant self. Some pastors were inclined
to call for "a violent warfare upon the impulses of our
nature." Under the governance of the habituated will,
self-control could become relentless oversight, rigid
self-possession, and inward repression.[81]

The prevailing mental philosophy drew critics. A few
argued that chemistry promoted balance more efficiently
than did casuistry. Benjamin Rush in Philadelphia
expounded an early version of medical psychiatry in his
Diseases of the Mind (1812), arguing that most mental

abnormalities stemmed from physical causes. Rush had noticed how heredity and illness could influence mental and moral capacities, and he hoped for a "medicine" that would cure even "moral diseases" and distorted religion: "Religious melancholy and madness, in all their variety of species, yield with more facility to medicine, than simply to polemical discourses, or to casuistical advice."[82]

In the popular lecture halls, the preferred alternative was not chemistry, but phrenology, an importation from Vienna that unlocked the secrets of the mind by explaining the bumps on the skull. The phrenologists located each of the mental faculties in a specific area of the surface of the brain. The size of the area indicated the strength of the faculty, so a tactile survey of the upper skull could reveal the mysteries of character. More important, exercise and practice could increase the size and capacity of each faculty. Phrenological analysis and prescription offered a "practical system of mental philosophy" that could ensure a balanced personality. And phrenologists appealed often to the ideal of balance. John Neal told the students at Brown that men of mind were heartless, men of bodily strength were mindless, and men of cultivated affections were weak in both body and mind. The solution was the "diligent cultivation of every faculty, whether bodily, mental, or moral, wherewith we are endowed by our creator."[83]

Few of the clergy had much use for phrenology (Henry Ward Beecher was the prominent exception). For them, balance was not achieved by bumps of equivalent size but by an invisible inner harmony of the soul. The harmony depended on divine grace, but God worked through human agencies, and ministers believed that with the proper balance of argument and sympathy in their pastoral care, they could serve God's purposes in the engendering of redeemed and harmonious souls.

Toward Self-Culture

Antebellum Protestants were of one mind in their admiration for the properly balanced self in which the will, the intellect, and the affections moved in harmonious unity. They were not of one mind about how to engender such a self. Some believed that balance required the suppression of self-assertion, a disciplined destruction of self-will. Others practiced an unabashed self-indulgence, designed to foster self-assertion. The resulting spectrum—which found expression in diet, dress, child-rearing, and religion—had innumerable shadings. In practice, therefore, Protestants still displayed no consensus about self-love. In Protestant theory, though, there was a widespread acceptance of the idea of self-love, and even an expansion of that idea in the direction of "self-culture."[84]

Both seventeenth-century Puritans and eighteenth-century Old Calvinists had accorded a limited acceptance to the notion of self-love. Samuel Willard, in seventeenth-century Boston, had taught that "every Man owes a Love to himself." Men and women were obliged to seek their own health, comfort, and salvation insofar as such acts of self-love enabled them to consecrate themselves to God. Even Richard Baxter, who believed self-denial to be close to the heart of piety, had conceded that self-love was "a principle useful to preserve the world, and to engage the creature in the use of the means of its own preservation." But in the early nineteenth century, the main source for the development of the idea of self-love was the British ethical tradition, and the main agency of its dissemination was the standard college course in moral philosophy.[85]

The most popular moral philosophy textbook in the first two decades of the century, William Paley's *Principles of Moral and Political Philosophy* (1785), taught that "private happiness," both here and hereafter, was the sole motive for virtue. His text followed an emphasis popularized in England by Samuel Clarke's *On Natural Religion* (1706), outlining our duties to God, to our fellow creatures, and "to ourselves." By 1830, Paley was out of fashion, but the tripartite outline was not. Although his critics derided his "selfish" system, most of them maintained the threefold ordering of duties, and they so expanded the range of duties to "ourselves" that self-love began to take on a new meaning.[86]

The initial step was to reassert the distinction between self-love and selfishness. The former, wrote the Scottish philosopher Dugald Stewart, was "inseparable from our nature as rational and sensitive beings." According to Francis Wayland, whose *Elements of Moral Science* (1835) was the most popular of the American texts, no one could doubt for a moment that men and women were "instrument[s] for the production of [their] own happiness." Self-love was simply the impulse to seek lasting happiness for the self. And it was subject only to the governance of the conscience: As long as the impulse of self-love did not "interfere with the happiness of others" or collide with a clear duty to God or to neighbor, it could be considered both innocent and beneficial. Only when it assumed the form of a disposition to promote the self at the expense of duties owed to others or to God did self-love become selfishness.[87]

By the 1820s, some New England theologians were combining British moral philosophy and the Old Calvinist heritage to argue that the choice of God as one's chief good was the result of a "desire for happiness" that could appropriately be called "self-love." Nathaniel William Taylor and the other New Haven theologians urged clergy to direct their evangelistic appeals toward self-love, which, they said, was nothing more than a rational desire for happiness. Bennet Tyler replied that the Taylorites, in suggesting that saints as well as sinners made their choices from a regard for their own happiness, had eradicated the distinction between holiness and sin. But most Protestant theologians had come to agree about the virtues of self-love. Even those who believed that Christian virtue consisted in "disinterested benevolence"—a selfless love for the well-being of God and the universe—no longer conceived of virtue as the antithesis of self-love. Charles Finney, for one, could accept self-love as "simply the constitutional desire of happiness."[88]

The moral philosophers, though, did not stop with the affirmation of self-love. In expounding their list of our "duties to ourselves," they also began to advance an ideal of "self-culture." In the late eighteenth century, John Witherspoon at Princeton instructed his students to fulfill their duty to themselves—first, by attending to "self-interest" through acquiring knowledge and preserving health, reputation, and possessions, and second, by a "self-government" that kept the understanding, the will, and the affections within the bounds of a "due moderation." By the mid-nineteenth century, the standard categories used in discussing duties to self were "self-control" and "self-culture." Both categories designated a duty to improve every "bodily and mental faculty" by securing a "complete self-development" through attention to diet, dress, physical exercise, cleanliness, knowledge, and growth in wisdom. Self-culture was not as much the realization of latent potentialities as the nurture of actual faculties, a tending of the self which refined "all that has been given."[89] It was, in fact, an enhancement of the very balance so admired by mental philosophers and pastoral theologians.

Among some of the clergy—especially the Unitarians—the ideal of self-culture shaded into an ideal of piety. William Ellery Channing spoke of self-culture as "the care which every man owes to himself, to the unfolding and perfecting of his nature." It was an "expansion" of the self that encompassed "all the principles of our nature"—thought, feeling, and volition—in a process of spiritual growth that overcame selfishness and nurtured devotion to God. Channing still preached of the need for self-denial, but looked upon self-denial as merely the subordination of immediate appetites and passions to the "moral and intellectual powers" that sustained growth toward "perfect character." Channing affirmed a continuity between self-culture—the unfolding of one's powers and capacities—and salvation: He finally decided that the "essence of the Christian religion" was God's perfecting our nature "in a career of endless improvement." For Channing, such a process was "the only true good."[90]

It would be misleading, however, to detach the antebellum notion of self-culture, even in its Unitarian forms, from its intellectual setting in evangelical Protestantism. Self-culture required the subordination of the self to "an ultimate rule." Channing believed that intellectual and moral perfection implied a growing capacity for "virtuous obedience" to "the will of our heavenly Father." The self-culture advocated by the moral philosophers required unremitting self-control: the control of appetites, passions, pride, envy, and covetousness. It required, as well, that men and women "cultivate the habit of obeying" the impulses of conscience as the most authoritative faculty of their nature. It entailed "frequent and rigid self-examination" before an infallible divine Judge for whom "character is every thing." It was suffused with the piety and ethics of the older Protestant culture. Self-culture was the conformity of the self to a higher reality; it was not a source or a criterion of ideals and values. Yet, for all that, it did represent an expansion of the notion of self-love in directions that many earlier Protestants would have found utterly disconcerting.[91]

To summarize the argument so far: In the seventeenth century, an image of hierarchy, derived from social experience and intellectual tradition, governed the Christian conception of the soul, of sin, and of salvation, and structured the practice of pastoral care. Even within that consensus about hierarchy, though, there were conceptual tensions that took shape in disagreements about the understanding and the will. In the eighteenth century, those tensions fed into the conflicts of the Great Awakening, with some pastors urging the superiority of the understanding, and others arguing that the affections were deeper—and hence more important—than the mere intellect. In trying to move beyond those conflicts and to attract the allegiance of an emerging middle class that valued practical rationality, tender sentimentality, and commercial enterprise, the antebellum pastoral theologians turned toward an ideal of balance. As theologians, they attempted to balance rationality, sentiment, and exhortation. As mental philosophers, they sought to describe (and to promote) the inner balance of reason,

157

sentiment, and volition. The combination of the theology and the mental science—in a setting of sensitivity to the class distinctions of urban society—defined gentlemanly counsel. And the ideal of self-culture was a natural extension of that vision of inner balance.

Most of the clergy had little use for Ralph Waldo Emerson's "Self-Reliance," and they never could have joined the chorus of Walt Whitman's "Song of Myself." When they spoke of self-culture, they had in mind something far more akin to the inner harmony of the faculties within the Christian who had been saved and sanctified by grace. They never spoke of self-culture without including self-control, watchfulness, obedience, and piety. Only in that sense did the idea of self-culture exercise a discernible influence on the forms of antebellum pastoral conversation.

But the idea did prepare the way for the new vision of pastoral care that would begin to develop after the Civil War. By that time, Ichabod Spencer's conversations would no longer exemplify the latest fashion in Protestant pastoral theology, though Spencer was still widely admired by the clergy. By that time, self-culture would begin to give way to "self-mastery," and the older ideal of balance would pale before a new appreciation of natural vitality. A city pastor, a gentleman who industriously visited his parishioners, Spencer combined reason, sentiment, and persuasion, much as the pastoral theologians advised. He embodied in his practice the social and intellectual tensions of his time. In the new atmosphere after the Civil War, however, Ichabod undoubtedly would have decided that the glory had departed.

5

The Natural Style

Sometime after the Civil War, the pastoral theologians lost their sense of balance. By the end of the century they would have little to say about the ideal of balance among the faculties or the notion of pastoral conversation as a balanced appeal to sentiment, reason, and volition. They spoke more often about the vitality of human nature—either the force of the will or the dynamism of subconscious impulse. They talked about power and energy, effort and mastery, force of character and boldness of decision, and "the natural processes of human life." Indeed, they wrote repeatedly of the "natural," and they began to reconceive their idea of nature: "Our whole modern conception of nature," stated one liberal theologian, "is dynamical; it is a problem of forces with which man has to do alike in his thought, his science, and his conduct." Nature was a "play of forces," and men and women were "powers" within that natural dynamism. Such a conception entailed a reevaluation of religious tradition, and by 1895, Washington Gladden could announce that the revision was complete: "Christianity is no longer anti-natural; it is in the deepest sense natural."[1]

But what did it mean to talk about natural powers and forces? And what did it imply? The first generation of postwar pastoral theologians thought they knew, but the problem became murkier as the century proceeded. They defined *nature* as force, power, and vitality; assumed that strength of character consisted of a capacity for forcefulness; and defined a "natural" style of pastoral conversation simply as the cultivation of a manly, cheerful, informal, and persuasive bearing. But the debates of psychologists and psychotherapists raised another possibility. Perhaps it was more appropriate to help people tap the resources of nature by engendering in them a capacity for receptiveness. In that case, the old methods of persuasion might well be inconsistent with what the liberal theologians liked to call "the method of the Divine working in and through nature."[2] By the time the Emmanuel Movement began to propagate the new psychotherapy within Protestant churches, a few pastors were attempting a redefinition of the natural.

The transition produced a relocation of the notion of Providence. The liberal theologians, at least, wrote not as much of conformity to God's transcendent providential Will as of communion with an immanent Person. "The first and foremost, the constant, the last, and the greatest study of the theologian," declared Henry Churchill King of Oberlin, "must be of persons and of personal relations." By 1901 King was claiming that a new constructive period in theology was at hand; its purpose was to restate theology "in terms of personal relation."[3] For the liberals, therefore, the primary locus of God's activity was within the subjectivity of faithful people. In making that assertion, they ensured that psychology—or at least the study of human subjectivity—would always hold a secure place within liberal churches.

The change entailed a certain tension between the themes of activity and receptivity in pastoral care. This tension was the fruit of an older theology which, in trying to reconcile divine sovereignty and human freedom, had spawned endless debates about the relationship between

God's will and the volitions of the faithful. The diminishing sense of a transcendent Providence, coupled with the activist temper of liberal Protestantism, resulted in a restatement of the older issue. On one level, it became a question of the relationship between activity and receptivity within the self; on another, of the relationship between an active immanent supreme Person and an active, though finite, person. The period began with a pronounced scorn for receptivity; it ended leaving some lingering doubts about the dominance of the active powers within the self. Hence the era marked the first crucial turning point in the history of American pastoral theology. It established the context for the twentieth-century pastoral care movement.

Transcendent Providence

The older methods lingered for decades, though they, too, underwent some subtle changes as the old rational orthodoxy gradually turned into Protestant fundamentalism. Pastoral theology within postwar conservative circles continued the old Baconian quest for an inductive rational science of pastoral care. It retained, as well, the supernaturalist preconceptions of seventeenth-century Scholasticism, linked firmly to the piety of antebellum revivalism. Such a work as the *Helps and Hints in Pastoral Theology* (1874), written by the Presbyterian William Plumer, exemplified the tenacity of the older rational orthodoxy as a guide to pastoral practice.

Plumer wrote that he had visited a sick young woman who surprised him by crying out desperately after he concluded his pastoral prayer: "Oh, I am dying unprepared; do pray for me again. I am going to hell! Oh, I am going to hell; do pray for me again!" Plumer immediately decided that she needed instruction as well as prayer, so he told her that Jesus was her only helper and urged her to seek his salvation.

But the young woman turned to her mother and cried: "Oh mother . . . I am dying. Do pray for your dying child. I never heard you pray in my life. Mother, I am going to hell. Do pray for my poor soul." As onlookers broke into sobs, Plumer could think only of the young woman's "horrible consciousness of being unprepared for the solemn exchange of worlds." So he addressed her with a long plea:

> Chloe, evidently you have but a short time to live, and it is a matter of the utmost importance that you should be prepared to die. Doubtless it is the anxious desire and prayer of all present, who know how to pray, that God would have mercy on your soul, prepare you for death, save you from hell, and fit you for heaven. But there is something which God requires *you* to do. The Lord Jesus Christ has died on the cross of calvary to atone for sin, that guilty sinners through faith in his name might be saved from destruction. God requires you now *to believe this truth*, and accept of the righteousness of his atoning blood as your covering from the guilt of sin. You are convinced that you are a sinner; you fear the wrath of God, and are afraid to die. The Lord Jesus, your only helper, your only Saviour, has opened the door of mercy, and invites you *now*, on your dying bed, to look to him for salvation. He requires you to repent of your sins, to believe in his name, and seek his pardoning mercy. Submit, yield up your heart, and resign yourself now into his hands, and Christ is able and ready to pardon your sins and save your soul from death.

The woman listened, fixed her eyes on the wall, and trembled. Plumer continued his exhortation: "Chloe, will you now accept the Lord Jesus Christ as your only Saviour from sin and hell, and submit your soul into his hands for salvation?"

"No, I can not!"

"Why, Chloe, are you not willing, and why *can* you not now, with dying breath accept of Christ for salvation?"

"It is too late," she answered. Within an hour she had died without saying another word.[4]

Plumer's report, interspersed with vivid details about Chloe's appearance, her faltering voice and inflammation, her anxiety and cold stare, bore considerable resemblance to the conventions of the popular antebellum novel and its voyeuristic attention to the dying prepubescent girl-child. It also illustrated the persistence of clerical rationalism. Plumer observed that the woman's "rational faculties" were still strong. Conceiving of religious faith as the acceptance of rational propositions, he therefore responded by appealing directly for a decision to believe a truth.[5]

Conservative pastoral theology concentrated on three themes: conversion, rationality, and the power of a transcendent spirit. The dean of Moody Bible Institute in Chicago, R. A. Torrey, outlined the standard "fundamentalist position" on "personal work." Its aim, he wrote, was to bring men and women to Christ. Its method was prayer, classification, and a "rational course" of persuasion. The classifications, of course, were those of the earlier textbook tradition: It was the pastor's task to decide whether the sick soul was indifferent, careless, anxious, deluded, ignorant, complaining, or skeptical. That decision would determine which kind of rational arguments would be most fitting.[6]

Torrey's own insistence on rational conviction was so unyielding that he refused to permit his parishioners any recourse to their feelings. When an inquirer would lament the absence of any "feeling" of assurance about salvation, for instance, Torrey always insisted that feelings counted for nought: "Ask him 'Are you going to believe God or your feelings?'" The only solution was the affirmation of biblical truth: "Do not ask him to look at his feeling, but . . . take him to some such passage as John 3:36." If reason and pleading did not succeed—and Torrey acknowledged that sometimes they did not—then the pastor must rely on the providential intervention of the Spirit. Thus did pastoral care proceed within fundamentalism. Torrey appealed to the older pastoral theology—he referred to the writings of Ichabod Spencer—but he had lost something of its breadth. He concentrated everything within the narrow sphere of conversion, defined as *rational assent*.[7]

163

Protestant fundamentalists were confident that their pastoral practice exemplified the highest reach of a Baconian scientific method. Writing in *The Fundamentals* in 1910, a Mississippi minister, H. M. Sydenstricker, marveled that "the penetration of scientific investigation into the erstwhile unknown regions of things is one of the wonders of the age." He insisted that even conversion—the divinely wrought new birth—lay within the range of "scientific investigation." The Scriptures, inductively surveyed, revealed the "purely scientific laws" that govern the steps to conversion, so that any pastor who began with prayer, applied the Word "with eloquence and reason," and cooperated with the Spirit, would be able to produce results with the same certainty as the chemist at work in the laboratory. "This result is as manifestly scientific as can be found in all nature."[8]

For a growing number of Protestant pastoral theologians, though, these notions of science and pastoral work seemed anachronistic and naive, and most abandoned hard-sell exhortation, though some persisted in such methods. The change was underway even while Plumer was at work. By 1899, E. L. Godkin, writing in *The Nation*, identified what he saw as a national trend: "This modern minister deems it his duty to fit his parishioners for the life that now is, as well as for that which is to come; and he looks upon his church as a centre and source of social regeneration and inspiration, in which the bodies and minds of men receive attention as well as their souls."[9] The modern physicians of the soul assumed the same duty, though they were never fully agreed on its implications.

The Transformation of Symbols

The movement toward a "natural style" of pastoral care proceeded on two levels. The first was the churches' accommodation to a new vocabulary in science, technology, and popular culture, an appropriation of the symbols that registered public sensitivity to social and intellectual change. The second was the assimilation of the New

Psychology into liberal theology. The two levels, though, were interrelated. Both the new psychology and liberal theology conceptually refined intellectual issues that had been dimly shadowed in the popular culture. And both levels of the movement toward the natural style raised similar questions about the relationship between activity and passivity.

In discussing the first level—the religious appropriation of scientific, technological, and popular symbols and images—one again engages the perplexing question of the relationship between social and intellectual change. The use of social and political metaphors in the hierarchical psychology of the seventeenth century illustrated one way in which social structures engender metaphors that overflow into other realms of discourse. The interconnection of middle-class urbanity and pastoral gentility in the early nineteenth century illustrated how social change can spread expectations that mold professional behavior. The same patterns—the overflow of language from one realm of discourse into another and the elevation of new social groups to positions of cultural importance—reappeared in the reshaping of pastoral theology after the mid-nineteenth century. One can isolate at least five reasons for the transformation of images and symbols which led to a more natural style of religious counsel. Each of the five contributed to a popular vocabulary replete with notions of power, virility, energy, and effort.

The first cause was the shift of interest in the natural sciences from geology to biology. It had not been easy for the educated antebellum clergy to accommodate themselves to geology, because the expanse of time required for the formation of fossil strata called into question the literal accuracy of Genesis. The new biology of the 1840s—symbolized by the publication in Britain of Robert Chambers' *Vestiges of the Natural History of Creation*—posed additional problems, partly because it brought into focus the untamed vitality—even brutality—of nature. A year before the publication of Charles Darwin's *Origin of Species* in 1859, the theologian Horace Bushnell was connecting the "disorder" of nature to the Adamic fall into sinfulness. In contrast to poets' "sentimentalizing among her dews and flowers," Bushnell depicted nature as a chain of causes and effects marked by deformity, "struggle," and the "deadly grapple" of combatants. Bushnell's "nature" was purposeful—it was, for one thing, a "gymnasium of powers designed to produce "character" through struggle—but it was not gentle.[10]

By the 1870s the liberal theologians were beginning to conclude that Darwin's theory of variation through natural selection merely expanded the old theological argument for design and purpose in nature. But they also recognized that the new evolutionary teleology required an acceptance of struggle and conflict as means to higher ends. Washington Gladden, in 1895, was writing blithely of the "struggle for existence and the survival of the fittest" as commonplace facts that any Christian would recognize. The result was a shift of theological metaphors: For an increasing number of theologians, *nature* seemed to connote power, energy, and force.[11]

The theologians found similar connotations in the language of technology. Josiah Strong announced in 1886 that the application of steam had initiated "a vast new life in the new world." It undoubtedly had initiated a new mode of theological discourse, especially among conservatives. To proceed very far into the literature of popular fundamentalism is to marvel at the repetition of technological metaphors. The conservative preachers spoke of the need to be "recharged with Divine energy," of prayer as a "celestial battery," of the Spirit as an "energizing cause," and of the Word as "the steam within the cylinder that drives the piston and carries forward his work." They compared pious solitude to electrical insulation, prayer to "chemical galvanism," and the power of the Spirit to the "vital energy" of "physical force." It is little wonder that the premillennialist W. E. Blackstone could see the "mighty forces of steam and electricity" as signs of Christ's imminent return. But the fundamentalists were not alone in their delight in technological metaphors. Liberals also could write about "the hydraulic force" of religion and compare the Church to a "powerhouse with . . . dynamos." The language of technology infused pious discourse with a recurring tone of power and energy.[12]

The Civil War—a third source of metaphorical change—provided not as much a new set of words as a new array of attitudes. By promoting a veritable cult of masculinity in intellectual circles, the war raised a question about the cure of souls: Was the whole enterprise perhaps "unmanly"? The question implicitly equated pastoral care with genteel and refined conversations that proceeded delicately in parlors and sitting rooms. Such an image of pastoral labor embarrassed ministers who had come to admire "the bold virtues."[13]

As American intellectuals sought to comprehend the suffering caused by the war, they began to interpret the carnage as a resounding negation of the early nineteenth century's "feeble sentimentalities." The "charming sentiments" of the philanthropists died with the soldiers who fell at Shiloh, Antietam, and Gettysburg. For the essayists, novelists, and journalists who watched, it seemed that the war called forth a new heroic and stoical ideal, contemptuous of softness, impatient with enfeebled humanitarians, opposed to "effeminacy." The fighting confirmed "the manly virtues." For a number of Americans it therefore redefined the meaning of *care*. The men and women who organized the public agencies for "care" during and after the war viewed themselves not as good samaritans but as tutors in the virtues of order and discipline, teaching the nation that tough-minded efficiency could heal physical and psychic wounds just as easily as it could run factories or armies. As a result, a vocabulary of toughness, realism, masculinity, and efficiency began to take hold—not only among novelists, intellectuals, and academicians but also among Americans whose vocation involved caring about other Americans.[14]

The economic consequences of the war intensified the cult of masculinity by glorifying the barons of industry who built the factories, railroads, and steel companies.

After the war the depiction of the "hero" in journalistic biographies underwent a marked change. In the new industrial era, the hero was not the person of refined character, but the man—not the woman—of power. In their biographical sketches the popular magazines and journals no longer spoke of refinement, gentility, and learning, but rather of forcefulness, fame, vision, and the capacity to hold sway over masses of people. The biographers admired Rockefeller, Carnegie, and Morgan—powerful capitalists who schemed and fought their way to economic dominion. And the preachers who attracted the adulation of the Gilded Age clearly resembled the barons of industry. The Victorian princes of the pulpit were forceful orators who could sway vast congregations, either as great preachers in splendid downtown churches or as mass revivalists who applied the techniques of corporate business enterprise to evangelical crusades. Some explicitly associated themselves with the captains of industry and cultivated a style of preaching designed to suggest masculine vitality. In his Yale lectures on preaching in 1892, Henry Ward Beecher urged theological students to "be manly" in their preaching—to "thrust" and "lunge" with vigor and vitality. "It takes a *man*," he said, "to refashion men."[15]

The economic changes altered the language even of those clergy who worried about industrialists. They began to speak of the world as ruled by "titanic industrial forces," and of property as "the concentrated force of power." "Human affairs in the last analysis are problems of forces," wrote the liberal ethicist Newman Smyth. The social liberals among the clergy acknowledged the need for laboring people to counter economic power with the power of collectivity—and for the "forces of religion" to enter into battle with the armies of Wall Street. The social crisis of the 1880s had aided in expanding the clerical vocabulary of power.[16]

By the 1890s a cult of virility pervaded popular culture. Youth counselors became so obsessed with physical culture that they could describe bodily weakness as a crime. The decade produced a virtual revolution in sports, as Americans, for the first time, began to admire heroes like the boxer John L. Sullivan and to take up tennis and bicycling as the first nationwide popular sports. The modern sports page first appeared in newspapers in 1896, in part because the colleges had so successfully touted football as a builder of manly character. The Y.M.C.A., which constructed its first gymnasium in 1869, had built some 450 by the end of the 1890s, when such liberal theologians as Washington Gladden were writing that the gymnasium should have a prominent place in the Church because physical health and strength were sacred possessions: "It is because this church aims to be a co-worker with God that it furnishes the gymnasium." Politicians called for "the strenuous life," philosophers extolled "the strenuous mood," and ministers described the education of the conscience as "athletic training, in the strenghthening of Christian manhood." The damning epithets coined during that period revealed the new values. Nobody wanted to be a "sissy," a "pussyfoot," or a "stuffed shirt." Nobody wanted to have "cold feet." It was the masculine era.[17]

From every side—from science, technology, the war, the economy, and popular culture—the message was the same: Power and vitality stood at the center of things. The imagery of power was by no means alien to the Christian tradition. The Old Testament exalted feats of physical strength; Jesus promised that his followers would "receive power"; Paul compared Christians to athletes competing in a race.[18] But antebellum Protestants had not made much of those themes. Only in the postwar cultural atmosphere did the churches recover (and distort and exaggerate) them. The result was a new religious setting for Protestant pastoral care.

Throughout the religious spectrum, ministers announced that Christianity was a source of power. The proponents of the fundamentalist and Holiness movements published scores of popular treatises: *The Power of a Surrendered Life, The Price of Power, Secret Power, How to*

Obtain Fulness of Power in Christian Life and Service.
Liberal apologists recommended Christianity for its
"living power," interpreted redemption as an infusion of
power that elevated Christians above the lower forces of
nature, and often followed Matthew Arnold in his
definition of God as "the power not ourselves that makes
for righteousness." The prophets of the social gospel
claimed that they were harnessing "the power of religion."
The practitioners of Christian Science insisted that the
main emphasis of the Bible was upon "the superiority of
spiritual over physical power" and that it imparted to
their followers "the healing power of Truth." The
advocates of New Thought claimed to know how to tap the
vitalizing reservoir of "Infinite Power." Religion was a
source of vitality and strength; religious experience was an
experience of power.[19]

This preoccupation with vitality coincided with the
growing popularity in England and America of "muscular
Christianity." Rooted in Thomas Carlyle's glorification of
work and of Old Testament morality, in Thomas Arnold's
notions of moral earnestness, and in John Robert Seeley's
depiction of a heroic Jesus in *Ecce Homo* (1865), muscular
Christianity reached a broad audience through the novels
of Anglican churchmen Charles Kingsley and Thomas
Hughes. The author of *The Manliness of Jesus* and *Tom
Brown's Schooldays*, Thomas Hughes, in 1870, lectured in
the United States on the virility of Christianity and the
forcefulness of its founder. He spoke mainly to middle-
class Protestants who admired toughness, athletic prow-
ess, and strength, whether physical or emotional. They
were pleased to hear that Jesus had maneuvered the rough
terrain of Galilee, trod dusty roads, physically challenged
money changers, and faced down hostile mobs. They liked
to think of him as a first-century counterpart of a Yale
fullback.[20]

The depiction of a muscular Christ appealed to a
spectrum of American preachers. Liberal theologians
described Jesus as "brave and valorous" ("he never was
afraid, never hesitated, never doubted"). The evangelical

170

Luther Gulick invoked the dynamism of Christ to persuade the Y.M.C.A. to promote team sports. And the revivalist Billy Sunday reassured his listeners that Christianity was neither "spineless" nor "effeminate" by reminding them that "Jesus was the greatest scrapper that ever lived." Thus could drum-and-trumpet Christianity march through the theological barriers that separated Victorian Protestants.[21]

The rhetoric of vitality also permeated the new ideal of character. By now, both Protestant and philosophical ethicists were affirming the ethical propriety of self-love. In *Christian Ethics* (1892), Newman Smyth expressed a liberal Protestant consensus when he insisted on the "duty of self-regard," and Protestant ethicists, like their predecessors, assumed that a pressing "duty" to oneself was the cultivation of "character." But the notion of *character* underwent a subtle change. Rather than urging the nurture of character through self-culture, the late-Victorian theologians preferred to speak of "self-mastery." Smyth considered the older ideal one-sided because it neglected "the physical laws of our being"; he liked the image of the "moral warrior" who realized ideals through conflict— "the mastery of good through effort." Theodore Munger spoke of character as an unfolding of the self which required that one throw oneself with "earnestness," and with all one's powers, into the service of others. Both liberals and conservatives could agree with Horace Bushnell in defining the "awful severity" of life as the means used by God for the training of character. When faced with the claim that the era's admiration for "the bold virtues" was a departure from primitive Christianity, Newman Smyth flatly denied it. He preferred to think that some of the vitalities latent in the early church had come to their blossoming in "chivalric virtue."[22]

Such notions of religious power, Christian virility, and self-mastery seemed to require a new style of pastoral care. The minister at the Lafayette Avenue Presbyterian Church in New York City, Theodore Cuyler, responded defensively when a western preacher asked him whether eastern clergymen regarded "pastoral" labors as really being altogether fitting for "an intellectual and manly ministry." Paul and Jesus had been manly, Cuyler replied, and they had valued personal interviews. Therefore no eastern pastor had to apologize to any western preacher. But it was not only the masculine ideal that raised questions about pastoral care. The pastoral theologians were concerned, too, about the social consequences of the increasing urbanization. And the urban professional ideal also raised some questions for them.[23]

By 1900 America was an urban and industrial nation. Immigrants from Europe and from the farms flowed into the cities, which grew into sprawling areas housing 40 percent of the country's population. As the social problems multiplied—as tenements decayed, laborers went on strike, the poor propagated themselves, and vices abounded—the middle classes began to worry about the new "urban menace." But the urban crisis helped to reshape the vision of the cure of souls. During the 1880s a host of urban reformers known as Progressives crowded into organizations for municipal reform, for direct initiative and referendum, for improvement of prisons, tenements, sweatshops, and mental hospitals, for the refurbishing of public education and the reformation of the professions. They called for compassion, but also for competence and efficiency. Members of the professional classes, the Progressives wished to protect their own standing in the social order, and they made visible progress. They organized the American Bar Association in 1878; reorganized the American Medical Association in 1901; pushed for accrediting agencies in public institutions; and transformed the best universities into preserves of specialty, each with its own learned society. Such reforms seemed especially necessary to professionals who worked in the cities, where anonymity allowed quacks to flourish while experts languished in obscurity. The reform of professions would be a natural prelude to the reform of society.[24]

This movement intensified a long-standing sense of

clerical insecurity. Earlier pastoral theologians had compared ministers with physicians and lawyers—and had lamented the differences. Professional reform prompted ministers to be even more suspicious that they were not as "professional" as their counterparts in medicine and law, and they now resumed the complaint— a lament that would continue throughout the Gilded Age—that popular regard for the clergy had declined, especially among the educated. Some explained the decline as the consequence of low salaries. Others argued that the other professions demanded more laborious preparation. A few believed that the mere proliferation of other professions after 1870 had altered the relative standing of the ministry. Whatever the case, the Progressive reform of the professions stimulated a call for a rethinking of professional ministry—and of the cure of souls.[25]

During the same period, ministers were compelled to adapt to another institutional change that had its roots in Progressivism. Between roughly 1870 and 1900, parish life underwent what one of the pastoral theologians called a "complete revolution." The symbol of change seemed to him to be the "church parlor." Growing numbers of churches had transformed themselves into centers that not only were open for worship and evangelism, but also were available for Sunday school concerts, church socials, women's meetings, youth groups, boys' brigades, girls' guilds, singing classes, reforming societies, and a host of other organizations and activities. While avoiding the hard issues that moved the social gospel preachers, the architects of the new parish used the same rhetoric. They claimed to be building the kingdom of God by bringing more and more people into the beneficial association of wholesome groups. In a few parishes, known as institutional churches, the growth of parish organizations coincided with the explicit aims of the social gospel by providing means of ministry to urban slums. But even in conventional parishes the imagery of the social gospel justified the new proliferation of meetings and social gatherings.[26]

Just as the spread of devotional groups before the war had altered pastoral duties, so now the growth of social organizations demanded new kinds of leadership. The pastor's skill in informal personal relationships counted for almost as much as eloquence in the pulpit or intensity in the prayer meeting. As early as 1872 Henry Ward Beecher could describe the new "social sympathy" within the parishes as "something which is coming into vogue," and he urged young pastors to "multiply picnics."

> No church ought to be built after this, in city or country, that has not in connection with it either a place set apart as a parlor, or a room which by some little change of seats could be made into a parlor. There ought to be, from week to week, or every other week, during the largest part of the year, such little gatherings as shall mingle the people together and make them like one another.[27]

One of Beecher's first projects at Plymouth Church in Brooklyn was the construction of such a room. By 1890 the "parlor" in some large churches was deemed "almost as necessary as a pulpit."[28]

The clergy were optimistic about the new sociology of the parish. Some of them believed that only "parish organization" could attract men into the churches: "They had rather serve on a committee than listen to preaching; and who can challenge their taste?" Others argued that social activities would call into service "the liberal culture of woman in our time" and that "social bands and guilds" would draw youth into church work. The new organizations would keep the churches entrenched in the center of city neighborhoods and small-town communities.[29]

It was no easy task to be a social director and still be a physician of the soul. The new kind of parish required a new kind of minister. The pastor "can no longer sit mewed constantly in his study, pondering the relations of sin to the greatest good, or of foreordination to free will," wrote one preacher. "He must be out among his people, with his eye, and often his hand, on every valve and lever of the church machinery."[30] The metaphor suggested an activist temper, a view of the pastor as mover and shaker. It entailed no necessary repudiation of any traditional notion of divine Providence, but the tenor of mainline progressive Protestantism—as of middle-class culture— was hostile to any hint of quietism or resignation. Late-Victorian Protestants were always busy doing God's work—pushing valves and pulling levers. Their inclination was to view their good works as expressions of an immanent Providence. They sought, therefore, a style of pastoral care that would express both their admiration for natural manly informality and their sense of active struggle with the evils of the world.

The New Pastoral Theology

Few ministers felt entirely comfortable while pulling levers and throwing switches in the new organizations, so the pastoral theologians assumed the task of telling them how to succeed. Or at least some of them did. A few of the postwar textbooks merely repeated the commonplace prescriptions of the antebellum writers. Stephen Tyng's *Office and Duty of a Christian Pastor* (1874) consisted of lectures in Episcopal seminaries before the war, and William Plumer's *Helps and Hints in Pastoral Theology* (1874) extended the old rational orthodoxy into postwar pastoral work. But other books—like the *Pastoral Theology* (1885) of James Hoppin at Yale Divinity School—reflected the new urban culture. Presbyterian Thomas Murphy wrote his *Pastoral Theology* (1877) because he found the modern minister overwhelmed with duties that were "scarcely in existence" when the older textbooks were written. Chicago Theological Seminary's G. B. Willcox published *The Pastor Amidst His Flock* (1890) because, as he put it, "the expanding sphere of modern life has broadened the sphere of the Pastor" to such an extent that the ability to compose and deliver sermons could not suffice to attract people of "liberal culture." "The organizations within the church are multiplying, calling

175

... for more and more attention," wrote Washington Gladden in *The Christian Pastor* (1898). In textbooks explaining how to live in this new ecclesiastical world, the pastoral theologians suggested that ministers were not equipped with the interpersonal skills necessary to engage the new tasks. They also promoted a style of religious counsel that corresponded to the activist temper of Protestant progressivism.[31]

It was no surprise when seminary faculties began to reorganize their curriculum into "practical" and "classical" branches—a distinction that had not previously served as the organizing principle for the courses of study. The schools also added one subject after another to their list of studies. As early as 1899 the Hartford School of Religious Pedagogy offered a course on the "Psychology of Religion." The University of Chicago offered a similar course (by correspondence) five years later. Boston University's theology school followed suit in 1905; by 1916 it was even offering a course on psychotherapy. But ministers complained that most seminaries had failed to teach them how to apply their theology, analyze the soul, understand their parishioners, or give counsel—in short, how to minister to congregations with new expectations.[32]

The pastoral theologians responded by suggesting that a deeper knowledge of human nature would guide the clergy in their new array of duties. The purpose of pastoral theology was still to teach more effective ways of appealing for a decision—a decision to believe, to reform, or to face difficulty bravely. But the pastoral writers now suggested that the ministers' manner in evoking the proper responses was almost as important as their message and that a different clerical style could produce a different kind of pastoral relationship.

The new prescriptions for the cure of souls often repeated the advice given in the older manuals. Believing that interpersonal skills could buttress the pulpit, the pastoral theologians urged the clergy to unearth, through interviews, "the antecedents and inner lives" of parishioners. Some wanted clergy to keep detailed record books which diagnosed the spiritual ills and registered the inner growth of each member. But although some of the techniques were familiar, the tone was innovative. The new textbooks promoted not as much a set of theoretical conclusions as a "natural style" of pastoral relationship.[33]

They agreed, first, that pastoral theology must come to terms with the revolt against sentimentality, though they did not always agree about how that was to be done. Everybody could decry the antebellum association between physical weakness and spiritual strength. James Hoppin at Yale told his students that their piety should be "of a healthy and athletic sort"—that piety and paleness were no longer synonymous. Their studies should therefore put them in touch with "masculine intellects"; their recreation should prepare them for "manful work"; their moral self-restraint, including sexual restraint, should undergird their "masculine power"; and their social relationships should exhibit "manly independence of character," but without surrendering refinement. Hoppins' Baptist counterpart at Rochester Theological Seminary, T. Harwood Pattison, regularly included in his lectures long discourses on clerical health (for Christ, after all, had chosen "robust men" as disciples) and on ministerial manliness. He used Thomas Hughes' study of the masculine Jesus as the authority for urging clergy to transcend slavish fear, intellectual subservience, social timidity, self-indulgence, and all other weakness of spirit and body.[34]

Hoppin and Pattison had adopted an image that permeated writings on the Protestant ministry during the late nineteenth century. A considerable number of clergymen believed that ministerial manliness would attract businessmen back into the churches, and they ridiculed "silken niceties" and "scented foppery" that would drive tough-minded men away. From the quadrangle of Yale Divinity School to the small towns of Indiana, the clergy seemed to agree that they wanted "men, not weaklings and invalids," to lead them; "It is manhood that appeals to people, not sentimentality." "I have myself," wrote the liberal Henry Churchill King, "a great deal of faith in the value of the coming muscular minister."[35]

The piety of sentiment still appealed to many Protestants, however, and even the champions of manliness could indulge in coying sentimentality. Henry Ward Beecher walked both sides of the street with ease, lunging and thrusting at his congregation while telling them that Christ was a man of "exquisite pity" and the Bible a book of "tender sympathy." Beecher's sermons on God's love and nature's beauty degenerated into gushy sentimentality, but without subverting his virile and robust image.[36]

The laity seemed baffled, unable to decide whether their pastors should be indulgent parents or straight-talking cops. As late as 1905, a small but nationwide poll of churchgoers revealed that 61 percent wanted their ministers to be sympathetic, benevolent, patient, fatherly, and kind, while 40 percent gave the highest ratings to clergy who were manly, strong, courageous, and possessed of good executive and business instincts. But both groups agreed that a minister should be a man of imposing physique, stately bearing, and well-proportioned limbs—a man who was six feet tall and exuded strength.[37]

The advocates of "heart religion" often identified sentimental piety and pastoral tenderness with feminine virtues, which some found preferable to all the lunging and thrusting of the virile set. Theodore Cuyler said outright that a pastor must be "womanly." One minister called for less preaching and more "mothering" by the clergy. Another argued that sympathy was a trait "half-masculine, half-feminine, and, therefore, wholly pastoral." The ministers were using the common sexual stereotypes to define a proper balance of activity and receptivity in pastoral labor. They were continuing the antebellum discussions of sentiment and rationality. But the identification of the older issues with sexual roles carried new shadings of evaluation that made some clergymen exceedingly uncomfortable.[38]

Some pastoral writers associated a masculine bearing with the pulpit and more feminine characteristics with pastoral conversation. One result of that association was a spirited debate over the usefulness of visiting, the usual means of conducting pastoral labors. The patterns of labor in the cities, observed G. B. Willcox, meant that a pastor, when calling, was "apt to find only the ladies at home." Visiting, then, seemed a glaring symbol of the union of the pastoral and the feminine. Phillips Brooks, at Trinity Church in Boston, wondered whether he, as a man, had any business in a vocation that accorded so much importance to household visits, and he declined the chaplaincy at Harvard when his congregation assured him that he could simply preach, without calling from house to house. Henry Ward Beecher advised ministers to visit, but he himself left "pastoral work" to assistants. He rarely visited the sick and dying, even among his friends, and on occasions when he did, his artistry with words failed him—"He lost control over his words and himself." Other clergymen were more consistent. They openly announced that they considered pastoral visits as mere occasions for "bell-pulls and card exchanges." Pastoral calling, they said, was "effeminate work" and "a tragic waste of a strong man's time." In their estimation, the pastoral visit precluded attention to weightier pulpit matters and no longer served as a fitting instrument for the cure of souls.[39]

For most clergy, though, the solution was less drastic. They called simply for a shift in the tone of pastoral conversation so that it would be more "natural and manly." By avoiding affectations, stiffness, and formality, the pastor would invite companionship; the best pastor was the "friend," the comrade. Only out of comradeship could natural counsel evolve—and comradeship required a mood of pastoral informality.[40]

The pastoral theologians therefore advised ministers to "be cheerful." One, G. B. Willcox, had heard it frequently said that no company was as "merry" as that of clergymen, and he urged them to carry that buoyancy into their pastoral duties. Because a sense of humor had been implanted in human nature, a winsome manner, devoid of pompous solemnity, would bring comfort and confidence.

Cheerfulness and wit seemed to be especially fitting in the sickroom. "Shed sunshine, make music," wrote one light-spirited adviser, "and you will cheer."[41]

The modern physician of the soul was therefore to shed any trace of the morbid and even to refrain from dwelling "morbidly" on religious themes. Ministers who attended the weak and dying were still allowed to ask "some very brief questions in regard to the state of the soul," but they were not to push for "repentance." And they were never to endanger any ill person by their efforts to guide or console. Theodore Cuyler even warned that in many cases of extreme illness the presence of the pastor could be an "unwise intrusion." A minister could help a parishioner acknowledge an impending death: "You are very sick," one might say, "and life is uncertain, and if it should please the Lord to take you, do you feel quite ready?" But in some instances, pastoral theologians warned, overt religious discourse would be a mistaken strategy in dealing with ill or distraught persons, especially if the words lacked cheer.[42]

The new mood was visible in the changing tone of clerical attitudes toward the grieving, especially in liberal churches. Henry Ward Beecher opposed traditional mourning customs and encouraged stricken families to "scatter flowers" rather than hang black crepe. When Beecher died, his own family staged a "flower funeral": A friend noticed that "no emblem of sorrow or parting was there." By 1913, the Protestant funeral could seem like an occasion for celebration. "We no longer shroud the house in black," wrote Lyman Abbott. "We make it sweet with flowers; for the hymns of grief we are fast substituting the hymns of victory; for words charged with a sense of loss we listen to words that hold wide the door of hope and faith."[43]

At such times, the pastoral theologians added, any thoughtless chatter might do as much harm as morbid talk. "Show your sympathy," suggested Willcox in 1890, more by "pressing the sufferer's hand in silence than by insisting prematurely on any Christian truth, however precious." It was a custom of Phillips Brooks to counsel with people in trouble or grief merely by sitting without saying anything, permitting them to do all the talking, and some pastoral theologians approved of such a practice. They urged pastors to learn the art of sympathetic insight; they told them to understand rather than condemn; they assured them that sympathy was manly. The antebellum writers, also, had encouraged silent sympathy, of course, but now the rationale was different: Silence was valued because it permitted "nature" to have its way. The pastor was never to assume that people crushed wih calamities would be "satisfied and calmed by . . . consolations." "Let them weep for a while," wrote Willcox. "Nature must have her way." The flow of tears was not only "manly" but a natural "safety-valve" of grief. Nature had her own wisdom and it required respect.[44]

The main appeal in pastoral counsel, though, was still directed at the will. Washington Gladden admired those physicians who used a "vigorous moral treatment." "They put much emphasis on the rousing of the patient's will, the strengthening of his self-control, the exercise of his rational and mental power."[45] So the pastoral theologians, too, assumed that their purpose was to teach ministers to move the will. That assumption held firm even after a few clergy began to describe their conversations as "psychotherapy." Indeed, one such instance of clerical therapeutics nicely illustrates the tone of a "natural style" of pastoral care.

Before the turn of the century, one W. T. McElveen, the pastor of the First Congregational Church in Evanston, recorded his interview with an alcoholic stranger who one day wandered into his office and thickly inquired whether the minister could help him stop drinking.

"That I can," said the pastor, who then launched into a short exhortation, which seemed to produce no noticeable result.

"What is your name?" the minister finally asked.

"MacDonald," the man answered.

"Are you Scotch?"

"Yes, sir, that's what I am. What's your name, Mr. Minister?"

"McElveen."

"You Scotch, too?"

"Yes," replied the minister, thereby evoking a hearty handshake from his visitor. The handshake helped suggest a clerical strategy.

"MacDonald," he said, "you're no Scotchman."

"What's that?"

"I say I don't believe you're a Scotchman—no pure Scotchman, I mean. You're a mongrel. You're mixed up with English; maybe some Irish, too. I could do something for a real Scotchman. But that combination is too much for me. You might as well go along."

The caller stormed and swore and finally demanded: "What makes you say I'm no Scotchman?"

"Well, MacDonald, you know yourself that one thing the Scotch are famous for all the world over is that they're so stubborn. Once they make up their minds, nothing can change them. Nothing in creation can drag them into doing what they don't want to do. They always keep their promises. But you here, MacDonald . . . You can't keep your promises."

The man vowed that he had no drop of blood that wasn't Scotch, but McElveen refused to believe him until the unhappy fellow burst out: "If you'll only believe I'm Scotch, I'll let you pray with me."

"No, it wouldn't be worthwhile," McElveen answered. "You've broken so many promises to God that I think it would be a good deal of an insult to bring you round to him again." But after the man pleaded further, the minister offered to pray for him on the condition that he would then pray for himself.

After the minister's prayer, the caller seemed to balk, so the pastor retorted with indignation: "Now I know you're no Scotchman. You've gone back on me."

"Get down again," the man said. "I'll pray." And he poured out his soul: "O God above, make this minister man know I'm a Scotchman, for Jesus's sake. Amen."[46] The minister's summary of the incident revealed one underlying supposition of the natural and manly style of counseling: "I knew I'd won then." The next chapter was inevitable—the alcoholic reformed and joined the church. The counseling session had, if we can believe the report, issued in a clear victory for the natural style. Hearty good cheer and tough persistence had enabled the counselor to overcome opposition and give new direction to another person's life.

McElveen's method gained the applause of at least one psychologist at Clark University, who saw in it an appeal to latent forces of character. To a later generation, his style bore the marks of low comedy or well-intentioned manipulation, but it serves as a reminder that one purpose of pastoral conversation of the time was to *win:* Pastoral writers spoke of winning souls, winning hearts, winning friends, winning confidence, and winning battles. Or as one minister put it, changing the metaphor, manly pastors were to be "promoters," but "the parish machine must not be a machine," for the parochial must be pastoral. In such a setting, the minister who did not win—who faced defeat from disease, weakness, or intransigence—carried a heavy burden indeed.[47]

The rhetoric of naturalness, cheer, and informality even appeared in the continuing arguments about penitential confession in the sacramental churches. The Roman Catholic bishop of Richmond, James Gibbons, insisted that a few minutes in the confessional could elevate men and women from shame and confusion to quickness of step, joy of countenance, and brightness of eye. The Episcopalians were not so sure about that, though some of them wanted to believe it. While the high-church party argued that private confession allowed the priest to "deal with sins as physicians deal with diseases," the low-church group claimed that auricular confession was "morbid," destructive of "healthy growth," and subversive of "moral stamina." The evangelicals complained that half-educated young priests simply wanted to be the directors of "morbid and lackadaisical men and 'silly women.'" They also charged that detailed confession was "filthy." They claimed, in brief, that the confessional was somehow unnatural. No argument could have been more convincing.[48]

The pastoral theological textbooks urged ministers to be natural and manly. The images suggested by science and technology led to the association of "nature" with "power," and the popular conceptions of masculine roles suggested an equation of manliness with vigorous activity. A "natural" style of pastoral counsel, then, consisted of little more than informal and cheerful persuasion. But by the 1880s, psychologists and liberal theologians were seeking more complex conceptions of the natural and having second thoughts about the disdain for receptivity. To be sure, their redefinitions of nature, the self, and God partially confirmed the intuitions of pastoral theologians like Willcox, Hoppin, and Pattison. But by the beginning of the twentieth century, conceptions of the "natural" were beginning to expand. Ideas of subconscious vitalities and divine immanence complicated the simple association of naturalness wtih forceful informality. While the new psychologists and the liberal theologians were clearly the children of the masculine era, they suggested, often reluctantly and gingerly, that it would be necessary for proponents of the natural to take into greater account the place of receptivity in human nature.

Psychology and Psychotherapy

In 1897 William James reported that Americans, especially those in the schools, were turning to psychologists with great expectations. The psychologists should respond, he urged, by "showing fruits in the pedagogic and therapeutic lines."[49] James hoped that psychologists and neurologists would join in a common quest for therapeutic fruitfulness. But first he had to convince the psychologists that they had misunderstood human activity, and the neurologists, that they had misinterpreted nature. He was not entirely successful; many of his fellow psychologists considered him a metaphysician in disguise. But he eventually reached a vast audience and transformed the popular understanding of psychology.

Most of the newly established psychologists were indifferent to James' summons. The last of the great mental philosophers—James McCosh at Princeton—was in no position to take the lead in such a venture. The younger psychologists had other things to do. Busily working to transform psychology into an exact science, they left healing to doctors and spent their time in psychological laboratories, isolating and classifying the contents of consciousness. Devoted to the scientific psychology of Wilhelm Wundt, who in 1879 had established in Leipzig the first of the European laboratories, the American "structural" psychologists constructed galvanometers, oscillographs, and recorders to measure degrees of attention and levels of sensory awareness. In the new academic departments that proliferated after 1888, psychology was to be the study of conscious mental states, which were accessible to introspection and the new tools of measurement.[50]

James took a leading position in a "functionalist" revolt against the reigning academic psychology. He had nothing against laboratories. He had a tiny one of his own at Harvard as early as 1876, and he and G. Stanley Hall, who founded the first "real" psychological laboratory at Johns Hopkins in 1883, quarreled about priority. But James thought that laboratories were worthless if they were used simply for classifying discrete moments of sensation. Such a project was unreliable and sterile because in real life the quality of any sensation—or any experience—was determined by the totality of changing circumstances in which it occurred. Like John Dewey, whose article on "The New Psychology" in 1884 argued that it was impossible to consider "psychical life as an individual, isolated thing developing in a vacuum," James believed that psychologists should attend to a concrete world of never-ending associations, in which sensations were related not only to other sensations, but to the purposive activities of real men and women. James had been impressed by the implications of Charles Darwin's *Origin of Species:* The Darwinian notion of change through spontaneous variation heightened his interest in free decisions that would make a difference in the environment; the Darwinian idea of adaptation stimulated his interest in the way mental functions helped an organism survive and flourish within an unyielding environment. It was less important to James that "mind" possessed classifiable contents than that it possessed specifiable uses. He, Dewey, James R. Angell, and others—the functionalists—were more interested in the mind's adaptations than in its elements.[51]

In an activist era, the psychologists became the experts on action. James' colleague Hugo Münsterberg unveiled an "action theory" of consciousness, according to which our readiness to act, registered in muscular tension, determines our perceptions of the world. James believed that the purpose of mental activity is always a bodily change or activity of some kind, that all mental effort is "for the sake of action." That is, every idea tends to pass into action—and would do so unless hindered by the presence of other ideas. James Mark Baldwin, the founder of the Princeton Psychological Laboratory, developed a law of "dynamogenesis," which stated that the nervous process is never complete until it issues in some form of action. And G. Stanley Hall at Johns Hopkins reached similar conclusions by studying the muscular system. Like the clerical theoreticians of character, the psychologists argued that thought and feeling come to their highest expression only in action.[52]

Just as the muscular Christians were weary of disembodied spirituality, the new psychologists were bored with disembodied minds. They wanted a "physiological psychology" that would demonstrate the unity of mind and body. James admired the *Physiological Psychology* (1887) of George Trumbull Ladd, a theologian and philosopher at Yale, and when James published his own *Principles of Psychology* in 1890, he described in great detail the work in physiology being done in England,

France, and Germany. To James, the unity of mind and body did not necessarily entail a materialistic claim that brain-states were the sole cause of mind-states, though he did assume their uniform correlation—that the activity of the cerebral hemispheres was a condition of consciousness. The notion of psychophysical unity, though, did indicate that physical vitality controlled psychological dispositions. "Our moods and resolutions," he wrote, "are more determined by the condition of our circulation than by our logical grounds."[53]

To James' clerical readers it seemed that the new psychology had discovered the physical conditions of intellectual and moral achievement. Laboratory research had shown the connection between muscular contraction and attention, muscular fatigue and depression, and "muscular tone and will-power." It had demonstrated that a surplus of nervous energy could undergird self-control, fatigue could alter perceptions, and bodily training could influence ethical judgment. To Henry Churchill King, the president of Oberlin, the new research suggested that an active life would promote a tranquil spirit.[54]

The ethical implications of a physiological psychology seemed particularly clear in James' famous chapter on habit. The president of Brown, W. H. P. Faunce, told a Yale audience in 1908 that the chapter had been "preached in a thousand pulpits." Henry Churchill King considered it "incomparable." James had defined habits as pathways of neurological discharge formed in the brain, and he had described habitual behavior as both an example of the organism's tendency toward action and a consequence of motor activity. Disciplined deeds and useful actions would convert the nervous system into an ally. Action formed character, passivity subverted it. "There is no more contemptible type of human character than that of the nervous sentimentalist and dreamer, who spends his life in a weltering sea of sensibility and emotion, but who never does a concrete manly deed." James urged habitual efforts to create good habits: "Be systematically ascetic or heroic in little unnecessary points, do every day or two something

for no other reason than that you would rather not do it."
By so creating and sustaining useful habits, he said, we
spin our own fates.[55]

The creation of habit was largely accomplished by
willpower. The new psychologists claimed that they no
longer believed in the existence of separate "faculties."
But when they dissolved the old faculty of will, they let it
seep downward through the whole organism, until finally
it suffused everything. They began to view all mental life as
infused with a purposive, voluntarist impulse. As early as
1881, James concluded that "the willing department in
our nature" dominated our thought and perception. He
meant not only that thought was always at the service of
action, but that the mind classified and ordered reality in
accordance with the "purposes" of the will.[56]

According to several of the new psychologists, the will
revealed itself most directly in "attention"—the capacity to
attend to one object rather than another. When James
published the brief version of his *Psychology* in 1892, he
argued that "effort of attention" was "the essential
phenomenon of will," that attention was inevitably selective, and that by their selective attention, men and women
partially created the world of which they were aware. In that
sense, the will even helped to construct the intelligible
world: Selective attention carved the contours of knowledge
within what would otherwise have been "one big blooming
buzzing confusion" of sensations. Münsterberg went so far
as to say that "the world we will is the reality." The normal
categories of classification and conception were not universal structures of a static reason—they were teleological
instruments of the purposive mind.[57]

The clergy took note of that "voluntarist trend" in
psychology. It confirmed their conviction that the secret of
"character" was self-mastery and self-control. "The
problem of character," wrote Henry Churchill King,
"becomes, thus, ultimately a problem of *fixing attention*."
King urged Protestants to move beyond introspection and
fix their attention on the world outside themselves. They
were to lose themselves by attending to something other

than themselves. Sports and games, service and good works, worship and activity in the world—all were occasions for "will-training."[58]

William James was by no means the only prominent American psychologist of his era, but in the eyes of the educated Protestant clergy, he did "more than any other to make psychology vital." To isolate a few popular themes from his *Psychology* is to do him an injustice—the book was one of the masterly productions of nineteenth-century America. It combined physiology, introspection, and observation into an exceedingly rich description of the stream of human consciousness which had enormous influence on analytic philosophy, phenomenology, and philosophical pragmatism in the twentieth century. But to nineteenth-century clergy, the important themes in the book had to do with the unity of mind and body, the centrality of action, the importance of habit, and the description of the willing self. Those were the themes that made sense in the masculine era (and the new psychologists touted the masculine virtues as insistently as did the clergy).[59]

But James also came to believe that an unremitting emphasis on the active powers led to a one-sided conception of the self. In his popular address on "The Energies of Men," in which he lamented that so few people could tap their "stored-up reserves" to live "at the maximum of their energy," he continued to accent the force of the will: "The normal opener of deeper and deeper levels of energy is the will." But in his equally popular essay "The Gospel of Relaxation," he called for repose and a toning down of moral and bodily tensions. Receptivity might be as reliable an access to power as active exertion.[60]

By 1890 James was becoming increasingly interested in the notion of a "subliminal self," a source of energy that was deeper than the level of conscious awareness. By the time he published his *Varieties of Religious Experience* in 1902, he was describing the "wider" subconscious self as a source of saving transformation. The "sick souls" who struggled with internal conflict and discord would not find their salvation in effort, but in surrender. James seemed impressed by the possibilities of relaxing, letting go, and opening the consciousness to a power outside it. He speculated that the source of that salvation—which he called the More—might be simply each person's own subconscious energies. But it might be more than that. In any case, it was real, for it produced real effects, and it explained how receptivity could unify and enhance the active life, how self-surrender could engender self-assertion. Transcendent Providence had become immanent power.[61]

The new notions of the subconscious, of relaxation, repose, and self-surrender were derived in part from the popular writers in the so-called New Thought tradition. By the 1890s, the leaders of New Thought—people like Ralph Waldo Trine and Orisen Swett Marden—were promising power and success to everyone who could learn the techniques of self-abandon through mental discipline, relaxation, and autosuggestion. James admired Annie Payson Call's best-selling *Power through Repose*, and the title of the book became a popular slogan among Protestant clergy. It was not the last time the dogmas of positive thinking would infiltrate Protestant traditions. But popular Protestantism, having substituted a gospel of good works for the older gospel of justification by grace, had no other way to refer to the relaxation of effort.[62]

The new ideas about repose and the subconscious therefore had the effect of expanding the popular Protestant conception of the natural. Those ideas suggested that the first generation of pastoral theologians might well have overemphasized the active power. Henry Churchill King, for one, read James and decided that "character, in the large sense, requires both self-assertion and self-surrender." That insight would appear repeatedly in early twentieth-century efforts to reevaluate pastoral conversation. But that reevaluation did not rest simply on the New Psychology or on New Thought. It drew also on the traditions of psychotherapy that had begun to arise within American medicine. It was the convergence of themes in both psychology and neurology that would produce the rethinking of the natural style of pastoral care.[63]

Ever since the 1880s, medical neurologists had assumed responsibility for healing maladies of the soul. But they were struggling to establish themselves as tough-minded empiricists rather than speculative quacks. They were therefore inclined to seek a "materialist" solution for every psychic ailment—from back pain to hysteria. They sought tiny anatomical lesions that might cause nervous and mental disorders, or they urged the strengthening of the nervous system. When George Beard, a physician in New York, published his celebrated diagnosis of *American Nervousness* in 1881, he explained that the seeming epidemic of "neurasthenia" in the United States was the result of tension between a competitive society and the nervous system. Modernity drained people of their "nerve force." But Beard's solution required waiting for nature to produce a neurologically superior human being.[64]

Few neurologists could afford to wait. So they improvised. They came up with ways to strengthen the body and help nature along. One group, led by S. Weir Mitchell, instituted a "rest cure" which compelled patients to remain in bed, utterly bored and isolated. Mitchell alone would break the monotony, applying "moral medication" in long sessions of exhortation, teasing, and pleading. One of his colleagues explained that the method was closely akin to the old religious effort to "break the spirit" of recalcitrant sinners. A second group, though, insisted that a rest cure was but a prelude to the more effective "work cure." The Boston neurologist Richard Cabot described the work cure, in which distressed patients were assigned useful tasks, as "the best of all psychotherapy."[65]

No neurologist could explain why work and rest cures proved effective. They were convinced that all ailments had some hidden physical cause, but some ailments responded to work and rest, while others did not. Why the difference? The neurologists offered an answer, but on close examination it was merely another way of posing the question. The answer, they said, could be found in the distinction between functional and organic illness. Some ailments were amenable to the physician's direct intervention—they they were organic. Others would yield only to "nature," with some indirect assistance from the doctor—and they were functional. The distinction seemed clear, and it permitted neurologists to hold on to their medical materialism. It meant that in 1908, someone like Richard Cabot could grudgingly agree to use the "terrible" word "psychotherapy."[66]

By 1908, though, the medical materialists were under siege. William James accused doctors of making a dogmatic superstitution of materialism, and along with such academics as G. Stanley Hall and Josiah Royce, he urged physicians to explore mental disorder from a purely psychological vantage point. Gradually, a few doctors, notably James Jackson Putnam and Adolf Meyer, announced that their colleagues who were seeking a physical cause for every ailment had gone astray. A professor of neurology in Harvard Medical School, Putnam concluded finally that doctors had to deal with "values and purposes" in a world of free persons.[67]

By the time Putnam began to criticize the "somatic style" of medical materialism, the psychotherapeutic movement that had begun in Europe in the 1860s was attracting attention in America. And that prompted some historical revisionism. The ideas of the eighteenth-century Viennese Franz Anton Mesmer—who had healed by including in his patients a "mesmeric sleep" that enabled him to shift the force of their "animal magnetism"— seemed no longer the ravings of an eccentric but the first glimmerings of psychotherapeutic insight. Staid American academics took a second look at the work of the Scottish surgeon James Braid, who in the 1840s had used "neuro-hypnotism" to kill pain during surgery and to cure what he called functional afflictions. They looked again at the experiments of Jean-Martin Charcot, whose use of hypnotism as a diagnostic device had impressed his student Sigmund Freud. And they also began to pay attention to the work of A. A. Liebault and Hippolyte

Bernheim at the University of Nancy in France, where hypnotism was viewed as a form of sleep induced by suggestion. Bernheim's conclusion that "suggestive" therapies could prevent serious illness influenced both medical practice and pastoral counseling in America.[68]

Americans took the therapeutic tradition and made it their own. They flocked to hear the lectures of the French physician Pierre Janet, who twice toured American medical school faculties to explain his theories about the psychological sources of hysteria and other disorders. In 1905 Americans began to read the English translation of Pierre Dubois' *Psychic Treatment of Nervous Disease*, which even Richard Cabot described as an epoch-making book that would convince the medical public that "there was such a thing as scientific mind cure." Dubois was a professor of psychotherapy at the University of Berne, and his book helped persuade American doctors to list *psychotherapy* as a separate topic in their 1906 official index of medical papers. By 1909 some ninety articles on the topic had already been published. By that time, moreover, the psychologist Morton Prince had introduced at Tufts Medical School the first American course in psychotherapy, and doctors were planning their first conference on the subject.[69]

The doctors who gathered at the 1909 conference were eager to hear the case for psychotherapy as a natural method of healing, but it was obvious that they shared no consensus about the meaning of *nature*. The result was open conflict over the means of pursuing therapy. Some doctors argued for the use of hypnotism. Others recommended the more modest method of verbal suggestion, believing that hypnotism itself was only a fancy form of suggestive therapy. But the opponents of suggestion worried that this degenerated into a "lie-cure" in which the therapist practiced well-meaning deceit, and they called instead for "creative assertion"—the therapist was to encourage rather than offer suggestive messages. The opponents of assertion worried that this appealed simply to the will and ignored rational reflection. They preferred

193

to follow the theories of Dubois, and they argued for a "rational psychotherapy" that would sharpen the judgment of patients by teaching them to see things as they really were. But the opponents of the rationalists worried that logic was insufficient. They thought clients should be compelled to face painful experience and attain inner unity by ethical commitment to a center of loyalty. But the opponents of "ethical" counseling worried that this failed to take into account the new insights of psychoanalysis. They thought Sigmund Freud should have a hearing.[70]

The extent to which the early therapists disagreed about the meaning of *nature* was evident in their writing about the notion of the subconscious or unconscious. Such an idea had been current in Europe since the 1870s, but neither Europeans nor Americans could agree about what it meant. The discussions in America unearthed a spectrum of possibilities. A few psychologists claimed that the term *subconscious* had no intelligible meaning. Most disagreed with that assessment, but the defenders of the concept were divided into at least four groups.

Some psychologists and neurologists were willing to use the word to describe any chemical or physical operation in the body of which the mind remained unaware. For practical purposes, they could disregard the subconscious. Richard Cabot said he felt no need to grope in "dusky vagueness" when counseling his patients, since psychotherapy was the education of character, and as such, required no reference to subconscious forces. A second group, though, had no choice but to grope in the dusk: They had patients who were split into multiple personalities. Yet each personality, it seemed, could think and reason, which suggested a "subconscious" that was itself amenable to reason and education. Morton Prince, for one, believed that the subconscious was suggestible, that rational suggestion could supply new meanings to restore a disintegrated person. A third group had less confidence in the rational domestication of the subconscious—it had more faith in its inherent creativity. The therapists

who followed William James used suggestion and auto-
suggestive techniques, forms of positive thinking that
tapped the creative subconscious powers within the
mind.[71]

By 1908 a number of American doctors were discovering
a fourth position. The Freudians wrote of an "unconscious" that was not a beneficent or creative force, but
primarily "repressed infantile material," chaotic psychic
forces which pounded the rational walls of consciousness—
seeking exit, donning disguises, battering at weakened
defenses, and eluding the searchlight of reason. In 1909 A.
A. Brill at Columbia University was telling Americans that
"no recent theories either in medicine or psychology have
evoked so many controversies as those of Freud." In the
same year, Freud himself journeyed to tiny Clark University in Worcester, Massachusetts, where his lectures on
psychoanalysis won the allegiance of James Jackson
Putnam, the Boston Brahmin whose respectability would
cushion the shock of the new ideas. And they evoked from
William James the prediction that the future of psychology
would belong to Freud.[72]

A small group had followed Freud for years in the
specialized journals, but his visit attracted the attention of
the popular press, the scorn of most academic psychologists (who sometimes depicted him as yet another ragtag
faith healer), and the uncritical adulation of the *literati* in
Greenwich Village salons. Brill found himself in demand,
though, not only in Mabel Dodge's soirees in New York but
in fashionable Episcopal churches in Boston as well. As
early as 1909 the associate rector of the Emmanual
Episcopal Church announced that he and his fellow
ministers ranged themselves on the side of Freud.[73]

The conceptual disagreements among psychotherapists
would reappear eventually among pastoral counselors.
But the initial effect of the controversy was to raise
questions about the meaning of *the natural.* The first group
of postwar pastoral theologians had assumed that nature
connoted power and forcefulness and that for a minister to
be "natural," he must be informal, cheerful, and manly.

195

Much of the New Psychology confirmed that older image. But all the talk about subconscious vitalities subverted, for only a few ministers at first, the old confidence in the rational dialectics of manly counsel. Nature itself seemed to demand surrender as well as assertion, receptivity as well as active mastery. What then were pastors to do? Should they argue and persuade? Or assert? Or offer subtle suggestions? Or probe unconsious meaning? The answer might have been more clear if everyone had understood *nature* in the same way, but the disagreements among psychologists and neurologists over the subconscious revealed that nature was far more mysterious than pastoral theologians had once supposed.

Liberalism and the Psychology of Religion

The problem would have been less difficult had liberal theologians not banked so heavily on the values of the natural. In 1858 Horace Bushnell had complained of "the tendency, on every side, to believe in nature simply, and Christianity only so far as it conforms to nature." His solution had been to rescue the supernatural by redefining the natural. Nature, he said, was a self-contained chain of causes and effects; the supernatural was anything that transcended the chain or acted on it from without. In that sense, human beings—creatures with originating wills— were supernatural beings, able to set the causes in nature to work in new combinations. Such a recognition of the supernatural in the human, Bushnell thought, would obviate objections to a supernatural God. But his later admirers could see other implications in his argument: It suggested that the supernatural was to be reinterpreted as "the realm of freedom," which was fully "as natural as the physical realm of necessity." At most, the supernatural was simply the immanent evolutionary telos of nature toward "an ethical purpose and end" in the "free world of the spirit." Such ideas became so familiar within Protestant liberalism that by 1894, William Newton Clarke, dean of the early liberals, could assert that "what is true is natural."[74]

196

The liberals believed that "the theology of any age is largely an expression of the Christian experience of that age." They tried to express the Christian experience of their own age by reinterpreting the meaning of the natural. In their doctrine of immanence, nature became the locus of the Divine and thus provided a way to talk about both surrender and assertion, receptivity and mastery, in Christian growth. At the same time, their constant appeal to experience ensured that a certain therapeutic temper would be deeply ingrained in the liberal traditions.[75]

Liberalism rationalized the relocation of divine Providence that was already implicit in Protestant activism. It transferred the locus of divine activity from the transcendent heights to the surface and depths of the mundane world. "The idea of God as transcendent," wrote Episcopal theologian A. V. G. Allen in 1884, "is yielding to the idea of Deity as immanent in His creation. A change so fundamental involves other changes of momentous importance in every department of human thought, and more especially in Christian theology." It involved, certainly, a revaluation of subjective experience.[76]

Increasingly, the liberal theologians began to think of salvation as the "experience of a power which delivers us from our weakness, our ignorance, and our sin, and transfers us into the glorious freedom of the children of God." They came under the sway of Hermann Lotze, a philosopher in Göttingen and Berlin, who argued that Christianity was the "absolute religion" because it best enabled men and women to overcome the lower forces of nature and fulfill their potential as spiritual persons. The German theologian Albrecht Ritschl appropriated that theme from Lotze and used it to argue that the unique quality of Christianity was the moral experience it could produce. The appeal to experience became the keynote of the liberals, Ritschlians or not, and provided a way to combine the themes of receptivity and activity. Salvation required a receptivity to the inward promptings of an immanent God, and it was precisely the receptivity that enlarged the scope of an active life of service and love.[77]

197

Such a notion of salvation presupposed that inward experience was trustworthy, that receptivity could truly put one in touch with God. And the liberals had confidence in the authority of their own experience, though they did not abandon the authority of Scripture, especially of the person of Christ as revealed in Scripture. Newman Smyth's *The Religious Feeling* (1877), which combined the vocabulary of German theological liberalism with the old Scottish philosophy, redefined Christian "evidence" by attempting to prove that there was a "valid experience"— a feeling or "perception" of absolute dependence—which revealed "the presence of real spiritual being and goodness without and above ourselves." By the end of the century, the mainline liberals concluded that the key to unlocking the mysteries of religion and reality was "in ourselves."[78]

It was the preoccupation with religious experience—a modern extension of the old Pietism—that stimulated the emergence of the "psychology of religion" as a powerful, though transient movement in American colleges and seminaries. The seminal figure in the movement was Granville Stanley Hall, a graduate of Union Theological Seminary in New York, who found in the experimental psychology and spiritual freedom of the German universities a new way of looking at the world. By 1889 Hall was the president of Clark University in Worcester, Massachusetts, an ambitious graduate school which was to be devoted to pure research, especially in the psychology of religion.

Heirs of a revivalist culture, Hall and his students turned their attention initially to the experience of conversion, interpreting it as a natural occurrence which usually accompanied the physical and emotional changes of adolescence. "However inexplicable," wrote Edwin Starbuck, "the facts of conversion are manifestations of natural processes." Starbuck was a Quaker who maintained a lively personal interest in religion, which he viewed through the lenses of philosphical idealism. Some other psychologists of religion advocated a thoroughgoing naturalism. James H. Leuba, a native of Switzerland with an intense dislike for orthodoxies, argued that conversion always had a "physical basis" and that religious experiences merely satisfied a natural instinct for self-preservation and organic pleasure. Most psychologists of religion reached conclusions more compatible with mainline liberalism. Their hope was to isolate a unique religious instinct, or to discover "the region of man's nature" from which religion chiefly sprang.[79]

They were mainly interested, however, in the function of religion—either its social uses or its enhancement of individual experience. Hall carried out his research with the idea that "efficiency for the conduct of life is the supreme criterion" of value in religion. His students and colleagues hoped to learn how religion helped adolescents to negotiate their crises and adults to find "harmony with the universal life," and how it helped social groups maintain inner stability. They believed that the primary value of religious experience was its capacity to unify the divided self, or facilitate a movement from egoism to altruism, or nourish the development of personality. And they hoped to "encourage the transformation of existing religious forms that they may become better adapted to their function."[80]

In touch with both the New Psychology and liberal theology, Hall's group began to redefine the *natural style* of pastoral care. They were interested in the way religious guidance should be practiced among pastors who understood the theological doctrine of immanence and the new theories of the subconscious. Even Leuba hoped that the "science of religion" could establish a wiser form of "soul midwifery."[81]

Their implicit—and often explicit—allegiance to a doctrine of divine immanence suggested the need to trust in natural processes. They insisted that the pastor who could identify the stages of natural "growth" had discovered "nature's way" of religious development. "Nature's way," wrote Starbuck, "is God's." By implication, a pastor would avoid narrow dogmatism, refuse to press for premature religious decision, and refrain from

199

encouraging morbid introspection. Religious feelings would ripen and mature in their own due time, along with the other powers of human nature.[82]

Normal religious development, the psychologists concluded, required a capacity for "self-surrender." Their study of conversion experiences convinced them of the need for a certain passivity, or receptivity, in the religious life. Leuba spoke of "abandon" or "absolute surrender." And religious development, properly nurtured, produced what Starbuck called an unselfing, an awakening into a larger spiritual insight which shattered the narrow boundaries of the ego. Conversion and growth transformed self-love into love for others, egoism into altruism, producing such an "extension of ego" that the true saint could live in "the universal life." The "wise teacher" would therefore use only incentives that accorded with the new life; narrowly self-serving appeals had no place in teaching or counseling intended to expand religious and ethical horizons.[83]

Pastors who took the psychology of religion seriously would hold their teaching to a minimum, in any case, recognizing that religion was a matter more of attitude and temperament than of intellectual belief. Leuba thought that Arthur Schopenhauer had aptly described the unconscious, emotional, striving force of nature; Hall thought that the German Romantics had discovered instincts, feelings, and sentiments vastly older and stronger than the intellect; William James thought that Frederic Myers in England had made the case for a "subliminal" consciousness. In each case, the early psychologists of religion set their sights on feelings, not doctrines. The pastoral implication was clear. Religious problems were not primarily intellectual. The wise pastor would probe more deeply.[84]

Some psychologists of religion, busily tabulating questionnaires or explaining complex mental states with diagrams of nerve paths, succeeded only in casting commonplaces into pompous jargon, but James' *Varieties of Religious Experience* synthesized the themes of his predecessors into a complex panoply of images and insights that would influence physicians of the soul for decades. His distinction between healthy-minded souls, whose temperaments were weighted on the side of cheerfulness, and sick souls, who were intensely aware of evil lurking around the next corner, accented the turbulence, chaos, and division within the self. His conclusion that men and women were in touch with a "wider self," through which they could be transformed, contained the seeds of a therapeutic enterprise. The pastors who attempted to put into practice a more "natural" style of care for souls drew on both sides of James' vision.[85]

By the early twentieth century a few theological liberals, followers of James and Dewey, were describing religion as an instrument used by the organism in adjusting to its environment. Edward Scribner Ames, at the University of Chicago, began as early as 1906 to explore the idea that theology was the handmaid of a "functional psychology." The truth of a theological idea, he said, simply lay in the fact that the idea aided people in their groping and stumbling efforts to live in the world. In that assertion, theology finally became therapy.[86]

Emmanuel

The first serious effort to transform the cure of souls in light of the new psychology and theology began in 1905 among some Episcopalians at the Emmanuel Church in Boston. Their Emmanuel Movement soon attracted support or emulation from Congregational clergy in Baltimore, Presbyterians in Cleveland, Unitarians in Portland, Baptists in Chicago, and Universalists in Brookline, Massachusetts. The movement spread to Rochester, Newark, Detroit, Buffalo, Brooklyn, and Pittsburgh. Lecturers traveled up and down the Pacific Coast, through the cities of the Midwest, and even to Europe, Asia, and Africa. By 1908 the movement had its own journal, *Psychotherapy*, which carried articles not only by theologians, biblical critics, and historians, but by neurologists and psychologists, medical materialists and orthodox Freudians, philosophical idealists and European therapists.[87]

The founders of the Emmanuel Movement announced that it sprang from "a new motive—the application of psychological principles to the problem of religion." Since every minister practiced "psychotherapy," whether intending it or not, they said, the church must face the question anew: Would the cure of souls be guided by tradition, or by sciences? Elwood Worcester, the rector of Emmanuel Church, and his associate, Samuel McComb, thought the church should choose science.[88]

A graduate of General Theological Seminary in New York, Worcester had earned a doctorate in philosophy from Leipzig, where he absorbed both the pragmatic religious idealism of Theodor Fechner and the experimental psychology of Wilhelm Wundt. When he became rector of St. Stephen's Church in Philadelphia, one of the members happened to be the neurologist S. Weir Mitchell, who encouraged him to reconsider the therapeutic office of the minister. When Worcester moved to Emmanuel in 1904, he initiated conversations with local doctors.

Church historian Samuel McComb had also studied abnormal psychology at Oxford, so both he and Worcester possessed credentials that gave them some standing with physicians. By 1905, therefore, they could join Joseph Pratt of Massachusetts General Hospital in applying the "law of suggestion" with small groups of indigent tuberculosis patients. In effect, they began a program of group therapy modeled on the example of medical practice. Believing that poverty and competition had produced an ominous increase in physical and mental illness, Worcester turned Emmanuel Church into a social settlement offering camps, clubs, and a gymnasium. Group therapy was to be one more tool for the amelioration of social injury.[89]

Another kind of relief was offered for the middle classes. Working with Richard Cabot and James Jackson Putnam, in 1906 the ministers sponsored a series of lectures on the moral and psychological treatment of nervous and emotional disorders. They concluded by inviting to a special meeting anyone interested in further counseling. The next day, 198 people crowded into the lecture room, like inquirers pushing toward a mourner's bench. For years, middle-class Bostonians visited the physicians who conducted diagnostic sessions at the church each week. The doctors referred some cases to physicians, others to the ministers at Emmanuel.

When Worcester touted the project nationally in 1908, his article in the *Ladies Home Journal* brought more than five thousand requests for treatment, even though he had discouraged any letters of inquiry. Other ministers briskly adopted the techniques that he and McComb recommended in their book *Religion and Medicine* (1909), written in consultation with their neurological adviser, Isador Coriatt, an early Freudian at Worcester State Hospital who was interested in the therapeutic value of religion. The book enjoyed remarkable success; even one of its critics described it as "the first book in which any attempt was made to point out the legitimate place of religious instruction as a part of psychotherapy," and readers were sufficiently numerous to support eight printings within seven months.[90]

Worcester believed that the popularity of the book and of the movement signaled the defeat of the "irrational healing cults" that threatened to siphon members from established churches. His followers painstakingly distinguished themselves from Christian Scientists, whom they believed to be unscientific and unacceptable to doctors. Worcester feared that the healing cults would sweep tens of thousands away from the church and, at the same time, undermine their faith in doctors. The Emmanuel Movement would unite doctors and ministers in an alliance to win the people back.[91]

The disclaimers of the Emmanuel apologists could not entirely erase the lines of kinship that linked them with their opponents. Like Christian Scientists and New Thought writers, they lectured and counseled mainly in the cities and viewed themselves as apostles to city dwellers swept by social uncertainties. Also like the Christian Scientists and New Thinkers, they depended heavily on the cooperation of women. One minister in Massachusetts attributed the success of the movement in his parish to the fact that his city, with several colleges, was a "woman's town." Some of the movement's critics charged that it was simply a ploy to attract neurasthenic women. In any case, in that era of muscular Christianity, few men would have wanted to acknowledge much weakness.[92]

The similarities between Emmanuel and New Thought extended also to ideas. While they criticized the soft, unscientific side of New Thought, the Emmanuel counselors could praise the substratum of "sound idealism" in the books of such writers as Horatio Dresser and Ralph Waldo Trine. Both movements were revolts against philosophical materialism. Both promised health and harmony to all who were, as the title of Trine's best-seller in 1897 put it, "in tune with the Infinite." The Emmanuel Movement, like its competitors, brought the gospel of faith as therapy.[93]

Like the New Thinkers, moreover, the pastors tried to hold together two conflicting visions of the healing power of nature. Worcester insisted that the curative power of nature—the *vis medicatrix naturae*—was the true agent in psychotherapy. But what was nature? Was it energy, or was it resistance? Did one tap its powers by surrendering to it, or by struggling against it? Did it yield more readily to submission, or to control?[94]

"We need," William James had said in 1906, "a new topography of the limits of human power. . . . We need also a study of the various types of human being with reference to the different ways in which their energy-reserves may be appealed to and set loose." James' own studies of energy reserves had helped to shape the ideas behind the Emmanuel Movement. Worcester believed that James' essay "The Energies of Men" had saved his life, and he distributed several thousand copies through his church. The central idea of his movement was that the "law" of effort and the "gospel" of relaxation belonged together: Receptivity was the underside of activity. Relaxation was the prelude to self-control; self-forgetfulness was a step toward the formation of character; and a symbolic moral holiday served to reinvigorate the moral will. The object of the movement was the creation of "stronger character and moral control"—but only by letting go could the self take hold again.[95]

The double aim of release and control influenced the Emmanuel pastors' thinking about the subconscious. McComb insisted that counseling did not depend on any one theory and that the movement could learn from Freud and Prince, Janet and James. At times he and Worcester could attribute to the subconscious, or unconscious (they used the terms without distinction), a "dominating role." The subconscious was fundamental, while the rational consciousness was acquired merely through maturation. They recognized that the subconscious could be filled with mischievous forces which outwitted the reason. But they derived their main inspiration not from Freud but from James, Arthur Schopenhauer, and Edouard von Hartmann, whose *Philosophy of the Unconscious* had ascribed rationality and creativity to the deeper workings of the subconscious. So they could assert that the subconscious was dominant, and then turn right around and argue that the powers of reason and will were ultimately "greater."[96]

The Emmanuel style of counseling illustrated this indecision. As the counselors in the movement interpreted pastoral counsel, it was a process that began with relaxation and moved toward rational consciousness. One Episcopal rector in Northampton, Massachusetts, displayed the pattern: He began each session by asking his client to be seated in a comfortable chair before a fire and practice rhythmic breathing, muscular relaxation, and visual imagery. He then led the client into "the silence of the quiet mind" by offering "tranquilizing suggestions," followed by healing suggestions, often interspersed with readings from the Bible or even a short "sermon." The purpose was to dislodge unwholesome thoughts from the subconscious; the assumption was that ideas given to the suggestible mind could penetrate to deeper levels. The rector also sometimes used candid conversations in which his visitors were confronted with unpleasant truths about themselves, but the more frequent technique was the substitution of confident thought in place of fear and worry. By reeducating the conscious powers while feeding positive thoughts to the subconscious, the Emmanuel counselors hoped to change individuals and save the church from Mary Baker Eddy.[97]

If the goal was to change faulty ideas, though, why not simply argue people into the ground, as Ichabod Spencer had done? Alternatively, if the goal was to reach a level deeper than reason, why not discontinue sermonic exhortations entirely? The Emmanuel counselors chose neither option. In view of their efforts, the older ideal of manly, cheerful persuasion seemed naive. But their own attempts to incorporate the subconscious into a new understanding of counseling seemed torn by indecision. It was not at all clear that pastoral counseling could or should be what they wanted it to be.

Some of the doctors decided it should not. The ministers had tried every way possible to satisfy the physicians. And at first some of them had been easy to please. They claimed to welcome the presence of the clergy with their patients, or they spoke of forming teams to cure nervous diseases resulting from defects of character. In return, the ministers had agreed to limit themselves to moral education or suggestive therapy, and even then to work under the direction of regular physicians. They almost had agreed to transform the cure of souls into a branch of medicine and work as physicians' aides.[98]

It was just such a transformation that worried doctors. If pastoral counseling became a medical enterprise, then doctors could do it better, they thought. By 1909 Richard Cabot was observing that the medical profession had become irritable about "anything done by clergymen for anyone who is, or has been, or ever will be, the patient of any doctor." Eventually both Cabot and Putnam withdrew their support, complaining that their association with the Emmanuel Movement had cost them their professional standing.[99]

By 1911 the popular press, which once had published sensational stories had forgotten about it, though the movement itself continued, in some form, well into the 1920s. Its confusions now seem more visible than its achievements. Yet the prominent names—especially that of Richard Cabot—would reappear in later debates. And the movement helped introduce the new psychology into the church at a time when it was barely understood within the hospital.

It could hardly be said, however, that the movement swept the seminaries and local churches. George A. Gorden, an influential liberal, called Worcester and McComb "crazy loons," and other clerics were equally hostile. Ministers became increasingly intrigued, however, by "the service of psychology," and no pastoral theologian who wished to influence the cure of souls could entirely neglect it.[100]

By the end of the century, then, the fascination with natural vitalities had subverted the older antebellum ideal of balance. But the pastors seeking a more natural style of pastoral relationship found it difficult to discover the real meaning of *natural*. Initially they took their cue from a fashionable scientific and technological vocabulary and a popular admiration for "masculinity." A natural style of pastoral care seemed to call for little more than a cheerful, forceful, assertive informality. But the growing interest in subconscious dynamics and in a liberal doctrine of Divine immanence helped to engender the conviction that it was perhaps more natural to trust the creative impulses of nature; to encourage a certain receptivity as the precondition of the active assertion of the will. Indeed, the quest for a more natural style of pastoral care eventually led the Emmanuel Movement in directions that the earlier muscular Christians would have considered decidedly unnatural.

In theological terms, the pastoral writers were rehashing the old issues of sin and spiritual growth. Like the antirevivalists of the eighteenth century, most postwar pastoral theologians emphasized sinful *acts* more than any inherent *condition* of sinfulness. And like the antebellum theologians, they tended to equate sin with acts of choice. The liberals, at any rate, defined *sin* as *self-will*, or sometimes as the downward tug of "the animal or lower side" of human nature. Except for the social gospel theologians, they located sinfulness mainly within the will. In their eagerness to affirm the sacredness of personality, moreover, some liberals also emphasized ethical potential far more than sinful incapacity. They adopted, implicitly, a notion that sin resulted from an interruption of natural development caused by a disorder of the will, and the optimists among them were confident that apt pastoral methods could cure the malady.[101]

They still spoke more of self-mastery than of self-realization. Though the language of self-realization was becoming popular among philosophers, not until the early twentieth century did it make pronounced inroads among theologians. Unlike the earlier idea of self-culture and the later one of self-realization, the image of self-mastery suggested the presence of powerful vitalities in the self which needed to be overcome or tempered, by force of will and strength of character. The Christian ideal, most agreed, was the "building" of character, the shaping of the emergent self. The later Victorians were less like gardeners than like blacksmiths, striving to hammer out the shape of their lives.[102]

The leaders of the Emmanuel Movement hoped to establish a pastoral "psychotherapy" that would build character by tapping the energies that were accessible through the subconscious. Their critics viewed them as pastors who were trying to be psychotherapists and hence were confusing theology with therapy. Josiah Royce identified the main problem when he observed that much of the debate over psychotherapy in America seemed to establish the health of the individual as a criterion of philosophical (and, by implication, theological) truth: "Whoever, in his own mind," wrote Royce, "makes the whole great world center about the fact that he, just this private individual, once was ill and now is well, is still a patient."[103]

6

From Adjustment to Insight

"Between 1919 and 1929 literate America, and much of illiterate America, were more deeply interested in the whats and whys and wherefores of the human mind than they ever were before, and than, it seems likely, they ever will be again." Or so it appeared from the vantage point of the 1930s. The ten years that followed the First World War seemed at the time to be "the Period of the Psyche"—a period of "psychological revival" that left no institution untouched. Assuredly, it touched the churches. The theologian Walter Marshall Horton of Oberlin complained in 1930 that the effort once given to Protestant social service now seemed to be devoted solely to private matters: "Books on the 'social gospel' have been largely set aside," he said, "in favor of manuals of devotion, studies of mystics, and books on applied psychology and mental hygiene."[1]

The change was real, though not as antagonistic to social service as Horton's lament suggested. The men and women who had transformed the cure of souls in Protestantism were, at heart, moral reformers. They wanted to reshape ethical sensibility and to reform the church and the

210

ministry, and they enlisted psychology in the service of that reform. They were also admirers of an American intellectual tradition that viewed reform as the negotiation of continuing adjustments between complex human beings and a complicated environment. Almost all bore, even if only in dim outline, an imprint of John Dewey. Hence the theme of "adjustment"—which Dewey had helped to popularize—organized their early thoughts about both the reform of churches and the cure of souls.

By the beginning of the Second World War, however, "adjustment" seemed no longer so absorbing. By that time, an experiment in clinical pastoral education had begun to revise the theory of the cure of souls in the light of repeated experience with men and women in crisis. The new theological temper, for that matter, was also not very congenial to the language of adjustment. The metaphors of "insight" seemed preferable. Not everyone traveled the road from adjustment to insight, but it proved to be the road into the postwar future.

The destinations of many Americans changed during the 1920s. For most, the old journey toward self-mastery seemed too limited, too narrow and restricted. After the First World War, Horton complained, people seemed more interested in "self-realization" than in service, more intent on self-expression than on the "building" of character. The self-realization of the 1920s was quite different, to be sure, from that of the 1960s. At least, the early theorists of self-realization could still take for granted the existence of communal supports and restraints to check and structure the push toward expressiveness. But already during the 1920s, the change in attitudes toward social mores, divorce, and birth control signaled a "repeal of reticence" that would turn "self-realization" into something its early proponents would hardly have recognized. That change, too, would leave its mark on the cure of souls.[2]

The Psychology of Success

In April 1917, a company of American psychologists banded together to offer their services in the crusade

211

against the Kaiser. More than 100 of them eventually served on the Surgeon General's staff, where under the guidance of Robert Yerkes they set up a program that would, by the end of 1918, expose about 1,700,000 soldiers to the mysteries of psychological testing. The testing of intelligence in the army was America's first direct encounter with psychological methods in the mass. The public was impressed.[3]

The war introduced the masses to psychology, but it was the reaction against the war, and against the society that had gone to war, that transformed psychologists and analysts into symbols of cultural freedom. Intellectuals, turning to Freud, argued that the social conventions of a corrupt society impeded individual fulfillment and that in a world ruled by industrialists who made bombs and machine guns, individual fulfillment was the last best hope. But popular psychology was not simply a symbol of rebellion. It also seemed to offer a scientific means of success and wisdom. Psychologists began to join the staffs of corporations and advertising agencies (the behaviorist John Watson left Johns Hopkins to become the head of his own agency). Psychiatrists studied the work forces in factories and department stores. Literary critics sought hidden psychological symbols in plays and novels. The Department of Labor published child-rearing manuals that bore the latest psychological discoveries. Newspapers carried articles on neuroses, complexes, and fixations. College students flocked into courses on applied psychology. The Sears Roebuck catalogue offered *Ten Thousand Dreams Interpreted* and *Sex Problems Solved*. And the psychiatrist as expert began to ascend before the American public: At the sensational trial of Richard Loeb and Nathan Leopold in 1924, ten psychiatrists sat in the courtroom—five for the prosecution, five for the defense.[4]

A journalist for the *Atlantic Monthly* aimed to convey a sense of the "psychological revival" simply by listing the book titles published between 1919 and 1928. It reads like a litany. Book buyers could read about:

Psychology and Common Life, Psychology and Sex Life, Psychology and Business Efficiency, Psychology and the Christian Religion, Psychology and Dramatic Art, Psychology and the Day's Work, Psychology and the Christian Day School, Psychology and Parenthood, Psychology and Politics, Psychology and Nursing, Psychology and Preaching, Psychology and Teaching, Psychology and Writing.

They also [could read] books explaining in detail the Psychology of Aesthetics, the Psychology of Athletics, the Psychology of Alcoholism, the Psychology of Beauty, the Psychology of Buying, the Psychology of Bolshevism, the Psychology of Business Success, the Psychology of the Christian Life, the Psychology of Citizenship, the Psychology of Coaching, the Psychology of Death, the Psychology of Dress, the Psychology of Fasting, the Psychology of Golf, the Psychology of Group Insurance, the Psychology of Jesus, the Psychology of Leadership, the Psychology of Learning, the Psychology of Marriage, the Psychology of Murder, the Psychology of Package Labels, the Psychology of the Poet Shelly, the Psychology of Selling Insurance, the Psychology of Your Name.[5]

The list, said the journalist, could continue for pages, and even then not communicate the full flavor of the cultural conversion to the psychological gospel.

The psychological revival resulted, in part, from the fascination with Freud. In 1913, A. A. Brill, who was translating Freud's writings, lectured at Mabel Dodge's salon in New York City. The event symbolized the infusion of Freudian notions into the literary culture. By 1915, Walter Lippmann, who had arranged the lecture, was writing in *The New Republic* that the new Freudian ideas had "set up a reverberation in human thought and conduct of which few as yet dare to predict the consequences." And Freud did not languish simply within the boundaries of the intellectual culture typified by Lippmann and *The New Republic*. By that time, articles on the "Diagnosis of Dreams" were also appearing in *Good Housekeeping*, and Freud was on his way to canonical status in the youth rebellion. The analyst Karl Menninger complained that as

213

a result of spectacular and superficial popularizing, "Freudian designations [had] become the symbol words of our generation." Menninger found himself taken for a modern magician—being asked, at a moment's notice in the midst of party chatter, to untangle human knots. "Soul-talking" had become a sport, and banter about complexes and defense mechanisms had replaced the old moralism with a new one that was fully as vague and uninformative as its predecessor.[6]

The rage for pop-Freudianism proceeded apace with the popularizing of yet another vision of psychological utopia. In 1914 John Watson published *Behaviorism*, which challenged the psychologists of consciousness (and of the unconscious). Watson's depiction of the "person" as a complex of patterns of conditioned behavior seemed to suggest limitless possibilities for social reform and self-improvement, and during the 1920s articles on the topic filled the popular magazines. Watson envisioned a world in which institutions built on behaviorist principles would, without unseemly sentiment, raise and train children to be citizens of a brave new rational world, and the Department of Labor agreed, at least to the extent of publishing a child-care manual that instructed parents to transcend indulgence and display behavioristic firmness.[7]

But neither Freud nor Watson did as much to popularize the therapeutic ideal as did the mental hygiene movement, which reached a peak in the late 1920s. As early as 1909, a growing interest in psychotherapy had led to the formation of a National Committee for Mental Hygiene, which called for the reform of hospitals and the creation of institutions that could detect and control incipient mental problems. Clifford Beers, the driving force behind the movement, was a young businessman who after a nervous breakdown had been committed to a hospital filled with straitjackets, padded cells, and violent attendants. While still a patient, he had decided to change such hospitals, and after being discharged in 1903 he published an exposé titled *A Mind That Found Itself*. The clergy were among his earliest supporters, and Beers organized the first of the state societies in a meeting at a minister's home in Connecticut. They saw the movement as a means of confirming an association between religion and health, and at least one member enthusiastically assigned to the pastor "responsibility for the health of his parishioners." But those expectations were modest, compared to the hope of a few secular enthusiasts: that mental hygiene would replace theology and philosophy and become a world-view that could coordinate all the sciences in the interest of human welfare.[8]

During the 1920s the more zealous converts to the movement believed that it could solve "practically every ill that beset the world, political, economic, social, and individual." Most of its adherents were more restrained. They desired simply to reform mediocre hospitals and promote "adjustment." The theme of adjustment—to other persons, to society, and to "the whole of things"— suggested a way to prevent serious mental illness and enhance human happiness. And that goal seemed plausible to thousands of Americans who by the 1930s had formed about fifty state and local mental hygiene societies.[9]

The burst of enthusiasm for psychology reflected, in some degree, the changing structure of the economy. After recovering from the brief postwar depression, the economy seemed to ascend along with the new Empire State Building—higher and higher. Industrial production almost doubled during those years, producing a striking change in the size and complexity of business and in the normal activities of thousands of workers. The increased mechanization of industry and the expansion of corporations called for more clerks and managers. The road upward seemed to lead from one secure place to another in a corporate bureaucracy. In 1929 Robert and Helen Lynd completed their first study of *Middletown*, a small American city of 38,000 people. They had concluded that the best way to classify its inhabitants was to distinguish between those who made things, and those who worked with people. The "business class," the merchants and professionals who sold or promoted products and ideas, constituted only about 30 percent of the population, but they dominated the culture, setting the tone in the churches and the civic groups. By the mid-1930s, when the Lynds returned to the city, depression had destroyed its prosperity but had not slowed the growth of white-collar classes. The number of "professionals" had increased by 56 percent, mainly because of the large nationwide corporations that had moved into Middletown. They were so numerous as to constitute a new middle class of salaried employees alongside the older local middle class of merchants and professional folk.[10]

It was probably not entirely coincidental that the people of Middletown checked out of their local library twenty-six times as many books on psychology and philosophy in 1923 as they had checked out twenty years earlier, even though the population had less than doubled. The change in the economy, exemplified both by the early prosperity and by the continued expansion of the white-collar middle class, helped to shift popular interest from the "building of character" to the creation of a "good personality"—a term that meant adaptability, cheer, and the ability to work smoothly with others. The popular psychological manuals told people how to "sell" things, including themselves, and the economy made such salesmanship seem increasingly necessary.[11]

At a popular level, then, psychology promised success. But success was exactly what many of the clergy felt they were lacking. During the "religious depression" of the era, church attendance fell, missions waned, and the sources of money ran dry. Or more precisely, Protestants seemed willing to dig into their pockets only for new buildings, not for the old causes. It was not a high moment for ministers, who often felt a certain condescension on the part of their fashionable parishioners, partially because of the churches' low educational standards. In 1926, only 33 percent of the Protestant ministers in 17 predominantly white denominations, and 7 percent of the ministers in three black denominations, were graduates of both college and seminary. (Protestants lagged behind their Catholic counterparts; 68 percent of Roman Catholic priests were college and seminary graduates.) In part, this reflected the economic status: In 1928, Protestant ministers earned an average annual salary of $1,407—an amount lower than the wages of most factory workers. But even the educated and better-paid ministers who drifted to the larger cities found it necessary to contend with a certain patronizing air. In Middletown, church members clearly felt affection and esteem for their ministers, but the undercurrent of condescension was visible in, for instance, a light-hearted newspaper article about a local sportsman who had broken his golf club. "Fortunately," the article added, "no ministers or women were present." Complained one clergyman in Middletown: "They won't talk to me because I'm a minister."[12]

The people of Middletown thought they knew what kind of minister they would talk to: He would be "a big regular man," a "regular 'he man,'" a "real fellow," a "good fellow among the men," and yet someone who was "spiritual" and "sympathetic." In that respect they were like most of the American laity, who seemed to desire, above all, that their ministers must possess "personality," but that they also "must want to understand [the people] and to understand the kind of life each leads."[13] They often seemed to assume, for some reason, that such a minister would resemble the vice president of a small but booming business enterprise. At least, that was the conclusion reached by the researchers who conducted Mark A. May's report on *The Profession of the Ministry:*

> In discussing the personal qualifications of their ministers, laymen in positions of the church were apparently dominated by the psychology of business. They desired a minister who believed in his wares, who was loyal to his organization, who could organize his sales force, who could advertise his product, who could balance his budget, and show certain dividends in increased membership and added prestige for his particular church.[14]

217

Such expectations helped to produce a flood of popular pastoral advice, promising success to clerical businessmen who knew how to use psychology.

These books and manuals instructed the clergy in how to advertise their churches, dramatize their teaching, improve their Sunday school attendance, build their congregations, solve their problems, and achieve success. They suggested that ministers who knew a little psychology could get people to do things. Such knowledge could also help pastors to counsel, satisfy needs, overcome doubts, bring assurance, and encourage "the struggling, fumbling, disheartened members of society to win out and walk in newness of life." The minister could serve—and conquer—the world by taking responsibility for other people: for their feelings, their pain, and their loneliness. But such a minister must overcome any lingering residues of effeminacy. "Football captains make first-rate pastors," wrote a clerical college president in 1916. And one might think that the authors of the popular tracts lived in fear of bullies who kicked sand in clerical faces. "Piety is looked upon as first cousin to effeminacy," lamented one writer. Another warned that all ministers should beware of "the effeminate streak which is so easily cultivated by their calling and check all development of it." The dean of Yale Divinity School complained that the minister had not always shown himself "a man among men"; he had spent his mornings with books and his afternoons with women and children. Such repetition of the complaint suggests that a number of Protestant ministers during the 1920s—nobody knows how many—suffered deeply from the feeling that they were ineffectual, or considered so.[15]

Some pastors confessed that they were especially baffled when they performed the traditional duty of pastoral visiting. The May report revealed that when most Protestant ministers referred to "pastoral" duties, they meant the "calling" from house to house, and many viewed such calls as "a channel through which the real intimate ministry can be performed." The ministers of Middletown, for instance, were manifestly proud of their diligence in calling: One reported that during one year he had made 957 pastoral calls of ten minutes or longer; another claimed that in four years he had made 2,700 pastoral calls. During the early 1930s, almost 80 percent of the Protestant clergy claimed that they held regular private conferences with parishioners about personal problems, often during their pastoral visits. But half of them reported that it was hard to make their pastoral calls count for something; many said they felt lost when asked to intervene in family difficulties; and most admitted that they found counseling difficult. "In regard to personal problems," one commented, "the minister has to establish a kind of clinic. I don't think the seminary ever touched it. A man has to feel his way along it. . . . A lot of ministers can't do it—it calls for a specialist."[16]

In one of those rare committee predictions that actually proved to be true, the May report announced in 1934 that "the work with individuals is to become one of the permanent and one of the most important aspects of the future ministry." The report did not foresee, however, that this trend would represent a revolt against both the prevailing understanding of the ministry and the popular understanding of psychology as a means to success. Leaders in the emerging pastoral care movement were dissatisfied with the current stereotypes of the ministry, with the notions that the clergy were the embodiment of bland moral conventions, were more interested in suppressing vices than in healing pain, and should have to prove themselves "regular fellows" in order to fulfill their calling. Some of the pastoral theologians, at any rate, turned to psychology as a revolt against a success-culture, not as a way to secure quick success.[17]

Harry Emerson Fosdick, at Riverside Church in New York, exemplified some of the new directions. Fosdick attempted to combine pastoral sensitivity with social reform. A pacifist, critical of laissez-faire economics and concerned that it was "sheer hypocrisy for the church to say that it cares about personality as sacred and then to do nothing about social conditions that impinge on personality with frightful consequences," Fosdick leaped into most of the social causes of his era. But the social gospel, he said, convinced him of the need for better individuals, and for that reason "personal counseling" was the center of his ministry.[18]

In his understanding of counseling, Fosdick was a transitional figure, reflecting the impulses of the popular culture while at the same time moving beyond them. In the 1920s he called for a Protestant version of the Catholic confessional. When other ministers criticized that suggestion, he turned for help to Thomas Salmon, the medical director of the National Committee for Mental Hygiene. Thereafter Fosdick spent much of his time each week in consultations with the distressed, laboring in a confessional built on the catechism of mental hygiene. His primary goal was the formation of character—to help people shoulder responsibility for themselves, transcend their petty self-preoccupation, and accept themselves with all their inner contradictions. His heroes were wracked, torn, and tortured souls. Yet Fosdick also could leap at the most facile ideas of the mental hygiene movement. He could sound like a prophet of New Thought as he urged people to release the power within themselves and exploit "the practical use of faith." His favorite psychologist was still William James, and in his counseling he still tried to induce a harmony of energy and repose, initiative and self-acceptance, with the purpose of enhancing a sense of personal power. And he still trusted a psychology of success. Yet he also had a vision of human suffering that kept him from succumbing to the worst excesses of the success seekers.[19]

Fosdick claimed that counseling, not preaching, was his central interest. Yet therein lies one of the ironies of his contribution to the cure of souls. Possibly more than any other person, it was Fosdick who persuaded a large segment of the liberal Protestant clergy to refashion the sermon in the image of the counseling session. He remarked that his own "preaching at its best has been personal counseling on a group scale." As one of the best-known Protestant preachers in America, with perhaps the largest radio audience of any clergyman of his day, Fosdick was a living illustration of the burgeoning therapeutic sensibility. Under his tutelage a generation of ministers constructed topical sermons on the mastery of depression, the conquest of fear, the overcoming of anxiety, and the joys of self-realization. Unfortunately, few of them shared Fosdick's other talents and sensitivities. Most sermons that masqueraded as personal counseling probably collapsed in banality.[20]

Yet Fosdick could serve as an example to those ministers who felt moved by the psychological revival but remained skeptical of the psychology of success, who saw the wisdom in the mental hygiene movement but hesitated to accept its more grandiose ambitions; who were eager to learn from Freud but disinclined to pronounce him a savior. The pastoral theologians of the 1930s did a considerable amount of stumbling around, but they laid the foundations for a postwar renaissance that would have surprised even them.

Adjustment and Self-Realization

"We are evidently at the opening of a new era in the history of the cure of souls," wrote John McNeill in 1934. "The new ministry to personality will be at once scientific and religious." Such optimism was widely shared. In 1937 the Federal Council of Churches created a Commission on Religion and Health, and its executive secretary, Seward Hiltner, announced that the mental hygiene movement was reshaping clerical attitudes toward social reform, sermons, and pastoral counseling. But what kind of reshaping was needed? At that time, there was no consensus in answer to that question. The pastoral care movement was undergoing an ideological transition in which the ideal of "adjustment" was giving way to the goal of "insight." In the background of that change could be seen the shifting attitude toward the relatively new theme of "self-realization."[21]

221

By the 1920s many academic ethicists in America had subscribed to an ethic of self-realization imported from Germany, or from British thinkers who had read the German Idealists. They believed that "goodness lay in the increasing growth of the individual's real self." The goal of the ethical life was to develop fully the potential of each person's self within the community of selves. In America, however, the ethic of self-realization initially was an expansion of the earlier ethic of character, not a reaction against it. In writing of self-expression and self-development, Americans had no intention of justifying pleasure "through the satisfaction of desires just as they happen to arise." Josiah Royce at Harvard, who appealed to that theme in developing his *Philosophy of Loyalty* (1909), advanced the common argument that the uninhibited expression of "natural desires" actually hindered self-realization. Because each self was a collection of conflicting impulses, instinctual self-expression would produce merely a "chaos of conflicting passions." The true self was deeper than its momentary impulses. The hope of self-realization, as John Dewey wrote in his early *Outlines of a Critical Theory of Ethics* (1891), lay in finding "that special form of character, of self, which includes and transforms all special desires."[22]

The notion of self-realization that was taught in the colleges and seminaries in the 1920s assumed that an individual's self could attain fullness of being only in relation to other selves. George Herbert Palmer at Harvard decided that the "real person" was a social self, defined by its relationship to other persons, not simply a "separate self" existing in atomistic isolation. True self-realization, then, might require the sacrifice of "separate" selfhood. Josiah Royce valued an ethic of loyalty because it alone could "unify" the divided self. But he believed that inner unity presupposed both union with others and oneness with the Eternal. The ethicists did not think, therefore, that institutions necessarily hindered self-realization. They usually claimed, in fact, that self-development reached its fullest expression only by serving the social institutions that past generations had established for promoting human welfare.[23]

The idea of self-realization therefore blended easily with an insistence that the self needed to make continual adjustment to the changing social and natural order. The more rich and complex the pattern of adjustments, the more the self would gain fullness of being and enhance the good, both for itself and for others. *Adjustment*, though, was not merely subordination to an environment or conformity to circumstances. It was an active assimilation which resulted in the "increase, or even reconstruction of the prior environment." It was the transformation of one's surroundings as well as of oneself.[24]

The man who did most to define the meaning of adjustment for the pastoral care writers of the early 1930s was John Dewey. His *Democracy and Education* (1916) might even be described as a hidden classic of the pastoral care movement. Filtered through the religious education traditions and assimilated into psychotherapeutic practice, the book's ideas would continue to echo among pastoral theologians well into the 1960s. Dewey defined education as a "reconstruction or reorganization of experience" which enhanced the meaning of that experience and increased the ability to direct the course of subsequent experience. Education therefore was a continual adjustment to an environment, but not in the sense of conformity to external conditions. "It is essential," Dewey wrote, "that adjustment be understood in its active sense of control of means for achieving ends." Adjustment required problem-solving.[25]

Dewey derived that idea of adjustment from Darwinism and functional psychology, and also from his prior assumption that the achievement of selfhood was a "process" and that selfhood's greatest good was "growth." By *growth* he did not refer to a movement toward a fixed end. Growth itself was the end, and the purpose of formal education was to organize the powers that would ensure further growth. Dewey might well have defined education as a movement of self-realization, though he was convinced that to make self-realization a conscious aim was to distract the attention from the very interests and relationships that brought about "the wider development of the self." Only as the self fully engaged the world did growth occur. But that engagement did enlarge and unify—and in that sense, "realize"—the self. The purpose of the process was the continual attainment of inner unity and the capacity to meet new demands from the natural and social environment.[26]

To Dewey, any claim that *growth* might refer to the realization of a self detached from social relationships and institutions suggested, at best, romantic illusion; any desire to perfect some "inner" personality was a sign of social pathology. "What one is as a person," he wrote, "is what one is as associated with others, in a free give and take of intercourse." And he did not assume that there was something wrong with institutional patterns of relationship that might happen to lack the qualities of warmth and intimacy: To view institutions as enemies of freedom, and social convention as merely an enslaving force, was to seek, consciously or unconsciously, a romantic return to nature that would lead to chaos. Dewey did not cast self-development into inevitable conflict with bureaucratic institutions. When his successors would begin to do so, they would alter the meaning of self-realization.[27]

His earliest admirers did not do so. Dewey's ideas found initial expression in the churches within the religious education movement, which also helped to secure a firm footing for psychology in the religious communities. With the collapse of the Emmanuel Movement, it seemed that the influence of psychology in the churches would depend entirely on the predilections of individual pastors. But the religious educators took up the slack. The launching of the Religious Education Association in 1903 signaled the beginning of an effort to reorganize the Protestant Sunday school in accord with the ideas of reformers like Dewey. The educational innovators argued that learning occurred when teachers managed to tap the lively interests and felt needs of their pupils, and they insisted that people learned by doing. Proposing that education be adapted to the stages of human development, they prepared "Sunday school materials and teaching guides for infants, toddlers, primary education pupils, older elementary children, junior high school youngsters, senior highs, older youths, young married adults, mature adults, and senior adults." Agreeing that education was a process in which the total personality passed through predictable stages of growth, they urged pastors to learn the intricacies—or at least the rudiments—of a developmental psychology.[28]

The patriarch of the movement was a philosopher of religion named George Albert Coe, who in 1909 became the professor of religious education at Union Theological Seminary in New York. Coe's research into the psychology of religion convinced him that the functionalists were right when they turned their attention from such well-worn topics as "perception" and "attention" and looked instead at persons' interests, preferences, and yearnings for self-realization. He therefore formulated the aim of religious education as promoting "the growth of the young toward and into mature and efficient devotion to the democracy of God, and happy self-realization therein." As early as 1902 he had suggested that religion was valuable because of its contribution to the forming of "the whole self," and like Dewey, he argued that the purpose of education was "to assist self-realization." In *Education in Religion and Morals* (1904) he left the impression that even God was expected to be of service in the quest for the realized self: "We believe in God primarily because we need God." By 1929 he was suggesting that we could offer a similar service to God: "He realizes himself by promoting our self-realization as persons."[29]

Self-realization was the result of a fitting adjustment, Coe believed, and it was the task of religious education to ensure that fit. All education assisted the movement toward "social adjustment and efficiency"; religious education helped to "adjust the race to its divine environment." But since God was immanent in the race, religious adjustment was, in practice, a certain kind of "social interaction"—the use of social activities to expand "social attachments" that would change the pupil's "outlook toward future social good." Self-realization required a social gospel.[30]

Coe sensed the therapeutic potential of such a view of religious education: The free interchange of views in a process of "cooperative thinking" could become a technique for releasing personality from its self-imposed limitations.[31] In fact, Coe and his colleagues developed so "functional" an interpretation of religious experience that therapeutic application seemed to be the next logical step. When they kept repeating that the important consideration in any religious experience was the result it attained, it became natural for religious education to shade into the therapeutic. Early in his career, therefore, Coe accented the tie between religious education and the cure of souls:

> Why should not the care of souls become an art—a system of organized and proportioned methods based upon definite knowledge of the material to be wrought upon, the ends to be attained, and the means and instruments for attaining them? Such an art would require scientific insight into the general organization of the mind, and especially into the particular characteristics of the child mind, the youth mind, and the mature mind.[32]

The religious educators quickly became cast as the "psychologists" within the seminaries and churches. Even friendly critics suggested that they talked too much about stimuli and inferiority complexes. But they set the stage for the appearance of "modern pastoral psychology."[33]

Long before there were any chairs of pastoral counseling in the Protestant seminaries, religious educators began to teach the subject. At Union Theological Seminary in New York, for instance, Harrison Elliott offered such instruction as early as 1921. One of his students, Carl Rogers, said that at Union Theological Seminary he had learned for the first time that "working with individual persons in a helping relationship could be a professional enterprise." (Rogers later became a virtual guru for the pastoral counseling movement.) Elliott also brought Harry Bone, a psychologist, and Seward Hiltner, a Presbyterian minister, to Union, where they developed pedagogical methods that became standard in the pastoral care courses of Protestant seminaries. By 1936 Harrison Elliott and his wife Grace published their own handbook on *Solving Personal Problems*. And at Southern Baptist Theological Seminary in Louisville, Gaines Dobbins, who had studied with both Coe and Dewey, in 1920 began a long campaign to "capture psychology for Christ." A professor of "Religious Education and Church Efficiency," Dobbins tried to convince the faculty that apart from the study of Scripture, psychology was "the most important single subject which should be mastered by one who all his life must deal at first hand with people." His courses in religious education introduced the new pastoral theology into southern conservatism. By 1927, the theological seminaries were offering a number of courses on "personality," but most of the instruction in counseling took place in the religious education classes.[34]

To the religious educators, pastoral counseling offered a means of "personality adjustment." To Dobbins, this meant the possibility of more "efficient" pastoral work. To Elliott, it meant that pastoral counseling was to be viewed as "problem solving." The counselor was to help men and women learn "habits of intelligent action," through which they could adjust to the requirements of the social environment, including its continual need for reform. Elliott taught his students the ideas of Freud and those of the post-Freudian analysts—Alfred Adler, Carl Jung, Otto Rank—but he filtered these ideas through the lenses of an "educational psychology" that emphasized the plasticity of human nature and the possibilities of "intelligent self-direction." Counseling was a way to solve the problems that hindered appropriate adjustment to the wider world.[35]

The vocabulary of adjustment made sense in the liberal

227

seminaries because it had permeated liberal theology so thoroughly. The emergence of a theology of adjustment can best be dated from the appearance in 1919 of Douglas Clyde Macintosh's *Theology as an Empirical Science*. A theologian at Yale Divinity School, Macintosh had moved from William James' pragmatism toward a conviction that theological conclusions could be scientifically verified. He came to believe that it was necessary for theologians to presuppose the reality of God in order to discern God's nature. It could turn out that *God*—the highest reality—was merely a name for the world-process, but the existence of some "highest reality" must be assumed in order to discover what it might be like. As a further hypothesis, assuming that the highest reality was consistent and constant, theologians, as believers, could adjust their lives to the Divine Object, variously defined, and then observe the results. That notion of "adjustment" became the bedrock of theological method.

In a preliminary way, Macintosh defined God as "a Power, not identifiable with our empirical selves, which makes for some dependable result . . . in and through us, when we relate ourselves to that Power in a certain discoverable way." His theory was that a "right religious adjustment" to that power consistently produced the qualities of peace, love, and joy in the pious soul. The theologian could then conclude that God was, at the very least, a Reality that would engender such qualities whenever the adjustment was adequate. To assume that God was a moral reality, however, and to respond accordingly, was to discover a richness of existence that would elude the person who responded with the assumption that the highest reality was merely a cosmic process inimical or indifferent to ethical values. Hence the process of trial and error, presumably in a community of persons who were diversely adapted to different conceptions of the highest reality, led to a knowledge of the divine nature. God was, in short, what God did, and through the adjustment of their lives to God, theologians could eventually discover the fruits—or the fruitlessness—of their initial hypotheses.[36]

Macintosh was by no means alone in popularizing the metaphor of theological adjustment. A number of theologians and psychologists of religion had adopted, in one form or another, Matthew Arnold's functional definition of God as "that power, not ourselves, which makes for righteousness" when we make appropriate adjustment to it. Theologians who never used the slogan often adopted the idea behind it. "The central religious problem," wrote Walter Marshall Horton, "is the psychological problem—how may personality be unified, energized, and directed to worthful ends?" By implication, the power that best unified and directed the personality was God. And theology was a guide to psychological and spiritual adjustment.[37]

Nowhere did the adjustment vocabulary have greater influence on theology than at the University of Chicago, where it became the common language of philosophers, sociologists, and theologians. The central issue for Henry Nelson Wieman, the most prolific of the Chicago theologians, was whether theology could discover the features in the universe that would bring peoples' lives to the largest fulfillment when the proper adjustment was made. The quest for those ultimately fulfilling realities was actually the search for God; religious experience was a process of adjustment to the ultimately real and valuable. God was, according to Wieman, the power and process within the world, which, by promoting value, unity, and mutuality, produced the greatest good and thus deserved the highest devotion. God was the "character of events" to which men and women needed to adjust in order to avoid the loss and fragmentation of their selfhood. And the theologian was the guide to proper adjustment.[38]

The metaphor of adjustment guided the pastoral theologians who published texts on the cure of souls during the early 1930s. When Charles Holman of the University of Chicago wrote *The Cure of Souls: A*

Socio-Psychological Approach (1932), he described "soul-sickness" as inadequate religious or moral adjustment. The task of the religious counselor was to facilitate adjustment by promoting devotion to noble causes and values, providing assurance of cosmic support in the struggle, and bringing people into the rich social environment of the Christian community. When Karl Stolz of the Hartford School of Religious Education published his *Pastoral Psychology* (1932), he explained that human life was a sequence of adjustments and that it was the pastor's responsibility to create in maladjusted persons the will and ability to reorganize themselves. Holman and Stolz appealed frequently to the psychoanalysts, especially to Carl Jung and Alfred Adler, but their main debt was to the older psychologists of religion, the religious educators, and the liberal theologians. It was from those sources that they learned about adjustment to reality.[39]

The publication of John Sutherland Bonnell's *Pastoral Psychiatry* in 1938 illustrated the principles of the academic pastoral theologians. Bonnell was a Presbyterian minister in New York, whose father, a staff member at Falconwood Hospital in Canada, had convinced him that religion would one day become "one of the extensively used forms of psychotherapy." Bonnell endeavored to fulfill his father's predictions in his own pastoral counseling, in which he combined three themes: He retained the conviction of the older pastoral theologians that a minister's first responsibility was to undergird the religious life; he believed that the goal of counseling was to assist the person in making a right adjustment to God; and he drew from Freudian revisionists, especially from the Viennese analyst Alfred Adler, the assumption that the person who understood truly would act rightly.[40]

Pastoral theologians who were interested in a post-Freudian dynamic psychology found themselves often drawn to the writings of Adler. In his own counseling Bonnell employed Adlerian techniques, such as asking clients to recall one specific event in their childhood and then trying to interpret its meaning. Breaking with Freud,

Adler had argued that feelings of inferiority, rooted in the frustration of a childhood drive for mastery, explained most later psychological difficulties. More important, he had insisted that the continuing drive for mastery led to an unending need to overcome difficulties that arose in the environment. Or as the Elliotts told their students, Adler believed that "treatment is a process of re-education in which the patient, either by uncovering fresh resources or by lowering the exaggerated ideal he has for himself, comes to an effective but realistic adjustment to life." Clearly, the focus on adjustment in Adler's "individual psychology" commended him to Americans. Adjustment was a theme they knew something about.[41]

The metaphor of adjustment carried something of the tone of the popular psychological revival, but its reformist overtones also represented a dissatisfaction with the more crass examples of pop-psychology—the advocates of adjustment were more interested in reform than in success. But adjustment was a slippery notion that could serve the purposes of hucksters as well as reformers, and it was hard to know exactly how to adapt it to concrete cases. Even as they were writing about adjustment, therefore, the pastoral theologians of the 1920s began to seek alternative metaphors to describe and guide their work. The most fruitful result of that search was a new method of training men and women for ministry.

The Clinical Traditions

During the 1920s, a small group of American ministers began to construct a program of professional training known eventually as clinical pastoral education—a long-term supervised encounter with men and women in crisis in hospitals, prisons, and social agencies. The purpose was not to discover new methods of pastoral counsel but to reshape the Protestant ministry. The founders of clinical training deplored the cultural image of clerical prissiness and were of the opinion that seminaries failed to train ministers to deal with a messy world, or even to

231

understand religion within it. They did not set out to train pastoral counselors; they intended to jolt the church. Yet one important consequence of their movement was a gradual shift in the understanding of pastoral counseling.

The movement toward clinical education for clergy paralleled educational changes in other professions. As early as 1871 some instructors at Harvard Law School had decided that improved pedagogy demanded the abandonment of lectures and the substitution of case studies. By the early twentieth century, the best medical schools and the new schools of social work had expanded the notion of case studies to include various forms of supervised clinical training. The founders of clinical pastoral education looked on with interest, for they, like earlier ministers, believed that the clergy had failed to keep pace with other professionals. They lamented that doctors "seldom welcomed" clergy as "allies in the struggle against suffering"; they argued that psychologists and social workers received "more adequate training in the meeting of human problems than the seminary offers"; they optimistically described the clinically trained pastor of the future as an "officer of health" who would be welcomed as an ally by physicians "as perhaps never before." Indeed, they hoped that clinical training would "deepen the community's respect for the minister" during a period when pastors who ministered to the urban middle classes felt most deeply the absence of public esteem.[42]

Almost from the beginning, the new forms of secular professional education raised ethical issues. The educators were torn between two ideals. Their engagement with intricate cases taught them that simple moral preconceptions could interfere with the intention to restore health and wholeness. The social worker Ida Cannon insisted that sympathy and objectivity were needed to preclude the subjective moralistic judgments to which untrained laity were prone. But there were others who felt that one of the main benefits of clinical education was the unique training it offered in the formation of moral judgments. Richard Cabot, who by now was a leading neurologist and

232

cardiologist, praised medical internships because of their effectiveness in indirectly teaching medical ethics. Cabot worked easily with Cannon, but clashed with other social workers over the issue.[43]

The question of ethics quickly surfaced in the movement for clinical pastoral education, though during the early years the disagreements were muted. The precursors of that training had simply assumed that ministers gave moral guidance. Elwood Worcester thought such moral and spiritual counseling should become more "scientific." Richard Cabot established a medical social service with the assumption that the study of character was the social worker's chief responsibility, and that it was the minister's, as well. And William S. Keller, a physician in Ohio, organized a summer school in social service with the hope of teaching pastors ethical values through social action. The early clinical innovations, then, were expressions of the Progressive social gospel.[44]

When Richard Cabot issued his "Plea for a Clinical Year in the Course of Theological Study" in 1925, he viewed it as a call for greater moral depth in the cure of souls. He later reprinted the address as the first chapter in a treatise titled *Adventures on the Borderlands of Ethics*. By 1925 Cabot was an imposing figure. The founder of medical social work and of clinical pathological conferences for medical teaching, a path breaker in the study of heart disease, a professor of medicine at Harvard, and a member of a wealthy and prominent New England family, he could be an intimidating figure. One colleague admitted later that in their entire period of association, he had never felt at ease with Cabot and had never failed to treat him with "due deference": "He was . . . quite conscious of the fact that he was a Cabot, and the Cabots were reputed to have a private line of communication with God. I always suspected that Richard Cabot believed that."[45]

In later years Cabot seemed to derive satisfaction from his own stoical demands on himself. He swam in the cold ocean, maintained a rigorous schedule of work, and even delivered a public lecture the day his wife died. Impatient with weakness either in himself or in others, Cabot felt that clinical training should give the clergy a realistic vision and moral toughness that would help them form and shape strength of character in their pastoral work. But what was the purpose of seriously considering character in the cure of souls and in the training of pastors? There were at least two answers to that question. One group of clinicians accented the ideal of ethical formation; a second group exalted freedom and autonomy. And underlying those disagreements about ethics were deeper disagreements about human nature. But despite the conflicts, both groups were feeling their way toward an ideal of pastoral work that, for better or worse, carried them away from the notion of adjustment.

When the liberal clergyman Anton Boisen began to train a handful of students at Worcester State Hospital in the summer of 1925—with Cabot's full support—he, too, took it for granted that clinical education would clarify the internalizing of ethical norms. In 1930 Cabot and Boisen joined with others in the formation of the Council for the Clinical Training of Theological Students. Cabot viewed it as an adventure on the borderland of ethics. Within two years, though, the men and women in that council were embroiled in a border war that split them into two antagonistic factions—one in Boston, the other with headquarters in New York. In 1933 Cabot was charging that "the psychological-medical group which today dominates public opinion almost as the medieval church did" was trying to substitute psychology for ethics. His views were not acceptable to the New Yorkers, who happened to admire psychologists, even psychoanalysts. And though Cabot mediated between the two groups for a few years, he was soon ousted from the presidency of the New York organization. The men and women who worked alongside him in Boston then formed their own organization: The New England Theological Schools Committee on Clinical Training. And they clearly felt comfortable with most of Cabot's ideas.[46]

The Boston Tradition: Counseling and Formation

The Boston movement initially tended to think that Cabot was correct when he insisted that "growth"—growth in such powers as sympathy, courage, honesty, tenacity, and knowledge—was the ethical absolute. Cabot viewed ethical growth with the aid of biological imagery and with the assumption that there is purposeful order within the self. He was confident that spiritual life was actually "the growth of each soul along the plan of its individual nature." He therefore hoped that clinical education would teach theological students to "listen" to the unspoken word and thereby discern the "growing edge" of the soul. Cabot derived the notion of a "growing edge" from physiology: The self was like a piece of human tissue, putting out new cells as it grew. Implicit in his vision of growth was an ethical and theological vocabulary which defined the self with metaphors of purpose, rationality, order, effort, will, freedom, and cumulative experience.[47]

Cabot's vision of human nature suggested an ethical program. He valued two principles above all others: stability and growth. By stability, he meant an integrity and unity that came from forming and adhering to purposes, plans, and agreements, both within ourselves and with others. By "growth," he meant a maturing that occurred through the exposure of our plans and purposes to "the facts." Agreeing with Alfred North Whitehead that "the ultimate basis of all authority" is "the supremacy of fact over thought," Cabot concluded that the primary hindrance to growth was self-deceit. The one theme in Sigmund Freud's writings that Cabot admired was his exposure of self-deceit, his admonition to face reality. One among several themes in Ralph Waldo Emerson's writings that Cabot liked was his charge to "banish your will and be transparent." Cabot believed that ethical formation was the consequence of attending to the real. His own moral imperative was the maxim "Thou shalt grow by learning Reality."[48]

It followed that any vivid encounter with reality was a moment in the ethical formation of the self. From John Dewey Cabot took the notion that duties were the acts required by a situation: "To study the situation and ourselves as part of it, in search of the act just now called for by the facts, is the business of ethical reflection." And when he advanced practical suggestions for promoting ethical growth, Cabot recommended many of the same methods he had advocated as the elements of clinical education: "Push up near enough to the situation to be in close range of the sights, sounds, and smells"—learn to listen, to get things straight, to write things down, to question yourself, to fail and admit failure, to give things their right names. Cabot viewed moral growth as the forming and ordering of our selves by conforming them to the Real, and he had the same view of clinical pastoral education.[49]

It could hardly be said that Cabot's ethical vision shaped all the goals and methods of the New England tradition of clinical education, but his aim of professional formation endured and, through his work and writing with Russell Dicks, began to inform a new outlook on the cure of souls. When Dicks became a chaplain at Massachusetts General Hospital, he hoped at first to secure it as a training center for the New Yorkers. But he soon felt more comfortable with the Boston counselors than with his old allies, even though his first meeting with Cabot had unnerved him. Cabot had asked why he was interested in sick people. Dicks replied that he once had been seriously ill himself. Cabot's response was brusque: "I'm glad you have." Dicks was offended, but he and Cabot soon developed a close though touchy relationship.[50]

A native of Oklahoma and orphaned at fifteen, Dicks had worked his way through college and then through Union Theological Seminary. A struggle with tuberculosis increased his interest in counseling the sick, and after his ordination as a Presbyterian minister he became the first full-time Protestant chaplain at Massachusetts General. There he maintained a program in clinical education for the clergy. He believed that the study of the immediate encounter between a student and a patient could reveal the congruence or disparity between the student's perceptions and intentions, on the one hand, and the realities of the situation, on the other. By insisting on written "verbatims" of conversations—word for word transcriptions—he was, in effect, applying Cabot's techniques of moral reflection.[51]

In 1936 Cabot and Dicks completed a book that helped to change the understanding of the cure of souls in American Protestantism. *The Art of Ministering to the Sick* embodied all Cabot's imagery of growth and stability. It popularized the metaphor of the "growing edge," and it assigned to the minister the responsibility for finding and cultivating that growing edge, largely through "good listening." Cabot and Dicks argued that the minister presented and represented the teachings of Jesus, especially his call for "confidence in God," but that the therapeutic imagery of the medical tradition provided the central theological metaphor. They defined God as a power of healing—the *vis medicatrix naturae*—or, altering Matthew Arnold's definition, "the power not ourselves that makes for righteousness," they defined God as "that great power in ourselves that makes for health." The minister, they thought, could enter the sick room confident in a purposive healing force within each person. By helping men and women discover the direction in which this immanent divinity was carrying them, helping them face and assimilate and obey the "plan" of God for their lives, the minister helped them grow. The pastor's task was to supply the atmosphere in which growth was favored.[52]

The best way to fulfill that task was to learn to listen, and therefore counseling should begin where persons already were. Dicks was intrigued with the notion of "directed listening," which sought to find the "better parts of the person's mind," and with the related notion of "quietness," the period in which the patient discovered his or her own "growing edge." Cabot added that such a discovery was more likely to occur if both counselor and patient concentrated on the presence of a "third" reality—a common goal, for example, or a project or an interest that drew them both beyond themselves. He suggested that every conversation should proceed as if a "third person" were present, someone or something greater than the immediate concerns of the two persons engaged in the conversation.[53]

A Unitarian layman, Cabot conceived of counseling largely as an ethical appeal to the will. Dicks obviously concurred, despite his desire to start where people "really were." He once reported a conversation with a patient who was believed to be dying: "She said, 'I think I am going to die.' I said, 'You are not afraid, are you?' After considering, she said, 'No, I am not afraid.'" And that, said Dicks, "is starting with a patient where you find her, and moving at once toward the point which the patient needs to reach."[54] Dicks' response was, in fact, an appeal to the woman's will, an appeal to the will to reach an exceedingly difficult goal.

He illustrated his style of counseling in 1939 when he published a series of verbatim reports of pastoral conversations. Often accompanied by critical comments, the descriptions revealed the practical implications of the theories Dicks and Cabot were developing. A conversation in a hospital with a bitter, uncommunicative old man who wore a stocking cap and broken spectacles, and had tobacco-stained whiskers, exhibited something of the method that Dicks was proposing.

The minister, who clearly was Dicks himself, began the conversation by helping the old man light a cigarette and then asking, "How long have you been here?"

"Thirteen weeks. . . . I'm just getting over spinal meningitis. . . . Bedam, that's something."

"That *is* something," said the minister. "How long have you had that?"

"*Two years,*" he said with emphasis.

"Been in bed all the time?"

"Yes, all the time. Bed and wheel chair. When I came in here they promised—they *guaranteed*—I'd be able to walk out in a month. I've already been here three months and still am."

"What did they do?"

"They did a lumbar puncture. . . . At the . . . hospital where I was they did twelve, trying to find a damn little bug. I've been in bed two years." His laugh was loud and raspy.

"That must have been very discouraging."

The man's eyes became misty and he took a deep breath. "They called me the miracle man. They didn't think I'd live through it."

For awhile neither man spoke. Then Dicks asked, "Do you have a family?"

The man answered indifferently: "Yes. Three—three counting my wife. Her mother lives with us. . . . But she's a grand old lady. Gives me hell," he said laughing. "I just stand, or lay and take it."

"And give it back to her?"

"No, I don't really. I just take it."

"How long has she lived with you?"

"Ever since we were married. I've got her insured for five hundred dollars and I tell her damned if she won't outlive me. She's nearly ninety." He became serious. "But I would miss the old lady."

"What was your work?"

"I was a machinist. I made good money." He laughed. "I made it and I spent it. During the good days I made a dollar and a quarter an hour with overtime."

"Ten dollars a day," said Dicks.

"Yes, and more."

"That was back a few years?"

"Yes, during the war."

There was a long pause before Dicks asked, "They operated on you here?"

"Yes, they did. . . . Who are you, a doctor?"

"No, I'm a minister."

"Well, well." The man's voice became quieter. He seemed embarrassed.

Dicks laughed. "Slipped up on you that time, didn't I?"

239

"Yes, you sure did."

"I'm in the hospital all the time," said Dicks. "I've been away, so I missed you. I don't try to see everyone. Only those who are here for quite a while."

"What denomination are you?" asked the old man. When Dicks, a Presbyterian, responded, the old man shifted in his bed and said that he was a Baptist.

"It doesn't make much difference here," said Dicks. "I see all denominations."

"No, it doesn't," said the old man. "Not in here. Not much anywhere."

"If you've been here thirteen weeks you were here during the hot weather."

"Yes. There were three days that were bad." The old man became silent.

After a time, Dicks took his leave: "Well, I'll see you again."

"I'm glad to have met you. Stop again."

Dicks did stop by the ward two days later, during the mid-morning. "Well," he said to the old man, "you're out early this morning."

"Yes, I'm the first one." The old man greeted him, holding out his hand.

"I guess they're getting tired of you."

"By Jesus, I'm getting tired of them too."

"It's pretty slow going, isn't it?"

"It certainly is." Then came a pause and a question: "You're Presbyterian, you said?"

"Yes." For a moment the two men were silent.

"You're Baptist," said Dicks.

"Yes." Again the pause.

"Well, there's only a little difference between the two in teaching."

The old man shifted his position: "Yes, I knew there was a little." As he looked at Dicks with a vacant stare, an orderly came by, taking a patient to the operating room. The old man watched them until they were out of sight.

"That's the only one from this ward who's going down this morning," he said.

240

"A little boy, wasn't it?"

The man nodded, and Dicks gestured toward the bed: "How do you sleep on this contraption?"

"I don't," he said.

"Just catnaps, eh?"

The old man responded with impatience: "Yes, you get catnaps. You have to. . . . I'd give ten years of life to get home and have a good sleep. And that would be about all I have left."

"You think that would about finish up your assignment?" asked Dicks.

"Yes. I do." Another pause.

"Is there anyone in the ward very sick?"

"Not very," answered the man, "and there's none very well either."

Nothing more happened until Dicks said good-bye: "I'll see you again. I wanted to stop by and see you a minute this morning."

"I'm glad you did."[55]

Dicks saw the old man frequently during the next four weeks. They talked of daily happenings, and Dicks believed the conversations were of value though they never went beyond the discussion of surface events. He seemed to have succeeded in gaining the man's goodwill and in helping him get some relief from his tension. By shifting the subject, by persisting even when the old man seemed irritable, and yet refusing to be aggressive, Dicks had helped a man deal with his illness and stress, and even with the prospect of "finishing up" his assignment.

It would seem to a later generation of pastoral theologians that Dicks had missed most of the old man's cues. When the man alluded to the "miracle" of having "lived through it," Dicks moved away from his implicit anxiety by asking about the family. When he mentioned his pain, Dicks picked up instead on the assessment of the hospital staff. When the old man, who had undergone a painful operation, drew Dicks' attention to another patient who was "going down there," Dicks asked about the bed. Dicks himself observed that he had failed to discover whether the old man's references to Baptists and Presbyterians were perhaps a subtle way of edging into deeper religious questions. But on the whole, Dicks approved of the interview. He had discovered, he said, that people were helped most when they were permitted to talk about what they wanted to talk about. So he urged pastors to listen, confident that men and women could discover their own growing edges. Dicks was convinced that by listening, questioning, and trusting, ministers could, without being judgmental, provide others the opportunity to accept "creative responsibility" for themselves.[56]

A disagreement about moral conduct drove Dicks and Cabot apart, but Austin Philip Guiles moved in quickly to take up the slack. In 1932 Guiles had broken with the New York training program and introduced clinical education at Andover Newton Theological Seminary. A debonair educational entrepreneur, he attracted Cabot's favor and held it even after being dismissed from Massachusetts General Hospital for practicing "psychiatry" in a manner that angered the doctors. Guiles' program at Andover Newton reflected the ideas of Cabot and Dicks. He had developed considerable interest in what he called the rather daring theories of the depth psychologists, but in his teaching, he concentrated on such subjects as the relationship between moral guilt and the unconscious guilt which disturbs "responsible life and behavior." Guiles placed psychology in the service of morality, and he sought to inculcate a certain moral self-control in his clinical students. His aim was to test the student's "patience," to further the "capacity to *control* embarrassment," to engender "the willingness to *see through* a difficult assignment." He taught theological students to value and embody persistence, effort, and self-possession; he conceived of clinical education as a disciplining that would produce competence. And Guiles brought those same values to the pastoral counseling centers which he opened at the Wellesley Hills Congregational Church and later at the Old South Church in Boston.[57]

By helping to organize the New England program into

an Institute for Pastoral Care in 1944, Rollin Fairbanks, a professor at the Episcopal Theological Seminary in Cambridge, reinforced the growing amity between clinical supervisors and seminary faculties in the Boston area. By establishing the institute, he also preserved some of Richard Cabot's vision of human nature and ethics. In later years, Russell Dicks observed that the Institute had been far more appreciative of Cabot's ideas and his own than had the Council in New York. And when Fairbanks opened a counseling center in cooperation with St. Paul's Episcopal Cathedral in Boston, social work was the model for his counseling methods, consistent with his disinclination to overemphasize what he called the pathological and the morbid within the personality. Fairbanks continued to speak out for rationality and freedom, even insisting that the doctrine of free will was a central Christian affirmation. And he continued for twenty years to lament the preoccupation with "pathology" among clinical supervisors and pastoral counselors.[58]

Fairbanks maintained that the clinical method developed "specifically pastoral skills by testing them with real people and submitting the results for evaluation." He believed, also, that the process required explicit moral judgments: Clinical supervisors—and the pastors they were training—should attend to "the dimension of judgment," the "obligatory," the "imperative"; the physician of souls should offer "clarity as to right and wrong." And like Josiah Royce, Fairbanks argued that neither religion nor pastoral counseling should become the handmaiden of health. The primary goal was to strive for the building of the kingdom of God through reconciliation. Health was, at best, a secondary benefit.[59]

The New Englanders quickly outgrew Cabot's narrow views of psychiatry, but the continuing influence of Boston personalism and other forms of theological liberalism helped to sustain their optimistic reading of the psychological literature and to confirm their commitment to moral growth. The personalist theologians at Boston—Borden Parker Bowne, Edgar Sheffield Brightman, and Albert

Knudson—had taught that the formation of moral personhood was a project demanded by the fact that "personality" was the primary attribute of God. The cure of souls was therefore more deeply in touch with reality when the pastor aided men and women to grow into maturity as persons. Both the training of pastors and the counseling of parishioners assumed the primacy of moral formation.

The New York Tradition: Counseling and Freedom

By 1938, the New Yorkers who wanted physicians of the soul trained through clinical education had begun to call themselves simply the Council for Clinical Training. Any number of issues divided them from their counterparts—and competitors—in Boston. Some of the leaders, marked by strong personalities, simply disliked one another. Henry Sloan Coffin at Union Seminary used to say, in reference to the quarreling, that "the personality adjustment people can't adjust." But the two groups also held conflicting views of the self and of what the self ought to be. The New Englanders, admiring the capacity for rationality and purposive growth within the personality, were interested in ethical formation. The New Yorkers wondered at the potential for chaotic impulsiveness within the self; they were interested in freedom—the freeing of persons from rigid and destructive social and personal expectations.[60]

The New Yorkers derived their dominant metaphors first from Anton Boisen, and then from the depth psychologists. Boisen was a graduate of Union Theological Seminary, a theological liberal who had studied social ethics with Cabot and abnormal psychology with William McDougall and Macfie Campbell at Harvard and at Boston Psychopathic Hospital. He also had conferred with Elwood Worcester at the Emmanuel Church in Boston. As a consequence, he decided that the theological schools needed a thorough overhauling, mainly because they failed to use scientific methods in the study of religious

244

experience. From Cabot, he had learned to value the firsthand study of "cases," and he hoped that his experiment in clinical training at Worcester State Hospital in 1925 would become both a model for theological education and a means of exploring religious experience.[61]

Boisen was himself a tortured soul who had, since childhood, suffered extraordinary guilt for having sexual fantasies and entertained an exceedingly negative concept of himself as a wretch and a failure. He had idealized his parents and also a young woman whom he had loved at a distance until her death drove him into psychotic withdrawal. Compelled on two occasions to hospitalize himself, he found that his own experience with mental illness served him well in his work as chaplain at psychiatric hospitals in Massachusetts and Illinois.[62]

Boisen's interest in the psychology of religion led him to interpret mental illness as an instance of religious experience. His *Exploration of the Inner World* (1936) advanced the notion that emotional collapse was a chaotic encounter with God which could lead either to a new integration of the personality or to a fall into total inner disarray. Boisen viewed clinical pastoral education, therefore, as a study of sin and salvation. The tormented souls whom he studied were "living human documents." And he believed that the key to understanding the self lay in its pathological eruptions. No sharp line divided the insane from the normal. Schizophrenic torment offered a clearer insight into the human personality than did any process of biological growth in tissues and cells.[63]

Boisen found Freud useful but shortsighted. Boisen's intellectual heirs who organized clinical training in New York felt more at home with the new depth psychologies. But implicit in his outlook and in that of his successors was an ethical and theological vision which defined the self with metaphors of struggle, conflict, impulse, nonrational feeling, and inner chaos. When they appropriated ideas from the psychologists, they, like the Bostonians, could still appeal to William James. They admired James—not because of his doctrine of the will but because of his vision of the sick soul, and Boisen, especially, criticized the liberal psychology of religion because of its optimism about human nature. The New Yorkers were impressed with the turbulence of the inner self.[64]

It is true that Boisen's ethics were not much different from Cabot's. Boisen admired self-control, self-discipline—even the control of thought and impulse. Throughout his life he patrolled his own inner walls like a prison guard and punished every deviant desire. He bound himself to Josiah Royce's high notion of loyalty, which he interpreted with the aid of George Herbert Mead's descriptions of the way we form our conscience by internalizing social standards. Boisen believed that mental illness exposed the failure to grow into higher social loyalties, as well as the effort to transcend that failure.[65]

As Boisen soon recognized, a number of his heirs in clinical work found themselves drawn to a Freudian analysis which highlighted inner turbulence and impulsive, even chaotic vitality, and a few began to propose a freedom "quite at variance" with his own rigorism. Some supervisors engaged in training physicians of the soul, Boisen charged, were treating patients with conflicts by "lowering [their] conscience threshold." Boisen interpreted the change as an instance of moral lapse. It would be more accurate to see it as a continuation of his own preoccupation with the understanding of inner conflict and struggle. During the 1930s, supervisors trained by Boisen riveted their attention on the drives and impulses of the personality. Like the nineteenth-century pastoral theologians, they argued that a new "knowledge of human nature" could undergird new forms of relationship between the minister and parishioners. But under the influence of the psychoanalytic movement, some of the leading figures in the Council for Clinical Training decided that the proper understanding of human nature entailed an alternative ethical ideal: liberation through insight.[66]

It was a matter of at least symbolic importance that Richard Cabot, the patriarch of clinical training for pastors in Boston, scorned Freudian theory, while the matriarch of the movement in New York was a psychiatrist named Helen Flanders Dunbar who had worked with Boisen at Worcester State Hospital and had studied psychoanalysis in both Vienna and Zurich. Having done scholarly research on Dante, medieval literature, devotional exercises, and psychosomatic medicine, Dunbar shared Boisen's hopes that the tortured symbolic visions of mental patients might well be the path to a new and deeper understanding of the self, though she supplemented Boisen's ideas with psychoanalytic notions that distressed him.[67]

Dunbar insisted in 1935 that the Council had not introduced psychoanalytic technique into clinical training, but that it did try to "give the student a clear conception of the place of psychoanalysis in psychotherapy." She eventually fell into disfavor and moved on to other tasks, but when Robert Brinkman became director in 1937, he turned to psychoanalytic doctrine not only to provide the student an understanding of "deeper motivation," but to interpret traditional Christian images. He tied this new understanding to an ethical standard: growth through the transcendence of "passivity." It was during Brinkman's tenure that Boisen began to worry about the uncritical acceptance of Freud—and even of Wilhelm Reich and his theories about sexuality and relaxation—within the Council. He complained that a genetic interpretation of mental illness by Spurgeon English and Gerald J. H. Pearson, *Common Neuroses of Children and Adults* (1937), had become "the law and the gospel in most of the centers."[68]

Brinkman's innovations created bitter conflicts. Some charged that he had lost interest in pastoral education. But even his critics found their work increasingly informed by depth psychology. Instructed by Freud and the neo-Freudians, they interpreted clinical training as a means of introducing pastors to "deeper motivations" in the self—to disorder, inner conflict, and guilt. Brinkman quickly lost influence, but the New Yorkers clung to Freud.[69]

As late as 1945, Thomas Bigham of General Theological Seminary could, it seems, represent a consensus within the Council by arguing that we understood "the spiritual heights of human nature" only when we opened our eyes to a full view of "human disorders." Bigham debated the issue with his Episcopal colleague in Cambridge, Rollin Fairbanks. "There is something to be said," he once told Fairbanks, "for a morbid view as a good thing." Such a view of the self enabled us to understand and accept our own drives and impulses, even when we found them repugnant. Such a view also helped the counselor accept the unacceptable within others. A recognition of disorder therefore brought with it a certain kind of freedom from moral and pastoral rigidity.[70]

During the 1940s, an articulate group of chaplain supervisors within the Council concluded that Protestant legalism and moralism were responsible for much of the emotional conflict and spiritual immaturity of the patients and students. Hence they called for an end to harsh moral judgments, negative views of sexuality, legalistic preaching, and above all, authoritarianism, which they deemed "essentially sinful." Throughout the 1930s the supervisors had counterposed their goal of "understanding" against the New Englanders' aim of pastoral competence. By the 1940s, *understanding* had taken on a fresh nuance of meaning. It connoted tolerance, an acceptance of feelings; of the body, the senses, and sexuality; and an opposition to rigidity and to condemnation. *Understanding* implied an ethical attitude, a willingness to sympathize with people rather than idolize conventions and rules.[71]

An interest in freedom was by no means absent from the New England tradition, and the New Yorkers also had some deep concerns about moral formation, but the differences in emphasis were pronounced. The two different visions reflected, to some extent, differences in educational background, social origins, and temperament. Even a hasty sampling of the leaders in the New England movement, for instance, reveals that about 80 percent of them had received their seminary education in Connecticut and Massachusetts. About the same percentage of the leaders in the Council had gone to seminary in New York, Chicago, and Evanston. They were the "fraternity of rebels"—suspected of Reichian heresies, criticized for exposing students to unnecessary emotional shocks, and viewed often as enemies of the theological seminaries. The division mirrored the tensions in medicine during the early debates over psychoanalysis. The anti-Freudian neurologists, like Richard Cabot, came largely from the upper classes, clustered in the vicinity of Boston, and held positions of considerable standing. The early psychoanalysts were from a lower social class (from which they were moving upward), came largely from small towns and provincial cities, and found more sustenance in New York than in Boston. Also, the pastoral supervisors in the New England programs felt at home in the region and in its established institutions, whereas the New Yorkers were more likely to feel themselves estranged from both the churches and the seminaries.[72]

For reasons both ideological and social, therefore, the diverse perspectives in the clinical movement never faded away completely, even though the two groups were beginning to cooperate and move toward union by the early 1940s. Though the nuances of difference remained, both groups had by that time moved quite some distance from the earlier theme of adjustment, which came under siege during the mid-1930s. Largely for theological reasons, adjustment by then seemed no longer an adequate metaphor to describe pastoral work. In any case, the clinical traditions had not found it useful in their work with students. The emerging consensus sought another guiding metaphor, and the gradual trend was toward "insight."

Insight

The change was underway by 1931. By that time some of the young theologians were charging that the language of adjustment, when used in theology, ran the risk of identifying finite cultural values with the Infinite Ground of values. It confused parental desires with divine commands, happiness with holiness, and success with sanctity. For those theologians, human beings did not seem to be makers and builders, shaping and adapting themselves to fit into God's purposes or making adjustments here and there that would bring in the kingdom. In the new vision prompted by political unrest and economic depression, human beings seemed limited, finite, anxious creatures, burdened with the responsibility of free decision and with the knowledge that no finite good could be identified with the Infinite.

In 1931 H. Richard Niebuhr at Yale complained of the tendency to define God in terms of God's "usefulness," to the neglect of divine holiness. The liberal tradition, he said, had conceived of religion as adjustment to a divine reality for the sake of gaining power. It was more realistic, he thought, to abandon pretensions of power and adjustment and to hear a revelation that brought criticism and judgment. The following year, Niebuhr translated Paul Tillich's critique of western culture, *The Religious Situation*—an argument that genuine religion was antithetical to the illusion that cultural values, even the values of human health and well-being, were the values of God. Tillich viewed Freud with favor, but initially not so much for his therapeutic methods as for his subversion of a calculating, technical rationality. By implication he suggested that the language of adjustment was merely a reflection of a capitalist culture that sought only control over mind, nature, and God. And for him, the divine was precisely the reality that resisted control: It was "absolutely hidden," transcending all experience and resisting every effort to "adjust" to it for transient ends.[73]

The theological realists—Tillich, H. Richard Niebuhr, Reinhold Niebuhr, George Richards, and others—claimed that the notion of "value" in liberal theology had wrongly taken precedence over the idea of "being." That is, the liberals had defined reality through the lenses of their own values. They had therefore felt compelled to demonstrate God's usefulness in the human search for justice, happiness, security, or emotional health. They had made "the gospel of God a means to an end." Rather than acknowledge that God stood in judgment over every finite value, they had defined God as the support and preserver of ideals. And they had done so by using—or misusing—the idea of adjustment.[74]

It took only a few years for theological realism to shape a new perspective on the cure of souls. In 1939 Rollo May published *The Art of Counseling*, a book not grounded in older American traditions but in the work of the European analysts: Freud, Jung, Rank, Kunkel, and Adler. Within a year, May published a second book, *The Springs of Creative Living*, dedicated to Paul Tillich, and with gratitude to Reinhold Niebuhr, who had read the manuscript as May was writing it. It was no surprise that May had some harsh words for liberal theologians, especially for Henry Nelson Wieman, who had failed, May said, to recognize the "otherness" of a God who judged all human pretension.[75]

When the two books appeared, May was a young pastor who had studied both at Adler's Vienna Clinic and at Union Theological Seminary. Having taught for a time in the Garrett Biblical Institute, a Methodist school connected to Northwestern, he had written *The Art of Counseling* as a series of lectures for ministers in Arkansas and North Carolina. The book quickly caught on; Anton Boisen described it as an "enlightened" presentation of psychotherapy for religious workers. Although May later studied at the William Alanson White Institute of Psychiatry, underwent analysis with Erich Fromm, and ventured into private practice and a writing career, his initial audience was composed mainly of pastors who were expanding their interests in "pastoral psychology."[76]

May believed in 1939 that men and women were "finite, imperfect, and limited," that their insecurity drove them to prideful self-will, and that they could overcome egocentricity only when the Christ—a concrete figure "outside" the closed circle of their own subjectivity—

reconciled them to "the structure of reality." He was wary of the older optimism about "growth," with its assumption that more enlightenment, education, and ethics could transform the personality. He believed that human life was marked by an unending conflict between freedom and determination: The self yearned for a total freedom that would transcend all structures, but egocentric freedom swamped the self in its own subjectivity and prompted a retreat into the security of unquestioning allegiance to a finite structure—whether it be a nation-state, an authoritarian moralism, or a fundamentalist religion. Following the lead of the psychoanalyst Fritz Kunkel, he argued therefore that the task of the counselor was to help people maintain a healthy tension between their freedom and the demands of reality, including the demands imposed by the "structure" of things.[77]

May was convinced that every problem in counseling held moral implications, but his commitment to psychoanalytic theory helped to convince him that any appeal to "conscious decision" was superficial. The goal of counseling was more modest; the counselor's task was to offer interpretations that would promote understanding and insight. May joined his teacher Adler in thinking that the person who understood truly would probably act rightly, but he added that true insight was not simply rational knowledge; it was also a capacity to trust. Insight was attained when the ego surrendered its pretensions and trusted the structure of reality.[78]

May ventured an example of a style of counseling which he believed embodied both psychoanalytic theory and theological truth when he reported one of his talks with a Mr. Bronson, a college instructor who had come to him complaining of unbearable tension. The tone of the conversation suggested that insight came through explanation; counseling meant psychological interpretation and theological clarification.

"It seems as though I must always have something driving me," said Bronson, "something compelling me to keep at my work."

"You mean driving you in your teaching?"

"Yes, but also in other aspects of my work, such as writing articles. . . ."

May took note of Bronson's jerky, nervous movement: "Yes, you do appear to work at a great strain. How long have you noticed the tension?"

"Always. At least, ever since I can remember. In high school I worked very hard and fast—I was quite small then, only four foot ten. . . ."

"Tell me more," said May, "about how this tension appears in your living now."

"The main trouble is that I cannot get accomplished what I want to," replied Bronson, explaining at length his overwrought and unproductive style of work.

"But have you never thought that you could do better creative work if you did not keep yourself at this great tension?"

"Yes, I have realized that often. But at other times I feel that I must have something compelling me from the outside. . . ."

To May, the inconsistency between Bronson's complaints about external compulsions and his desire to retain them reflected an unconscious conflict. "Have you ever had a breakdown under these strains?" he asked.

"Yes, when I was a senior in college I had a nervous collapse," said Bronson, who then added reports of other incidents. He continued to "talk it out," responding to May's questions, adding details, undergoing what May called the period of "confession." Finally May began to seek specific information about Bronson's age, his family, and his friendships. Believing, with Adler, that a child's position in the family shapes the personality, he considered it important that Bronson was the younger sibling. His questions initiated the interview's "stage of interpretation."

"You appear to have a tremendously strong ambition," he said.

"Yes, I am very ambitious. . . ."

"Now we know that an exaggerated ambition, when

the individual is not able to keep up his striving, is very often connected with some deep inferiority feeling."

Bronson interrupted: "I certainly have had an inferiority complex. It was connected with my being so small in high school, and I had to strive to make a place for myself."

"Do you know what your position in the family indicates?"

Bronson did not, so May explained to him that the second child typically developed a prominent ambition.

"Yes, this seems to fit my case perfectly. When I was very young I can remember always trying to outdo my sister."

May then asked Bronson if he could relate an early childhood memory. (Adler had argued that an early childhood memory was like a closeup snapshot of a personality.) Bronson told May of once having been carried home from a fair. He also added a memory of a childhood dream in which he repeatedly climbed a ladder, only to fall when he reached the top.

"That early memory doesn't help us much," said May, "but the dream is very interesting. We can now see some rather distinct things about your personality pattern, Mr. Bronson." And May then explained to Bronson that his tension expressed an exaggerated ambition connected to a feeling of inferiority which had developed in part from his position in the family, and which was manifested in the dream. "Have you always been afraid of falling, or let us say, of failing?"

"Why, yes, as a matter of fact I have been—very much so."

"Why should you be afraid of failure?"

"I don't know. . . ."

"You appear to fear some catastrophe. This usually arises out of a basic distrust of life—a feeling that one must watch carefully or some disastrous thing will happen. Do you have that feeling?"

"Yes. I've never thought of it in that way, but I guess I

am distrustful and suspicious of life. . . . I have never been able to accept that statement of Jesus, 'Be not anxious.' I believe in God, but yet I have a fear and deep distrust—rather inconsistent, isn't it?"

After another short exchange, Bronson asked for advice. May refused to give it. "You wish rules on the matter," he observed. "You want these rules to compel you from the outside. And you'll follow them with the same strain and tension which you manifest now." May suggested that Bronson must relax that tight grip. "And to do that you must understand yourself better and get over that basic distrust of life. . . . Why do you feel you must be driven from the outside?"

"Well, as you said, it is connected with my family position. I got into the habit of striving too much when I was young, and I've just been keeping it up."

"No, it does not help simply to blame the habit. It's a deeper matter. . . . It is more fruitful to assume that your present exaggerated tendency to strive arises out of the same factors in your personality pattern which gave rise to your similar striving ten years ago. And what we need to understand is those factors. . . . Do you have a dread of being imperfect?"

"Yes, I do—very strongly so."

"But you realize that nobody achieves perfection in this world?"

"Yes, that's right."

"You see, if you always demand perfection, you'll never do anything. You will never take the last step on the ladder for fear you'll fail. One needs the courage of imperfection to live creatively. . . . Bronson, why do you distrust life?"

"I don't know."

May explained again that the distrust of life could be the result of an early feeling of inferiority, accentuated by small size and family position. But he ended the interview by returning to the theological themes: "You can afford to trust more. You can develop the courage of imperfection, and in that way you'll relax much of that driving ambition. . . . That means trusting and affirming life more."[79]

May's report condensed a two-hour conversation into a few pages of print, but he revealed a style of counsel that was beginning to appeal to some ministers during the late 1930s. From a later perspective, May's use of psychological "explanations" would seem terribly wooden. He told Bronson what to feel, and Bronson felt it. He explained Bronson's dilemma, and Bronson accepted his explanations without demur. A later generation, sated with psychological jargon, would find it difficult to understand the power of early counseling techniques, which often seemed to push and shove every "symptom" until it fit some explanation, which was then communicated with flourish to the counselee. Yet at that time the language was still fresh, the method innovative. And the psychological language seemed consistent with a theology that had rediscovered the meaning of faith as trust, rather than as assent to propositions, had recovered a sense of inner conflict in place of the older liberal optimism and that rebelled against the legalism that often marked the older language of adjustment.

The theological realists were beginning to recover a traditional Protestant doctrine of sinfulness that the liberals had forgotten. Most took a position like that of Reinhold Niebuhr, who argued that the human capacity for transcending self invariably produced anxiety and thus spawned a futile effort in all of us to secure our existence by making absolutes of mere relative and finite values. Sin was the pride and sensuality that flowed out of unchecked anxiety. At the heart of sinfulness, then, was idolatry, a trust in cultural values as if they embodied the divine. Theological realism was an attempt to shatter the idols and redirect trust toward the God above idols.

May's conversation with Bronson was intended to elicit just such trust by combining the insights of post-Freudian analysis and realist theology. Bronson's anxiety had caused him to make an idol of his own success. May offered insight into the idolatry—and an exhortation to "trust life." The movement from adjustment to insight, then, was a transition from a notion of sinfulness as a false adaptation to the divine, to a conception of sin as an inability to transcend idolatry. It marked a recovery of older Calvinist and Lutheran themes that had been subdued, or absent, for half a century.

The realists, though, found it difficult to talk about spiritual growth, especially if that were supposed to refer to some kind of self-realization, as the liberal theologians had believed. May's reflections on counseling illustrated the beginning of a transition in ways of thinking about self-realization. The collapse of confidence in "adjustment" reflected the theological critique of culture. The criticism of cultural values, in turn, subverted ideals that the earlier theorists of self-realization had taken for granted. The earlier writers had believed that self-realization should proceed in accordance with the highest and best values of the culture, which were to be embodied in both social conventions and social institutions. Secular reformers and liberal theologians had agreed about that. But the theological criticism of "culture religion" removed one of the props that supported the older ideal. If every cultural value stood under judgment, then how could any of them be trusted to define the direction of self-realization? One possible solution was to abandon the emphasis on self-realization—to argue that the very notion of self-realization constituted a subtle form of idolatry. Most of the realist theologians followed that path. Another solution was to redefine self-realization as a transcending of social convention. The pastoral theologians of the 1940s would find that answer tempting.

The reevaluation of pastoral care in the 1920s, then, had its roots in a postwar psychological revival, an economic shift toward a white-collar economy, and a pragmatist intellectual tradition which had used the idea of adjustment as an instrument of social reform. When the early twentieth-century seminary teachers of pastoral theology—whether called pastoral theologians or Christian educators—incorporated the post-Freudian analytic methods into their instruction, they initially read Freud in the light of their own theories and theologies of adjustment. The clinical pastoral education movement, however, began the search for more adequate ways to understand pastoral counsel. Some of the clinical supervisors moved toward a program of "formation"; others moved toward the study of "sin and salvation" in "living human documents"; still others, toward an ideal of inner liberation. No group entirely abandoned the older rhetoric of adjustment, but by the early 1930s the theological realists, led by the Niebuhr brothers and Paul Tillich, initiated a vigorous criticism of adjustment as a guideline for theological and pastoral work. The theological critique helped to ensure that the idea of insight, a term with deep roots in the psychotherapeutic traditions, would take hold in Protestant pastoral care. But the new theology also raised questions about self-realization as a form of Protestant spirituality—questions that would reappear after the Second World War, when Americans seemed intent on the creation of a therapeutic culture.

7

Acceptance and Self-Realization

Pastoral counselors began to speak a new language after the Second World War. Gone from pastoral conversations were the labored explanations and the bits and pieces of well-meant advice. Gone was the tendency to view counseling as theological debate or moral exhortation. And gone also was the assumption that pastors were supposed to inform people that they suffered from compulsiveness or an inferiority complex. Or so it might have seemed to anyone who chanced to read one of the postwar textbooks. In fact, most American ministers probably continued to exhort and instruct in the office as well as in the pulpit. But among pastoral theologians in the nation's mainline schools of theology—among the new theoreticians of the cure of souls—exhortation and advice were out of fashion.

In the background of the new pastoral style stood the American psychologist Carl Rogers, who for more than a decade exercised enormous influence on pastoral theologians. But why the change in pastoral style? And why Rogers? On one level the answer is simple: The pastoral theologians were men and women of goodwill, seeking better ways to respond to pain and hurt. On another, the answers are multilayered: a theological revolt against legalism, the recovery of older Protestant doctrines, a white-collar economy, a burgeoning cultural preoccupation with psychology, postwar affluence, the constraints of seminary training, a critique of mass culture, and an ethic of self-realization. All those pieces fit together in a larger picture of religious adaptation to new cultural demands.

The new style of pastoral care seemed to blend with a resurgent ethic of self-realization. The postwar pastoral theologians maintained that pastoral care not only could alleviate pain but that it could enhance growth, nurture the development of the self's hidden potentialities. In advancing that proposal, they did not depart very far from the opinions of their predecessors, except in one telling detail. The earlier proponents of self-realization had supposed that social institutions, however much in need of periodic reform, both promoted and guided the growth of individuals. They had located the possibilities of self-realization within trust-worthy social structures. But the psychologists and social critics who informed postwar pastoral theology—Erich Fromm, Karen Horney, Carl Rogers, and others—tended to view most social institutions as bureaucratic impositions on human freedom and dignity. It was, after all, an era of bureaucrats, dictators, and demagogues. But self-realization as an ethic of individual growth, counterposed against social institutions, was quite different from self-development within a setting of shared corporate aims and commitments. For the pastoral theologians, then, self-realization, variously understood, was a commendable aim, but it also was a problem.

Popular Psychology

Since the beginning of the present century, popular American interest in psychology and mental health has risen during each period of war and subsequent prosperity. Even more than the First World War, the second exposed vast numbers of American to the mystique of the psychologist. The army employed more than 1,500 psychologists and hundreds of psychiatrists who studied the enemy, tested and treated their own troops, and instructed military leaders. After the war, even General Eisenhower began to deliver lectures on mental health, and the newspapers ran optimistic stories about peacetime applications of wartime psychiatry. *Life* magazine observed that the war had produced the "greatest upsurge" of psychological interest in the nation's history.[1]

The ending of the war did nothing to dampen the upsurge. The servicemen and women who had met the psychologist in training camps met them again when they returned to factories and executive suites. In 1927, some psychologists hired by the Western Electric Company to study the morale of its workers had discovered that productivity went up when wattage in the plant's lighting was increased, but then they also had found that productivity climbed when the wattage was decreased. Production rose when workers received special privileges, but it also rose when the privileges were taken away. After five years, it struck the bemused researchers that the workers were not responding to any single innovation, but to the attention they were receiving. The research made them feel important and work harder. And that was precisely what business wanted. Hence the demand for "industrial psychologists" accelerated, and factories were more than willing to accommodate the psychologists who were departing from the army after the war. By 1954 almost half the members of the American Psychological Association—or close to 7,000 psychologists—were laboring as efficiency counselors, personnel managers, vocational advisers, pollsters, and advertising consultants. General Motors hired seven simply to investigate Chevrolet's "sounds and smells." By 1952, one-third of the nation's corporations were using personality tests to screen prospective managers. A journalist of the period marveled that the application of theory to "practical

261

problems, in business and elsewhere, is rapidly becoming the psychologists' chief occupation."[2]

Suddenly it seemed that there were not enough psychologists and psychiatrists to go around. During the late 1940s the newspapers published a flurry of articles on the need for more. The New York Times reported in 1949 that the nation needed at least 27,000 more psychiatrists, and a Corporate Foundation for Research and Training in Psychiatry was soon endeavoring to convince American businesses to spend $9 million a year to train psychiatrists and support their research. Subcommittees of the House and Senate issued regular reports on the number of Americans who suffered from mental ailments, and they joined presidential commissions, federal committees, and the Public Health Service in decrying the "personnel shortage" in mental health.[3]

One after another, the large foundations responded. The Rockefeller and Macy foundations began with modest grants during the 1940s. By the next decade the Ford Foundation was providing grants of half a million dollars to university departments, $6 million to selected research centers, and $15 million for general research in behavioral sciences. In 1953 the Social Research Foundation gave Yale University alone $6 million for research in psychiatry; and other universities with smaller grants dramatically expanded the size of their departments of psychology and psychiatry. With the help of big business, embodied in the big foundations, psychology was on its way to becoming a big business itself.[4]

The advance quickly won the support, and the dollars, of the federal government. In 1946 Congress passed a National Mental Health Act, calling for federal funds to establish a nationwide program. The resulting National Mental Health Foundation expanded slowly, but by the 1950s, when President Eisenhower called on Congress to spend millions for research and signed the bill to permit federal grants for research and training in state institutions, it was disbursing amounts of up to $16 million per college for training mental health workers, conducting research, and expanding services.[5]

Certainly the country had not become the psychiatrist's utopia. As late as 1954, only 2 percent of medical research funds were available for the study of mental illness. The treatment of mental patients in state and private hospitals was still so disgraceful that the F.B.I. infiltrated the state institutions to gather evidence for criminal charges. The new president of the American Medical Association declared that the handling of mental patients was "a national disgrace." But even the complaints, with the attendant publicity, pressed home the new importance of psychiatry and psychology, and when in 1959 Blue Cross Health Insurance extended its benefits to include medical care for psychiatric conditions, it was clear that the old crusaders for mental hygiene had won their battle.[6]

The foundations, the universities, and the government had joined in a chorus commanding the psychologists and psychiatrists to be fruitful and multiply. And that they did. In 1940 there had been 3,000 members of the American Psychological Association; by 1957, there were 16,000, working alongside more than 9,000 psychiatrists. *Life* magazine reported in that year that the country had "more psychologists and psychiatrists, engaged in more types of inquiry and activity, than all the rest of the world together." In the entire world, moreover, there were only 1,400 psychoanalysts, and half of them were native-born Americans. Sigmund Freud's disciple and biographer Ernest Jones made a pilgrimage to this new Mecca in 1956, and he announced that in psychoanalytic work, too, the United States led the world.[7]

In growing numbers, Americans began to seek psychological counsel. The postwar period saw a flood of popular counselors, hypnotists, specialists in human relations, tutors in relaxation, experts in positive thought, truth healers, and "metaphysical" therapists. The journalist Lee Steiner, in an effort to discover where people "took their troubles" in 1945, found America awash with healers pushing one or another form of popular psychology. But

Steiner also found an expanding number of therapists who used established techniques of psychotherapy, and in 1947 the American Psychological Association felt it necessary to offer universities a detailed training program for clinicians. By 1951, Carl Rogers could claim that "professional interest in psychotherapy" was "in all likelihood the most rapidly growing area in the social sciences today." Rogers marveled at the change since 1940, when only a handful of psychologists had much interest in therapy; in 1951, nearly 20 percent of the members of the American Psychological Association offered psychotherapy.[8]

Americans seemed eager to hear psychological wisdom on every topic, and the new band of experts was ready to offer it. They became the interpreters of the society, scurrying from one big issue to another, and the newspapers faithfully reported their messages of hope and doom. Venturesome doctors began to provide social criticism, observing that the defense economy undermined "emotional security," or that the persistent optimism in the nation signaled "the absence of mental health," or that American society, above all others, was adept at "driving people nuts," or that the entire world was neurotic and in need of a new scientific cure. They also offered political and social analysis, claiming that political partisanship reflected personal unhappiness, or that white racists were mentally ill, or that psychiatry could remove the causes of war. They ventured into aesthetic criticism as well: One psychiatrist suggested that dissonance in the current music revealed a "universal neurosis" sweeping through the world. By 1956 the critic Alfred Kazin was complaining, with ample justice, that Americans had fallen prey to an "increasing tendency to think that *all* problems are psychological."[9]

The new psychological interests quickly infiltrated the institutions of popular culture. It did not take Hollywood long to discover the newly ascendant psychiatrist, or for screen directors to make their own explorations into the recesses of the psyche. The wartime fascination with the subject found initial expression in such films as *The Lodger*

(1943) and *Spellbound* (1944), which offered psychological interpretations and dream sequences that probed at unconscious motives. *Spellbound* featured not one but two psychiatrists, one of whom brought comfort and healing to the other. In other pictures—like *Lost Weekend* (1945) and *Snake Pit* (1948)—the film makers turned their full attention to the treatment of mental illness. As early as 1945, *Hollywood Quarterly* was publishing periodic articles on the screen's "discovery" of psychiatry, and by 1947 the industry was producing more than twenty films a year defined by the Motion Picture Association as "psychological" in story line. During the next decade, the definition was applied to at least 10 percent of the movies distributed each year. During the 1950s, the stage also fell into line: There were psychiatrists in the cast of characters of at least five successful Broadway plays in 1957. Critics complained that some of the new psychological films were "horrendous," and psychiatrists worried about their inaccuracy, but on the whole, the film writers portrayed psychiatrists as decent and competent people—neither villains nor troubled eccentrics, but experts in a difficult enterprise.[10]

The book buyers shared the tastes of the moviegoers. The publication in 1946 of Mary Jane Ward's novel *The Snake Pit*, which preceded the film by two years and became a best seller with about 600,000 purchasers, started the trend for novels about psychiatric problems. When Lucy Freeman told the story of her psychoanalysis in her *Fight Against Fears*, curious readers bought over 335,000 copies, and many returned to buy her *Hope for the Troubled*. There were some surprises: During the fifties the Modern Library edition of *The Basic Writings of Sigmund Freud* sold over 250,000 copies. But psychological self-help books, unsurprisingly, accounted for most sales. In 1948 Dale Carnegie's *How to Stop Worrying and Start Living* hit the best-seller lists. Invariably the staples of popular psychology were the manuals of inspirational self-help which reappeared each year with advice and exhortation for the multitudes who aspired to "live 365 days a year" or find "release from nervous tension," or learn the "magic of believing." Repetitive, often banal, frequently adorning common-sense maxims with pretentious jargon, these handbooks for the discontented were the secular prayer-books of a therapeutic era.[11]

Psychology, like God, seemed omnipresent, if not omnipotent. Parents sought psychological counsel from best-sellers on child care; teachers learned to recognize the covert meanings of drawings, essays, and polite exchanges; popular magazines—*Journal of Living, Your Personality, Your Life*—offered psychological wisdom for twenty-five cents; nine out of ten major American newspapers carried at least one column of psychological advice; and some apartment complexes on the West Coast included psychological assistance for tenants in their rental fee. In the United States, announced *Life* magazine in 1957, "This is the age of psychology."[12]

One journalist concluded that the psychological preoccupation of the culture had made for a change "comparable in the magnitude of its effect to the original American revolution." Alfred Kazin declared that it was the "greatest revolution of all." Such claims were somewhat overwrought, but assuredly, the pop psychology altered some of the great institutions of the society, if only for a time. The religious revival of the 1950s, for example, was in part a consequence of a successful reinterpretation of religion as "God's psychiatry." The popularizers of the new piety hailed the psychological benefits of faith and invited the faithless to regain their composure in a cult of reassurance. "Whatever aids mankind in its quest for self-fulfillment," wrote Rabbi Joshua Loth Liebman in *Peace of Mind* (1946), "is a new revelation of God's working in history."[13]

Liebman's joining of psychology and liberal religion was, on the whole, a sober and restrained presentation of the accepted psychological wisdom, but by 1952 such sobriety was giving way to exaggerated optimism about the efficacy of psychological techniques and the equation of homely self-help formulas with Christian doctrines. Norman Vincent Peale's *Power of Positive Thinking* (1952) blended traditional Christian language with the old nineteenth-century tradition of New Thought. Peale drew on both the apostle Paul and Ralph Waldo Trine; on both Jesus and William James. His central message, which reflected the tone of much of the religious revival, was that "applied Christianity" consisted of the mastery of mental techniques that would assure health, energy, and success. He recommended all the formulas of suggestion and autosuggestion that had appeared in the old Emmanuel Movement—mental relaxation, repetition of positive thoughts, envisioning of success—and made them seem easy to master by summarizing them in five-point rules and ten-point worry-breaking techniques. A slogan adopted by the New York Protestant Council—See What God Can Do for You—summed up both the gospel of Peale and the message of the religious revival.[14]

The mainline postwar pastoral theologians found the popular revival embarrassing. Like Peale, they advertised the benefits of psychology for ministry, but they hated to be lumped with the positive thinkers. In 1957 the journal *Pastoral Psychology* published the lament that "whole segments of liberal religion have so reformulated themselves as to represent an integration of a cheapened psychiatry with a smooth, facile, surface religion." Wayne Oates of Southern Baptist Theological Seminary summarized the complaints about the "cult of reassurance." The positive thinkers, he said, treated personality as a reflex mechanism subject to prudential ethics and wishful voluntarism; they ignored the self's internal contradictions; they overlooked the necessity for people to accept their limitations; and they conceived of religion merely as a crutch to be used for narrowly personal benefits. Seward Hiltner acknowledged that the mental techniques might "work" for a time, but he believed them to be manipulative and thought that they impeded genuine growth.[15]

Yet the combination of pop psychology and religious revival clearly helped to stimulate the postwar interest in pastoral care, and both trends reflected the same social conditions. It was evident that the small entrepreneur had finally given way to a "new" middle class of white-collar workers—managers, salaried professionals, office workers, salespeople—who labored in large bureaucratic organizations. As early as 1940 only about 20 percent of the working population had been self-employed in their own small businesses, while 25 percent held white-collar positions, primarily in large corporations or bureaucracies. One percent of all the firms in the country had provided employment for more than half the people working in business. By 1956, white-collar occupations engaged more than half the population.[16]

As a result, increasing numbers of Americans discovered that their economic success and social standing required "a shift from skills with things to skills with persons." Working as members of staffs, faculties, committees, and management teams, they needed to be adept at handling people and manipulating abstract symbols. Their task was to maintain the morale and high motivation of people who worked under them, while adapting themselves to the expectations of superiors who valued a "well-rounded personality." In 1951, C. Wright Mills described the new economy in *White Collar*, a depiction of the "new universe of management and manipulation," populated by salaried specialists and secretaries, junior partners and entry clerks, middle managers and county agents, salespeople and social workers, laboratory assistants and bureaucrats, and thousands of others who labored in "new hierarchical organizations of educated skill and service" and worried about their standing in the "personality market." "By their mass way of life," Mills argued, "they have transformed the tang and feel of the American experience."[17]

Such an economy could not have been better designed to stimulate interest in the nuances of "personal relations," and the nation's social institutions promptly responded. The U. S. Office of Education initiated in 1946 a Life Adjustment Movement which encouraged teachers in the public schools to nurture their pupils' ability to work with others. Large corporations began to value good scores on "personality tests" as much as experience or intellectual ability. The housing industry, revolutionized when William J. Levitt brought mass-production techniques to house building, advertised the new suburbs (which increased by over 50 percent during the 1950s) as nurseries of congeniality and "belonging." Churches presented themselves as preservers of the family or as havens of friendliness. In the corporate society, observed David Riesman, social competence was becoming more important than technical skill, cooperation more rewarding than competition, and adjustment more esteemed than autonomy.[18]

The mainline pastoral theologians were uneasy with the new cultural ethos, but they also flourished within it. The interest in personal relations and popular psychology created such expectations of the minister's work that "pastoral psychology" seemed suddenly very relevant. Seward Hiltner recognized that "the peculiarly psychological intellectual climate" was a "mode of thinking . . . unique to our time." Unless modern men and women could realize that the psychological language could "also be a theological language," he said, they would be disposed to lose interest in theology and in the church. By implication, unless the minister learned more about human relations and pastoral counseling, the troubled souls within the congregation would look elsewhere. The postwar pastoral theologians were confident that they could find a solution to both problems.[19]

The Renaissance of Pastoral Psychology

About 8,000 chaplains had marched off to the Second World War, and when they arrived, they discovered that servicemen and women wanted to talk more than they wanted to listen. A large part of chaplaincy was counseling. But all the listening achieved mixed results. The common military experience helped to change some popular stereotypes of the minister, but when the service people began to talk to the chaplains, something often

269

seemed awry. A study of veterans after the war revealed that their complaints about the wartime clergy returned almost invariably to one issue: The chaplains too frequently lacked the skills appropriate to the cure of souls. And the chaplains, sensing the same lack, flocked into seminars on counseling throughout the war. Close to 8,000 attended the Army Chaplain's School at Harvard, which by 1944 had established a curriculum in pastoral care. When the war ended, they sought still further instruction as they returned to their parishes. A commission on the ministry sponsored by the New York Academy of Sciences during the 1950s concluded that the experience of the chaplains had helped to make pastoral counseling a "special part" of the work of the minister in postwar America.[20]

They returned to a prosperous society that could well afford to offer them—and other ministers—ample opportunities for learning. In 1945 the gross national product of goods and services in the United States was $215 billion—well over twice the prewar total. The change was staggering. There was virtually no unemployment, and consumers were buying cars and houses, filling restaurants, taking vacations, creating an expense-account society, and moving to the suburbs. As individuals, the clergy failed to profit much by the new affluence. Their average salary of $2,412 in 1949 was only slightly higher than the salary of factory workers, locating them in the lower third of the labor force. But the affluence opened a new world of opportunity for ministers who sought professional self-improvement. The shift in the economy did not dictate any particular style of pastoral care, but it did ensure that pastoral theologians now possessed the resources and the institutions to popularize whatever methods appealed to them.[21]

The movement to improve pastoral care became a veritable crusade, and the economy was expansive enough to permit some impressive victories. In 1939 few theological schools had even bothered to teach counseling courses that would introduce students to the newest psychological theories. By the 1950s, almost all of them did, over 80 percent were offering additional courses in psychology, and 80 percent could list at least one psychologist on their faculty. When H. Richard Niebuhr of Yale conducted a lengthy investigation of theological education in 1955, he concluded with some alarm that the study of pastoral care and counseling within the Protestant seminaries was threatening to develop a separate existence as a speciously complete form of ministerial training. Within Roman Catholic seminaries, as well, there was a "flurry of activity" directed toward training in counseling methods. And by the mid-1950s at least seven universities, including the University of Chicago, had established advanced graduate programs in personality and theology, pastoral psychology, pastoral counseling, or pastoral theology. The foundations and the government provided financial help. The National Mental Health Institute gave Harvard, Yeshiva, and Loyola universities substantial grants in 1956 to develop curriculum for theological students; the Old Dominion foundation backed the new program in psychiatry and religion at Union Theological Seminary; the Lilly Endowment provided support for the program at the University of Chicago. In a relatively brief period, therefore, pastoral theologians had secured their place in academia.[22]

Clinical educators, often competing with the seminaries, refused to lag behind. By the end of the 1950s they had established 117 regular centers for clinical pastoral education, formed alliances with more than 40 theological schools to offer clinical experiences for students, and cemented ties to such medical centers as the Washington School of Psychiatry and the William Alanson White Institute in New York. An interdenominational commission on the ministry announced in 1955 that about 4,000 Protestant clergy had already been trained in clinical centers, and the president of Union Theological Seminary, Henry P. Van Dusen, described the clinical movement as one of the most important developments "in religious circles during the past half-century." The clinical educators received support not only from foundations but also from the National Council of Churches, which in 1954 began to provide scholarship aid for ministers who wanted the training. Once the rebellious outsiders of theological education, clinical educators were well on their way to a prominent position in an affluent church.[23]

The expansion of the clinical movement helped bring about a gradual reconciliation between the Boston and the New York supervisors. During the 1930s, the executive secretary of the Council for Clinical Training, Seward Hiltner, found it almost necessary to defy the director, Helen Flanders Dunbar, merely to exchange notes with leaders in the Boston group. Her response to his independence was to replace him with someone else. But by the end of the war the kind of interchange that Hiltner had attempted became a regular feature of clinical education. By the 1960s the two traditions were moving toward organizational unity.[24]

The seminary courses and clinical centers were not able to meet the demand for training in pastoral counseling. By the mid-1950s at least 35 institutes and seminars—such as Reuel Howe's Institute for Advanced Pastoral Studies, located in a suburb of Detroit, and Thomas Klink's Program in Religion and Psychiatry at the Menninger Clinic in Kansas—met regularly to propagate the new methods. By 1956 the National Council of Churches had established a Department of Pastoral Services, and a broad grouping of religious leaders and psychiatrists had founded the National Academy of Religion and Mental Health. And with the inception of such periodic meetings as the Institute on Mental Hygiene for Seventh Day Adventist clergy in Ohio, it was manifestly clear that the preoccupation with counseling methods was to reach even Protestants who earlier had been indifferent or hostile.[25]

Some of the ministers who were trained in the new methods—and some of their teachers—began to form centers for pastoral care outside the traditional parishes. The establishment in 1937 of the American Foundation for Religion and Psychiatry in New York, which created a pastoral counseling center connected to the Marble

Collegiate Church, began a movement that mushroomed after the war. By the end of the 1950s there were at least 84 Protestant counseling centers staffed by ministers, psychiatrists, and social workers, and they promoted counseling on a new and vast scale. One single center at Boston University conducted 11,000 conversations in one year.[26]

Pastoral counseling "specialists" who chose not to work in one of the new centers, moreover, began to find openings in hospitals and other institutions. In 1940 only a handful of Protestant hospitals employed full-time chaplains; there was no regular chaplaincy in Veterans Administration hospitals; no state mental hospital had a plan for including chaplains on its staff. By the 1950s, almost 500 full-time chaplains were serving in general hospitals; at least 200 more worked in mental hospitals; and in the Veterans Administration alone there were 241 clergy as chaplains. Ministers drawn to counseling now had an opportunity to work in an expanding range of institutions—including prisons, reform schools, and other agencies—which required mainly some special skill in private relationships.[27]

The pastoral theologians began to distinguish pastoral counseling, therefore, as a special form of pastoral care. By *pastoral care*, they were referring to the broader range of pastoral duties; by *pastoral counseling*, they had in mind a more specific actiyity resting on knowledge of the psychotherapeutic traditions. They tried to avoid a one-sided preoccupation with counseling, but that was hard to do. Most pastors who followed their writing closely made it clear that counseling was their strongest interest. It might have been true, as Russell Dicks said in 1950, that 90 percent of the clergy were doing "little effective pastoral work or personal counseling of any kind," but an increasing number of ministers at least were under the impression that their parishioners were assigning them new responsibilities as counselors. A study by Samuel Blizzard at Princeton revealed that the clergy believed themselves to be devoting 175 million hours a year to pastoral counseling. That figure, which was quite unbelievable, served at least as a sketch of pastoral self-consciousness in an age of psychology. And there were indications that the public did turn with an increasing frequency to the clergy as counselors. A survey conducted during the 1950s by the National Institute of Mental Health showed that 42 percent of all people who sought help for emotional problems turned first to their ministers. "A good minister cannot now escape personal counseling," wrote Harry Emerson Fosdick in 1960. "It is in the air." Indeed it was. The ethicist Gibson Winter at the University of Chicago complained that ministers were coming to think of counseling as "*the* pastoral care of the Church," even though they might lack the time to do much of it. "The atypical case," Winter charged, "is becoming the norm of the Church's pastoral function."[28]

The proliferation of courses, centers, institutes, and chaplaincies both signaled and shaped a changing sensitivity among a large contingent of American ministers. The institutional strength of the pastoral counseling movement, undergirded by the expanding economy, intensified the interest in books and articles on pastoral care and counsel. And the size of the market began to alter the product. Riding the economic crest, the pastoral writers produced a veritable flood of books, articles, and journals. In 1947 the clinical educators founded a *Journal of Pastoral Care* and a *Journal of Clinical Pastoral Work*. By 1950 an even larger readership seemed ready for the periodical *Pastoral Psychology*, which in the opinion of its first editor evoked an "overwhelming response" from "every area of the country" and soon attracted 16,000 subscribers, of whom about 14,000 were ministers. Russell Dicks claimed that there was more being published in the field of pastoral care in one month than there had been in an entire year during the 1920s or 1930s. Indeed, he said, the pastoral theologians were, by 1950, producing more in any one year than had been written on the topic during the entire first quarter of the twentieth century.[29]

Four pastoral theologians assumed a position of intellectual leadership in the postwar renaissance. Seward Hiltner, a Presbyterian minister who had been associated with the Federal Council of Churches before joining the faculty of the University of Chicago, drew on social and cultural anthropology in preparing his *Pastoral Counseling* (1949). Carroll A. Wise, a professor of pastoral psychology and counseling at Methodist Garrett Biblical Institute, based his *Pastoral Counseling: Its Theory and Practice* (1951) on personalist theology, dynamic psychology, and Rogerian theories of counseling. In *The Christian Pastor* (1951), Wayne Oates, a professor of pastoral care and the psychology of religion at Southern Baptist Theological Seminary, attempted to combine traditional Protestant language with a theory of "psychosocial role behavior" taken from the social sciences. And Paul Johnson, a Methodist professor of psychology at Boston University, drew on Rogerian methods, interpersonal psychiatry, and personalist theology for his *Psychology of Pastoral Care* (1953).

It could hardly be said that four writers monopolized the topic. The expanded institutions provided work for a host of pastoral writers who had a lot they wanted to say. They wrote on the psychology of religion, the psychology of aging, and the psychology of small groups; alcoholism and delinquency; human development and human crisis; death and grief; medical work and chaplaincy; marriage, the family, and sexuality; illness and health; theology and psychoanalysis; prisons and reform schools; social ethics and social policy. The pastoral journals were devoting entire issues to the stages of grief, to aging, and to middle-age crises during the 1940s and 1950s—long before such issues became fashionable issues in the churches. Hardly a topic escaped the notice of some devotee of religion and psychology.

It seems foolhardy to isolate one theme woven through the mass of pastoral writings. No single issue encompassed everything. But if any topic recurred consistently, as either an explicit issue or an implicit criterion, it was the theme of self-realization. It is that topic which uncovers the presuppositions—and the problems—in the postwar pastoral theology movement.

The Burden of Social Convention

Postwar pastoral theologians looked for guidance not only to Carl Rogers, but to Freud and such revisionist Freudian analysts as Erich Fromm, Karen Horney, and Harry Stack Sullivan. Following the lead of the neo-Freudians, they adopted, explicitly or implicitly, an ethic of self-realization which defined *growth* as the primary ethical good. Such a position had characterized the pastoral theology tradition ever since the 1920s, but the rise of European and Asian dictators and American demagogues (like Senator Joseph McCarthy), and the complexities of mass culture, had established a new setting for a self-realizationist ethic.

The older theorists had located self-fulfillment within a set of trustworthy religious, civic, educational, and political institutions which provided directions and standards. They also had assumed that the deepest form of self-realization would result in an enhanced capacity for service within such institutions. But the new theorists of self-realization could trust neither social conventions nor the current social institutions, which they viewed largely as alien impositions on selfhood. They spoke still of "social usefulness" and service as the goal of self-fulfillment; they were by no means the proponents of a narrow hedonism or self-indulgence. But they were wary of becoming "tools of the culture" by imposing social mores on people. They tended to envision self-realization, therefore, as a process that stood in tension with both social conventions and the mass social structures of American society.[30]

The distrust of social conventions reflected the "revolt against moralism," a movement in Christian ethics that had begun in the 1930s and gradually permeated the theological schools. Directed against theological liberals who had often defined the Christian faith as commitment

276

to high ethical ideals, the new ethic called for free
obedience to a free God whose command could not be
encapsulated within any "eternal principles." The distrust
of social institutions reflected the critique of "mass
society," a European intellectual movement that had
emerged in the 1930s and gradually penetrated American
thought after the war. Only in the light of those two
intellectual movements—the revolt against moralism and
the critique of mass culture—can one understand the vast
influence of Carl Rogers in American pastoral care.

An early omen of the new emphasis on Christian freedom
appeared in 1923 with the first American translation of
selections from the writings of the nineteenth-century
Danish theologian Sören Kierkegaard. By the mid-1940s,
the translations of Kierkegaard's works were appearing at
the rate of three and four a year, each inveighing against
conventional and legalistic religion. Kierkegaard claimed
that the leap of faith might well require a break with the
ethical norm; that the dizziness of freedom was so
overwhelming that it produced anxiety; but that only
narrow-minded philistines would attempt to escape
freedom by trying "to be like the others, to become an
imitation, a cipher in the crowd." Americans found in
Kierkegaard an insistence that "only the exercise of
freedom, in the face of life's contradictions," can enable
one to "discover" oneself. Isolation, anxiety, the unifying
of the personality, self-affirmation, and freedom—all this
made it seem as though Kierkegaard had "anticipate[d]
psychotherapy."[31]

The revolt against legalism intensified during the 1930s.
Hiltner, writing later in *Pastoral Psychology*, observed that
Christian ethical thought had been in a ferment ever since
1932. In that year Reinhold Niebuhr's *Moral Man and
Immoral Society* pointed out the ambiguity of ethical
judgments about social policies, and Emil Brunner's
Divine Imperative asserted that the content of Christian
ethics must vary with varying circumstances lest the
Christian become entrapped with legalism. For Brunner, a
theologian at the University of Zürich, legalism (the

attempt to be a good person by scrupulous adherence to universal ethical principles) was "the worst kind of corruption," a form of "un-freedom" rooted in self-preoccupation, a false sense of autonomy, and commitment to abstractions rather than to persons. The Christian, he thought, was to remain open to the unpredictable command of God, which was always a command to love, but the content of that love could vary within different settings.[32]

By the mid-1950s, American theological students were being increasingly exposed to the writings of the European neo-orthodox theologians who had already joined full force in the crusade against a legalistic ethic. In his study of *Jesus and the Word*, translated into English in 1934, Rudolf Bultmann at Marburg had written that Jesus' insistence on radical obedience to God freed men and women from the endless and useless task of searching for commands and prohibitions, freed them from cultural values and ideals, freed them from general ethical principles, freed them even from the ideal of self-realization, and by wholly separating obedience from "legalism," threw them back on their own judgment, requiring only that they be totally obedient within each new situation. By 1951 Bultmann was touring American theological schools from Boston to Atlanta, from New Haven to Chicago, insisting that to be truly free was to be obediently open to "the unknown future that God will give." Such freedom, he added, was a freedom to be oneself.[33]

The English translation of Dietrich Bonhoeffer's *Prisoner of God*—his letters and papers from prison—appeared in 1953 and continued the onslaught against a legalistic moralism. "It is easier by far," Bonhoeffer wrote, "to act on abstract principle than from concrete responsibility." Free responsibility depended on a God who demanded bold action as the free response of faith, with the promise of forgiveness to those who might sin in the process. And in his *Ethics*, which was published in English in 1955, he expanded the message: Christ did not propound ethical abstractions and principles. God "command[ed] freedom"

278

to men and women who, rather than being "fettered by principles" were to be formed in the likeness of the incarnate, crucified, and risen One.[34]

Even Karl Barth, whom many Americans first mistakenly described as the leader of a retreat into an older orthodoxy, announced in his vast *Church Dogmatics* that the era of legalism was dead: The Christian was to remain open to God's unpredictable command in each concrete situation. The first volume appeared in English in 1936, but not until 1957 did Barth's discussion of ethics reach the broad mainstream of American theological students and pastoral theologians. And a strange discussion it seemed to be: "The grace of God," said Barth, "protests against all man-made ethics as such." He seemed almost unwilling to answer the recurring question, What are we to do? We are to do, he would say, simply whatever corresponds to the grace given us in Jesus Christ. We are to be free. We are to obey a command that is a permission, a command that orders us to be free and sets us free, a command to which we are to respond anew in each "specific situation" without relying on any universally valid rules. We are to live as men and women "to whom grace has come."[35]

By the 1950s, the mainline American theological schools were becoming outposts in a battle against "absolute moral laws." As early as 1941 Paul Tillich had told his students at Union Seminary in New York that Christian love was "above law." Love was an unconditional demand, to be sure, but it also was a power that should break through all conditional demands. Four years later Tillich published his essay on the "transmoral conscience"—the conscience that does not make its judgment in obedience to a "moral law" but in accord with its participation in a realm of free grace. In 1953 Paul Lehmann, the professor of applied Christianity at Princeton Seminary, claimed that even Emil Brunner had fallen into legalism. By declaring that "law" revealed God's command, Lehmann said, Brunner had unwittingly espoused an ethic "of obligation rather than of free response." Lehmann intended to extend and purify Brunner's insight by insisting that an ethic within the Christian fellowship always must be "concrete and contextual." Christians sought no absolute and eternal principles; they tried instead to remain open to the activity of a God who willed forgiveness, justice, and reconciliation, but who also "command[ed] freedom" to the community of men and women who sought to discern the varying meanings of forgiveness, justice, and reconciliation in shifting circumstances. Joseph Sittler at the University of Chicago added that to speak of a law of love was to contradict the nature of love. The words of Jesus, he said, were "non-legal," inexhaustible, principle-transcending," and instead of affirming a Christian ethical "system," Sittler preferred to speak of an uncalculated Christian ethical "style" that would witness in "mad obedience" to God's demand and gift. It is no wonder that by 1959 Joseph Fletcher was lecturing about the "new look" in Christian ethics.[36]

Most of the pastoral theologians accepted the new look. They saw themselves as the critics of an authoritarian Church, the opponents of repressive religious moralism, the enemies of dogmatism. They found the ethicists to be their allies in an effort to defend the claims of moral autonomy against the moralistic pretensions of a static cultural religion. "Most of the leading Protestant and Jewish theologians," wrote Hiltner in 1950, "are as anti-moralistic or anti-legalistic as any psychoanalyst, and equally cognizant that such a view runs against the mores of American society."[37]

The *Journal of Clinical Pastoral Work* carried regular broadsides against moralism and advertised the anti-legalistic intentions of clinical pastoral education. "We look at the student's attitudes," wrote Ernest Bruder, a chaplain at St. Elizabeth's Hospital in Washington, D.C., and help the student learn to understand rather than condemn. Bruder sought the "spiritual emancipation of the individual—be it from psychological or religious dogmas, the coercion of home or supervisors." He believed that persons should be free—and be freeing of others—from moral authoritarianism and institutional impositions.[38]

Seward Hiltner began as early as 1945 to explore what he called "the theology of conscience." Hiltner accepted the Freudian notion of the superego as an unconscious inheritance from childhood—activated by fear, antagonistic to "the real needs" of the person, and devoted unceasingly to the repression of instinctual strivings. He compared the idea of the superego to the Christian doctrine of bondage to the Law. Appealing to Tillich's "transmoral conscience," Hiltner argued that psychotherapy could well be considered analogous to a process of repentance in which the sinner directly confronted the "law-conscience," objectified it, and transcended it through a relationship that would produce a more rational and relevant ethical concern.[39]

When Hiltner published his text on *Pastoral Counseling*, he clearly intended to counter the "moralizing" which had marked many pastoral conversations. Hence he distinguished sharply between moral clarification and moral coercion in pastoral care. "It is tempting to speculate," he wrote, "why we pastors have such a predilection for moral judgment even when it clearly defeats our larger purposes." Thereupon he speculated whether perhaps the clergy often felt obliged to meet the unconscious expectations of church members who viewed them as caretakers of morality; or perhaps they took so seriously their symbolic position as moral guides that they felt vaguely uncomfortable in suspending moral judgments. But the result, he concluded, was rarely happy: "In counseling, moral judgments in place of understanding and clarification are especially likely to be disastrous."[40]

Hiltner made it clear in *The Counselor in Counseling* (1950) that he did not intend for ministers to hide their ethical convictions, "provided they [were] not of the legalistic variety." He encouraged them to feel free to "define the difference" between their views and the views of someone seeking counsel. Oates took a similar position: He considered legalism to be idolatrous; the "unforgiving legalist" had surrendered freedom to an idol. But Oates also believed that the Christian pastor frankly acknowledged that "ethical values make a difference in the mental health of the person," so though he preferred a "permissive" style in counseling, Oates also permitted an open exchange of ethical opinions between pastor and parishioner.[41]

When Carroll Wise published *Pastoral Counseling* in 1951, however, he seemed wary of pastoral efforts to "define the difference" or exchange ethical opinions with persons whom they counseled. Wise, a graduate of Boston University's School of Theology, had served as a counselor for the YMCA and taught at Boston before moving first to Ohio and then to the staff of the Hennepin Avenue Methodist Church in Minneapolis, where he had engaged in full-time pastoral counseling. He then became the pastoral theologian at Garrett Bible Institute. A feisty, spirited man, he delighted in debate with theologians whose work he considered too "abstract." Dismayed by the "compulsive legalism" in the church, he hoped that pastors would not view counseling as another occasion "to change behavior." Its purpose was to form a relationship which conveyed acceptance and understanding, not "approval or disapproval." "As counselors," he wrote later, "our chief goal is not to change a person's values," but to value persons.[42]

Paul Johnson agreed with Wise. A gentle Methodist liberal who had been attracted to the personalist theology of the Boston tradition, Johnson taught for many years at Boston University School of Theology. In his *Psychology of Pastoral Care* he urged ministers to "respect a person as worth more than the mistakes he has made" and to forego moralistic judgments in counseling. Indeed, Johnson seemed at times to preclude any judgments at all: "To the extent that we object to another person's behavior and want to change him, we are rejecting him as unworthy." The differences among the mainline pastoral theologians, however, were more of nuance than of substance. In the struggle against a legalistic ethic, they were united.[43]

The new look in ethics coincided with a criticism of mass culture which convinced some of the pastoral writers, at least, that the "bureaucratic" institutions of the postwar capitalist society had imposed coercive and alien expectations. They derived many of their social opinions from such writers as Erich Fromm, whose *Escape from Freedom* (1941) described the antagonism between the aims of modern society and the full development of persons, and whose *Man for Himself* (1947) described the emergence within the new capitalism of a distinctive form of human character: a "marketing" orientation that compelled men and women to "sell" their personalities in a social market which rewarded charmers and back-slappers. They read the works of Karen Horney, whose *Neurotic Personality of Our Time* (1937) described modern Western culture as competitive and isolating, and those of Harry Stack Sullivan, whose *Conceptions of Modern Psychiatry* (1947) depicted an insuperable tension between the current social order and the mental health of the people who lived in it.

Such views aroused widespread attention in America in the 1950s. At the beginning of the decade, David Riesman expanded Fromm's image of the commercial personality in an influential essay titled *The Lonely Crowd*, in which he argued that Americans were becoming increasingly "other-directed," seeking to find their source of direction from the cues and signals of other people. He contrasted them to the "inner-directed" Americans of the nineteenth century, who, in childhood, had internalized the values of their parents and then had maintained them as if balanced by an inner psychological gyroscope, despite the tug of alternative values. A culture that had once exalted strength of character, he wrote, now elevated the pleasing personality. Riesman's book encountered some stiff criticism, but it reached a wide audience, and other authors seemed to recognize the same trends. In 1956 William Whyte, Jr., published *The Organization Man*, a criticism of the "bureaucratic ethic" of social adjustment that pervaded the establishments where Americans worked, the schools where they learned, the suburbs where they lived, and the churches where they worshiped. The new patterns of work and leisure in the society, Whyte

283

argued, had made idols of the virtues of "togetherness" and "belonging."[44]

But the critic of mass culture who influenced the pastoral theologians most deeply was Erich Fromm, a refugee from Germany who combined a modified theory of psychoanalysis with a critique of capitalist economics that had been sharpened during his work in the Institute for Social Research at the University of Frankfurt. His particular blending of psychology and sociology evoked the wrath of his former colleagues in Frankfurt, but some American pastoral writers found him appealing because he offered reassurance that the religious quest was "basic" to human nature, while at the same time criticizing authoritarian religion; and he reasserted the claims of the rational conscience at the same time he was deploring authoritarian ethics. When *Pastoral Psychology* devoted most of a 1955 issue to his work, the journal's editor, Seward Hiltner, pinpointed the theme that ensured Erich Fromm's popularity in the pastoral theology movement. In social theory, Hiltner wrote, "Fromm's devil is 'authoritarianism.'"[45]

Fromm's distaste for authoritarian structures reflected his revision of Freudian psychoanalytic theory. Unlike Freud, who explained behavior almost entirely as the expression of intrapsychic drives, Fromm believed that human nature was, in the main, a "cultural product." A combination of inner needs and external conditions— primarily economic—formed in each person a "character structure." What puzzled Fromm, who had a firsthand knowledge of Nazi Germany, was that the "character structure" of so many people seemingly impelled them to surrender their freedom.[46]

Fromm's solution to the puzzle, as outlined in his first popular American publication *Escape from Freedom*, was to note the ambiguity of autonomy. To become an individual in any era, but especially in the present era, was to realize one's powers and yet to recognize one's insecurity. The social changes of the late medieval and

Renaissance periods—movements toward guilds, monopolies, and a nascent competitive capitalism—had exalted "individuals" while also accentuating their sense of isolation. In the modern capitalist economy, the ambiguity of autonomy had become, for many people, simply unbearable. The massive organizations were intrinsically isolating and alienating, and the yearning to overcome the isolation overwhelmed the desire to be free. The result was a profound, often unconscious readiness to conform to social expectations, to submerge individuality in order to escape the loneliness of freedom.[47]

By 1947 Fromm had developed a typology of character in the modern world as he saw it. In their styles of relating to others, the people tended to be "receptive" (dependent on outside sources of support and reward), or "exploitative" (determined to take what they wanted), or "hoarding" (stingy with their goods and their feelings), or "marketing" (eager to sell themselves in a personality market). Such "nonproductive orientations" were destructive adaptations to the culture, overwhelming the productive modes of accepting, taking, preserving, and exchanging that express the truly human powers. Fromm believed that the various orientations of character were usually blended in each person, but he also maintained that "the dominance of any specific orientation depends to a large extent on the peculiarity of the culture" in which the individual lived. And he was convinced that twentieth-century capitalism had been especially prone to produce receptive and marketing types—people oriented toward consumption (whether of material things or of other people) and selling (whether of their products or of their personalities). Such were the consequences of life in a world of "automaton conformity."[48]

Like Fromm, the other psychologists who influenced the pastoral counseling movement were men and women who were deeply impressed with the studies by the cultural anthropologists. They had read the books of Margaret Mead, Ruth Benedict, Edward Sapir, and John Dollard—books arguing that conceptions of the "normal" varied

285

with the culture. A psychoanalyst whose cultural studies and interpretations of psychology especially attracted the pastoral writers was a onetime colleague of Freud, Karen Horney, who had worked at the Berlin Institute for Psychoanalysis. "Of the many persons in the field of psychiatry, psychology, and psychoanalysis from whom the pastor may profitably learn," wrote Seward Hiltner in *Pastoral Psychology*, "perhaps no living person has as much to teach as Karen Horney."[49]

By the time Horney arrived in the United States in 1932, Fromm had already convinced her that cultural differences altered the form of neuroses, and her comparisons of American and European society confirmed her suspicion that the driving force in character disorders was not instinctual, as Freud had supposed, but social. Neurotic reactions grew out of disturbed human relationships in cultural settings that produced anxiety. Horney found some of the roots of anxiety in childhood experiences, but she argued in *Neurotic Personality of Our Time* that the competitiveness of Western culture also generated excessive anxiety in "practically everyone." And she outlined the typical neurotic defenses against anxiety—disproportionate cravings for affection, power, and status—that marked the modern era.[50]

A number of pastoral theologians found such social analysis convincing. It seemed to them that American society was extraordinarily competitive and that such competition distorted the growth of the individual. Wayne Oates worried about "the moralizing mechanisms of mass thinking" and feared that "the age of McCarthyism, orthodoxy hunts," and academic pendantry would encourage "unforgiving legalism" in the society. He was concerned also that both religion and psychiatry would "take conformity to the least common denominator of society" as a criterion of righteousness and health. A product of a South Carolina mill town, Oates always sustained a certain sympathy with southern populism. After a clash with the supervisors in the Council for Clinical Training who refused to "accredit" him in their organization, he founded his own clinical program at Kentucky State Hospital in Danville and forged links with Southern Baptist Theological Seminary. He felt that even the pastoral care movement had cast its lot too quickly with the urban middle class, neglecting rural folk and the lower classes. His determined insistence on retaining the language of biblical tradition in pastoral care reflected his sense of identification with a southern rural culture that did not entirely fit in with the broader competitive mass society.[51]

Both Oates and Seward Hiltner were quite taken with Erich Fromm's criticisms of Western society. Hiltner wrote a doctoral dissertation at the University of Chicago that dealt at length with Fromm. He considered Fromm's *Escape from Freedom* a "brilliant" book, and he and Fromm met often for discussion. Hence in 1959 Hiltner announced in his *Christian Shepherd* that the critics of mass society had uncovered "the dominant characterological trend of our time." His earlier interpretation of the Kinsey Reports on sexual behavior had confirmed his conviction that "cultural and social pressures and influences" constituted "the most weighty influence" in determining how men and women thought and felt about most matters. Hiltner therefore came to believe that the class structure and social pressures of American society pushed toward a subtle kind of conformity and that American clergy ran a peculiar risk of becoming "unwitting fosterers of the organization man."[52]

A good number of the influential pastoral theologians, then, felt a sense of unease with both the moral conventions of American society and the social institutions that enforced them. They joined in the revolt against moralism and accepted the critique of mass society. They claimed that selfhood was a product of social relationships, but they could not entirely trust either the institutions that structured those relationships or the cultural definitions of the good, the beautiful, and the true that had once nurtured and shaped the Protestant concept of character. These pastoral theologians saw the self as standing in almost inevitable tension with its society. Self-realization had become a problem.

Self-Realization

Many of the European theologians who led the revolt against moralism disliked the notion of self-realization. They criticized religious legalism not because it hindered the growth of selfhood, but because it precluded obedience to the commands of a living God as revealed in a suffering Jew. The European social psychologists like Fromm and Horney, however, opposed legalism for the sake of a self-realization rooted in obedience to the imperative of human nature. How could one then unite the two perspectives? The pastoral theologians tended to forge alliances between them: They argued that genuine obedience to God presupposed a capacity for growth in the self. As a mediator between the two worlds, nobody could surpass Paul Tillich, who declared that self-realization was the precondition of obedience to the command to love. The moral imperative was to realize one's "essential" nature as an integrated and free person, but the content of that realization was an expanding ability to love. And love brought liberation "from the bondage to absolute ethical traditions, to conventional morals, and to authorities that claim to know the right decision perhaps without having listened to the demand of the unique moment." The revolt against moralism and the quest for self-realization belonged together.[53]

Most pastoral theologians, then, believed in an ethic of self-realization, or at least implicitly accepted it. The good for which they aimed was "growth." But some of them recognized from the beginning that a self-realizationist ethic presupposed communal structures and corporate commitments which could provide at least tacit guidelines for defining what was appropriate growth and what was not. This was the issue that shaped the debates in the pastoral counseling movement well into the 1960s. To understand the enthusiasm for Carl Rogers, and yet the nagging uneasiness with Rogerian methods of counseling, even on the part of some of his advocates within the churches, one must recognize that those methods were linked to a concept of the self and society that seemed both inviting and increasingly problematic to the pastoral theologians who propagated the Rogerian gospel.

The theorists who influenced the notion of self-realization within the pastoral care movement tended to distinguish between a "real" self and a public self. Erich Fromm believed that within the "pseudo self" that each person displayed while meeting social expectations and fulfilling conventional roles, there resided a deeper self, an "original" self capable of self-realization through the spontaneous activity of the integrated personality, waiting to blossom and flourish. He envisioned the "truly human self" as being the organism's inherent tendency to actualize its potentialities. There was in everyone, he thought, an inner drive toward growth and integration, a tendency toward productive love. The task was to protect the real self against the blows of an authoritarian society in which the tyrannical authority was all the worse for being so often hidden and anonymous.[54]

Fromm's own ethical position, developed in 1947 in his popular *Man for Himself*, took the form of a "humanistic ethic" of self-realization. Virtue was the expression of one's "unique individuality," born of one's capacity to love, to affirm both oneself and other persons. Such an outflowing of human potential need not subvert rational authority, he insisted. Indeed, it would welcome and use any guidelines, as long as they were subject to "constant scrutiny and criticism." But on the basis of what authority could one criticize a false authority? Fromm's answer was utilitarian: The criterion was human welfare. And human welfare entailed nurturing the needs and potential of the real self.[55]

The "humanistic conscience," therefore, was the voice of one's "loving care" for oneself, the affirmation of one's "real interests." Fromm criticized the Calvinists and the Kantians for their depreciation of "self-love." Only those who truly loved themselves could truly love others, he maintained. And only in love for others could one realize one's own potential by finding a form of union that would preserve "one's integrity, one's individuality." That was the message of Fromm's best-selling treatise on *The Art of Loving* (1956). The spontaneous affirmation of others, whatever its additional values, was a way of preserving one's own freedom.[56]

The counterpart of a nonauthoritarian ethic would be a "humanistic religion." Fromm reasoned that since every person needed a "frame of orientation and an object of devotion," every person also needed a religion, but not an "authoritarian" religion which required obedience to some higher external power. Fromm disliked even Carl Jung's notion of religion as a surrender to the "higher power" within the unconscious levels of the self and the race. Humanistic religion entailed the exaltation of the self, not its depreciation. It spoke of God as a symbol for human powers and capacities, for a "spiritual reality which we can strive to realize in ourselves and yet can never describe or define." So interpreted, religion was a stimulus to self-realization and a source of autonomy. The tragedy of religion was that it perverted that freedom by becoming encased in "mass organizations governed by a religious bureaucracy." The glory of religion was that it served the self.[57]

Underlying Fromm's confidence in an ethic of spontaneous love was a faith that the self-actualizing powers of human nature would move naturally toward "ethical" ends. Underlying his faith in a humanistic religion was a conviction that the need for an object of devotion was rooted in the conditions of human existence. Fromm believed that there were "immutable laws inherent in human nature" that could not be violated without serious damage to the personality. Human life bore an inner telos, a goal, a purposiveness, a movement toward independence, integrity, and the ability to love. Fromm's psychology and his ethic implied an ontology, even a theology. It is no wonder that Rollo May could describe him as a "theistic humanist."[58]

Fromm's confidence in an immanent, nameless God, in fact, led him by 1955 to the belief that some radical changes in the social order, removing the conflicts between society and human nature, would lead to a "sane society." The solution was simply to "implement political democracy" in the realms of governance and economics. Paul Tillich was of the opinion that this vision was utopian— and indeed it seemed a far cry from Fromm's earlier analysis of the tension within the "character structure" that made men and women willing to surrender their freedom. But the seeds of the later optimism had been present from the beginning. The villain for Fromm had always been authoritarian social institutions, "bureaucratic" impositions on the autonomy of the self. *The Sane Society* (1955) was his testimony to the providential power of the immanent God of human potential to break through social encrustrations.[59]

Karen Horney remained more sober, but as early as 1939 she also was developing an ethic of self-realization that distinguished between a true and a public self. In *New Ways in Psychoanalysis* she wrote that "true moral problems" were involved in "every neurosis"; she soon came to believe that distorted morality was at the heart of psychological disorder. In her book on *Our Inner Conflicts* (1945), Horney argued that the most unyielding neurotic solution to anxiety was the self's creation of an "idealized image." In subsequent years the concept of self-idealization became the central theme of her work. Horney believed that children, and later adults, overwhelmed by a threatening world, unconsciously compensated for their anxiety by creating an ideal image of themselves—the "idealized self"—which gradually constituted their sense of who they were. The result was their self-imposed subjection to "the tyranny of the should." The search for glory, the effort to meet the perfectionist image, inevitably trapped them within a "pride system" which veiled a hidden self-contempt and alienation. Life became a series of hostile inward encounters, with the "actual" self living in a constant tension, torn between the tyrannical demands of the "ideal" self and the insistent efforts of the submerged "real" self to express its need for spontaneous growth.[60]

When she published *Neurosis and Human Growth* (1950), Horney acknowledged that she was proposing a "morality" in which the criteria were human growth and self-realization. She had argued for years that therapy presupposed value judgments, that therapists inevitably exposed their own values, and that the aim of psychoanalysis was to uncover moral pretenses and help patients face real moral issues. By the 1950s she was expounding an ethic grounded in the possibilities of human nature. In the struggle against the alienating power of the culture, she said, the real self could move toward autonomy, growth, and fulfillment. With the weakening of the pride system through psychotherapy, the "constructive forces" of the real self would be given an opportunity to grow. She never explained precisely why "growth" should be considered a moral criterion.[61]

The theologians sometimes complained that Horney and Fromm had lost any real "feeling for the irrational," but they did feel drawn toward an ethic of growth. In 1942 Carroll Wise, in *Religion in Illness and Health*, had included a thoroughly functional interpretation of religious symbols. The most important problem with religious beliefs, he said, was not their truth, but their function; he believed that the "central function" of religion was to develop a symbolic world-view that could aid in the "integration and growth" of the personality. Impressed by the work of Walter B. Cannon and Helen Flanders Dunbar in psychosomatic medicine, and by the psychoanalytic theory of Karl Menniger and Karen Horney, Wise contended that religious symbols offered a way for a person to express inner "meanings" and discover values and ideals. The deepest purpose of religion was the fostering of self-realization. Such a perspective informed Wise's later writings on counseling. In 1947 he wrote that the function of religion was to "produce new and deeper integration of personality," and throughout his book on *Pastoral Counseling* he assumed that the goal of the counselor was to facilitate the "growth and fulfillment of the personality."[62]

Seward Hiltner also had argued, as early as 1943 in his *Religion and Health*, that a "healthy" religion could enhance the "whole personality" by helping people integrate their lives in accord with the "worshipful reality" in the universe, transcend their egocentricity, and overcome their dependence on limited cultural values. (He believed that religion contributed to health in part by relativizing "mere cultural standards.") When Hiltner published his manual of pastoral counseling in 1949, he set his whole discussion within the context of his ethics. He began by outlining the assumptions about human nature that undergirded counseling in the United States. Some counselors assumed, he wrote, that emotional difficulties emerged out of inadequate "adjustment" to the social order. Hiltner feared that such an assumption risked subordinating persons to social conventions. Other counselors assumed that their duty was to release creative capacities. With such a view, Hiltner was sympathetic. He believed that pastoral counseling would improve to the extent that pastors recognized the practical importance of "inner release"; it should provide "the operating center of the counselor's daily work." But Hiltner felt that the notion of inner release should be set within a broader ethical vision. Certain minimal demands of the personality, he wrote, were "part of essential human nature." And those demands were "undergirded by the structure of the universe itself." Self-realization, in some form, was more than a luxury—it was a requirement imposed and supported by the very structure of things.[63]

Though Hiltner fully acknowledged "the darker aspects of the unconscious," he also emphasized the "creative dynamic forces" in the personality. He believed that people were truly eager to assert the positive and creative impulses buried within themselves and that they had an inner capacity for autonomous growth beyond the limits imposed by their pasts. By 1951, in *Self-Understanding*, he moved toward Fromm's view of the "humanistic conscience" as the voice of our "true selves," summoning us to become what we "potentially are." Like Fromm, Hiltner proposed to push aside "the obstacles in the way of human growth" in order to "permit the release of the self's most creative powers."[64]

Few pastoral theologians went as far as did Paul Johnson in praising the virtues of "growth." "The greatest thing about a person," he wrote, is the "capacity to grow and outgrow." There were, in fact, reservations about self-realization as early as 1951, when Wayne Oates insisted that the "central objective" of all pastoral care and personal counseling was that "Christ be formed" in the personality of the person who sought help. But most of those who wrote in the leading journals assumed that some form of self-realization was the primary object of counseling, even though they may have expressed that assumption in traditional religious language. Indeed, it was the trust in the powers of growth within the self—and the distrust of moralism and "authoritarian" institutions—that lay in the background of the Rogerian revolution in the liberal churches.[65]

Acceptance

Throughout the 1930s Anton Boisen had focused his attention on the dynamics of the inner life. During the same period, Russell Dicks and Richard Cabot had emphasized the relationship between the pastor and the person seeking help. Hiltner and Wise began to merge the two points of view by paying attention to a third dimension of pastoral care: the attitude and intention of the pastor. The change in perspective reflected the growing importance within the clinical movement and the seminaries of three patterns of thought and practice: psychoanalytic theory, psychosomatic medicine, and Rogerian therapy. The result was a growing emphasis on the minister's capacity to offer "acceptance" and facilitate "self-acceptance."[66]

The new confidence in the efficacy of "acceptance" grew

naturally out of the revolt against moralism and the critique of mass society. According to the Rogerian theory, an atmosphere of thoroughgoing acceptance in counseling provided people with temporary relief from rigid moral expectations and alien institutional constraints. The brief respite from the tyranny of expectations gave people a chance to get to know and appreciate themselves and marshal their capacities for growth. That was a welcome word to a generation of liberal pastors who had come to dislike the image of the minister as the dispenser of advice and exhortation. But the theme of acceptance was more than simply a therapeutic motif. It became part of the theological atmosphere, and it helped to define the pastoral implications of the ethic of self-realization.

The publication in 1942 of Rogers' book *Counseling and Psychotherapy* created hardly a ripple among academic psychologists, but it quickly became a standard text among clinical groups and in theological seminaries. It was the first systematic theory of psychotherapy that attracted widespread support among the clergy, and one reason for its popularity lay in Rogers' seeming success in presenting scientific evidence that the counselor's acceptance of unacceptable impulses in persons seeking aid would open the way to their own self-acceptance and self-realization.[67]

Carl Rogers intended to make psychotherapy a science, but an aura of liberal Protestant ethical idealism always lingered in the background whenever he spoke about acceptance. As a young man he had abandoned the "strict and uncompromising" religious conservatism of his parents, partly because a trip to China in 1922 with the World Student Christian Federation taught him that "sincere and honest people could believe in very divergent religious doctrines." His alternative was to follow the way of Protestant liberalism, locating the source of religious authority in individual experience. When he decided to enter the ministry, he resisted his father's attempts to send him to conservative Princeton Seminary. He enrolled instead at Union Seminary in New York, which he believed to be "the most liberal in the country." There he studied with Fosdick, A. C. McGiffert, Harrison Elliott, and others who, he recalled, "believed devoutly in freedom of inquiry." Although he decided that he could not enter a profession that required him "to believe in some specified doctrine," and hence after a few years crossed the street to study clinical psychology at Columbia Teacher's College, Rogers never abandoned the liberal Protestant spirit, or the liberal optimism about human nature, or its ethical preoccupation with the fulfillment of personality. Such were the values that guided his early efforts to define a "non-directive" form of counseling.[68]

His work with children in Rochester soon led Rogers to conclude that a supportive environment could release an inner "drive to health" and that any "coercive" relationship in counseling was never more than superficially effective. His emerging vision of nondirective counseling, which showed traces of the liberal religious education movement and of his earlier reading in John Dewey, expanded as he absorbed the ideas of colleagues who had studied under Otto Rank. A onetime Freudian, Rank had developed a "will therapy" which accented the patient's inner strength as a source of growth, the therapist's role as a supporter and helper, and the importance of the patient's growing self-acceptance as counseling proceeded. By the time Rogers moved to Ohio State University, where he produced *Counseling and Psychotherapy*, he had decided that it was the counselor's "acceptance of both the mature and the immature impulses, of the aggressive and social attitudes, of the guilt feelings and the positive expressions," that permitted a person to achieve insight and "acceptance of the self" as a prelude to growth.[69]

The counselor was not to respond as much to the substance of what was said as to the feelings that were expressed, with the expectation that "the free release of the client's feelings and emotionalized attitudes in an accepting type of counseling relationship" would lead "inevitably to insight." *Insight*, for Rogers, implied not only an expanding capacity to see old facts in new patterns, but a new perception of the intricate interweaving of all the impulses within the self. Such a perception, he argued, engendered self-acceptance, which issued in growth.[70]

By 1951 Rogers had decided that even the counselor's clarification of the other person's feelings in a therapeutic session implied a subtle lack of respect, because it suggested that only the counselor knew what those feelings were. He now believed that the counselor should try to adopt the client's "frame of reference"—that is, to see the world as the other person saw it, even to see the other person as if from that person's own perspective—in a form of perception Rogers called empathy. Rollo May, drawing on the writings of Alfred Adler, had been chiefly responsible for directing the attention of pastors to the idea of *empathy* when, in *Art of Counseling*, he called it the key to good counsel, observing that it required a temporary loss of the counselor's own identity. Psychiatrist Harry Stack Sullivan had also used the word, but not in connection with psychoanalytic therapy. In fact, psychoanalysts had been somewhat wary of the notion. But Rogers found the term useful as a way to denote not some "loss" of the counselor's identity, but rather the counselor's acceptance and understanding of the client's feelings and attitudes. Rogers spoke now of client-centered rather than of "non-directive" counseling, precisely to signal the change from a preoccupation with a "method" to an interest in the warm personal relationship that conveyed "acceptance of each fluctuating aspect" of another person.[71]

In *Client-Centered Therapy*, published in 1951, Rogers described the theory of personality on which his notion of acceptance rested. The human organism, he thought, was marked by an inherent tendency toward self-actualization as a social and sociable person. In contrast to the tragic Freudian vision of enduring conflict in the depths of the self, Rogers depicted the personality as having a "forward-moving tendency" toward "growth and enhancement." Unfortunately, though, no person—or organism, as Rogers preferred in his more technical writing—could mature simply by realizing inner potential. The human being became a "self" through social interaction and symbolization. Persons became who they were by negotiating a delicate compromise between their own sensory and visceral perceptions and values, and their internalizing of perceptions and values that originated in other persons (such as parents) and social institutions. But the negotiation was never perfect, and the result was a divided self. Everyone saw the world with double vision: The inner wisdom of the organism stood in tension with the internalized patterns of interpretation imposed by others—patterns that were always distorted because their origin in external evaluations remained hidden.[72]

Out of the conflict between the organism and its culture, between the innate capacity to symbolize experience and the learning of "distorted symbolizations," emerged a "self-concept"—a picture of the self—so powerful that it could determine the content of consciousness. People simply learned to ignore, deny, or distort whatever failed to fit their deeply rooted but invariably distorted conceptions of who they were. Their conceptions of themselves stood always in tension with their "real" organic nature, and the conflict was so severe that all people lost, in varying degrees, the capacity to symbolize and evaluate their experiences correctly.[73]

The counselor's empathetic, nonjudging attitude of "positive regard" would assure people that they were accepted as they were and thus permit them to feel and to articulate the experiences they had denied or distorted. The counselor's support of the personality's innate forward movement would result in the growing ability of people to accept themselves and to transcend the burdens imposed by an unaccepting culture.[74]

By 1954 Rogers was arguing that if self-acceptance were good for the client, it would be good for the counselor, too. He began to insist that the therapist should also be free to accept and trust inner feelings and attitudes. "It seems extremely important," he said, "to be real." The technical term he soon used was *congruence,* which meant that "the feelings that the therapist is experiencing are available to him, available to his awareness, and he is able to live these feelings, be them, and able to communicate them if appropriate." By the mid-1950s he was describing the proper atmosphere of the counseling session as one of "unconditional positive regard," a willingness by the self-accepting counselor to accept the client without reservation or evaluation.[75]

Rogers bridled at external impositions on the autonomy of the self. His discomfort with such constraints stood in the background of his dislike of "interpretation" in counseling, with its implicit suggestion that "the counselor knows best," and it also found expression in stormy episodes throughout his career. There was something in Rogers that always disliked fences, that defined personal fulfillment as being in opposition to institutional structures. As a young man he had rebelled against religious restrictions, whether legalistic or liberal. He later left Ohio State protesting against the rigidity of its Psychology Department. He battled the Medical School of the University of Chicago, where he went in 1945 to establish a counseling center. After joining the faculty of the University of Wisconsin, he soon informed the Psychology Department there that he doubted whether it "would ever be possible" for him to "work out a suitable pattern for my own activities" within their "self-defeating" graduate program. By the end of his career he was envisioning a "radical new budding of persons" whose "deepest antipathies" would be directed toward highly structured and bureaucratic institutions. The problem, he thought, was that institutions imposed rigid expectations which led to distorted self-perceptions and thus undermined self-acceptance. Like the theorists of mass culture, Rogers viewed contemporary social conventions as alienating, partly because they were the source of the "social evaluations" that precluded self-acceptance.[76]

In spirit, though not in creed, Rogers always remained an old-time Protestant liberal who was, as he once put it, "too religious to be religious." The phrase echoed with the historic call for an ethically sensitive religion that would

299

honor human nature, exalt mutual love and forbearance, and find religious truth in human experience. Rogers was one of the last of the old liberals, a preacher without a pulpit, fighting fundamentalists of every stripe, trusting to the end in the truths of heartwarming experience.[77]

When Reinhold Niebuhr criticized the psychotherapists for excessive optimism about growth and self-realization, and for insufficient awareness of the impulse toward selfishness which existed "at the very heights of human personality," Rogers could only shake his head in wonderment. Niebuhr, he said, was offensive, pretentious, and dogmatic. Rogers insisted that the freely functioning human being was constructive and trustworthy. People were not the victims of self-love. They were rational and realistic, and only confidence in the human capacity for self-actualization could safeguard the possibility of acceptance and self-acceptance.[78]

In the debate between Rogers and Niebuhr, the pastoral theologians stood with Rogers. In 1949 Seward Hiltner effectively introduced Rogers' ideas to the clergy in *Pastoral Counseling*, and by 1956, that book was the most frequently used text in the pastoral care courses of American seminaries. A survey of the graduates of two prominent schools—Yale Divinity School and Union Theological Seminary in New York—revealed that they considered Hiltner's book "the most significant" one they had read. Wise further popularized the Rogerian style in his textbook on *Pastoral Counseling* in 1951; Oates was cautious but affirmative in *Christian Pastor* (1951); and Johnson based much of his *Psychology of Pastoral Care* (1953) on Rogers' *Client-Centered Therapy*.[79]

It was symbolic that in 1950 the first volume of the new journal *Pastoral Psychology* ran a long article by Rogers and Russell Becker which presented the Rogerian method as a "basic orientation" for counselors who permitted clients to "own" their experiences—that is, claim them as integral to themselves—and therefore move toward self-actualization. Thereafter the journal regularly published articles by and about Rogers, whom Hiltner described as "more concretely influential in American psychology than any other person." Walter Horton expressed a common sentiment in 1957 when he claimed that Rogerian counseling embodied "essentially the attitude that good Christian priests and ministers have always intuitively maintained."[80]

Carroll Wise illustrated the new ideal by including in his textbook a model conversation meant to transcend the older methods. Recognizing that written records of counseling could leave a false impression, he nevertheless ventured to offer an example of an interview which he thought clarified a young woman's feelings and conveyed a sense of the counselor's acceptance.

"I have felt much better this week," she began. "And I have had a pretty good week. I have discovered that when I feel blue I don't try to snap out of it. . . . I just go on feeling blue. I don't live up to my own standards. I should do something about it, but I don't. That gets me down."

"You get discouraged because you don't do as you feel you should," said the counselor.

"Take smoking for example," she said. "I don't approve of smoking. But I still do it. Then I feel bad because I do it. But I don't stop doing it."

"Feeling bad doesn't help you change it."

"That's right. I think the trouble is that I have no goal in life. I just seem to live from day to day. I ought to have a goal. I do have one, in a way. But still I don't do much about it. I don't know if I am mixed up or what. Sometimes I feel it is a matter of security. I have never felt I had a home—that is, a real home. I had a place to live. But I never felt my parents cared for me."

"It seems it has something to do with not having a goal and not feeling secure and loved at home?"

"I have taken full responsibility for myself since I was in high school. They don't care what I do. They have no interest in me. I am completely on my own. And I can't see any future in my job."

"You have to look after yourself completely, and now you have nothing to look forward to."

301

"I have nothing to look forward to. Most girls my age look forward to marriage. I suppose I should, too, but I can't seem to. Yet I wish I could. But I don't want a marriage like my parents'. All they ever did was fight. That's all I can remember about my childhood. . . . I know I don't have a chance."

"Your experience with your parents . . . left you pretty discouraged about your possibilities for a happy marriage."

"I know I don't have a chance," she said. "My ideals are too high. I know that, too. I demand perfection from others. Yet I am far from perfect. I wouldn't have enough to offer the kind of man I want. Sometimes I get so that I want to hit something and scream at the top of my lungs."

"Part of your discouragement is in your high ideals and sometimes it makes you want to let it out rather forcefully?"

"Yes, it does. I suppose it all revolves around me. I should think of others. I always think of myself. That isn't right but again I don't seem to do anything about it. It is mostly in my attitude of mind."

"Thinking about yourself is another thing that you do not handle as you think you should."

"That's right. I am always tense. I am nervous. I can't sit quietly. I build up everyday situations until they are big problems. I exaggerate them. I think I have a lot of anxiety."

"You feel anxious and tense and tend to build up small happenings," said the counselor.

"Yes. I don't like myself. I do the things I shouldn't do. I don't mean morally wrong things, but like smoking."

"You dislike yourself for doing things that conflict with your ideals."

"I give in to my moods easily," she said. "I do nothing about them. I keep blaming myself. I see that the solution lies in my own hands, but I'm not doing anything about it."

"The solution is in your hands, but you do nothing about it; you feel you are letting yourself down."

"That's it," she said. "I always feel lost in a crowd, or in groups. The groups at the church. I feel better in a big group than in a smaller one. No one really feels close in a big group. But a small group—I don't feel I belong."

"You don't feel at home in a small group," said the counselor.[81]

And so the conversation proceeded until gently and gradually, the counselor began to draw it to a close. By intonation, careful rephrasing, and attention to feelings, the pastoral counselor conveyed, Wise thought, an attitude of acceptance—an attitude that permitted and encouraged foward movement and growth.

Rogers offered a method of counseling that could be taught—or at least introduced—in the brief period available in the seminary curriculum. One pastoral theologian who observed Rogers' "determining influence" on pastoral counseling remarked that he offered "a relatively safe method for a counselor of limited training." The Rogerian method could prevent a minister from doing any harm. But Rogers was popular with the religious liberals because they liked his optimistic image of the self as capable of growth and change, because their distaste for moralistic legalism corresponded to his notion that conventional social expectations inhibited the true self, and because his accent on progress confirmed the growing sense in Protestant liberalism that "openness" to the future was a prime mark of Christian faith.[82]

A few older pastoral theologians held out against Rogers: Russell Dicks, writing in 1949, called for a "directive listening" that would include support, interpretation, and reassurance. "There is no such thing as non-directive counseling," he said, "for there are many ways of being directive without asking questions." Rogers' admirers could have agreed with that judgment, but they still found that his "formulation of the concepts of simple acceptance, understanding, and clarification" offered so preferable an alternative to the older approaches that the criticism seemed irrelevant.[83]

Yet even Rogers' admirers proposed some modest

correctives, and implicit in their proposals was a lingering reservation about the Rogerian notion of self-realization. Seward Hiltner, for instance, preferred to speak of an "eductive approach," which accepted the "basic intention" of Rogers, "drawing more and more of the solution to the situation out of the creative potentialities of the person needing help," but left the pastor free to vary details of method. Hiltner considered such a modification necessary in order to understand the pastor's "precounseling work"— that is, pastoral work with troubled parishioners who had not yet come to the point of being able to seek or use pastoral counseling. But to speak of precounseling was to assume an institutional setting—a context for pastoral care that Rogers did not presuppose. Such a context opened the possibility of defining self-realization in ways that were not available to either Rogers or Fromm.[84]

Carroll Wise shared similar reservations. He complained that both Rogers and Hiltner paid too much attention to "the point of view of the counselor" and not enough to the "interaction" between counselor and client. To Wise, the "essence of counseling" was "communication" —the conveying of experiences in terms of their personal meanings—and the indispensable condition for success was "the relationship that the pastor creates with his people." Ministers could not separate their counseling from their "general pastoral relationship," which helped define the very meaning of communication and response in pastoral work.[85]

Wayne Oates believed that the Rogerian insights were indispensable, although he was more reserved than the others, partly because he was intrigued by the "symbolic role of the pastor" as the representative of a specific community and tradition. Using a notion of "social role" derived in part from the social psychology of Gardner Murphy at Columbia University, Oates urged ministers to be sensitive to a community's ways of expressing its expectations of the clerical role. He did not propose that they simply conform to the expectations, but he thought they could learn to use communal expectations in

304

understanding why people would come to them in search of aid, rather than to other counselors. He also felt that the ministerial "role" properly affected the minister's method of counseling. Though it was often wise to follow Rogers' advice and simply "reflect . . . feelings back to the person," he said, ministers also should acknowledge certain broad objectives they were seeking to accomplish. They could therefore feel free to take more initiative in their counseling than Rogers would permit.[86]

Even as they appropriated Rogers' ideas, then, the pastoral writers advanced a number of claims and proposals that stood in tension with the Rogerian presuppositions about self-realization. Their notions of context, relationship, and communal tradition provided a counterweight for the images of self-actualization that undergirded Rogers' methods. And as popular versions of self-fulfillment began to pervade American culture during the 1960s, the writers became increasingly restive. Few proposed to abandon Rogers entirely; they continued to deplore the "abuses" of ministers who mistook exhortation and advice for counseling. But increasingly, they raised questions about the adequacy of a Rogerian style.

The early enthusiasm for Rogers had surfaced in an affluent postwar culture that was intrigued by the therapeutic potential of psychology. On one level, the attraction to Rogerian ideas reflected a distaste for that culture—a conviction that its social conventions were legalistic and its mass institutions either trivial or oppressive. Rogerian permissiveness seemed to counter the legalism and undercut the bureaucratic ethos. On another level, though, Rogers' ideas could suggest an ethic that was eminently compatible with the very social patterns it was supposed to counter. The sharp dichotomy between a "true" self, seeking realization and fulfillment, and an inauthentic public self, oppressed by social and institutional expectations, reappeared continually among the hucksters of mass advertising who sold the dream of private happiness in a society of isolated consumers.

Despite their debt to Rogers, therefore, the pastoral

theologians never fully accepted the Rogerian presuppositions, though some were more enthusiastic than others. They did not wish the Christian pastor to discard the wisdom of a specific historical religious tradition; or to define a spiritually healing relationship too narrowly, as a "therapeutic encounter"; or to forget that the realization of selfhood occurred only within a community of language and commitment, which would provide guidance and direction.

How, though, did such an awareness of context and tradition guide the day-to-day practice of ministers who were called on to offer counseling to people in pain? What was the difference between pastoral counseling and psychotherapy? What was the relationship between growth, as Rogers or Fromm understood it, and the traditional concept of spiritual growth in the religious communities? How were theologians to use the wisdom of psychologists without abandoning their own wisdom as theologians? The pastoral writers worried about those questions for decades. Hence to dwell on the theme of self-realization is to see only one side of the effort to build bridges between psychology and theology.

Increasingly, theologians raised further questions about self-realization and growth. By the 1960s even Paul Johnson, one of the most enthusiastic of the early proponents of Rogerian methods, was asserting that Rogers had wrongly espoused "a capsule theory of personality" as something self-sufficient and self-contained.[87] But Rogers had advanced such a view partly because he had found that social institutions and traditions no longer seemed to nourish people. Did an alternative view of "growth" require a new look at institutional structures? Some of the pastoral theologians thought so, and by the mid-1950s they were turning with renewed interest to the notion of a "context" for pastoral care. They began to search for a communal criterion by which to evaluate both growth and the pastoral practice designed to elicit it.

8

The Context of Pastoral Care

"**G**auged both by consumer demand and by the clergyman's self-evaluation, the chief business of religion in the United States is now—as it probably has long been—the cure of souls." So it seemed to the historian William Clebsch in 1968. Writing in an era when the churches were widely engaged with vast social issues, Clebsch argued that religion was penetrating society far more profoundly through "pastoral care" than through all the social activism aimed at shaping official policies. Because it was the primary activity parishioners expected from their religious leaders, he said, the cure of souls was "the most flourishing religious function in American society."[1]

Clebsch observed, though, that the vocabulary of religion had too often drawn attention to sins and debilities rather than to the possibilities of "developing spiritual strengths." He believed that "the opportune challenge before the cure of souls today is to hammer out a vocabulary describing how sacral powers contribute to the fulfillment of human personhood." In so arguing, he was echoing a powerful cultural mood. Many Americans were looking for ways to "fulfill" their personhood. The critic Philip Rieff observed the American landscape in 1959 and discerned that its symbolic center was no longer the church building or the legislative hall, but the hospital. A certain therapeutic sensibility had begun to permeate the nation's social institutions, and it was becoming common for middle- and upper-class Americans to evaluate themselves and other people in terms of such internal psychological criteria as contentment, joy, and fulfillment, as opposed to the traditional standards of achievement in the marketplace. They were increasingly interested in self-expression and self-direction and more deeply concerned about interpersonal relations than about their standing within organizational hierarchies. In brief, they were moving in some of the very directions the pastoral theologians had thought they ought to move. But some of the pastoral writers were having second thoughts.[2]

By 1968 the culture was seemingly awash in therapeutic possibilities. Modes of therapy that once had been relatively hidden in clinical settings designed for the deeply distressed now attracted the attention of the merely dissatisfied. Programs of psychotherapy that had appeared eccentric when they first were proposed had come to be viewed as avenues toward the expansion of consciousness. In 1957 few people even noticed the death in prison of iconoclastic therapist Wilhelm Reich, but the mid-1960s saw a resurgence of interest in his argument that the human body, in its tight muscles and rigid bearing, displayed a psychological history of defensiveness and inhibition. In 1950 Frederick S. Perls, who had been one of the Reich's patients, published a treatise on *Gestalt Therapy*, calling for emotional spontaneity and a sensitivity to the body that could engender moments of insight, enhancing awareness, expressiveness, and feeling. Nobody paid much attention then, but by 1967 the Esalen Institute in northern California, where Perls worked as a therapist, was grossing over $1 million a year. By that time, moreover, the therapists were popularizing dozens of techniques: psychodrama, a role-playing therapy developed by the Viennese physician Jacob Moreno; guided fantasy, a systematic method for daydreaming; biogenetics, a bodily therapy invented by a student of Reich; rolfing, a form of deep-muscle manipulation created by a biologist turned therapist; psychosynthesis, a combination of group and individual methods. All the new and exotic techniques had existed in the 1950s but were then unknown outside the circle of a few initiates. In the 1960s they became the objects of entertaining distraction in popular journalism, so that even people who had never even thought of trying such methods began to be vaguely aware that the therapists were offering new avenues to "fulfillment."[3]

By 1968, in fact, the interest in the therapeutic had even started to shape a popular vocabulary, to imprint itself in the register of American slang. It seemed neither fashionable nor healthy to be uptight or to have hangups; the idea was to hang loose, to be free, to experience your own inner space. A counterculture of young Americans alienated by the war in Vietnam and the slow pace of political change in the United States launched a quest for a "new consciousness" that would create new possibilities for self-development.

Consequently, the 1960s witnessed an enormous expansion in the number of small groups devoted to therapeutic ends. In 1946 the Research Center for Group Dynamics at the Massachusetts Institute of Technology, established by social psychologist Kurt Lewin, had sponsored a summer workshop on the study of small groups. That event led to the creation of the National Training Laboratories in Bethel, Maine, which founded training groups (or T-groups) to train people in the skills needed to change institutions. With the introduction into the Bethel groups of new staff members in psychiatry and clinical psychology, the focus of the sessions became interpersonal events in the groups themselves, and the Bethel Laboratory became a model for hundreds of human relations groups, encounter groups, and sensitivity sessions. Conducted in institutions ranging from the Esso-Humble Oil Company to the Methodist Church, the small-group sessions used therapeutic motifs to define both communal intimacy and working relationships.[4]

What had been a scattered, occasional series of departures from Freudian and behaviorist psychological theories during the 1950s, moreover, came to be known in the early 1960s as a movement in "humanistic psychology." Such theorists as Abraham Maslow, Carl Rogers, Gardner Murphy, and Gordon Allport proposed an approach to psychotherapy that would accent the potential for growth, fulfillment, and creativity. They soon began to think of themselves as constituting a "third force" in psychology, a loose coalition devoted to the understanding of such human capacities as creativity, love, and self-actualization. By the time they had organized themselves into an Association of Humanistic Psychology in 1962, they had concluded that it was those higher capacities, rather than unconscious conflicts or habits, that most deeply defined the self.

The practitioners of the new therapies, the founders of the small-group movement and the humanistic psychologists intermingled throughout the early 1960s. One result of their collaboration was what later came to be known as the "human potential movement," a panoply of growth groups and training centers which promised the elevation of consciousness and the transformation of the self. On its outer fringes, the nascent movement encouraged experimentation with intense modes of emotional interaction, and also with sex, unfamiliar Eastern religions, and drugs. But focusing attention on the more sensational moments would miss the more subtle social import of the emerging therapeutic culture—namely, that it was the bearer of a coherent ethic. Its proponents were bringing to public awareness, in fact, the kind of ethic that was implicit in the newer definitions of private therapeutic relationships.

Close to the heart of the therapeutic ethic was the familiar distinction between the conventional public self and the true inner self. Such a distinction found expression in a persistent tendency to exalt the values of honest self-expression and communal intimacy. To say that the good of the individual lay in the awareness and expression of the inner self was to emphasize the virtue of honesty. It was to criticize a self-restraint governed by the conventional expectations of social propriety, which came to be viewed as hypocrisy or conformity to deadening role expectations. It was also, by the way, to foster a certain distrust of an "analytic rationality" that would preclude intuitive awareness of the self's deeper affective impulses. To say that the good of the community lay in respect for the true selfhood of others was to emphasize the virtue of tolerance. It was to value social institutions insofar as they facilitated the kind of open, honest encounter that would result in greater intimacy and mutual understanding. It was also to foster a distrust of the "technical reason" that manipulated people for bureaucratic ends. Hence a familiar litany of honorific words became part of the popular vocabulary during the 1960s: freedom, openness, honesty, tolerance, sensitivity, and self-realization.[5]

The pastoral theologians felt drawn to those terms, many of which seemed congruent with their own assumptions about growth and self-realization. But they were also wary. Seward Hiltner would later look back with "fear," feeling that he had contributed unintentionally to the one-sided preoccupation with "self-realization and self-development" in the culture. From the beginning, pastoral theologians had retained a sense for the limits of self-realization—limits that many of the popular writers in the therapeutic culture seemed often to ignore. Moreover, though they shared the popular distaste for authoritarian structures, the pastoral writers worked within an institution and tradition that had historically embodied authoritative claims. The earlier practitioners of the cure of souls, for instance, had assumed responsibility for ethical guidance that therapists like Carl Rogers did not want to see counselors assuming. And most of the pastoral writers recognized, finally, that self-realization could not be equated simply with the ideals of spiritual growth that had marked the religious traditions.[6]

The pastoral counselors did share many of the same goals with the secular therapists. Some of them even began to see "pastoral psychotherapy" as their central purpose. Few would have been entirely happy with Clebsch's observation in 1968 that the traditional pastoral functions of healing and guiding had been effectively captured by medicine and psychotherapy, leaving the clergy the duty of "sustaining" people through periods of loss and sorrow and serving as agents of "reconciliation" for those who felt estranged from one another. We should not, Carroll Wise argued, "surrender an essential ministry aimed at the deeper levels of human need to the so-called secular priests of healing."[7] And indeed the methods proposed for use by pastoral counselors were often indistinguishable from accepted psychotherapeutic practices. But what distinguished those counselors from the therapists? What was distinctive about "pastoral" counseling?

In an effort to qualify and define what they meant by *growth* and *self-realization* and to describe the distinctiveness of pastoral counseling, the theologians turned increasingly to the theme of "context." "Something in the whole setting and context of the minister's work," wrote Hiltner in 1958, "affected what was relevant and what could be appropriated."[8] But it was by no means clear how the "context" should be defined or what difference it would make in counseling.

They addressed the problem in three ways. All agreed, first, that the formation of selfhood occurred through interpersonal relationships and that therefore the interpersonal dimensions of counseling were of primary importance. Most also argued that in speaking of "pastoral" care or counseling, a "context" of God's activity in the world was presupposed. But what concrete difference did it make to say that the pastoral counselor presupposed the trustworthy activity of a faithful God? Did such an assumption of faith have any bearing on counseling itself? In trying to answer such questions, a few pastoral theologians decided to push the question of context one step further: Pastoral counseling, they argued, pre-supposed the concrete institutional context of the church. The institutional setting, with all it symbolized, gave "pastoral" counseling its distinctive meaning. But not all pastoral writers were willing to accept such limits, and a few ministers were, in fact, establishing themselves as private counselors. The issue therefore divided the pastoral care movement.

When we explore the theme of context on each of its three levels—interpersonal, theological, and ecclesiastical—we begin to understand why the pastoral writers increasingly sought alternatives to the counseling methods of Carl Rogers. But the discussion of context held implications beyond the choice of one or another approach to counseling. It also signaled a broader historical mood. The theologians were attempting to move beyond the postwar loss of confidence in the institutions and cultural conventions of mass society. Their attempt represented a lingering awareness that the realization of the self—whether defined as psychological development or as spiritual growth—required a tacit reliance on a communal wisdom that transcends the self.

The Interpersonal Context

Speaking to a conference of clinical educators in 1951, Thomas Bigham, of the General Theological Seminary in New York, observed that psychoanalytic theory has, "like every other field of learning, philosophical presuppositions and, like every other practice, ethical presuppositions." And he considered it "impossible" that psychoanalysts engaged in the practice of therapy "could hold to any ethic other than that of self-realization." The same statement could have been made about the pastoral predilection for Rogerian methods of counseling: Those methods implied that the "good" life consisted of the increasing realization of the self's capacities and powers. But as the ethicist A. T. Mollegen observed the following year, words like self-realization and growth were empty of meaning when used outside the specific tradition that informed their content. Casual talk about self-realization could imply that the self possessed "a potential structure which, given the proper environment . . . will simply achieve the fulfillment of itself." But in fact it made sense to speak of growth and maturity only as concrete processes within historical traditions: One could speak of Christian maturity, perhaps, or Buddhist maturity, or maturity according to the vague canons of middle-class society in the American suburbs or of one or another therapeutic tradition. But there was no such thing as maturity in itself; there was no universally accepted norm of appropriate growth. So how could one ensure that the ideal of self-actualization implicit in the client-centered modes of counseling would be informed by the norms of spiritual development that grew out of the Christian tradition? Were the two traditions even compatible?[9]

These questions required the pastoral theologians to specify the meaning of growth or self-realization more precisely, and in the conception of "development," they found an inviting way to do so. From the beginnings of American theology a vision of spiritual development had been deeply embedded in the language of spirituality. It was no surprise that the postwar resurgence of interest in developmental psychology attracted the attention of pastoral writers. As early as 1951 Lewis J. Sherrill at Union Seminary in New York was defining growth as a series of transitions "through certain stages as one moves toward the complete fulfillment of life," but not until the pastoral theologians had time to assimilate the work of such developmental theorists as Robert Havighurst, Arnold Gesell, and especially Erik Erikson, did they begin to ponder seriously the implications of "life-stages" for understanding both human growth and pastoral counseling. By 1957 Wayne Oates was seeking to outline the religious dimensions of personality development; by 1959 Hiltner was describing how patterns of pastoral "shepherding" changed in accord with the changing stages of the life cycle, from early childhood through old age.[10]

314

The pastoral writers varied, however, in the ways they appropriated the developmental metaphors. One group, influenced by psychoanalytic theory, emphasized that the development of the personality proceeded by means of a painful series of inner conflicts. Like the eighteenth-century revivalists, they felt that inward change would probably require periodic crises. Hiltner drew on both Freudian and educational psychologies to argue that the metaphor of growth, which suggested only expansion without pattern, was inadequate for understanding a dialectic of stability and change that was marked by spurts and plateaus, contraction and expansion, unfolding and crisis. Wayne Oates took a similar position: He agreed with Hiltner in repudiating the image of "unfolding gradualism" and insisted that the "developmental pilgrimage" was "attended by conflict at every stage." Oates preferred, therefore, to draw on the imagery of Robert Havighurst at the University of Chicago, who had mentioned the difficulty of developmental "tasks." Or again, Thomas Klink at the Menninger Foundation defined the movement toward "identity" as a series of efforts to maintain a fusion of constructive and destructive instinctual drives. Some pastoral theologians, then, still felt drawn to the Freudian vision of enduring inner conflict. They sounded much like the early New Yorkers in the clinical training movement: For them, self-realization required a struggle with inner chaos.[11]

A second group of pastoral writers felt the pull of the new humanistic psychologies. For them, development seemed not so much a series of crises as an unfolding of inner potential. Like the opponents of the eighteenth-century revivals, they preferred to accent the self's inner strengths. Paul Johnson, for example, drew increasingly on the writings of Gordon Allport and Abraham Maslow to argue that "the power of growth" could "hardly be overestimated." The "growing personality, with zest for living," he said, "wants to exercise his powers and actualize his enlarging capacities." To Johnson it seemed that psychoanalytic theory, however useful for limited purposes, was too severely restrictive in its attention to instinctual drives and unconscious mechanism. He proposed to emphasize the "resources for mental health and growth" within every person. Johnson sounded much like the early New Englanders in the clinical movement: For him, self-realization was a gradual expansion of the powers of true selfhood.[12]

About one matter, though, both groups agreed. Despite their conflicting views of growth, they shared a common conviction about the social formation of the self. They were attracted to a psychology that accorded a significant place to an interpersonal "context of relationships." Their interest in an interpersonal psychology reflected the continuing influence of Anton Boisen, who was still arguing in 1951 that "what is lacking in most of the current psychoanalytic thinking is the recognition of the social basis of personality as set forth by such thinkers as Mead and Dewey." But the social psychology of the neo-Freudians—like Fromm, Horney, and Harry Stack Sullivan—and the small-group movement that emerged out of Kurt Lewin's experimentation in group dynamics, also caught the attention of pastoral theologians.[13]

The interest in interpersonal psychology, in fact, went hand in hand with what one minister, writing in 1964, called the "remarkable . . . proliferation of small group activity" in the churches. As early as 1950 two brothers named Clinton and Clifton Kew—one an Episcopal rector and the other a senior psychologist at the clinic associated with Peale's Marble Collegiate Church—were advertising the possibilities of group therapy in church settings. But the main impetus came from the laboratories for group dynamics that had grown out of Kurt Lewin's research and the experiments at Bethel. Hence the movement represented the blending of two traditions—one flowing from medical practice and the other from social science research. The pastoral writers, though, viewed it also as the recovery of yet another neglected tradition in Protestant churches—the older Pietist and revivalist practice of creating societies, meetings, and classes for

316

devotional purposes. Small groups seemed to offer the possibility of healing, community, and intense emotional experience. Rollin Fairbanks attended a summer laboratory in 1955 and came away with a sense of religious fervor: "Again and again, one may find himself saying this is the way God intends us to live—honestly, actively, and in real and close relationship with one another."[14]

Robert Leslie, a pastoral theologian at the Pacific School of Religion, thought that small groups, by providing a way to deal with individual feelings and interpersonal relationships simultaneously, gave people a chance both to feel the acceptance of others and to be confronted with limits and boundaries. It was that kind of group interaction, he wrote, that could foster "healthy personality growth." By accenting the primacy of interpersonal relations, moreover, the groups seemed to reflect the rediscovery that human beings became "persons" in and through "community." Hence the small groups provided a setting in which ethical reflection would of necessity take into account communal restraints and responsibilities.[15]

The proponents of the small-group movement found theoretical guidance in Kurt Lewin's social psychology. Lewin had taken concepts from physics, mathematics, and the psychology of perception to develop a "field theory" of human behavior. Rather than seek a single cause for a person's action—some identifiable "stimulus," for example—Lewin preferred to locate the person at a point of intersection in a field of interdependent forces. Changes in human behavior, he believed, usually resulted from a complex alteration of all the forces within the relevant field.

Lewin thought that psychologists, therefore, should view a person as a unitary system in process, surrounded by a larger field of continually altering systems and forces. By arguing that the state of any part of the field depended on every other part, he implied that a counseling procedure that emphasized the interacting forces would be preferable to one that attended only to the internal state of an individual, or to the past events of childhood. His

317

work with small groups, for instance, suggested that group therapy, which located persons within a shifting pattern of interpersonal processes and relationships, might have some advantages over the traditional one-to-one counseling.[16]

By the end of the 1960s, Carroll Wise was complaining that some pastoral theologians had become so enamoured of group approaches as to believe that one-on-one pastoral counseling was merely "pseudo-psychiatry." Most of them, though, continued to assume that individual counseling would be a central part of the minister's work. But even they had begun to rethink counseling in the light of interpersonal psychology.[17]

A few theologians found guidance in the writings of Harry Stack Sullivan, one of the founders of the Washington School of Psychiatry, which was devoted for years to the promulgation of Sullivan's "interpersonal theory of psychiatry." Sullivan died in 1949 and his principal books appeared only in the early 1950s; Seward Hiltner observed in 1952 that Sullivan's views were "not widely or clearly known." But his friendship with Anton Boisen and his support of Boisen's work had helped ensure that the pastoral writers would be among his early admirers. In 1954 Carroll Wise noted with approval that the central theory behind Sullivan's work was "the concept of personal relationships" and that he therefore truly understood the therapeutic interview as a "relationship." In 1955 Wayne Oates observed, also with approval, that Sullivan viewed therapy as a process of "reciprocal participation." Sullivan offered, in short, a vision of counseling that took seriously that "interpersonal context" of human growth.[18]

Sullivan had become interested in the interpersonal causes of psychiatric illness while he was a young man working at St. Elizabeth's Hospital in Washington. He learned a great deal from Adolf Meyer, head of the psychiatry department at Johns Hopkins, but by 1927, when Sullivan began to use the term interpersonal relationships, the notion of the social formation of the self was becoming part of the mental furniture of American academic thought. Sullivan read Edward Sapir's studies of language, George Herbert Mead's social psychology, and Charles Cooley's theories of "social communication." By 1933, when he helped form the William Alanson White Foundation in Washington, Sullivan was ready to abandon Freud and propound his own vision of psychiatry.[19]

At the center of that vision was Sullivan's social theory of personality: It was a relatively enduring pattern of activity resulting from a lifelong series of interpersonal relationships. It was the register of a person's perceptions of treatment or evaluations by others, especially others whose esteem was crucial, such as parents. The most prominent feature of the personality was the "self-system"—all the interpersonal actions, attitudes, and processes which a person used to ward off anxiety and ensure security. Comprising all the "security operations" that protected self-esteem, the self-system was therefore to be the primary object of the therapist's attention. And just as the self-system was the result of interpersonal encounters, so also was therapy to be a real interpersonal engagement between the counselor and the patient.[20]

In his book on *The Psychiatric Interview*, published in 1954, Sullivan therefore presented a description of counseling quite unlike anything the Rogerians were advocating. He believed that the therapist was a "participant observer" whose involvement with the patient was itself an interpersonal relationship which altered self-evaluations. He also believed that the heart of the interview consisted of the straightforward exploration of current and past relationships and interpersonal crises. In such an exploration, the therapist, rather than reflect feelings, was free to ask questions, probe into details, and express judgments. Sullivan's own procedures sometimes bordered on the dramatic: When a patient responded to a question with a patently misleading reply, for instance, Sullivan was known to remove his glasses, gaze at the patient, and exclaim, "Extraordinary!" Or he was inclined at times to utter rhetorical questions: "What's so wrong about that?" Counselors were not neutral, nor were they merely "accepting" figures; they were participants in an "expert-client" relationship, and their clients had every right to expect that they not only would have an expert grasp of the intricacies of interpersonal relations but would take an "active role" in guiding and conducting the therapeutic interview.[21]

No pastoral theologian ever advised the clergy to adopt Sullivan's therapeutic methods, but his arguments clearly appealed to them. Sullivan was moving in directions that they, too, were traveling, insofar as he was examining the interpersonal setting for self-fulfillment. And they liked the ethical implications of his ideas. Albert Outler at Yale thought that Sullivan's ideal of love in human relationships was "surprisingly Christian in all save its name and reference." Wayne Oates believed that Sullivan's concepts of interpersonal relations could, with careful imagination, "be correlated with the concept of the covenant relationship in the Hebrew-Christian view of personality in society and under God." An interpersonal psychology seemed to provide guideposts that kept an ethic of self-realization from becoming a justification for self-indulgence.[22]

Interest in interpersonal psychologies tempered the theologians' enthusiasm for Carl Rogers. By the mid-1960s, Paul Johnson concluded that Rogers' notions of self-actualization entailed "a sterile and introvert narcissism of I for Me by Myself." By 1965, Howard Clinebell, a pastoral theologian at the Claremont School of Theology in California, announced that "the client-centered approach" had "dominated pastoral counseling literature too long." Clinebell disavowed any intention to return to "pre-Rogerian abuses," but he had decided that a "relationship-centered counseling," aimed explicitly at enhancing a person's ability to form satisfying relationships with other people, should supersede the Rogerian reflection of feeling.[23]

There were a few appeals to the clergy to abandon psychotherapeutic methods altogether. The psychologist O. Hobart Mowrer, for instance, decried the emphasis on "acceptance" in counseling as a form of "cheap grace." Mowrer felt that religion ought to be a matter of rules, laws, and demands. The churches should insist on confession and changed behavior—indeed, on a strict adherence to moral laws—rather than accept any "psychoanalytic view" of human life. Mowrer valued religion because its doctrines of law and condemnation promoted a route to self-realization through acknowledgment of guilt. But he made few conversions.[24]

The movement away from Rogers was more visible in the attention given to themes of "judgment" and "confrontation" in counseling. Without at all abandoning the ideal of "acceptance," some pastoral writers began to talk about the importance of "confronting" people with the need to face and change their destructive patterns of living. And even those who felt uneasy with the idea of confrontation began to put greater emphasis on ethical "judgment." Seward Hiltner suggested in 1965 that his own position had "mellowed." He was by then more convinced than ever of the importance of moving toward judgments in counseling—not arbitrary judgments imposed from without, which would merely reactivate psychological mechanisms of defense, but "shared appraisals" which respected the other person's capacity to assimilate a gentle nudge. "Acceptance," wrote Carroll Wise in 1966, "involves and includes judgment," and its goal should be to encourage "self-judgment and evaluation." An acceptance that overlooked a person's ethical confusion, insisted the Baptist Samuel Southard, did not constitute "loving care."[25]

The new emphases led the pastoral writers in diverse directions. Carroll Wise attempted to present a view of pastoral care as "the art of communicating the inner meaning of the Gospel to persons at their point of need"—not by verbal reassurance, but through a relationship in which deep feelings could find expression and acceptance, though still with the goal of helping another person find "full self-realization." Paul Johnson amplified a notion of "responsive counseling" which he had been developing since 1945: It combined interpersonal psychology and a "neo-personalist" theology in a counseling strategy that sought "growth through relationship." Seward Hiltner still argued that all counseling proceeded through accepting, understanding, and clarifying inner conflicts, but Howard Clinebell began to urge pastors to concentrate less on eliciting "insight" and more on helping people deal directly with interpersonal conflicts and problems. And Wayne Oates outlined a distinctively "Protestant" style of counseling that could either apply or abandon "nondirective" methods, as required, in the interest of "personal, adult decision."[26]

Underlying some of the diversity was a continuing difference of opinion concerning conflict and growth. Some writers—such as Hiltner and Oates—continued to believe that the main goal of counseling was the clarification of inner conflicts. For a long time, Hiltner had distinguished pastoral counseling from pastoral care by observing that in counseling, both the pastor and the parishioner recognized that they were dealing with inner conflicts. Other writers—such as Johnson and Clinebell—moved away from the traditional psychoanalytic accent on inner conflict to emphasize instead the potential for growth. Clinebell insisted that pastoral counselors had become too dependent on psychoanalytic suppositions. He much preferred, with the humanistic psychologists, that the emphasis be placed on the actualizing of potential.[27]

The overarching theme of interpersonal relationship, though, cut across all the differences, in large part because it promised to clarify the connection between the psychological ideal of self-realization and the theological understanding of spiritual growth. Hiltner said, in 1958, that the idea of the "social self" could "prove to be the key to the relationship between psychology and religion." Albert Outler believed that the theory of interpersonal relations held by such therapists as Harry Stack Sullivan contained "more points of contact with Christian notions than any other single perception in modern psychotherapy." An interpersonal psychology suggested possibilities of linkage with biblical themes such as "covenant," ethical notions such as "love," descriptions of the Church as an "organic body," and religious motifs such as "encounter" with the divine Presence. It also provided a set of analogies for referring to God as the subject of an I/Thou relationship. Among the theologians most admired by pastoral writers was the Jewish mystic Martin Buber, whose distinction between the impersonal relation of "I" to an "It" and the personal relation of "I" to a "Thou" became a standard idea within the pastoral theology movement.[28]

For most of the pastoral writers, however, the appeal to social psychology, however important it might be, did not fully clarify the difference between "the psychiatric goal of mental health" and "the theological goal of spiritual growth." Or to phrase the issue differently, it failed to define adequately the relationship between psychological wholeness and salvation. In the churches' initial rush of enthusiasm for psychotherapy, there had been a tendency to identify salvation and health. By the 1960s, though, when both the National and the World Council of Churches sponsored consultations on health and salvation, most pastoral writers were inclined to emphasize the differences. To be sure, they usually viewed mental health as in some degree a prerequisite for participation in a process of salvation. Carroll Wise maintained that one could "hardly expect to find a creative, mature Christian experience in a person of childish or immature ego development." Others described health as a "base" for salvation or spoke of salvation as "potential" in health. But most pastoral writers eventually agreed, in Hiltner's words, that "health in any modern sense is not to be equated with salvation; it does not substitute for salvation, and it does not guarantee salvation." Edward Thornton of the Southern Baptist Theological Seminary argued, for instance, that emotional health was, at best, only an implicit and penultimate preparation for salvation, which also could occur "in the midst of disease, death, and depravity."[29]

But what difference did it make if pastoral counseling were viewed in the context of language about salvation?

What did theology add to interpersonal psychology? Writing in 1965, Daniel Day Williams posed the issue in a form that had occupied pastoral theologians for decades: "Psychologists speak of anxiety, egocentricity, acceptance, integration, freedom, love. The Christian faith speaks of anxiety, sin, forgiveness, faith, freedom, love. Sometimes the words are the same; sometimes not." So how, then, were they related? And how did the wider context of Christian language—and the claims that it embodied—affect either conceptions of self-fulfillment or procedures of pastoral counseling?[30]

The Theological Context

The pastoral writers who were seriously interested in theology—and not all of them were—turned their attention also to contextual themes. They spoke of the need to locate interpersonal psychology within a "larger context." Or they spoke of conceptions of God as "attempts to characterize the ultimate context" in which self-fulfillment occurred. Hiltner claimed that every statement about human beings implied "some context" and that any consideration of men and women apart from "the context of [their] relationship to God is a straight abstraction from the Christian point of view." Hence the theologians tried to discern the meaning of the "Christian context" for both psychotherapy and pastoral counseling.[31]

The result was a renewed effort to define the relationship between theology and psychology. As early as 1940 a number of theologians, sociologists, psychiatrists, and psychologists—Paul Tillich, Seward Hiltner, Gotthard Booth, Ruth Benedict, David Roberts, Rollo May, Harrison Elliott, and others—had begun to meet monthly in what they called the New York Psychology Group. During the same period, systematic theologians began to participate in psychiatric institutes and seminars. Albert Outler, the Dwight Professor of Theology at Yale, commuted weekly to the Williamson Alanson White Foundation. David Roberts of Union Seminary in New York—along with several other theologians—worked in the influential Columbia University Seminar on Religion and Health. And by the late 1940s, a few theologians were ready to begin announcing their conclusions.

In 1950 David Roberts published his *Psychotherapy and a Christian View of Man*. His purpose was to work toward a "synthesis" of theology and psychotherapeutic theory, a task that seemed to him especially pressing in view of the neo-orthodox tendency to isolate theology from the secular disciplines. Roberts believed that therapists presupposed theological claims and that theologians needed to incorporate the new therapeutic insights into their definitions of doctrine. The concepts of theology and psychotherapy were "correlative."[32]

One part of Roberts' argument, then, was that psychotherapy could not "understand its own task aright except within the framework of a Christian view" of God and humanity. The therapist's confidence that men and women could move toward inner harmony made sense "only if the dynamic structures which undergird such harmony are more far-reaching than anything man alone can determine or control." The quest for integration within the self required a trust in possibilities that human beings alone could not invent or create; it presupposed a "drive for integration" within being itself: "Healing power is latent in men because it is latent in the nature of things." For Roberts, that claim was tantamount to an affirmation of divine immanence. And he found in the biblical depiction of Christ "the supreme disclosure" of that truth.[33]

The prominent part of Roberts's argument, though, was his insistence that psychotherapeutic theory enriched the theologian's understanding of Christian doctrine. By describing the function of feelings and unconscious motives in the formulating of religious beliefs, it illumined the inner dynamics of faith and faithlessness. By affirming natural vitalities as latent assets and by clarifying the human capacity for integrity and harmony, it helped to redefine the doctrine that human beings were created in the image of God. By undercutting the Pelagian exaltation of willpower and uncritical assertions of free will, it subverted authoritarian moralism. By its attention to inner conflicts and internal bondage, it helped theologians appropriate from their Augustinian heritage a more meaningful understanding of human sin. And by exploring the deeper meanings of healing as the result of changes occurring through a personal relationship of trust and acceptance, psychotherapeutic theory provided a way of understanding salvation that could accord proper weight to both the initiative of God and the responsiveness of human beings. Clearly, Roberts' most significant emphasis lay in his intention to show how psychotherapeutic theory could deepen theology.

In 1954 Albert Outler published his *Psychotherapy and the Christian Message*. He praised Roberts' book, and he, too, tried to find areas of agreement between psychotherapy and theology, but his tone and approach were different: "Christianity and psychotherapy are both wisdoms-about-life," he wrote, "and it is by no means clear that they are the same wisdom." Rather than concentrate on locating the ways in which psychology could enrich theology, Outler emphasized the need for theology to check and limit the uncritical pretensions of a secularist psychotherapy. He saw himself as standing in the tradition of James Jackson Putnam, the turn-of-the-century Harvard neurologist who had helped to ensure Freud's success in America, but also had demanded that psychoanalysts deal more forthrightly with their own philosophical assumptions about the self and its freedom, the good and its realization, and the reality and relevance of religion.[34]

Outler agreed that clerical exposure to the theories of psychotherapy had improved pastoral practice. It had encouraged self-awareness in pastoral counselors, checked clerical moralism, demonstrated the hidden and distorting sources of much religious thought and feeling, compelled a greater sense of respect for troublesome people, clarified the processes of human growth, and illumined for ministers "the subpersonal and inter-personal matrix of human life." He did not want the churches to lose sight of the "practical wisdom" of psychotherapy. But his main purpose in writing was to question the naturalistic presuppositions which often characterized a certain psychotherapeutic "faith."[35]

Outler was convinced that the Christian world-view provided a perspective for psychotherapy more adequate and valid than any secularist faith could offer. Christian theologians recognized that our consciousness of ourselves as natural beings manifested our capacity to transcend nature and therefore to exercise some degree of "responsi-ble freedom" even within the natural causal order. The theologians understood, moreover, the discrepancy be-tween human possibility and human actuality to be the result of a refusal to accept finitude, and hence of an unfaith and mistrust deeper than any specific neurotic maladjustment. They saw that self-fulfillment presupposed "a power at work in life and history . . . which moves in us and draws us into it mysterious workings." And finally, they glimpsed the paradoxical truth that self-realization required self-denial (specifically, the "denial of self-importance") as its invariable condition. "Self-denial, rightly understood," wrote Outler, "is the master key to the right ordering of life."[36]

Outler felt that such a "context" of theological affirma-tion could affect the procedures of psychotherapy. To speak of God as being "compresent" in every situation, including the counseling session, was to suggest a triadic relationship which both imposed restraints and created possibilities. It clarified the meaning of healing by compelling both the counselor and the person seeking counsel to recognize the intractability of human limita-tions; it thus undercut any facile optimism about counseling. It precluded manipulation and control by the counselor, who must recognize "the presence of God who judges as man must not judge, who redeems as man cannot redeem." And it required that the counselor consider ideas, especially ethical ideas, as more than simply "psychological material." Outler was not proposing that ministers suddenly begin talking about religion in their counseling sessions. He believed, for one thing, that the religious content of the neurotic superego was typically infantile and that therefore religious debates could never serve as substitutes for pastoral counseling. But he did maintain that a religious perspective informed by a neo-orthodox theology would not only help ministers recognize that they, too, were "human, all too human," but also would encourage them to seriously consider the moral and spiritual attitudes of people who were caught within a web of "self-frustrations."[37]

Roberts emphasized, then, that psychotherapy should deepen theology; Outler emphasized that theology should deepen psychotherapy. Each view had supporters, though most pastoral writers found Roberts' proposal the more appealing. Carroll Wise worried that Outler's critique would discourage lay people from seeking therapy. By 1954, however, many of the writers believed they had discovered a theological system that would permit them to strike precisely the right balance between therapeutic wisdom and theological insight. The entrance into prominence of Paul Tillich, on the one hand, and the process theologians, on the other, created an environment in which it seemed that pastoral counseling could be enriched by both psychology and theology.[38]

The pastoral writers liked Tillich and the process theologians for a variety of reasons, but it seems useful to focus on one theme as a way of exemplifying the methodological questions. No single idea was more important for the pastoral theologians than the idea of "acceptance," and the same idea also attracted the interest of the systematicians. Much of the discussion about the relation between theology and psychotherapy, therefore, returned again and again to that concept. Indeed, the similarities between the language of the psychologists and that of the theologians created a bridge that permitted pastors to adopt psychotherapeutic ideas about acceptance as merely the practical expressions of what the theologians had been talking about.

The postwar period witnessed a striking wave of enthusiasm in America for Tillich's theology. A refugee in 1933 from Hitler's Germany, Tillich had only slowly achieved eminence in the United States. Not until 1948, with the publication of *The Protestant Era* and a series of sermons called *The Shaking of the Foundations*, did he emerge into the public light. But the first volume of his *Systematic Theology* (1951) and the publication in 1952 of his best-selling *The Courage to Be* established Tillich as a theological celebrity. Before long he was lecturing to crowds of up to 7,500 people, appearing on the cover of *Time* magazine, receiving special invitations to presidential inaugurations, and accepting honorary degrees and governmental honors from all over the world. A teacher for twenty-one years at Union Theological Seminary in New York, then a University Professor at Harvard, and the first Nuveen Professor of Theology at the University of Chicago Divinity School, Tillich himself marveled at his popularity in post-war America, a period he described as his "harvest-time." And it was no accident that the Tillichian harvest coincided with the flowering of pastoral counseling in the mainline Christian churches.[39]

With no group was Tillich more influential than with the American pastoral theologians. Seward Hiltner claimed that Tillich's relationship with *Pastoral Psychology* was "in many ways the greatest thing that happened to the journal." The writers liked him, for one reason, because he seemed to have a way of relating psychological concepts to theological tradition. Ever since 1929, when the neurologist Kurt Goldstein and the psychologist Adhemar Gelb at the University of Frankfurt encouraged Tillich to study psychiatric theory, he had incorporated a psychological vocabulary into his thought. Equally important, he had developed a systematic "method of correlation," according to which the philosophical or psychological analysis of existence and the questions it raised shaped the form of the Christian answer presented by the theologian. That was precisely what some of the pastoral theologians, intensely aware that they lived in a therapeutic era, had been seeking. "He has provided the pastoral psychologist with a theological method for translating the power of the gospel into the idiom of twentieth century thought, namely a psychological way of thinking," wrote Wayne Oates. Tillich was confident that the "substance" of theology would not be lost, whatever the "form" of its language might be, so he welcomed the translation of theological concepts into a psychological vocabulary.[40]

Tillich's treatment of acceptance nicely exemplified his theological method. In his sermons in *The Shaking of the Foundations*, he proclaimed that the Protestant doctrine of justification by grace through faith, translated into modern idiom, simply meant that the unacceptable were accepted. In Paul's understanding of Jesus as the Christ, Tillich said, the apostle had found himself accepted in spite of the fact that he had been rejected. And that was the message of grace for modern men and women:

> You are accepted. You are accepted, accepted by that which is greater than you, and the name of which you do not know. Do not ask for the name now; perhaps you will find it later. Do not try to do anything new; perhaps later you will do much. Do not seek for anything; do not perform anything; do not intend anything. Simply accept the fact that you are accepted. If that happens to us, we experience grace.[41]

Tillich had engaged in an almost lifelong battle with his own sense of guilt and weakness, and on the original manuscript of the sermon "You Are Accepted," he had written: For Myself. Acceptance, for Tillich, as for the psychotherapists, was no peripheral matter but a recurring preoccupation. It stood at the heart of theology: "Present theology can say again that acceptance by God of him who is not able to accept himself is the center of the Christian message."[42]

One aim of Tillich's method, then, was to translate the older Protestant language about justification into the

330

psychological idiom of the mid-twentieth century. He acknowledged that clinical therapeutic practice provided both the language and the inspiration for his new understanding of grace. The psychoanalytic method had taught him what it meant to speak of accepting the unacceptable. The word *grace* had regained "a new meaning by the way in which the analyst deals with his patient. He accepts him," Tillich wrote in *Pastoral Psychology*. "The psychoanalytic pattern of nonjudging and nondirecting acceptance of the mentally disturbed became the model for Christian counseling; and through counseling, for teaching; and through teaching, for theological inquiry." Hence Tillich could say that Sigmund Freud had helped Christians rediscover "the central Christian message, the good news of acceptance."[43]

Tillich did not believe, though, that Christian acceptance was merely the mirror reflection of a psychiatric technique. His method of correlation had redefined acceptance by locating it within a wider theological vocabulary. He insisted that the acceptance offered by counselors represented and embodied a "power of acceptance" that transcended any finite relationship. "No one can accept himself who does not feel that he is accepted by the power of acceptance which is greater than he, greater than his friends and counselors and psychological helpers." Each instance of acceptance and self-acceptance was an expression of the "power of being," or what Tillich called being-itself, the unconditioned Ground and Power that undergirded and suffused everything that exists. When Tillich published *The Courage to Be*, he argued that both self-acceptance and the capacity to accept another person presupposed universal participation in an ontological order which sustained and empowered—and hence affirmed—each human being. Every person shared to some extent in the "self-affirmation of being"—its resistance to non-being. Every person was therefore acceptable, despite brokenness and estrangement. The method of correlation, then, recast traditional religious language by translating it into a modern vocabulary, but it also transformed modern language by locating it within a context of theological assertions.[44]

Tillich always argued, one should add, that it was necessary to distinguish between therapeutic and religious acceptance. The therapist dealt with anxiety and neurosis rooted in unsolved conflicts among structural elements of the personality, and the medical expert could facilitate the healing of that pathological anxiety. But there was also an "existential" anxiety, rooted in the fact that human beings, as finite powers, were partially united with, but partially estranged from, the deeper power of being. The healing of that existential brokenness could occur only through the awareness that one had been "accepted by that which infinitely transcends one's individual self."[45]

It was fitting that Tillich's final public appearance before his death in 1965 was a dialogue with Carl Rogers, and it was not surprising that they found much on which they could agree. But on a few questions, they politely clashed. Rogers claimed that the capacities for self-actualization in a person seeking counsel were so powerful that the counselor needed only to create a sphere of freedom in which they could unfold. Tillich maintained that human nature is more ambiguous than Rogers suggested and that the ambiguity would make it exceedingly difficult, if not impossible, for any counselor to create such a sphere of freedom. Rogers believed that "estrangement" was imposed by cultural institutions. Tillich was convinced that it was a tragic and inevitable component in any process of maturation. Rogers argued that for the modern world, God was dead, and he wondered why Tillich continued to use a religious vocabulary. Tillich insisted that scientific language is always limited in scope and that only the language of religious symbol and myth could point beyond itself to the unconditioned Ground of all existence. Both men agreed about the importance of self-affirmation and acceptance, but Tillich added that the acceptance experienced in a human relationship was a prelude to an awareness of being accepted within "the dimensions of the Ultimate."[46]

Tillich's method, then, seemed to offer a way for theologians to conduct a dialogue with psychology without abandoning theological insight. It appeared to deepen theology and enrich psychology, and yet maintain the distinctions. The problem, though, was that the method could be used in diverse ways and lead to conflicting conclusions.

Paul Johnson, for instance, agreed with Tillich that the theologian was to "correlate the questions of human life with the answering response that comes from the reality beyond us." Though his theological views differed from Tillich's, he too used a "method of correlation" to construct a position he called neo-personalism or, more frequently, dynamic interpersonalism. It was a "theology of relationship," which would, he hoped, serve as a guide for a program of "responsive counseling," with each person in a counseling interview continually listening and responding to the other. Johnson's main interest, then, was to discover a "theology for the counselor," and his tendency was to seek forms of theological language that were directly congruent with his theory of counseling. In effect, he interpreted the theological vocabulary by means of his interpersonal psychology.[47]

Johnson stood in a liberal personalist theological tradition which grew out of the work of the late-nineteenth-century philosophical theologian Borden P. Bowne at Boston University. The Boston personalists—Bowne, Edgar Sheffield Brightman, Albert Knudson—had always argued that the external world was the visible expression of an underlying Mind. Hence they believed that the investigation of finite minds could provide evidence by which to derive inferences about Ultimate Reality. On that point, Johnson agreed with his Boston predecessors. He regretted, though, their exclusive attention to the conscious experience of individuals. He proposed to enrich personalism by looking closely at unconscious dynamics and interpersonal relationships. A more adequate psychology, he reasoned, would furnish a more useful set of images and metaphors for the theologian.[48]

333

For Johnson, therefore, correlation primarily referred to the use of psychological insights to enrich theology. The language of interpersonal psychology continually found its way into Johnson's theological assertions. He spoke of God, for instance, as a Presence, a Thou, with whom men and women established relationships marked by conflicts, resistance, forgiveness, and acceptance. He also interpreted historic Christian affirmations with metaphors from psychology. Johnson was prone to speak of Jesus, for example, as a masterly psychologist, gifted with unique "insight" and "empathy," intensely aware of the fears and anxieties that crippled freedom, and able to accept people as they were and therefore to help them grow. For Johnson, then, a method of correlation led down the same road that David Roberts had traveled. It became a way to use psychology for interpreting theology.[49]

Wayne Oates, however, used correlation to continue Albert Outler's program of formulating theological criteria for evaluating psychological assertions. Oates had studied under Tillich and had taught alongside him; he believed that Tillich's method "opened the door once again for the use of the psychological method in theology." But for Oates, a method of correlation primarily meant that theology could provide clues to the deeper meaning of psychological processes; in practice, it usually meant that theologians were to judge psychological theories in the light of such Christian doctrines as creatureliness, sin, decision, suffering, and vocation.[50]

Oates stood in a neo-orthodox theological tradition that reasserted the importance of Christology as the clue to understanding human existence. In his *Christ and Selfhood* (1961), he argued that "the claim to uniqueness of the Christian understanding of the personality resides wholly in the Person of Jesus Christ." He also shared the prevailing neo-orthodox fascination with the destructive power of "idolatry," the misdirected focusing of ultimate loyalties on conflicting finite values. And he worried that psychology itself would become still another idol. So when he wrote *Protestant Pastoral Counseling* (1962), Oates warned against the tendency of pastoral counselors to seek a "borrowed identity" derived from psychotherapy. He hoped to find in the religious tradition an imagery and language to guide pastoral practice.[51]

While Johnson was describing Jesus as an insightful psychologist, therefore, Oates was worrying about his becoming merely "a symbol for our own selfhood." There were times when he, like Johnson, sought to reinterpret traditional religious language by borrowing ideas from psychologists; it was his opinion, for instance, that the field theory of Kurt Lewin could illumine the doctrine of the Trinity. But more often he used the religious language—*cross, covenant, idol, sin, justification*—to interpret the meaning of the psychological categories—identity, development, and therapeutic acceptance.[52]

Tillich's method, then, seemed to lead theologians in opposite directions, and some of the writers sought an alternative. Thomas Oden at Drew University believed that Karl Barth's neo-orthodox theology of grace, with its unyielding insistence on the priority of biblical revelation, offered the best starting point, a position that several European pastoral theologians were also defending. God's gracious acceptance of humanity through the incarnate word, Jesus Christ, had its analogue in the counselor's responsiveness; theological language, by implication, interpreted the meaning of therapeutic vocabulary. But Barthian theology did not command widespread approval among pastoral writers. Most of those who sought alternatives to Tillich looked elsewhere.[53]

The problem with Tillich was that his method of correlation seemed weakened by his claim that the theologian could make only symbolic statements about God. Such a claim, some pastoral writers observed, failed to recognize the deeper linkage between theological and psychological statements. It failed, therefore, to illumine the ontological foundations for notions such as acceptance. "The concept of therapeutic acceptance," wrote Don Browning of the University of Chicago, "should be applied to God analogically . . . rather than symbolically."

And for some theologians, the perspective that best clarified the relation between psychology and theology—and best illumined the analogy between human and divine acceptance—was process theology, an American movement that had its deepest roots in the writing of the philosopher Alfred North Whitehead.[54]

The son of an Anglican vicar, Whitehead turned to religious issues only after he had left the University of London and traveled to Harvard late in his career. In 1926 he published *Religion in the Making,* a book which more than a few theologians found baffling. It was, in fact, the bafflement of the theologians at the University of Chicago that provided the immediate impetus for the rise of a process theology. The Chicago theologians, especially Shailer Mathews and Shirley Jackson Case, had long been interested in religion as a social process, but Whitehead's language left them confused, so they invited Henry Nelson Wieman, then teaching at Occidental College, to give them an explanation. Before an overflowing audience in the common room of Swift Hall, Wieman interpreted the book in a performance so impressive that in 1927 he was invited to join the faculty. And when Whitehead published his massive and difficult *Process and Reality* in 1929, it was Wieman who announced in the *Journal of Religion* that the influence of the book would "radiate through concentric circles of popularization until the common man will think and work in the light of it, not knowing whence the light came." Wieman's prediction was exaggerated, yet oddly perceptive. By the 1950s, many American pastors were working, knowingly or unknowingly, in the glow of Whitehead's refracted light.[55]

Process theology always possessed an esoteric aura because of Whitehead's arcane philosophical vocabulary, but in 1928 Charles Hartshorne joined Wieman at Chicago, after having served as Whitehead's teaching assistant, and by the time Hartshorne published *Man's Vision of God and the Logic of Theism* in 1941, he could summarize the whole of the new theology in "three words, God is love." This summary, to be sure, was deceptively simple. Hartshorne's language was sometimes obscure, and he never reached a wide popular audience, among either the clergy or the laity. Certainly he was never as well known as Tillich. But through his insistence on developing a theology adequate to the religious idea of God as love, Hartshorne unfolded the themes that would link process thought to psychology—especially to the therapeutic idea of acceptance.[56]

Hartshorne believed that the traditional philosophical concepts used to interpret the idea of God had failed to do justice to the religious vision of God as "the all-loving and supremely efficacious friend . . . of all creatures." In particular, the older notions of God's perfection and immutability had resulted in an illogical, contradictory, and religiously unsatisfying depiction of God as a static Being unrelated to the world. The solution, thought Hartshorne, was to be found in a redefinition of the divine perfection which would entail a dual perspective on the nature of God. From one perspective, God was "abstract"—that is, unchanging—in the sense that the divine nature permanently structured, embraced, and endured all change in the world. From another, more fundamental perspective, however, God was supremely "concrete," in the sense that God's "knowledge," and hence God's very reality, included all the processes and events that constituted the world. God was therefore related to all creatures in such a way as to draw them into the divine life; their experiences became part of God's experience. Every creature in the changing world participated in the divine reality, and that participation continually transformed and enhanced the concrete nature of God. Hartshorne redefined divine perfection to mean God's capacity to be uniquely "self-surpassing" and self-increasing by unfailingly embracing every changing reality of space and time in the world.[57]

He spoke of God's all-inclusiveness as "divine relativity," meaning that God was internally related to every event, process, and person; and following the example of

Whitehead, Hartshorne defined the modes of divine relativity by using a vocabulary full of seemingly psychological analogies. Whitehead had called every event an "occasion of experience"; he had said that each unit of experience was marked by a certain "enjoyment" (or intrinsic value and reality); he had described the relations between occasions of experience as "feelings." Neither Whitehead nor Hartshorne assigned such words their ordinary psychological meanings, but gave them highly general definitions that could refer to changes in atomic structures or rock formations as easily as to transitions in personality. The dean of the Divinity School at the University of Chicago, Bernard Loomer, felt compelled, as late as 1949, to deny that the concept of "feeling" in process thought was "psychological."[58]

The very denial suggests, however, that process theologians did speak of the divine relativity with words peculiarly suited to adaptation by the pastoral theologians. "God orders the universe," Hartshorne wrote in *The Divine Relativity* in 1948, "by taking into his own life all the currents of feeling in existence." God not only "knew" but also "felt" each creature. Each event "influenced" the Divine Reality, who was therefore a "social" God related to all beings by a "sympathetic union surpassing any human sympathy." God's relationship to the world was marked by a "sensitivity" which permitted us to "enrich" God's own life "by contributing the unique quality of our own experience to the more inclusive quality of his, by virtue of his sympathetic interest in us."[59]

One of Hartshorne's colleagues at Chicago, Daniel Day Williams, expanded the argument in his 1949 work, *God's Grace and Man's Hope*, wherein he contended that process theology provided a way to discuss both God's creative and redemptive presence in history and the "growth in grace" which occurred in the human creature through divine forgiveness. Before long, Williams was writing about the analogies between theological and therapeutic language—specifically, between divine forgiveness and therapeutic acceptance. To speak of acceptance, he said, was to speak of a "creative process" which disclosed, by analogy, "something about all of life." It also disclosed the meaning of the Christian doctrine of atonement and divine love: The experience of human acceptance clarified the claim that God would "stand by the guilty one," would bear with us even in "our present life of fear and distrust." Indeed, the therapeutic relationship, which Williams illustrated with a long excerpt from a Rogerian counseling session, revealed something about the creative divine life: "When a broken self finds healing and strength, the healing process belongs neither to the self nor to another who acts as psychiatrist or pastor. It belongs to a power operative in their relationship." The possibility of acceptance reflected the fact that Reality, in its deepest dimension, was accepting.[60]

By the 1950s the process theologians had spread their gospel to at least a few of the pastoral theologians, including the prolific Seward Hiltner, whose books avoided the technical vocabulary, but presupposed the philosophical results of process thought. Hiltner was initially wary of any theological position that seemed to require a metaphysical world-view, but even in 1949 he expressed his indebtedness to Henry Nelson Wieman, and after he joined the faculty of the University of Chicago in 1950, Daniel Day Williams and Bernard Loomer convinced him that he was failing to see the metaphysical claims implicit in his own thought.[61]

By 1951 Hiltner was writing that God was not a "wholly other" reality, but rather an immanent power that "creates and sustains in every atom of the universe at every moment in time." The psychotherapist, he added the following year, must assume the reality of "a healing and integrating power," and though Hiltner was reluctant to advertise his allegiance to process theology in his pastoral writings, in 1953 he would describe his philosophy as "Whiteheadian."[62]

One advantage of process thought, according to Hiltner, was that it permitted the theologian to take into consideration the empirical studies of the natural scientist and the clinical psychologist. One could begin one's theological reflections within the empirical discipline, or one could begin with questions posed by Christian revelation, and then move back and forth between the two, seeking more adequate ways of formulating both the theological and the psychological assertions. Hiltner always insisted on "the determinative significance of the theological context," but he believed that the systematic theologians had neglected the concrete data available in "other contexts." Process theology, though, seemed amenable to interdisciplinary conversation. Indeed, some of the process theologians believed that any statement about the self or the world could be taken as a theological statement, under certain circumstances. Hiltner felt that a psychological generalization could itself be a part of Christian anthropology if it illumined, explicitly or by implication, the relationship between God and the self. Hence the line of distinction between theology and other disciplines was occasionally blurry. A method of analogy, after all, emphasized the extent to which empirical and religious statements could refer ultimately to the same reality.[63]

Process theology proved increasingly attractive to the pastoral theologians, but by the late 1950s a few—especially Oates and Hiltner—were beginning to wonder whether the pastoral theology tradition had taken a wrong turn by concentrating so intensely on the linkage between theology and psychology. Without abandoning the effort to clarify the disciplinary interconnections, they proposed a new enterprise: the formulation of a pastoral theology grounded in the study of concrete pastoral activity. The proposal, Hiltner said, continued and extended the earlier work of Anton Boisen, who had always urged that pastoral theologians study "living human documents." In the new pastoral theology, therefore, the living human document would be the minister at work.[64]

Hiltner had suggested earlier that pastoral counseling itself might serve as a ground for theological writing, and in 1958 he published *Preface to Pastoral Theology*, an effort

340

at "reflection upon pastoral operations seen from the shepherding perspective." Pastoral theology was henceforth to be something other than "merely psychology or psychiatry interpreted by theologians." It was to be a disciplined inquiry into the "healing, sustaining, and guiding" activities of the minister and the church.[65]

Hiltner's method was to distinguish three overarching "perspectives" on pastoral activity: shepherding, communication, and organization. Each perspective, he said, could lead to a separate branch of theology. It would be the task of "pastoral theology" to find within the shepherding activities—the activities of healing, sustaining, and guiding—a theological wisdom that could illumine all the church's functions. This did not mean that writers should seek "practical applications" of theology; it meant that the church's practice itself was a source for the writing of theology.[66]

Hiltner presupposed that the church had a grasp on a revelatory gospel; pastoral theology would serve, he thought, as one way to explicate that gospel. The "field theory" of Kurt Lewin and others provided a metaphor to clarify that explication. The Christian gospel was like a "focus" in a field of forces; everything within the field had some relationship to the focus; and indeed, the shifting configurations of the field altered one's point of view on the focus itself. A pastoral counselor's struggle with a marriage problem or a family conflict, therefore, could provide a new insight into the gospel—an insight perhaps available through no other source. To illustrate his proposal, Hiltner wrote an extended essay on Ichabod Spencer's pastoral sketches, showing how the kinds of issues brought to Ichabod Spencer by nineteenth-century parishioners could lead the alert pastor into a deeper "consideration of more ultimate dimensions." Concrete cases of pastoral care could provide insight into the relationship between sin and illness, or salvation and healing, or similar theological issues.[67]

Some reviewers considered *Preface to Pastoral Theology* to be an "event" of momentous importance in the history of pastoral theology. A few pastoral theologians—Edward Thornton of Southern Baptist Theological Seminary, for instance—followed Hiltner's book with others that attempted to show precisely how understanding of the "pastoral function" could contribute to theology. But Hiltner sensed little response from most of his colleagues. He later acknowledged that he felt "alienated" by the absence of attention to his efforts to promote a new vision of pastoral theology. It seemed to him that there was simply not much interest in theology or fundamental theory in the pastoral care movement.[68]

It was still unclear, in any case, how the theological insights, however they were derived, would alter the methods of the pastoral counselor. How did the theological context affect the procedures of the counseling session? Hiltner's book did not completely answer that question, but it did suggest one solution. It was not enough, he implied, simply to specify the theological presuppositions that governed the pastor's understanding of counseling. It was also necessary to locate pastoral counseling within a specific institutional context. The setting would alter the meaning and tone of the counseling; the setting—and all it suggested—would distinguish "pastoral" counseling from secular psychotherapy.

The Church as Context

In 1955 a Commission on the Ministry sponsored by the New York Academy of Sciences had observed that a minister's work was always "distinguished by the religious setting in which it is done." A minister was a "representative leader of a religious community." For Wayne Oates, chairman of the commission, such a description raised some questions about the burgeoning interest in pastoral counseling; he therefore advised that the clergy not be encouraged to regard counseling as a religious or professional "specialty."[69]

Such sentiments were frequently expressed during the late 1950s. Gibson Winter at the University of Chicago complained that the prevailing inclination was to think of pastoral work as "the resolution of individual tensions" rather than as the nurturing of a larger community. James Dittes at Yale Divinity School, observing the clerical fascination with counseling, warned that it offered an illusory "hope of relevance" and urged ministers to use psychology to understand the communal setting in which they worked, rather than to master skills and techniques as counselors.[70]

Few pastoral writers had any serious quarrel with the observation that a minister's work was distinguished by its "religious setting." The more pressing issue, for many of them, was finding a way to determine how the setting imparted a distinctive tone to clerical work, especially to pastoral counseling. Seward Hiltner, for instance, during the mid-1950s, began to reflect on the notion of "context" as a way to define the differences between counseling by pastors and counseling by other professionals. He thought that such reflection might help the clergy understand counseling as part of their "central task"—to bring people to recognize and acknowledge their dependence on Jesus Christ.[71]

Beginning in 1956, Hiltner and Lowell Colston, an intern at the University of Chicago counseling center, began an experiment designed to reveal whether pastoral counseling was different because of its context. Drawing frequently on the research and methods of Carl Rogers, they established a counseling program in two settings—one secular and one religious. Colston offered regular counseling to a group of clients in a counseling center and to another group in a local church. The goal of the project was to measure the progress of each group; the conclusion was that the people who sought help from a pastor tended to move ahead slightly further and faster. But though Hiltner and Colston bolstered their case by using standardized tests on both groups, they acknowledged that the differences were "very slight"; the significance of the study lay not in its conclusions about effectiveness and progress, but in its effort to define the distinctiveness of pastoral counseling by considering the physical setting of the church building, the continuing network of pastoral relationships within which pastoral counseling occurred, and the clients' special expectations of a pastor. It was the setting and the expectations associated with it that made pastoral counseling distinctive.[72]

Hiltner and Colston had offered a modest proposal—one that would not alter significantly the client-centered methods of the clerical Rogerians—though Hiltner also reemphasized his earlier ideas about "pre-counseling," arguing that pastoral writers should pay as much attention to the pastoral relationships that preceded counseling as to the counseling itself. Within a year, Wayne Oates went a step further. In his *Protestant Pastoral Care* (1962), he criticized the "subprofession" of pastoral counseling, contending that pastors should do their counseling solely within the church. He also insisted that they should view counseling as a "covenantal" relationship which did not derive its criteria and methods from psychoanalysts, but from the history of the church. The free-church traditions, especially, he said, had always recognized the need for rebellion against spiritually incestuous family attachments, the need for adult decision, communal discipline, and openness to the mysterious movement of the Spirit. He found in those ideas the basis for a vision of pastoral counseling as "the creation of a permissive atmosphere in which the negations, the aggressive no, and the rising up of the individuality of the person in freedom can be affirmed."[73]

To a considerable number of pastoral theologians, Oates and Hiltner sounded excessively conservative and conventional, especially in their insistence that counseling be located solely within the context of pastoral work in the church. One member of the American Association of Religious Therapists accused Hiltner of being "timid" and "dated." By 1961, moreover, some writers were issuing a call for pastoral counseling specialists—to work in counseling centers or even to carry on private pastoral practice. They also proposed to form a national association

344

of pastoral counselors to set standards for accrediting counseling programs.[74]

In 1963, they did convene an international conference of pastoral counselors. The initiative came from leaders of the American Foundation of Religion and Psychiatry in New York, the financial support from positive-thinking insurance magnate W. Clement Stone. The conference resulted in the formation of an American Association of Pastoral Counselors, an organization initially designed for specialists in counseling—not for ordinary parish ministers. Most of its members were associated with pastoral counseling centers (there were more than 150 such centers) and some of the founders also supported the idea of private pastoral practice.[75]

Frederick Kuether, director of clinical training at the American Foundation of Religion and Psychiatry, directly challenged the idea that pastoral counseling belonged exclusively in churches. He also argued that a distinction should be made between counseling and pastoral care, though he did not have in mind the kind of distinction that most pastoral writers were accustomed to making. Counseling was intended, he said, to help persons come to terms with themselves; pastoral care referred to activities that brought people closer to the church. Counselors dealt with the inner lives of individuals; pastoral care was devoted to building institutions. And the two activities often stood in tension: Counseling might well be a means to free individuals from the constraints of institutions. In any case, counseling was not an aspect of "pastoral care." It was a "religious" activity insofar as it dealt with the religious dimensions of personal problems, but it was not a church activity. To locate counseling exclusively within the institutional church, Kuether maintained, would be to deny its deepest meaning.[76]

Not all the founders of the new association were prepared to accept Kuether's version of the difference between religious counseling and pastoral care. Howard Clinebell argued that the counseling specialist simply supplemented the work of the parish minister. But he, too, disagreed with Hiltner's suggestion that the ecclesiastical context defined the distinctiveness of pastoral counseling. He predicted, in fact, that the recent impulse toward specialization in pastoral counseling centers would "push us toward the discovery of new facets of the answer to the complex question, 'What is the unique contribution of the minister-counselor to the helping of troubled persons?'"[77]

Clinebell did believe, however, that pastoral counselors were unique because of their theological training, their public role as religious authority figures, and their use of religious symbols and practices. They were also distinguished by their "explicit goal of spiritual growth." Clinebell approved of the move toward specialization in pastoral counseling, partly because he thought it would stimulate the creation of new ways to help people "grow toward fulfilling their potentialities." And he called on pastoral counselors, whether specialists or parish ministers, to develop a "variety of tools"—from family group therapy, transactional analysis, and crisis intervention to reality therapy, existential psychotherapy, and role-relationship marriage counseling—to facilitate self-actualization. But it was not fully clear in Clinebell's writings why spiritual growth, so defined, constituted a "unique contribution of the minister-counselor," or how those clerical tools differentiated the pastoral counselor from the psychotherapist.[78]

Hiltner charged that the movement toward specialization was an effort to turn ministers into cryptopsychologists and psychiatrists, and he accused the new pastoral counselors' organization of encouraging a move toward "private practice." But *private pastoral* practice, he said, was a contradiction in terms. Oates agreed with Hiltner; he claimed that private pastoral practice was "a violation of the basic character of the ministry," perhaps even a violation of professional ethics. For both Oates and Hiltner, pastoral counseling was merely one function of the broader ministry of pastoral care within the church.[79]

By the late 1960s, the members of the American Association of Pastoral Counselors were also having some second thoughts. They voted to oppose the private practice of pastoral counseling; they also opened the organization to parish ministers who were not counseling specialists. By that time, moreover, some of the pastoral theologians were even complaining about the one-sided emphasis on counseling throughout the pastoral care movement. Ever since the 1950s, for instance, Seward Hiltner had spoken of pastoral care as "shepherding." By the 1960s he was counterposing the shepherding imagery against the narrow image of counseling or interviewing. By the time he published *Ferment in the Ministry* in 1969, he had relatively little to say about pastoral counseling. Like a number of other theologians, he was turning his attention to new issues (or, perhaps more accurately, to older ones).[80]

The interest in the context of pastoral counseling, then, failed to produce a consensus—in part, because it was susceptible to various interpretations. Everyone shared the fascination with contextual notions, but some writers had in mind only the interpersonal context described by the new interpersonal psychologies; others emphasized the theological context; still others insisted that pastoral counseling should occur only within the specific context of the church. It was difficult to know, moreover, precisely how the sensitivity to context informed the actual counseling. It was clear that interpersonal psychology raised some questions about Rogerian methods. It was clear that sensitivity to the context defined by theology shaped the pastoral counselor's interpretation of what was happening in a counseling session, though it was not clear that it had much influence on what really was happening. And it was also clear that the ecclesiastical context—the symbols and roles and architecture associated with the church and the minister—somehow affected the tone and feel of pastoral counseling. But most writers who emphasized the ecclesiastical context—those who thought pastoral counseling was only one aspect of pastoral care—wrote more about the expectations the people brought to the counselor than about the pastoral counselor's own style of dealing with issues or the way the institutional context altered that style.

347

The discussions of the context of pastoral counseling did, however, reflect a growing awareness that self-realization and spiritual growth were not necessarily the same thing. By the 1960s the theorists of pastoral care were earnestly seeking to uncover their own presuppositions. And they were discovering that the Christian vision of salvation might well enhance and correct the cultural ideal of self-realization. It might even redefine, once again, the church's understanding of the cure of souls.

Epilogue

Pastoral conversation—whether understood as counsel or as counseling—has never been a disembodied activity, isolated from social and cultural expectations and ideals. The strategies of pastoral discourse, the tone and vocabulary of private communication between the minister and the person in distress, always have borne the dim reflection of a public order. One begins to understand something about pastoral counseling by looking closely not only at prevailing conceptions of theology and psychology but at popular culture, class structure, the national economy, the organization of the parishes, and the patterns of theological education. And one must also look at the past.

A representative selection of pastoral conversations in the late twentieth century would probably encompass the whole history of pastoral counseling in America. Some ministers today still speak in the tightly rational accents of the seventeenth century; some still worry about eighteenth-century understandings of sin, conviction, and rebirth; some still strive for the appearance of gentility; some affect an easy and informal manner; some offer diagnoses couched in psychological jargon; some nod sympathetically and strive to reflect the right feelings. To adopt a certain style, to say some things and leave other things unsaid, is to locate oneself within a specific tradition and a specifiable history. Every pastor, wittingly or unwittingly, adopts some "theory" of pastoral counseling, whether it be derived from the seventeenth century or from the twentieth.

The history of pastoral counseling does not yield itself to interpretation solely through the tracing of ideas. The pastor has always been immersed in a society. Sometimes the social order has provided the conceptual terms used for analyzing the soul, as it did when casuists described the faculties as princes and councilors. Sometimes the social setting has exercised a more profound influence on the counseling session. The magisterial bearing of the seventeenth-century casuist embodied the hierarchical assumptions of the society. The eighteenth-century exaltation of self-love—and the demand for a "gentler" style of counsel—reflected the new evaluation of individual achievement in a commercial order. The expansion of mercantile capitalism, with the resulting growth and spread of towns, clearly created an expectation of clerical gentility and thus stimulated the first wave of attention to "pastoral theology" in the seminaries. But what the social order had engendered, the social order could also suppress. The changes in America during and after the Civil War, combined with the Progressive response to urbanization, helped to fashion a new receptivity to a more natural style of pastoral counsel, one in which gentility gave way to cheerful informality. And social and economic change also lay behind the expanding twentieth-century interest in psychology; one can hardly understand the interest in Rogerian methods of counseling, for instance, without taking into account both the movement toward an affluent white-collar economy and the dramatic expansion of bureaucratic institutions which were perceived as impositions on human creativity.

Just as pastoral counseling methods have mirrored vast social changes, so they also have registered transitions in the organization of the Protestant churches. The hierarchical style of the seventeenth century presupposed a church with sharply defined levels of authority, and the eighteenth-century debates over styles of counsel were also arguments over whether the church should be a body of regenerate saints or a more comprehensive institution with wider membership. Just as the gentlemanly counsel of the early nineteenth century seemed, moreover, to fit the urban churches swept by the new devotionalism and its array of small-group meetings filled with disproportionate numbers of women, so the search for a natural style of pastoral conversation represented a later concept of the church as a social center with parlors and picnics as well as prayers. Something of that concept endured in the religious education movement, which turned the Sunday schools into temporary havens for psychology. But the emergence of clinical pastoral education revealed a frustration with the late-nineteenth-century image of the church as a congenial social group. And it is not entirely amiss to interpret the proliferation of counseling centers and institutional chaplaincies in the past three decades as a reflection of widespread unease in the parish churches. In one way or another, the structures of the parish have always influenced the prevailing point of view on appropriate pastoral counseling.

One cannot turn, then, simply to the history of ideas. But one also cannot ignore the transitions in thought. It is an oversimplification, of course, to trace a neatly defined movement from self-denial to self-love, from self-love to self-culture, from self-culture to self-mastery, and from self-mastery to self-realization. The different patterns often can be found side by side; they overlap and merge in unpredictable combinations. And yet each era has, I think, been characterized by a dominant pattern, fashionable among the people who stipulate what is currently acceptable and what is not. And the changing styles of pastoral conversation have closely paralleled those

351

changing conceptions of the self in Protestant religious culture.

The divergent views of the self have, in turn, paralleled changing notions of sinfulness. Sixteenth-century ideas of sin as transgression, faithlessness, disobedience, and disorder have been remarkably persistent, but they, too, have assumed different meanings through time. In the hierarchical suppositions of the seventeenth and eighteenth centuries, it seemed natural to think of sin as an offense against a sovereign God. The activist piety of the early nineteenth century, the preoccupation with reform and respectability, tended to engender an image of sin as a specific act—a vice, perhaps, or a wayward thought—but in any case, a voluntary decision. That emphasis on the will endured throughout the late nineteenth century. It permeated liberal concepts of sinfulness, and it remained implicit within the early theories of self-realization. But the dethronement of the will in the post-Freudian era, combined with the revolt against moralism in Protestant theology, helped to revive older notions of sin as distrust or as false pride rooted in anxiety. Among the modern pastoral theologians, sin came to be defined as an orientation of the self toward the world—not as a specific act within the world. Pastoral counseling, therefore, became less a matter of correction and exhortation than an effort to elicit a disposition of trust.

In the late twentieth century, the people who drew most frequently on the vocabulary of development, growth, actualization, and self-realization often seemed impatient with too much dreary talk about sin; for some, the language of actualization appeared to provide an alternative. In the seventeenth century, in contrast, it was the acute awareness of sin that made it seem necessary to talk about development. Inner development—defined as an increasing "sanctification"—was construed precisely as a struggle against sin. But as early as the eighteenth-century Awakening, the language of growth was beginning to stand in tension with the vocabulary of sinfulness. And by the late nineteenth, the language of growth and development

352

helped to define the very meaning of sin. The psychologists of religion, in any case, ensured that the notion of development would be deeply ingrained in liberal theology; and the religious education movement used that same notion to reform and structure the omnipresent Sunday school. Anyone familiar with the history of American Protestantism—with Calvinist and Wesleyan debates over sanctification, with Horace Bushnell's *Christian Nurture* or Josiah Royce's philosophical idealism, with the perennial return to perfectionist themes, with the ethical thought of Protestant liberalism—could certainly understand why developmental psychology proved so attractive to the pastoral theologians. For the same reason, anyone familiar with that history should also find it easier to understand why developmental psychologies have proliferated so freely in the secular culture of American universities. The spirit of an earlier piety still lingers silently in the background.

It is not only in the late twentieth century that theologians, whether pastoral or systematic, have availed themselves of psychological theory. The seventeenth-century casuists presupposed a hierarchical faculty psychology, even as they endeavored to transcend the static connotations of their references to isolated "faculties." They were not as naive as their successors believed them to be, and in the grasp of a powerful mind like that of Jonathan Edwards, the faculty psychology could become a subtle and fluid conceptuality to illumine the hidden places of the soul. Some of that subtlety was lost in the old mental philosophy courses, but even the mental philosophers, whatever the limitations of their methods, enriched the language of Protestant piety through their tidy but suggestive descriptions of the human dispositions. By the late nineteenth century, with the emergence of the "new psychology" and the European psychotherapies, the pastoral writers began to expand the practical implications of psychological theory. Whether they worked with James' theories of habit and the subliminal consciousness, or with Freud's theories of libido and the unconscious, they began to explore more deeply the link between psycho-therapeutic techniques and clerical practice. In the later adoption of therapeutic images of adjustment, or insight, or acceptance, the twentieth-century pastoral writers continued that exploration.

Styles of pastoral counsel have also reflected the prevailing theological patterns. Seventeenth-century casuistry exhibited a typical blending of natural and revealed theology, as well as a habit of thinking about theological issues in hierarchical and supernatural terms. The pietistic Calvinism of the eighteenth century prompted the scrupulous caution of the revivalists, while the expanding accent on human ability and integrity suggested the advisability of a gentler, more reassuring form of pastoral counsel. By the early nineteenth century, most Protestants shared, despite their intense disagreements, a common allegiance to a pattern of theology which I have called rational orthodoxy. Preoccupied with proof, argument, and logical consistency as theologians, they conceived of counseling as a form of earnest but genteel debate, aimed at persuasion. As theologians, they combined rationalism, sentimentalism, and an intense interest in volition to create an evangelical theology; and the same combination marked their understanding of counsel.

Much of that aura of refined ratiocination endured into the late nineteenth century, but when the liberal theologians began to emphasize divine immanence and the authority of religious experience, the pastoral writers started to discuss a teleological movement within the self—a movement that proceeded through natural stages of development and made argumentation seem unwise. By the early twentieth century, the theologians and the theorists interested in the cure of souls seemed to have achieved an effortless accommodation: The language of adjustment provided a bridge between theology and psychotherapy. But the synthesis proved satisfying finally neither to the therapists nor to the theologians. The emergence of theological realism, with its distaste for "culture religion," helped to push the theme of adjustment into the distant background. And by the mid-twentieth century, during the theological revolt against moralism, adjustment seemed to be merely another form of legalistic conformity to culture.

The pastoral theologians of the mid-twentieth century have been especially interested in the "correlation" between theology and psychology. Hence they often have been attracted to such writers as Paul Tillich or the process theologians, who also seemed interested in correlating psychology or natural science with theological traditions. In an era of religious doubt within individuals and self-doubt within religious institutions, however, the temptation to allow the psychological language to overwhelm or define the religious tradition has often been irresistible. In sometimes proposing a facile equation of self-realization and spiritual growth, some of the early-twentieth-century pastoral writers overlooked the fact—I take it to be a fact—that historic traditions of language are possessed of an unyielding integrity that resists a simple translation into the terms of another realm of discourse. To say that Jesus was a "good psychologist," or that therapeutic acceptance and Christian love are the same, is to render trivial both psychology and a religious tradition.

Pastoral theologians have ample access to the language of both worlds. They are better served when they live in both, letting each check the imperialistic tendencies of the other, than when they smooth out the differences or assume that religious and psychological concepts merely designate the same reality with different words. Of course the two realms of discourse are not absolutely distinct. If they were, one realm could not in any way illumine the other. But the best illumination often occurs through emphasis on their differences. The contrast between therapeutic acceptance and sacrificial love might tell us more about both love and acceptance than would the quest for analogies between them.

Despite some excessive enthusiasm, Protestant clergy have profited vastly from the new sensitivity to pastoral counseling. The problem is that our era has evidenced a singular preoccupation with psychological modes of thinking—modes which have tended to refashion the entire religious life of Protestants in the image of the therapeutic. When Harry Emerson Fosdick referred to the sermon as counseling on a large scale, he forgot that Protestant sermons, at their best, have interpreted an ancient text that resists reduction to the psychological. When religious educators transformed the church school in accord with the canons of psychological relevance, they often forgot that education in the church should sometimes invite Christians to encounter a body of knowledge that satisfies no immediate or utilitarian needs. When theologians translated traditional categories into psychological terms, they often inadvertently consigned religious discourse to the sphere of the inward and private. Pastoral counseling—a counseling rightly sensitive to psychological wisdom—can best flourish when it is not exalted as the paradigm of clerical activity.

To trace the history of clerical counseling in America is to attain a distinctive vantage point from which to understand both the culture's indebtedness to its Protestant past and Protestantism's adaptation to the changing patterns of the culture. The introspective piety in the American Protestant heritage—the preoccupation with inwardness, rebirth, conversion, revival—was easily translated into a secular psychological piety. And the new vocabulary of the psychologists and psychotherapists then reshaped the older Protestant vision. The writings of pastoral theologians have reflected the transitions in the church and the culture. In their proposals concerning pastoral counsel and counseling, one can discern the broader Protestant journey "from salvation to self-realization."

Notes

1: Theological Traditions

1. Thomas Fuller, *The Cause and Cure of a Wounded Conscience* (London, 1647), p. 92.
2. Philip Rieff, *The Triumph of the Therapeutic: Uses of Faith after Freud* (New York: Harper & Row, 1966).
3. John T. McNeill, *A History of the Cure of Souls* (New York: Harper & Brothers, 1951), pp. 112-35, 287-306.
4. John H. Leith, ed., *Creeds of the Churches* (Garden City, N.Y.: Doubleday & Co., 1963), pp. 405-7.
5. *The Catechism of the Council of Trent*, trans. J. Donovan (Baltimore, 1839), pp. 16, 194. See also Henry Charles Lea, *A History of Auricular Confession and Indulgences in the Latin Church* (Philadelphia, 1896) 2:254.
6. *Catechism of the Council of Trent*, pp. 181-82, 192-93.
7. Reuben Gold Thwaites, ed., *The Jesuit Relations and Allied Documents* (New York: Pageant Books Co., 1959) 36:163-64, 193; H. Shelton Smith, Robert T. Handy, and Lefferts A. Loetscher, *American Christianity: An Historical Interpretation with Representative Documents* (New York: Charles Scribner's Sons, 1960) 1:34. See also such works as Philip Salvatori, S.J., *Practical Instruction for New Confessors* (New York, 1887; 1st ed., 1885); St. Leonard of Port Maurice, *Counsels to Confessors*

(Dublin, 1875); Laurence Vaux, *A Briefe Fourme of Confession* (Antwerp, 1576).

8. Martin Luther, *Three Treatises* (Philadelphia: Fortress Press, 1960), pp. 210, 212-14; Martin Luther, "Commentary on Galatians," in *Martin Luther*, ed. John Dillenberger (Garden City, N.Y.: Doubleday & Co., 1961), pp. 130, 141, 163; Martin Luther, *Early Theological Works*, ed. James Atkinson (Philadelphia: Westminster Press, 1962), pp. 276-95.

9. Baird Tipson, "How Can the Religious Experience of the Past Be Recovered? The Examples of Puritanism and Pietism," *Journal of the American Academy of Religion* 43 (1975): 695-707; Theodore Tappert, "The Influence of Pietism in Colonial American Lutheranism," in *Continental Pietism and Early American Christianity*, ed. F. Ernest Stoeffler (Grand Rapids: William B. Eerdman, 1976), pp. 13-22; F. Ernest Stoeffler, *The Rise of Evangelical Pietism* (Leiden: E. J. Brill, 1965), pp. 240-41; Carl J. Schindler, "The Psychology of Henry Melchior Muhlenberg's Pastoral Technique," *The Lutheran Church Quarterly* 16 (1943): 54-55; C. Charles Bachman, "The Development of Lutheran Pastoral Care in America" (Ph.D. diss., Boston University, 1949), p. 70.

10. Schindler, "Psychology of Muhlenberg's Technique," p. 55; Kurt M. Enger, "Private Confession in American Lutheranism" (Ph.D. diss., Princeton University, 1962); E. Clifford Nelson, ed., *The Lutherans in North America* (Philadelphia: Fortress Press, 1975), pp. 70-71.

11. Leith, *Creeds of the Churches*, pp. 270-71; C. F. Allison, *The Rise of Moralism* (New York: Seabury Press, 1966), p. 202.

12. J. Sears McGee, *The Godly Man in Stuart England: Anglicans, Puritans, and the Two Tables, 1620–1670* (New Haven, Conn.: Yale University Press, 1976), pp. 163, 238, 248; David Little, *Religion, Order, and Law: A Study of Pre-Revolutionary England* (New York: Harper & Row, 1969), pp. 132-225.

13. George Herbert, "A Priest to the Temple; or, The Country Parson, His Character and Rule of Holy Life," in *The Clergyman's Instructor; or, A Collection of Tracts on the Ministerial Duties* (Oxford, 1807), pp. 68-93; Thomas Wood, *English Casuistical Divinity During the Seventeenth Century* (London: S.P.C.K., 1952), pp. x, 54.

14. John Calvin, *Institutes of the Christian Religion*, ed. John T. McNeill (Philadelphia: Westminster Press, 1960) 2:1:4:245.

15. Cited in McGee, *Godly Man in Stuart England*, p. 71.

16. Henry Holland, "Introduction," in Richard Greenham, *The Works of the Reverend and Faithful Servant of Jesus Christ, M. Richard Greenham* (London, 1599); William Ames, "To the

Reader," in *The Workes of the Reverend and Faithful Minister of Christ William Ames* (London, 1643).

17. Ames, "To the Reader."
18. William Perkins, "The Whole Treatise of the Cases of Conscience," in *The Works of That Famous and Worthy Minister of Christ, William Perkins* (London, 1617) 2:20. See E. Brooks Holifield, *The Covenant Sealed: The Development of Puritan Sacramental Theology in Old and New England, 1570-1720* (New Haven, Conn.: Yale University Press, 1974), p. 40.
19. Perkins, "Whole Treatise," in *Works*, p. 20; Richard Sibbes, "Introduction," in *The Soule's Conflict with Itselfe and Victory over Itselfe by Faith* (London, 1635).
20. Thomas Fuller, "The Life of Mr. Perkins," *The Holy State* (Cambridge, 1648), p. 85.
21. Fuller, *Cause and Cure of a Wounded Conscience*, p. 92.
22. Leith, *Creeds of the Churches*, p. 413.
23. F. Ernest Stoeffler, *German Pietism During the Eighteenth Century* (Leiden: E. J. Brill, 1973), pp. 13-18; Tipson, "How Can Religious Experience of Past Be Recovered?" pp. 695-707.
24. Leith, *Creeds of the Churches*, pp. 274-76.
25. William Perkins, "The Whole Treatise of the Cases of Conscience," in *William Perkins 1558-1602*, ed. Thomas Merrill (Nieuwkoop, Netherlands: B. DeGraf, 1966), p. 103 (hereafter cited as Merrill).
26. Thomas Shepard, "The Sound Believer: A Treatise of Evangelical Conversion," in *The Works of Thomas Shepard* (Boston, 1853) 1:115-284; Edmund Morgan, *Visible Saints: The History of a Puritan Idea* (Ithaca, N.Y.: Cornell University Press, 1963).
27. Edmund Morgan, ed., *The Diary of Michael Wigglesworth 1653-1657* (New York: Harper & Row, 1946), pp. 121-22.
28. Tipson, "How Can Religious Experience of Past Be Recovered?" pp. 695-707.
29. E. Brooks Holifield, *The Gentlemen Theologians: American Theology in Southern Culture 1795-1860* (Durham, N.C.: Duke University Press, 1978), pp. 142-43.

2: A Hierarchical World

1. George H. Williams, "The Life of Thomas Hooker in England and Holland, 1583-1633," in *Thomas Hooker: Writings in England and Holland, 1623-1633*, ed. George Williams et al. (Cambridge, Mass.: Harvard University Press, 1975), pp. 4-6.
2. Edward W. Hooker, *The Life of Thomas Hooker* (Boston, 1849), p. 21.

3. John Hart [Jasper Heartwell], *The Firebrand Taken Out of the Fire; or, The Wonderful History, Case, and Cure of Mrs. Joan Drake, Sometime the Wife of Francis Drake of Esher, in the County of Surrey* (London, 1654), pp. 4-12, 17.

4. Ibid., pp. 23, 45, 63.

5. Ibid., pp. 119, 124, 148.

6. Richard Baxter, *The Reformed Pastor* (New York, 1839; 1st ed. 1656), pp. 45, 68, 71, 74, 81-83; Winthrop Hudson, "The Ministry in the Puritan Age," in *The Ministry in Historical Perspectives,* ed. H. Richard Niebuhr and Daniel Day Williams (New York: Harper & Row, 1956), p. 193; William A. Clebsch and Charles R. Jaekle, *Pastoral Care in Historical Perspective* (Englewood Cliffs, N.J.: Prentice-Hall, 1964), pp. 32-66.

7. E.M.W. Tillyard, *The Elizabethan World Picture* (New York: Macmillan Co., n.d.), pp. 27-28, 38-82.

8. Hart, *Firebrand.*

9. Perkins, "Whole Treatise," in Merrill (see ch. 1, n. 25), p. 101; idem, "A Discourse of Conscience" (1608), in Merrill, pp. 5, 63.

10. Perkins, "Whole Treatise," in Merrill, p. 70; Keith Thomas, *Religion and the Decline of Magic* (New York: Charles Scribner's Sons, 1971), pp. 218-85; Howard Feinstein, "The Prepared Heart: A Comparative Study of Puritan Theology and Psychoanalysis," *American Quarterly* 22 (Summer 1970): 166-76.

11. Thomas Clap, *The Greatness and Difficulties of the Work of the Ministry* (Boston, 1732), pp. 6-7, 15, 17, 32; Ernest Lowrie, *The Shape of the Puritan Mind* (New Haven, Conn.: Yale University Press, 1974), p. 67.

12. Samuel Willard, *A Compleat Body of Divinity in Two Hundred Fifty Expository Lectures on the Assembly's Shorter Catechism* (Boston, 1726), pp. 1-4.

13. Lowrie, *Shape of the Puritan Mind,* pp. 47, 51-52.

14. Willard, *Compleat Body,* pp. 13-16.

15. Seymour Van Dyken, *Samuel Willard, 1640–1707: Preacher of Orthodoxy in an Era of Change* (Grand Rapids: William B. Eerdman, 1972), p. 21.

16. Samuel Willard, "A Brief Account of a Strange and Unusual Providence of God Befallen to Elizabeth Knapp of Groton" (1672), in *Remarkable Providences,* ed. John Demos (New York: George Braziller, 1972), pp. 358-71.

17. Ibid., p. 371.

18. Perry Miller, *The New England Mind: The Seventeenth Century* (Boston: Beacon Press, 1961; 1st ed., 1939), pp. 111-41. Walter J. Ong, S.J., *Ramus, Method, and the Decay of Dialogue* (Cambridge, Mass.: Harvard University Press, 1958), and Wilbur Samuel Howell, *Logic and Rhetoric in England,*

1500–1700 (Princeton, N.J.: Princeton University Press, 1956), also clarify Ramean logic.

19. Perkins, "Whole Treatise," in Merrill, pp. 118-19.
20. Willard, "Brief Account," p. 366.
21. Perkins, "Discourse of Conscience," in Merrill, p. 5.
22. Perkins, "Whole Treatise," in Merrill, p. 124.
23. William Ames, *Of Conscience, and the Cases Thereof* (London, 1643) 1:13-14.
24. Miller, *New England Mind,* p. 128.
25. Perkins, "Whole Treatise," in Merrill, p. 120.
26. Perry Miller and Thomas Johnson, eds., *The Puritans: A Sourcebook of Their Writings* (New York: Harper & Row, 1963; 1st ed., 1938) 1:195.
27. Kenneth A. Lockridge, *A New England Town: The First Hundred Years, Dedham, Massachusetts, 1636–1736* (New York: W. W. Norton & Co., 1970), p. 12; Philip J. Greven, Jr., *Four Generations: Population, Land, and Family in Colonial Andover, Massachusetts* (Ithaca, N.Y.: Cornell University Press, 1970), p. 45; Jackson Turner Main, *The Social Structure of Revolutionary America* (Princeton, N.J.: Princeton University Press, 1965), p. 8; Stephen Foster, *Their Solitary Way: The Puritan Social Ethic in the First Century of Settlement in New England* (New Haven, Conn.: Yale University Press, 1971), p. 27; Bernard Bailyn, "Politics and Social Structure in Virginia," in *Seventeenth-Century America,* ed. James Morton Smith (Chapel Hill: University of North Carolina Press, 1959), p. 100; James A. Henretta, "Families and Farms: Mentahté in Pre-Industrial America," *William and Mary Quarterly,* 3d ser. 35 (1978): 3-32.
28. Norman H. Dawes, "Titles as Symbols of Prestige in Seventeenth-Century New England," in *Class and Society in Early America,* ed. Gary B. Nash (Englewood Cliffs, N.J.: Prentice-Hall, 1970), pp. 89-99; Foster, *Their Solitary Way,* p. 28; Rowland Berthoff, *An Unsettled People: Social Order and Disorder in American History* (New York: Harper & Row, 1971), p. 86; Greven, *Four Generations,* p. 47.
29. Berthoff, *Unsettled People,* p. 88; Lockridge, *New England Town,* p. 16; Nash, ed., *Class and Society,* p. 6; G. M. Brydon, *Virginia's Mother Church and the Political Conditions Under Which It Grew* (Richmond: Virginia Historical Society, 1947), p. 23.
30. Douglas Adair, ed., "The Autobiography of the Reverend Devereux Jarratt, 1732–1763," *William and Mary Quarterly,* 3d ser. 9 (1952): 346-93.
31. For Hubbard, see Miller and Johnson, *The Puritans* 1:247, 251. Willard is cited in Foster, *Their Solitary Way,* p. 25. See

also Sumner C. Powell, *Puritan Village: The Formation of a New England Town* (Garden City, N.Y.: Doubleday & Co., 1956; 1st ed., 1963), p. 151; Charles Sydnor, *American Revolutionaries in the Making* (New York: Macmillan Co., 1956; 1st ed., 1952), p. 60. For Quakers, see Berthoff, *Unsettled People*, p. 86.

32. Frederick Lewis Weis, *The Colonial Churches and the Colonial Clergy of the Middle and Southern Colonies 1607–1776* (Lancaster, Mass.: n.p., 1939), pp. 17-18.

33. For New England, see David Hall, *The Faithful Shepherd: A History of the New England Ministry in the Seventeenth Century* (Chapel Hill: University of North Carolina Press, 1972), pp. 91, 152, 121-51. For Virginia, see James Blair, "A Memorial Concerning Sir Edmund Andros" (1697), in *Historical Collections Relating to the American Colonial Church*, ed. W. S. Perry (New York: A.M.S. Press, 1969; 1st ed., 1870) 1:16; William Seiter, "The Anglican Parish in Virginia," in *Seventeenth-Century America*, ed. Smith, p. 132; Brydon, *Virginia's Mother Church*, p. 412; Arthur Pierce Middleton, "The Colonial Virginia Parson," *William and Mary Quarterly*, 3d. ser. 26 (1969): 426, 436; see also Spencer Ervin, "The Established Church of Colonial Maryland," *Historical Magazine of The Protestant Episcopal Church* 24 (1955): 232-92.

34. Larzer Ziff, ed., *John Cotton on the Churches of New England* (Cambridge, Mass.: Harvard University Press, 1968), p. 112; Clap, *Greatness and Difficulties of the Work*, p. 16.

35. William T. Youngs, Jr., *God's Messengers: Religious Leadership in Colonial New England, 1700–1750* (Baltimore: Johns Hopkins University Press, 1976), p. 14; Weis, *Colonial Churches and Colonial Clergy*, p. 3; Frederick Lewis Weis, *The Colonial Clergy of Virginia, North Carolina, and South Carolina* (Boston: n.p., 1955), pp. 1-157; Brydon, *Virginia's Mother Church*, pp. 419-21; Nelson Rightmeyer, "The Character of the Anglican Clergy in Colonial Virginia," *Historical Magazine of The Protestant Episcopal Church* 19 (1950): 120. For colleges, see Weis, *Colonial Clergy of Virginia, North Carolina, and South Carolina;* idem, *Colonial Churches and Colonial Clergy;* idem, *The Colonial Clergy of Maryland, Delaware, and Georgia* (Baltimore: Genealogical Publishing Co., 1978). See also Dawes, "Titles as Symbols of Prestige," p. 95.

36. Cotton Mather, *Magnalia Christi Americana; or, The History of New England* (New York, 1852) 2:410-15.

37. On New England, see Bernard Bailyn, *The New England Merchants in the Seventeenth Century* (New York: Harper & Row, 1964; 1st ed., 1955), p. 135; Foster, *Their Solitary Way,*

appendix. For Virginia, see Bailyn, "Politics and Social Structure," p. 111; Middleton, "Colonial Virginia Parson," p. 427. For quotation, see Eliphalet Adams, *Ministers Must Take Heed to Their Ministry* (New London, Conn., 1726), p. 15. See also David J. Rothman, *The Discovery of the Asylum: Social Order and Disorder in the New Republic* (Boston: Little, Brown, & Co., 1971), pp. 30-56.

38. Philip Greven, *The Protestant Temperament: Patterns of Child-Rearing, Religious Experience, and the Self in Early America* (New York: Alfred A. Knopf, 1977).

39. Perkins, "Whole Treatise," in Merrill, pp. 125-26.

40. Ibid., pp. 125-46; Samuel Sewall, "Diary," in *The Puritans*, ed. Miller and Johnson, 2:512.

41. Norman Fiering, *Moral Philosophy at Seventeenth-Century Harvard: A Discipline in Transition* (Chapel Hill: University of North Carolina Press, 1981), p. 63-103.

42. Ibid., pp. 111, 113, 119, 122, 127, 129, 130-32.

43. Richard Baxter, "Treatise of Self-Denial," in *The Practical Works of the Rev. Richard Baxter*, ed. William Orme (London, 1830) 11:58, 116-17.

44. Sacvan Bercovitch, *The Puritan Origins of the American Self* (New Haven, Conn.: Yale University Press, 1975), pp. 13, 17, 18; Baxter, "Treatise of Self-Denial," pp. 77, 128, 139, 150; Thomas Shepard, "The Parable of the Ten Virgins Unfolded," in *The Works of Thomas Shepard* (Boston, 1853) 2:55.

45. Bercovitch, *Puritan Origins*, p. 18; Baxter, "Treatise of Self-Denial," p. 58.

46. Willard, *Compleat Body*, pp. 194-95; John Locke, *An Essay Concerning Human Understanding* (New York: Dover Publications, 1959) 1:449, 460, 466; Lowrie, *Shape of the Puritan Mind*, pp. 79, 82-83.

47. Locke, *Essay Concerning Human Understanding* 1:449.

48. Ibid., p. 462.

49. Lowrie, *Shape of the Puritan Mind*, p. 76.

50. Willard, *Compleat Body*, pp. 118, 122, 123.

51. Ibid., p. 122.

52. Gail Thain Parker, "Jonathan Edwards and Melancholy," *New England Quarterly* 41 (1968): 195, 197; Ames, *Of Conscience* 1:13.

53. Willard, *Compleat Body*, p. 211.

54. Shepard, "Parable," pp. 112, 230, 233-34.

55. Willard, *Compleat Body*, p. 211; Shepard, "Parable," p. 230.

56. Quotation cited in John Demos, *A Little Commonwealth: Family Life in Plymouth Colony* (New York: Oxford University Press, 1970), p. 137, see also pp. 135-38; Emil Oberholzer, Jr.,

Delinquent Saints: Disciplinary Action in the Early Congrega-tional Churches of Massachusetts (New York: Columbia University Press, 1956), pp. 173-76; Edmund Morgan, *American Slavery, American Freedom: The Ordeal of Colonial Virginia* (New York: W. W. Norton & Co., 1975), p. 150.

57. Fiering, *Moral Philosophy*, pp. 110, 113, citing William Partridge, commencement thesis, Harvard College, 1686.

58. Ibid., pp. 121-24.

59. Thomas Hooker, *The Application of Redemption* (London, 1657), p. 279.

60. Fiering, *Moral Philosophy*, pp. 122, 127, 129, 132.

61. Miller and Johnson, eds., *The Puritans* 1:301-6.

3: Understanding and Affections

1. Ebenezer Parkman, "Extract from the Diary of the Reverend Ebenezer Parkman," in *Remarkable Providences* (see ch. 1, n. 16), pp. 158-62.

2. On the Awakening, see C. C. Goen, *Revivalism and Separatism in New England* (New Haven, Conn.: Yale University Press, 1962); Edwin S. Gaustad, *The Great Awakening in New England* (New York: Harper & Brothers, 1957); C. H. Maxson, *The Great Awakening in the Middle Colonies* (Gloucester, Mass.: Peter Smith, 1958); and Alan Heimert and Perry Miller, eds., *The Great Awakening* (Indianapolis: Bobbs-Merrill, 1967).

3. Gaustad, *Great Awakening*, pp. 104-5; Youngs, *God's Messengers* (see ch. 2, n. 35), p. 49.

4. Jonathan Edwards, "Unpublished Letter," "Colman's Abridgement," and "A Faithful Narrative of the Surprising Word of God," in *Jonathan Edwards, The Great Awakening,* ed. C. C. Goen (New Haven, Conn.: Yale University Press, 1972), pp. 106, 109, 119-20, 123-24, 162, 164, 166.

5. Heimert and Miller, *Great Awakening*, p. xxxix.

6. Solomon Stoddard, *An Appeal to the Learned* (Boston, 1709), p. 36.

7. Heimert and Miller, *Great Awakening*, p. 595.

8. Jonathan Edwards, *The Great Concern of a Watchman for Souls* (Boston, 1743), p. 9; Edwards, "Unpublished Letter," and "Some Thoughts Concerning the Present Revival of Religion in New England," in *Great Awakening*, ed. Goen, pp. 109, 392; Parker, "Jonathan Edwards and Melancholy" (see ch. 2, n. 52), p. 206.

9. For Old Lights, see Charles Chauncy, *An Unbridled Tongue a Sure Evidence That Our Religion Is Hypocritical and Vain* (Boston, 1741), pp. 12, 28; Alexander Garden, *Regeneration and the Testimony of Spirit* (Boston, 1740), p. 8. For New

Lights, see Gilbert Tennent, *The Unsearchable Riches of Christ* (Boston, 1739), p. 25; idem, *A Persuasive to the Right Use of the Passions in Religion* (Philadelphia, 1760), pp. 5-6; Jonathan Dickinson, *The Witness of the Spirit* (Boston, 1743; 1st ed., 1740), p. 20; Jonathan Edwards, *A Treatise Concerning Religious Affections* (1746), ed. John E. Smith (New Haven, Conn.: Yale University Press, 1959), pp. 127-90.

10. For New Lights, see Tennent, *Unsearchable Riches*, p. 1; Samuel Blair, *The Great Glory of God Which Is Displayed in the Gospel of Christ* (Boston, 1739), p. 31; Jonathan Dickinson, *The Nature and Necessity of Regeneration* (New York, 1743), p. 14. For Old Lights, see Charles Chauncy, *The New Creature* (Boston, 1741), p. 18.

11. For New Lights, see Blair, *Great Glory of God*, p. 31; Tennent, *Unsearchable Riches*, p. 1. For Old Lights, see Chauncy, *New Creature*, pp. 9, 18; Garden, *Regeneration and Testimony*, pp. 8, 10.

12. Chauncy, *New Creature*, pp. 7-13.

13. Jonathan Dickinson, *A Display of God's Special Grace* (Philadelphia, 1743), p. 18; idem, *Nature and Necessity*, p. 14.

14. Charles Chauncy, *Seasonable Thoughts on the State of Religion in New England* (Boston, 1743), p. 12; Nathanael Appleton, *The Clearest and Surest Marks of Our Being So Led by the Spirit of God as to Demonstrate That We Are the Children of God* (Boston, 1753), p. 16; idem, *God and Not Ministers to Have the Glory of All Success Given to the Preached Gospel* (Boston, 1741), p. 27; Gilbert Tennent, *The Duty of Self-Examination* (Boston, 1739), p. 137.

15. Jonathan Dickinson, *The True Scripture-Doctrine Concerning Some Important Points of Christian Faith* (Boston, 1741), p. 149; Joseph Sewall, *The Holy Spirit Convincing the World of Sin, of Righteousness, and of Judgment* (Boston, 1741), p. 91; William Williams, *A Discourse on Saving Faith* (Boston, 1741), p. 7; Heimert and Miller, *Great Awakening*, p. 128; Blair, *Great Glory of God*, pp. 93, 98; Solomon Williams, *A Vindication of the Gospel-Doctrine of Justifying Faith* (Boston, 1746), p. 36.

16. Edwards, *Religious Affections*, p. 272; Jonathan Edwards, "Miscellanies," #728, in *The Philosophy of Jonathan Edwards*, ed. Harvey Townsend (Eugene: University of Oregon Press, 1955), pp. 113-26.

17. Edwards, "Miscellanies," pp. 115-19; Edwards, *Religious Affections*, p. 205.

18. Fiering, *Moral Philosophy* (see ch. 2, n. 41), p. 143; Dickinson, *True Scripture-Doctrine*, p. 164; Charles Chauncy, *The Only Compulsion Proper to Be Made Use of in the Affairs of*

Conscience and Religion (Boston, 1739), p. 11; John Thomson, *The Doctrine of Convictions Set in a Clear Light* (Philadelphia, 1744), p. 18; Garden, *Regeneration and Testimony*, p. 10.

19. Samuel Davies, *A Sermon on Man's Primitive State and the First Covenant* (Philadelphia, 1748), pp. 17, 19; Blair, *Great Glory of God*, p. 93.

20. Jonathan Edwards, *Freedom of the Will*, ed. Paul Ramsey (New Haven, Conn.: Yale University Press, 1957), pp. 141, 144, 145, 148, 217.

21. Ibid., p. 220; Jonathan Edwards, "Concerning Efficacious Grace," in *The Works of President Edwards in Eight Volumes* (London, 1817) 8:408.

22. Jonathan Edwards, "A Divine and Supernatural Light," in *Works* 8:9; Charles Chauncy, *The Gifts of the Spirit to Ministers Consider'd in Their Diversity* (Boston, 1742), p. 8; Chauncy, *Seasonable Thoughts*, p. 422; Heimert and Miller, *Great Awakening*, p. 248.

23. Chauncy, *Seasonable Thoughts*, pp. 324-25, 422.

24. Edwards, "Thoughts Concerning the Present Revival," pp. 296, 298.

25. Edwards, *Religious Affections*, p. 101.

26. Tennent, *Duty of Self-Examination*, p. 137; Dickinson, *Display of God's Special Grace*, p. 18.

27. Nathanael Appleton, *Evangelical and Saving Repentance, Flowing from a Sense of the Dying Love of Christ, Distinguished from a Legal Sorrow* (Boston, 1741), p. 19; David Harlan, *The Clergy and the Great Awakening in New England* (Ann Arbor, Mich.: U.M.I. Research Press, 1979), p. 59.

28. Edwards, *Great Concern of a Watchman*, pp. 28, 42-47.

29. Thomas Foxcroft, *A Practical Discourse Relating to the Gospel Ministry* (Boston, 1718), p. 37.

30. Adair, "Autobiography of Devereaux Jarratt" (see ch. 2, n. 30), p. 377; Clap, *Greatness and Difficulties of the Work* (see ch. 2, n. 11), p. 14.

31. Edward Holyoke, *The Duty of Ministers of the Gospel to Guard Against Pharisaism and Sadducism of the Present Day* (Boston, 1741), p. 35; Edwards, *Great Concern of a Watchman*, pp. 45-46.

32. Appleton, *God and Not Ministers*, p. 27.

33. Appleton, *Clearest and Surest Marks*, p. 20.

34. Chauncy, *Gifts of the Spirit*, pp. 6-14.

35. Samuel Finley, *Clear Light Put Out in Obscure Darkness* (Philadelphia, 1743), pp. 6-7; John Gerstner, *Steps to Salvation: The Evangelistic Message of Jonathan Edwards* (Philadelphia, 1960), p. 41; Dickinson, *Witness of the Spirit*, p. 5.

36. Appleton, *Clearest and Surest Marks*, p. 80; Thomson, *Doctrine of Convictions*, p. 39.

37. Thomson, *Doctrine of Convictions*, p. 34; Heimert and Miller, *Great Awakening*, pp. 487-89; Chauncy, *New Creature*, pp. 35-36.
38. Thomson, *Doctrine of Convictions*, p. 31.
39. Dickinson, *Display of God's Special Grace*, p. 30; Richard L. Bushman, ed., *The Great Awakening: Documents on the Revival of Religion, 1740–1745* (Chapel Hill: University of North Carolina Press, 1970), pp. 12, 76; Williston Walker, *Ten New England Leaders* (New York: Silver, Burdett & Co., 1901), p. 114.
40. Thomson, *Doctrine of Convictions*, p. 63.
41. Walker, *Ten New England Leaders*, p. 272; Chauncy, *Seasonable Thoughts*, pp. 2, 7-32.
42. Heimert and Miller, *Great Awakening*, pp. 50-55, 345, 487-89.
43. Finley, *Clear Light Put Out*, pp. 50, 55-56; Dickinson, *Witness of the Spirit*, pp. 25-26; William Williams, *Discourse on Saving Faith*, p. 20.
44. Edwards, *Religious Affections*, p. 95.
45. Edwards, "Faithful Narrative" and "The Distinguishing Marks of a Work of the Spirit of God," in *Great Awakening*, ed. Goen, pp. 176-77, 286.
46. Edwards, *Religious Affections*, p. 275.
47. Ibid., pp. 107, 251, 263, 278, 295, 320.
48. Heimert and Miller, *Great Awakening*, p. 173.
49. Ibid., pp. 248, 400; *A Protestation Presented to the Synod of Philadelphia, June 1, 1741* (Philadelphia, 1741), p. 11.
50. Joseph A. Conforti, *Samuel Hopkins and the New Divinity Movement* (Grand Rapids: William B. Eerdman, 1981), pp. 9-15, 26-27; James W. Schmotter, "The Irony of Clerical Professionalism: New England's Congregational Ministers and the Great Awakening," *American Quarterly* 31 (1979): 150-52; James W. Schmotter, "Ministerial Careers in Eighteenth-Century New England: The Social Context, 1700–1760," *Journal of Social History* 9 (1975): 253; Harry S. Stout, "The Great Awakening in New England Reconsidered," *Journal of Social History* 8 (1974): 28.
51. Edmund Morgan, *The Gentle Puritan: A Life of Ezra Stiles, 1727–1795* (New Haven, Conn.: Yale University Press, 1962), p. 32.
52. Bushman, *Great Awakening*, p. 76.
53. Edwards, *Great Concern of a Watchman*, p. 45; Samuel Hopkins, *The Life and Character of the Late Reverend, Learned, and Pious Mr. Jonathan Edwards* (Northampton, Mass., 1804), p. 55.
54. Edwards, "Faithful Narrative," pp. 175-76.
55. Ibid.

56. Finley, *Clear Light Put Out*, p. 49.
57. Thomson, *Doctrine of Convictions*, p. 35; Heimert and Miller, *Great Awakening*, pp. 487-89.
58. Chauncy, *Gifts of the Spirit*, pp. 8-11.
59. Thomson, *Doctrine of Convictions*, p. 34.
60. E. Clifford Nelson, ed., *The Lutherans in North America* (Philadelphia: Fortress Press, 1975), p. 64; Tappert, "Influence of Pietism in Lutheranism" (see ch. 1, n. 9), pp. 29-30; Schindler, "Psychology of Muhlenberg's Technique" (see ch. 1, n. 9), p. 55; Lea, *History of Auricular Confession* (see ch. 1, n. 5) 2:329. See also Philip M. Salvatori, S.J., *Practical Instruction for New Confessors* (see ch. 1, n. 7); St. Leonard of Port Maurice, *Counsels to Confessors* (see ch. 1, n. 7).
61. William McLoughlin, ed., *Isaac Backus on Church, State, and Calvinism: Pamphlets, 1754–1789* (Cambridge, Mass.: Harvard University Press, 1968), pp. 207, 218, 219, 222; Goen, *Revivalism and Separatism*, p. 215; see also William McLoughlin, *Isaac Backus and the American Pietistic Tradition* (Boston: Little, Brown & Co., 1967).
62. Samuel Hopkins, *Animadversions on Mr. Hart's Late Dialogue* (New London, Conn., 1770), p. 10; Joseph Bellamy, *A Careful and Strict Examination of the External Covenant* (New Haven, Conn.: 1770), p. 128; Stephen West, ed., *Sketches of the Life of the Late Rev. Samuel Hopkins, D.D., Pastor of the First Congregational Church in Newport, Written by Himself* (Hartford, Conn., 1805), pp. 29, 42; Edwards A. Park, *Memoir of the Life and Character of Samuel Hopkins, D.D.* (Boston, 1854), pp. 36-37.
63. William Hart, *A Letter to the Rev. Samuel Hopkins* (New London, Conn., 1770), p. 9; Moses Dickinson, *An Answer in the Form of a Familiar Letter* (New Haven, Conn., 1770), p. 6; Moses Mather, *The Visible Church in Covenant with God* (New Haven, Conn., 1770), pp. 36, 40, 49.
64. Heimert and Miller, *Great Awakening*, pp. 547-78.
65. Charles Chauncy, *Twelve Sermons* (Boston, 1765), p. 337; Chauncy, *Five Dissertations, On the Scripture Account of the Fall and Its Consequences* (London, 1785), p. 191.
66. L. A. Selby-Bigge, ed., *British Moralists* (Indianapolis: Bobbs-Merrill, 1964; 1st ed., 1897), pp. 33, 72, 104, 193, 199, 240, 355.
67. Jonathan Edwards, *The Nature of True Virtue* (1765) (Ann Arbor: University of Michigan Press, 1960), pp. 45, 47. Edwards had flirted with the Lockean notion that personal identity consists of self-consciousness and memory, but he eventually decided that God's creative power, rather than any autonomous self-consciousness, constitutes the enduring

self. See Edwards, "The Mind," in *Philosophy of Jonathan Edwards*, ed. Townsend, pp. 31, 70.

68. Jonathan Mayhew, *Seven Sermons* (Boston, 1749), pp. 123-29; Samuel Johnson, *Ethices Elementa; or, The First Principles of Moral Philosophy* (Boston, 1746), pp. 12, 61.

69. Mather, *Visible Church in Covenant*, pp. 5, 11-15, 145.

70. Conforti, *Samuel Hopkins and New Divinity Movement*, pp. 109-24.

71. Morgan, *Gentle Puritan*, p. 50; Fiering, *Moral Philosophy*, p. 371; Merle Curti, "The Great Mr. Locke: America's Philosopher, 1783–1861," *Huntington Library Bulletin* 11 (1937): 107-51; Daniel Walker Howe, *The Unitarian Conscience: Harvard Moral Philosophy, 1805–1861* (Cambridge, Mass.: 1970), p. 36.

72. Edwards, *Freedom of the Will*, pp. 142, 156-59, 172, 225.

73. James Dana, *An Examination of the Late Reverend President Edwards's "Enquiry on the Freedom of the Will"* (Boston, 1770), pp. 17-18.

74. Samuel West, *Essays on Liberty and Necessity, In Which the True Nature of Liberty Is Stated and Defended* (Boston, 1793), pp. 13-14; idem, *Essays on Liberty and Necessity . . . Part Second* (New Bedford, Mass., 1796), pp. 7-24.

75. Fiering, *Moral Philosophy*, pp. 147-206; Norman Kemp Smith, ed., *Descartes' Philosophical Writings* (New York: St. Martin's Press, 1952), pp. 288, 306.

76. Edwards, *Nature of True Virtue*, p. 71; John Witherspoon, "Lectures on Moral Philosophy," in *The Works of John Witherspoon* (Edinburgh, 1805) 7:25. I think that Garry Wills, *Inventing America: Jefferson's Declaration of Independence* (Garden City, N.Y.: Doubleday & Co., 1978), is entirely correct in emphasizing the influence of the Scottish philosophy on Jefferson's moral thought; I do not agree, however, with his further suggestion that Jefferson adopted the technical epistemology of the Scottish philosophers.

77. See Foster, *Their Solitary Way* (see ch. 2, n. 27), p. 7.

78. Lockridge, *New England Town* (see ch. 2, n. 27), pp. 93-164; Foster, *Their Solitary Way*, pp. 99-126; Nash, ed., *Class and Society in Early America* (see ch. 2, n. 28), pp. 18, 158, 174; Allan Kulikoff, "The Progress of Inequality in Revolutionary Boston," *William and Mary Quarterly* 28 (1971): 376; Main, *Social Structure of Revolutionary America* (see ch. 2, n. 27), pp. 164-96; Berthoff, *Unsettled People* (see ch. 2, n. 28), p. 87.

79. Heimert and Miller, *Great Awakening*, pp. 6, 559, 578; James A. Henretta, *The Evolution of American Society, 1700–1815* (Lexington, Mass.: D. C. Heath & Co., 1973), p. 99; Edmund S. Morgan, ed., *Puritan Political Ideas* (Indianapolis: Bobbs-

Merrill, 1965), p. 340; Chauncy, *Seasonable Thoughts*, pp. 319-25; Edwards, *Nature of True Virtue*, p. 35; Samuel Williams, *The Influence of Christianity on Civil Society* (Boston, 1780), p. 13.

80. J. Hamilton Moore, *Young Gentleman and Lady's Monitor* . . . , 6th ed. (New York, 1790).

81. Arthur M. Schlesinger, *Learning How to Behave: A Historical Study of American Etiquette Books* (New York: Macmillan Co., 1946), pp. 8-14; John Gregory, *A Father's Legacy to His Daughter* (Philadelphia, 1775), p. 13; see also Hester Chapone, *Letters on the Improvement of the Mind, Addressed to a Young Lady* (Worcester, Mass., 1783), p. 71.

82. Main, *Social Structure of Revolutionary America*, pp. 68-115; Henry May, *The Enlightenment in America* (New York: Oxford University Press, 1976), p. 78.

83. Joseph Lyman, *The Approbation of God, the Great Object and Reward of the Gospel Ministry* (Norwich, Conn., 1780), p. 15; Nathan O. Hatch, "The Christian Movement and the Demand for a Theology of the People," *Journal of American History* 67 (1980): 545-67.

84. John Wingate Thornton, ed., *The Pulpit of the American Revolution; or, The Political Sermons of the Period of 1776* (Boston, 1860), pp. 168, 267, 273, 362; Samuel Cooper, *A Sermon Preached Before His Excellency John Hancock* (Boston, 1780), p. 3; Frank Moore, ed., *The Patriot Preachers of the American Revolution* (Boston, 1860), pp. 206, 226; Edmund S. Morgan, "The Puritan Ethic and the American Revolution," *William and Mary Quarterly* 24 (1967): 3-43; Bernard Friedman, "The Shaping of the Radical Consciousness in Provincial New York," *Journal of American History* 56 (1970): 781-800.

85. Merle Curti, *Human Nature in American Thought: A History* (Madison: University of Wisconsin Press, 1980), pp. 97, 105-46; Roy P. Fairfield, ed., *The Federalist Papers* (Garden City, N.Y.: Doubleday & Co., 1961), p. 155.

4: Balance, Gentility, Self-Culture

1. J.D.B. DeBow, *Statistical View of the United States* (Washington, D.C., 1854), pp. 126-27; Ichabod Spencer, *A Pastor's Sketches*, 2d series (New York, 1866; 1st printing, 1853), pp. v-viii; John Todd, *The Pulpit* (Northampton, Mass., 1834), p. 61.

2. William Sprague, ed., *Annals of the American Pulpit* (New York, 1858) 4:711-20.

3. Ichabod Spencer, *A Pastor's Sketches*, 1st series (New York, 1851; 1st printing, 1850), pp. 157-59.

4. Alan Dawley, *Class and Community: The Industrial Revolution in Lynn* (Cambridge, Mass.: Harvard University Press, 1976), pp. 11-41; Eugene Genovese, *Roll, Jordan, Roll: The World the Slaves Made* (New York: Random House, 1974); Stuart Blumin, "Mobility and Change in Ante-Bellum Philadelphia," in *Nineteenth-Century Cities: Essays in the New Urban History,* ed. Stephen Thernstrom and Richard Sennett (New Haven, Conn.: Yale University Press, 1969), pp. 165-208.

5. Edward Pessen, *Jacksonian America: Society, Personality, and Politics* (Homewood, Ill.: Dorsey Press, 1969), pp. 114-15; Paul E. Johnson, *A Shopkeeper's Millennium: Society and Revivals in Rochester, New York, 1815–1837* (New York: Hill & Wang, 1978), pp. 37-61; George Rogers Taylor, *The Transportation Revolution 1815–1860* (New York: Rinehart & Co., 1951), pp. 207-28; review by John William Ward, *The New York Times Book Review* (August 30, 1981), p. 1.

6. Taylor, *Transportation Revolution,* pp. 15-31, 132-52, 176-206; Leo Marx, *The Machine in the Garden* (New York: Oxford University Press, 1964), pp. 3-33.

7. Pessen, *Jacksonian American,* p. 121; Taylor, *Transportation Revolution,* pp. 229-49; Blumin, "Mobility and Change," p. 201.

8. Donald M. Scott, *From Office to Profession: The New England Ministry, 1750–1850* (Philadelphia: University of Pennsylvania Press, 1978), pp. 148-51; Pessen, *Jacksonian Democracy,* pp. 116-19; Nancy Cott, *The Bonds of Womanhood* (New Haven, Conn.: Yale University Press, 1977), pp. 5-7.

9. Rothman, *Discovery of the Asylum* (see ch. 2, n. 37), p. 57; Joseph F. Kett, *Rites of Passage: Adolescence in America* (New York: Basic Books, 1977), p. 36; Taylor, *Transportation Revolution,* pp. 3-5; Richard D. Brown, "The Emergence of Urban Society in Rural Massachusetts, 1760–1820," *Journal of American History* 61 (1974): 29-50; Leonard Curry, "Urbanization and Urbanism in the Old South: A Comparative View," in *The Many-Faceted Jacksonian Era: New Interpretations,* ed. Edward Pessen (Westport, Conn.: Greenwood Press, 1977), pp. 82-97.

10. Horace Bushnell, *Prosperity Our Duty* (Hartford, Conn., 1847), p. 21; Philip Schaff, *America: A Sketch of Its Political Ideas and Religious Character,* ed. Perry Miller (Cambridge, Mass.: Harvard University Press, 1961; 1st ed., 1855), pp. 52-53; Henretta, *Evolution of American Society* (see ch. 3, n. 79), p. 198; Berthoff, *Unsettled People* (see ch. 2, n. 28), p. 187; Pessen, *Jacksonian America,* pp. 114-15. See also Anthony F. C. Wallace, *Rockdale: The Growth of an American Village in the Early Industrial Revolution* (New York: Alfred A.

Knopf, 1978); Johnson, *Shopkeeper's Millennium;* Holifield, *Gentlemen Theologians* (see ch. 1, n. 29); Pessen, ed., *Many-Faceted Jacksonian Era,* pp. 7-47, 114-41.

11. Schaff, *America,* p. 54; Johnson, *Shopkeeper's Millennium,* p. 19; Richard Carwardine, *Trans-Atlantic Revivalism* (Westport, Conn.: Greenwood Press, 1978), p. 23; Edward Pessen, *Riches, Class, and Power Before the Civil War* (Lexington, Mass.: D. C. Heath & Co., 1973), pp. 169-247; Berthoff, *Unsettled People,* p. 226; Holifield, *Gentlemen Theologians,* pp. 5-23; Anon. to C. B. Dana, 1 March 1858, Dana Papers, Louisiana State University.

12. Francis Wayland, *The Apostolic Ministry* (Rochester, N.Y., 1853), p. 60; Neil Harris, *Humbug: The Art of P. T. Barnum* (Boston: Little, Brown & Co., 1973), pp. 61-89; Carl Bode, *Antebellum Culture* (Carbondale, Ill.: Southern Illinois University Press, 1970; 1st ed., 1950), pp. 119-30; E. Douglas Branch, *The Sentimental Years 1836–1860* (New York: Appleton-Century Co., 1934), pp. 257-88.

13. Branch, *Sentimental Years,* p. 172; Fred Lewis Pattee, *The Feminine Fifties* (New York: Appleton-Century Co., 1940), pp. 57, 284. See also Meade Minnigerode, *The Fabulous Fifties* (New York: G. P. Putnam's Sons, 1924), p. 135; Bode, *Antebellum Culture,* pp. 7-89; Ronald G. Walters, *Primers for Prudery: Sexual Advice to Victorian America* (Englewood Cliffs, N.J.: Prentice-Hall, 1974).

14. Enoch Pond, *The Young Pastor's Guide; or, Lectures on Pastoral Duties* (Bangor, Maine, 1844), pp. 20, 23; Holifield, *Gentlemen Theologians,* p. 20; Edward A. Lawrence, *The Life of Rev. Joel Hawes* (Hartford, Conn., 1871), p. 54; Benjamin Bacon, *Theodore Thornton Munger: New England Minister* (New Haven, Conn.: Yale University Press, 1913), p. 79; Scott, *From Office to Profession,* pp. 64-75; Spencer, *Pastor's Sketches* (1853), p. viii.

15. Charles Grandison Finney, *Memoirs of Rev. Charles G. Finney* (New York: Fleming H. Revell Co., 1911; 1st ed., 1876), pp. 88-89, 289, 293, 366; Richard Carwardine, "The Second Great Awakening in the Urban Centers," *Journal of American History* 59 (1972): 327-40; Timothy L. Smith, *Revivalism and Social Reform* (New York: Harper & Row, 1965; 1st ed., 1957); Carwardine, *Trans-Atlantic Revivalism,* pp. 3-56.

16. Brian Heeney, *A Different Kind of Gentleman* (Hamden, Conn.: Shoe String Press, 1976), pp. 93, 117-18, 151-61.

17. Raymond J. Cunningham, "From Preachers of the Word to Physicians of the Soul," *Journal of Religious History* 3 (1965): 330; Leonard Woods, *History of the Andover Theological Seminary* (Boston, 1885), pp. 147, 158; *Addresses at the*

Observance of the 100th Anniversary of the Establishment of the Harvard Divinity School (Cambridge, Mass., 1917), p. 16; Edward H. Roberts, *Biographical Catalogue of Princeton Theological Seminary, 1815–1932* (Princeton, N.J., 1933), p. xx. See Roland Bainton, *Yale and the Ministry* (New York: Harper & Brothers, 1957).

18. William B. Sprague, ed., *Annals of the American Pulpit* (New York, 1858) 3:603; Pond, *Young Pastor's Guide*, p. iv; Archibald Alexander, *Thoughts on Religious Experience* (Philadelphia, 1850; 1st ed., 1844), p. 7; James Spencer Cannon, *Lectures on Pastoral Theology* (New York, 1859), p. 575.

19. Adam Clarke, *The Preacher's Manual* (New York, 1820), pp. 108-9; Wayland, *Apostolic Ministry*, pp. 59, 74.

20. John Holt Rice, editorial, *Virginia Evangelical and Literary Magazine* 6 (1823): 424; George Howe, *A Discourse on Theological Education* (New York, 1844), p. 118; Holifield, *Gentlemen Theologians*, pp. 33-34; Edwards A. Park, "Introductory Essay," in *The Preacher and the Pastor* (Andover, N.H., 1845), p. 12; Scott, *From Office to Profession*, p. 115; Wayland, *Apostolic Ministry*, p. 79; Pond, *Young Pastor's Guide*, pp. 37, 73.

21. Scott, *From Office to Profession*, p. 43; Heman Humphrey, *Thirty-Four Letters to a Son in the Ministry* (Amherst, Mass., 1842), p. 17; Pond, *Young Pastor's Guide*, p. 125. See Sidney E. Mead, "The Rise of the Evangelical Conception of the Ministry in America," in *Ministry in Historical Perspectives*, ed. Niebuhr and Williams (see ch. 2, n. 6), p. 229; Holifield, *Gentlemen Theologians*, p. 22.

22. Samuel Miller, *Letters on Clerical Manners and Habits* (New York, 1827), pp. 42, 93-94, 132; Cannon, *Pastoral Theology*, p. 550; Stephen H. Tyng, *The Office and Duty of a Christian Pastor* (New York, 1874), p. 72, based on lectures given during the antebellum period.

23. Miller, *Clerical Manners*, p. 339; Barbara Welter, *Dimity Convictions: The American Woman in the Nineteenth Century* (Athens: Ohio University Press, 1976), pp. 21-47, 84-94; William H. Chafe, *Women and Equality: Changing Patterns in American Culture* (New York: Oxford University Press, 1977), pp. 27-34; Joan Jacobs Brumberg, *Mission for Life: The Story of the Family of Adoniram Judson* (New York: Free Press, 1980), pp. 79-106.

24. Miller, *Clerical Manners*, pp. 19, 104.

25. Burton J. Bledstein, *The Culture of Professionalism: The Middle Class and the Development of Higher Education in America* (New York: W. W. Norton & Co., 1976), p. 216.

26. Kett, *Rites of Passage*, p. 107; John Foster, *Decision of*

Character and Other Essays (New York, 1830); Miller, *Clerical Manners*, p. 396; Charles F. Kemp, *Physicians of the Soul: A History of Pastoral Counseling* (New York: Macmillan Co., 1947), p. 56; Lawrence, *Life of Hawes*, p. 118.

27. Spencer, *Pastor's Sketches* (1853), pp. 123-33.

28. Pond, *Young Pastor's Guide*, p. 67; Welter, *Dimity Convictions*, pp. 21, 47, 84-91, 129; Ann Douglas, *The Feminization of American Culture* (New York: Avon Books, 1978), pp. 107-91.

29. Charles C. Jones, *The Religious Instruction of the Negroes in the United States* (New York: Negro Universities Press, 1969; 1st ed., Savannah, Ga., 1842), pp. 179, 192-219, 232; Edward P. Wimberly, *Pastoral Care in the Black Church* (Nashville: Abingdon Press, 1979), pp. 24-29; Scott, *From Office to Profession*, pp. 95-132.

30. T. O. Summers, ed., *Sermons and Essays by Ministers of the Methodist Episcopal Church* (Nashville, 1857), pp. 4-5; Pond, *Young Pastor's Guide*, p. 20; Miller, *Clerical Manners*, pp. 19, 104; James M. Hoppin, *The Office and Work of the Christian Ministry* (New York, 1869), p. 467; Holifield, *Gentlemen Theologians*, pp. 36-43.

31. Cannon, *Pastoral Theology*, pp. 543-44; Miller, *Clerical Manners*, p. 153.

32. Increase Tarbox, ed., *Diary of Thomas Robbins, D.D., 1796–1854* (Boston, 1887), 1:263, 423, 472-74, 481, 2:641; Cunningham, "Preachers of the Word," p. 333; Wayland, *Apostolic Ministry*, p. 73; Miller, *Clerical Manners*, p. 153; Hoppin, *Office of Christian Ministry*, p. 523; Pond, *Young Pastor's Guide*, p. 65.

33. Alexander, *Thoughts on Religious Experience*, p. 6; Samuel Tyler, *A Discourse of the Baconian Philosophy* (Frederick City, Md., 1844), p. xx; Theodore Dwight Bozeman, *Protestants in an Age of Science: The Baconian Ideal and Antebellum American Religious Thought* (Chapel Hill: University of North Carolina Press, 1977), pp. 44-70.

34. "Thoughts on the Mental and Moral Character of Christian Ministers," *The Biblical Repertory and Theological Review* 8 (1831): 283; Bozeman, *Protestants in an Age of Science*, pp. 44-70; Tyler, *Baconian Philosophy*, p. 65; A Baconian Biblist, *A Practical View of the Common Causes of Inefficiency in the Christian Ministry of the Congregational and Presbyterian Churches of the United States* (Philadelphia, 1830), p. 4.

35. Alexander, *Thoughts on Religious Experience*, pp. 6, 26-27; Miller, *Clerical Manners*, p. 135; Hoppin, *Office of Christian Ministry*, pp. 656-66.

36. Holifield, *Gentlemen Theologians*, p. 142; Alexander, *Thoughts on Religious Experience*, pp. 79-205; Pond, *Young*

Pastor's Guide, p. 87; Marie Caskey, *Chariot of Fire: Religion and the Beecher Family* (New Haven, Conn.: Yale University Press, 1978), pp. 26-27.

37. Pond, *Young Pastor's Guide*, p. 292; Park, *Preacher and Pastor*, p. 13.
38. Spencer, *Pastor's Sketches* (1853), pp. 29-34.
39. Humphrey, *Thirty-Four Letters*, pp. 235-36.
40. Jonathan B. Condit, "Introduction," in John A. James, *An Earnest Ministry the Want of the Times* (Philadelphia, 1848), p. viii. Miller, *Clerical Manners*, pp. 136-38.
41. Ibid., p. 148.
42. Humphrey, *Thirty-Four Letters*, p. 231. See also Hoppin, *Office of Christian Ministry*, p. 562; Eliza Buckminster Lee, *Memoirs of the Rev. Joseph Buckminster, D.D., and of His Son, Rev. Joseph Stevens Buckminster* (Boston, 1849), pp. 177, 184. Douglas, *Feminization of American Culture*, pp. 151-73, emphasizes the sentimentality in a one-sided manner. Daniel Walker Howe, *Unitarian Conscience* (see ch. 3, n. 71), pp. 69-92, gives a balanced account of the dialectic of rationality and sentiment in Unitarian thought.
43. Enger, "Private Confession in American Lutheranism" (Ph.D. diss., Princeton, 1962), p. 157; F. L. Hawks, *Auricular Confession in the Protestant Episcopal Church* (New York, 1850), pp. 42-44, 82, 106; Edmond F. Prendergast, ed., *Diary and Visitation Record of the Rt. Rev. Francis Patrick Kenrick* (Lancaster, Pa.: n.p., 1916), p. 107.
44. Holifield, *Gentlemen Theologians*, pp. 77-84.
45. Joseph Haven, *Mental Philosophy: Including the Intellect, Sensibilities, and Will* (Boston, 1857), p. 23; Asa Burton, *Essays on Some of the First Principles of Metaphysicks, Ethicks, and Theology* (Portland, Maine, 1824), p. 4; James Marsh, "Preliminary Essay," in *Aids to Reflection*, vol. 1 of *The Complete Works of Samuel Taylor Coleridge* (New York, 1863) 1:81; Bacon, *Theodore Thornton Munger*, p. 68.
46. Nathan Fiske, "The Value of Mental Philosophy to the Minister of the Gospel," in *Memoir of the Rev. Nathan W. Fiske*, ed. Heman Humphrey (Amherst, Mass., 1850), p. 320.
47. Archibald Alexander, *Evidences of the Authority, Inspiration, and Canonical Authority of the Holy Scriptures* (Philadelphia, 1836), p. 11; Holifield, *Gentlemen Theologians*, pp. 88-90.
48. Holifield, *Gentlemen Theologians*, p. 100.
49. Thomas Ralston, *Elements of Divinity* (Nashville, 1871; 1st ed., 1847), p. 361.
50. Alexander, *Evidences*, pp. 190, 200.
51. Cited in Howe, *Unitarian Conscience*, p. 153.
52. "Proceedings of the First Ten Years of the American Tract

Society Instituted at Boston, 1814," in *The American Tract Society Documents 1814–1925* (New York: Arno Press, 1972), pp. 9-20.

53. *The Address of the Executive Committee of the American Tract Society to the Christian Public* (New York, 1825), p. 5; *The Second Annual Report of the Executive Committee of the American Tract Society* (New York, 1827), p. 10.

54. Howe, *Unitarian Conscience*, p. 160; Alexander, *Thoughts on Religious Experience*, p. 232; E. H. Chapin, *The Crown of Thorns: A Token for the Sorrowing* (Boston, 1847), pp. iv, 16, 24; G. T. Bedell, *It Is Well; or, Faith's Estimate of Afflictions* (Philadelphia, 1832), pp. 15, 25; A. P. Peabody, *Christian Consolations* (Boston, 1847), p. 54; Henry Bacon, *The Christian Comforter* (Boston, 1854; 1st ed., 1850), pp. 20, 23, 24, 32.

55. Jonathan Cole, *Meditations for the Sick* (Boston, 1837), pp. 10, 19, 57-81, 68; J.F.W. Ware, *The Silent Pastor* (Boston, 1863), p. 66; M. J. Bishop, *Thoughts in a Sick-Chamber* (Boston, 1859), pp. 18, 74.

56. Scott, *From Office to Profession*, pp. 138-40; Chapin, *Crown of Thorns*, p. 28; Douglas, *Feminization of American Culture*, p. 143; Welter, *Dimity Convictions*, pp. 84-93.

57. E. A. Park, "The Theology of the Intellect and that of the Feelings," *Bibliotheca Sacra and Theological Review* 7 (1850): 536, 545, 551, 554; Horace Bushnell, "Our Gospel a Gift to the Imagination," in *Building Eras in Religion* (New York, 1881), pp. 249-85.

58. Holifield, *Gentlemen Theologians*, p. 187.

59. Ibid., p. 189.

60. Ibid., pp. 189, 191, 201.

61. Ibid., p. 192.

62. William Ellery Channing, *A Selection from the Works of William E. Channing* (Boston, 1855), pp. 9-10; Howe, *Unitarian Conscience*, pp. 67-68; Nathaniel William Taylor, "Review of Spring on the Means of Regeneration," *Christian Spectator* 1 (1829): 17-21.

63. Charles G. Finney, "Sinners Bound to Change Their Own Hearts," in *Notions of the Americans 1820–1860*, ed. David Grimsted (New York: George Braziller, 1970), pp. 78, 82.

64. John Wesley, *Thoughts on Christian Perfection*, in *John Wesley*, ed. Albert Outler (New York: Oxford University Press, 1964), pp. 286-98; Nathaniel W. Taylor, *Concio ad Clerum* (New Haven, Conn., 1828), pp. 8, 13; Eleazar T. Fitch, *Two Discourses on the Nature of Sin* (New Haven, Conn., 1826), p. 5; Finney, "Sinners Bound to Change Their Hearts," p. 82; H. Shelton Smith, *Changing Conceptions of Original Sin* (New York: Charles Scribner's Sons, 1955), pp. 86-136.

65. *Historical Sketch of Union College, Founded at Schenectady, New York, February 25, 1795* (Washington, D.C., 1876), p. 30; Park, *Preacher and Pastor*, p. 14; Ezra Stiles Ely, *Conversations on the Science of the Human Mind* (Philadelphia, 1819); Fiske, *Memoir;* Enoch Pond, "Philosophy in the Church," *Southern Presbyterian Review* 4 (1850): 157.

66. Burton, *Essays*, p. 82.

67. Alexander, *Evidences*, p. v; Fiske, "Value of Mental Philosophy," p. 355.

68. Witherspoon, *Lectures on Moral Philosophy* (see ch. 3, n. 76), p. 18; see also Ely, *Conversations*, pp. 218-28.

69. Locke, *Essay Concerning Human Understanding* (see ch. 2, n. 46) 1:159; Thomas Reid, *Essays on the Active Powers of the Human Mind*, vol. 3 of *The Works of Thomas Reid*, ed. Dugald Stewart (New York, 1822) 3:2; Dugald Stewart, *The Philosophy of the Active and Moral Powers of Man* (Boston, 1828) 1:2; Thomas C. Upham, *Elements of Mental Philosophy* (Boston, 1832; 1st ed., 1831), pp. 168, 484 (an expanded version of his *Elements of Intellectual Philosophy*).

70. Burton, *Essays*, pp. 11, 53-61, 91.

71. Ibid., pp. 91, 138-46.

72. Upham, *Elements of Mental Philosophy*, pp. 20, 30; Frederick A. Rauch, *Psychology; or, A View of the Human Soul* (New York, 1840), p. 181; R. H. Rivers, *Elements of Mental Philosophy*, ed. T. O. Summers (Nashville, 1872; 1st ed., 1861), p. 253; S. S. Schmucker, *Psychology; or, Elements of a New System of Mental Philosophy, on the Basis of Consciousness and Common Sense* (New York, 1843; 1st ed., 1842), p. 30; Haven, *Mental Philosophy*, p. 36.

73. Reid, *Works* 2:74, 90; Holifield, *Gentlemen Theologians*, pp. 110-26.

74. Dugald Stewart, "The Life and Writings of Thomas Reid," in Reid, *Works* 1:19; Reid, *Works* 2:44, 83; Schmucker, *Psychology*, p. v; Fiske, "Value of Mental Philosophy," p. 27.

75. This paragraph is based on my reading of Rivers, *Elements of Mental Philosophy;* Schmucker, *Psychology;* Haven, *Mental Philosophy;* Rauch, *Psychology;* Ely, *Conversations;* and Upham, *Elements of Mental Philosophy.*

76. Rauch, *Psychology*, pp. 88-147; Haven, *Mental Philosophy*, pp. 22, 399-401; Fiske, "Value of Mental Philosophy," pp. 339, 355.

77. Horace Bushnell, *God in Christ* (Hartford, Conn., 1849), p. 73; Haven, *Mental Philosophy*, p. 378. For this idea I am indebted to Fiering, *Moral Philosophy* (see ch. 2, n. 41), p. 183; Erich Kahler, *The Inward Turn of Narrative* (Princeton, N.J.: Princeton University Press, 1973), pp. 5-7, 66-67; Walter Ong,

"Reading, Technology, and the Nature of Man," *Yearbook of English Studies* 10 (1980): 132-49.

78. Haven, *Mental Philosophy*, pp. 24, 532.

79. Thomas Upham, *A Philosophical and Practical Treatise on the Will* (Portland, Maine, 1834), pp. 60, 72.

80. Ely, *Conversations*, p. 19.

81. Fiske, "The Fearfulness of Man's Mental Constitution," in *Memoir*, p. 246; Pond, *Young Pastor's Guide*, pp. 293-94; Holifield, *Gentlemen Theologians*, p. 143; Thomas Smyth, "The Province of Reason, Especially in Matters of Religion," *Southern Presbyterian Review* 7 (1853-54): 279.

82. Benjamin Rush, "The Influence of Physical Causes on the Moral Faculty" (1786), in *American Philosophic Addresses*, ed. Joseph L. Blau (New York: Columbia University Press, 1946), p. 339.

83. Madeline B. Stern, *Heads and Headlines: The Phrenological Fowlers* (Norman: University of Oklahoma Press, 1971), p. xii; John Neal, "Man" (1838), in *American Philosophic Addresses*, ed. Blau, p. 378.

84. See Greven, *Protestant Temperament* (see ch. 2, n. 38).

85. Willard, *Compleat Body* (see ch. 2, n. 12), p. 584; Baxter, *Christian Directory*, vol. 2 of *Works* (see ch. 2, n. 43) 2:460-61.

86. William Paley, *Principles of Moral and Political Philosophy* (Boston, 1821), pp. 46, 248.

87. Francis Wayland, *Elements of Moral Science*, ed. Joseph Blau (Cambridge, Mass.: Harvard University Press, 1973; 1st ed., 1835), pp. 57-58, 97-99.

88. Taylor, "Review of Spring," pp. 20-22; Bennet Tyler, *Lectures on the Origin and Progress of the New Haven Theology* (New York, 1827), pp. 157, 160; Charles G. Finney, *Finney's Lectures on Systematic Theology*, ed. J. H. Fairfield (Oberlin, Ohio, 1878; 1st ed., 1846-47), pp. 141, 181.

89. Witherspoon, *Lectures on Moral Philosophy*, pp. 67-68; R. H. Rivers, *Elements of Moral Philosophy*, ed. T. O. Summers (Nashville, 1861; 1st ed., 1859), p. 195; Laurens P. Hickok, *A System of Moral Science* (Schenectady, N.Y., 1853), pp. 87-89.

90. William E. Channing, *Self-Culture* (Boston, 1845), pp. 21, 26-27; idem, *The Works of William E. Channing* (Boston, 1890), pp. 340, 343, 1004-5.

91. Hickok, *System of Moral Science*, p. 106; Channing, *Works*, pp. 1004, 1012; Rivers, *Elements of Moral Philosophy*, p. 203.

5: The Natural Style

1. Newman Smyth, *Christian Ethics* (New York, 1892), pp. 479, 495; Washington Gladden, *Ruling Ideas of the Present Age* (Boston, 1895), p. 294.

2. William Jewett Tucker, *My Generation: An Autobiographical Interpretation* (Boston: Houghton Mifflin Co., 1919), p. 91.
3. Henry Churchill King, *Reconstruction in Theology* (New York: Macmillan Co., 1901), pp. v, 234.
4. William S. Plumer, *Hints and Helps in Pastoral Theology* (New York, 1874), pp. 274-76.
5. Leslie A. Fiedler, *Love and Death in the American Novel* (New York: Stein & Day, 1960), pp. 262-72; Plumer, *Hints and Helps*, p. 276.
6. H. M. Sydenstricker, "The Science of Conversion," in *The Fundamentals* (Chicago: Testimony Publishing Co., 1910) 8:69; R. A. Torrey, *How to Bring Men to Christ* (New York: Fleming H. Revell Co., 1910), pp. 70, 20-93.
7. R. A. Torrey, *The Baptism with the Holy Spirit* (New York, 1895), pp. 12, 56-57.
8. Sydenstricker, "Science of Conversion," pp. 64-65, 70, 72. See George M. Marsden, *Fundamentalism and American Culture* (New York: Oxford University Press, 1980).
9. F. L. Godkin, "The Clergyman of Today," *The Nation* 69 (October, 1899): 311.
10. Horace Bushnell, *Nature and the Supernatural* (New York, 1858), pp. 187, 191, 211, 213, 258.
11. Gladden, *Ruling Ideas*, p. 9; William Newton Clarke, *An Outline of Christian Theology* (New York, 1894), pp. 86, 117; Smyth, *Christian Ethics*, p. 28.
12. Josiah Strong, *Our Country*, ed. Jurgen Herbst (Cambridge, Mass.: Harvard University Press, 1963), p. 14; Torrey, *Baptism with the Holy Spirit*, p. 74; A. C. Dixon, ed., *The Person and Ministry of the Holy Spirit* (Baltimore, 1890), pp. 3, 87; J. Stuart Holden, *The Price of Power* (New York: Fleming H. Revell Co., 1908), p. 14; Arthur T. Pierson, "Divine Efficacy of Prayer," in *The Fundamentals* 9:82; D. L. Moody, *Secret Power* (Chicago, 1881), p. 12; W. E. Blackstone, *Jesus Is Coming* (New York: Fleming H. Revell Co., 1908), pp. 225-30; Walter Rauschenbusch, *Christianity and the Social Crisis* (New York: Macmillan Co., 1907), p. 6; Washington Gladden, *The Church and the Kingdom* (New York, 1894), p. 25.
13. Smyth, *Christian Ethics*, p. 379.
14. George M. Frederickson, *The Inner Civil War: Northern Intellectuals and the Crisis of the Union* (New York: Harper & Row, 1968; 1st ed., 1965), pp. 68-110, 211-13; James H. Moorhead, *American Apocalypse: Yankee Protestants and the Civil War* (New Haven, Conn.: Yale University Press, 1978), pp. 146-49.
15. Theodore P. Greene, *America's Heroes: The Changing Models of Success in American Magazines* (New York: Oxford

University Press, 1970), pp. 59-165; Henry Ward Beecher, *Yale Lectures on Preaching* (New York, 1892), pp. 120, 192.

16. Gladden, *Ruling Ideas*, p. 77; Newman Smyth, *Passing Protestantism and the Coming Catholicism* (New York: Charles Scribner's Sons, 1908), p. 13; Rauschenbusch, *Christianity and Social Crisis*, p. xii; Smyth, *Christian Ethics*, p. 446; Strong, *Our Country*, p. 150.

17. John Higham, "The Reorientation of American Culture in the 1890's," in *Writing American History: Essays on Modern Scholarship* (Bloomington: Indiana University Press, 1970), pp. 77-100; C. Howard Hopkins, *History of the Y.M.C.A. in North America* (New York: Association Press, 1951), p. 245; Gladden, *Ruling Ideas*, p. 125; Smyth, *Christian Ethics*, p. 13. See also Bledstein, *Culture of Professionalism* (see ch. 4, n. 25), p. 153; Frederickson, *Inner Civil War*, pp. 223-34; Kett, *Rites of Passage* (see ch. 4, n. 9), pp. 163-77.

18. Acts 1:8; I Cor. 9:25.

19. For conservative examples, see J. Wilbur Chapman, *The Power of a Surrendered Life* (New York: Fleming H. Revell Co., 1901); J. Stuart Holden, *The Price of Power* (New York: Fleming H. Revell Co., 1908); Dwight L. Moody, *Secret Power* (Chicago, 1881); A. C. Dixon, ed., *The Person and Ministry of the Holy Spirit* (Baltimore, 1890); Torrey, *Baptism with the Holy Spirit*; R. A. Torrey, *How to Obtain Fullness of Power in Christian Life and Service* (New York, 1897). For liberal examples, see Clarke, *Outline of Christian Theology*, pp. 27, 39, 150, 442; T. T. Munger, *Character Through Inspiration* (London, 1897), p. 6; Gladden, *Ruling Ideas*, p. 10; Smyth, *Passing Protestantism*, p. 5. For social gospel imagery, see Rauschenbusch, *Christianity and Social Crisis*, pp. xii, 6, 119; Walter Rauschenbusch, *A Theology for the Social Gospel* (Nashville: Abgindon Press, 1978; 1st ed., New York: Macmillan Co., 1917), pp. 11, 12, 40, 72, 75, 87, 139, 165; Gladden, *Church and the Kingdom*, pp. 10, 11, 33, 39; George Herron, *The Christian State: A Political Vision of Christ* (New York, 1895), p. 24. For Christian Science, see Mary Baker Eddy, *Science and Health with Key to the Scriptures* (Boston, 1899; 1st ed., 1875), pp. 25, 28, 79, 124, 166. For New Thought, see Ralph Waldo Trine, *In Tune with the Infinite* (New York, 1897), pp. 11-12.

20. William E. Winn, "*Tom Brown's School Days* and the Development of 'Muscular Christianity,'" *Church History* 29 (1960): 64-73.

21. Smyth, *Christian Ethics*, p. 405; Munger, *Character Through Inspiration*, pp. 55-72; Kett, *Rites of Passage*, p. 203; William

G. McLoughlin, Jr., *Billy Sunday Was His Real Name* (Chicago: University of Chicago Press, 1955), pp. 141, 179.

22. Smyth, *Christian Ethics*, pp. 243, 246, 334-35, 379; Munger, *Character Through Inspiration*, pp. 9, 55-72, 132; Horace Bushnell, *Forgiveness and Law* (New York, 1874), pp. 134-35. See also Newman Smyth, *Old Faiths in New Light* (New York, 1879), p. 125.

23. Theodore Cuyler, *How to Be a Pastor* (New York, 1890), p. 18.

24. Paul Boyer, *Urban Masses and Moral Order in America 1820–1920* (Cambridge, Mass.: Harvard University Press, 1978), pp. 123, 130; Bledstein, *Culture of Professionalism*, p. 46; Robert Wiebe, *The Search for Order* (New York: Hill & Wang, 1967), pp. 2-121.

25. Kemp, *Physicians of the Soul* (see ch. 4, n. 26), p. 94; G. B. Willcox, *The Pastor Amidst His Flock* (New York, 1890), pp. 145-46; Thomas Murphy, *Pastoral Theology: The Pastor in the Various Duties of His Office* (Philadelphia, 1877), p. 3; Rauschenbusch, *Christianity and Social Crisis*, p. 302; H. K. Carroll, "The Pay of Preachers," *The Forum* 17 (1894): 741-52; [John James Tigert], *The Preacher Himself: Homely Hints on Ministerial Manners and Methods* (Nashville, 1889), p. 22; Cuyler, *How to Be a Pastor*, p. 125; Bledstein, *Culture of Professionalism*, p. 138.

26. Willcox, *Pastor Amidst His Flock*, p. 107.

27. Beecher, *Yale Lectures on Preaching*, pp. 155, 159.

28. William C. Beecher and Samuel Scoville, *A Biography of the Rev. Henry Ward Beecher* (New York, 1888), p. 231; Willcox, *Pastor Amidst His Flock*, p. 107.

29. Albert Joseph Lyman, *The Christian Pastor in the New Age* (New York: Thomas Y. Crowell & Co., 1909), p. 139; Willcox, *Pastor Amidst His Flock*, pp. 109-10.

30. Willcox, *Pastor Amidst His Flock*, p. 9.

31. Murphy, *Pastoral Theology*, p. 3; Willcox, *Pastor Amidst His Flock*, pp. 7-10; Washington Gladden, *The Christian Pastor and the Working Church* (New York: Charles Scribner's Sons, 1909), pp. 210-11. See also John Watson, *The Cure of Souls* (New York, 1896).

32. For changes in the seminary curriculum, I am indebted to Robert Lynn of the Lilly Foundation, who is engaged in a major study of the history of theological education in America. See also Kemp, *Physicians of the Soul*, pp. 243-44; Francis Strickland, "Pastoral Psychology: A Retrospect," *Pastoral Psychology* 4 (1953): 9.

33. Willcox, *Pastor Admidst His Flock*, pp. 10, 145. See also Murphy, *Pastoral Theology*, p. 19; Gladden, *Christian Pastor*, p. 95; the references in Kemp, *Physicians of the Soul*,

pp. 61-63; Lyman, *Christian Pastor*, p. 94; James M. Hoppin, *Pastoral Theology* (New York, 1885), p. 413.

34. Hoppin, *Pastoral Theology*, pp. 152, 176, 178, 195, 196, 207; T. Harwood Pattison, *For the Work of the Ministry* (Philadelphia: American Baptist Publication Society, 1907), pp. 4, 26.

35. Howard Henderson, *The Ethics and Etiquette of the Pulpit, Pew, Parish, Press, and Platform* (Cincinnati, 1892), p. 6; [Tigert], *Preacher Himself*, p. 128; Willcox, *Pastor Amidst His Flock*, p. 16; Charles F. Thwing, *The Working Church* (New York, 1889), p. 69; Robert Allen, *Letters of an Old Methodist to His Son in the Ministry* (New York: Fleming H. Revell Co., 1904), p. 11; Henry Churchill King, *Rational Living* (New York: Macmillan Co., 1905), p. 60.

36. Hoppin, *Pastoral Theology*, p. 155; Beecher, *Yale Lectures on Preaching*, 3:10; Clifford E. Clark, Jr., *Henry Ward Beecher: Spokesman for a Middle-Class America* (Urbana: University of Illinois Press, 1978), pp. 82-86.

37. David Spence Hill, *The Education and Problems of the Protestant Ministry* (Worcester, Mass.: Clark University Press, 1908), pp. 16-18.

38. Cuyler, *How to Be a Pastor*, p. 18; Allen, *Letters of an Old Methodist*, p. 76; Lyman, *Christian Pastor*, p. 57.

39. Willcox, *Pastor Amidst His Flock*, pp. 144-45; Hill, *Education and Problems of Protestant Ministry*, p. 36; Paul A. Carter, *The Spiritual Crisis of the Gilded Age* (Dekalb: Northern Illinois University Press, 1971), p. 12; Alexander V. G. Allen, *Life and Letters of Phillips Brooks* (New York: E. P. Dutton & Co., 1900) 2:104; Beecher, *Yale Lectures on Preaching* 1:100; Cunningham, *Journal of Religious History* 3 (1965): 327-46; Hoppin, *Pastoral Theology*, p. 14.

40. Hoppin, *Pastoral Theology*, pp. 181, 416; Milton Sernett, "Behold the American Cleric: The Protestant Minister as 'Pattern Man,' 1850–1900," *Winterthur Portfolio* 8 (1973): 15; Lyman, *Christian Pastor*, pp. 4, 8; [Tigert], *Preacher Himself*, p. 30.

41. Willcox, *Pastor Amidst His Flock*, pp. 46, 146; Henderson, *Ethics and Etiquette*, p. 75.

42. Hoppin, *Pastoral Theology*, p. 422; Willcox, *Pastor Amidst His Flock*, p. 147; Cuyler, *How to Be a Pastor*, p. 37; Henderson, *Ethics and Etiquette*, p. 75; Kemp, *Physicians of the Soul*, pp. 94, 97.

43. James J. Farrell, *Inventing the American Way of Death, 1830–1920* (Philadelphia: Temple University Press, 1980), pp. 81-82, 94.

44. Willcox, *Pastor Amidst His Flock*, p. 147; Henderson, *Ethics*

and Etiquette, p. 55; Allen, *Life and Letters of Phillips Brooks*, 2:776; Cuyler, *How to Be a Pastor*, p. 48.
45. Gladden, *Ruling Ideas*, p. 267.
46. Edward Weaver, *Mind and Health* (New York: Macmillan Co., 1913), pp. 128-30.
47. Ibid., p. 127; Lyman, *Christian Pastor*, p. 119.
48. James Gibbons, *The Faith of Our Fathers* (Baltimore, 1877), p. 377; Milo Mahan, *On Confession* (New York, 1872), p. 15; William Bacon Stevens, *Auricular Confession and Private Absolution* (Philadelphia, 1880), pp. 25, 26; A. Cleveland Coxe, *The Penitential* (New York, 1882), p. 8; William Walter Webb, *The Cure of Souls* (New York, 1892).
49. William James, *On Vital Reserves: The Energies of Men, The Gospel of Relaxation* (New York: Henry Holt & Co., 1911), p. 43.
50. A. A. Roback, *History of American Psychology* (New York: Library Publishers, 1952), pp. 180-216; Henryk Misiak and Virginia Staudt Sexton, *History of Psychology: An Overview* (New York: Greene & Stratton, 1966), pp. 46-78, 147.
51. John Dewey, "The New Psychology," *Andover Review* 2 (1884): 285; Philip P. Wiener, *Evolution and the Founders of Pragmatism* (New York: Harper & Row, 1965; 1st ed., 1949), pp. 97-128; Roback, *History*, pp. 214-48; Misiak and Sexton, *History*, pp. 131-33.
52. Roback, *History*, p. 96; William James, *Psychology, Briefer Course* (New York, 1892), pp. 4-6, 424; King, *Rational Living*, pp. 145-75.
53. James, *Psychology, Briefer Course*, p. 6.
54. King, *Rational Living*, pp. 55-102.
55. W.H.P. Faunce, *The Educational Ideal in the Ministry* (New York: Macmillan Co., 1911), p. 4, 158, 187; King, *Rational Living*, p. 91; James, *Psychology, Briefer Course*, p. 149.
56. William James, *The Will to Believe and Other Essays in Popular Philosophy* (New York: Dover Publications, 1956; 1st ed., 1897), p. 120.
57. James, *Psychology, Briefer Course*, pp. 16, 18; King, *Rational Living*, pp. 171-75; Bruce Kuklick, *The Rise of American Philosophy: Cambridge, Massachusetts, 1860–1930* (New Haven, Conn.: Yale University Press, 1977), pp. 196-214.
58. King, *Rational Living*, pp. 91, 145-46, 176-209.
59. Ibid., p. 176; Kuklick, *Rise of American Philosophy*, pp. 212-13; James, *Psychology, Briefer Course*, p. 148.
60. James, *On Vital Reserves*, pp. 25, 66, 78.
61. William James, *Varieties of Religious Experience* (New York: Random House, 1902), pp. 77-124, 475-509.
62. James, *On Vital Reserves*, p. 66; King, *Rational Living*, p. 34;

Gail Thain Parker, *Mind Cure in New England* (Hanover, N.H.: University Press of New England, 1973), pp. 12-81.

63. King, *Rational Living*, p. 34.

64. Donald Meyer, *The Positive Thinkers* (New York: Doubleday & Co., 1965), pp. 21-28.

65. Richard Cabot, "The Use and Abuse of Rest in the Treatment of Disease," *Psychotherapy* (1909) 2:2:23; Ilza Veith, *Hysteria: The History of a Disease* (Chicago: University of Chicago Press, 1965), pp. 217-18; Richard Cabot, "The Literature of Psychotherapy," *Psychotherapy* (1909) 3:4:19; idem, "Work Cure," *Psychotherapy* (1909) 3:1:27-28; 3:2:20.

66. Richard Cabot, "The American Type of Psychotherapy," *Psychotherapy* (1908) 1:1:5, 8-9; Veith, *Hysteria*, p. 227; Richard Cabot, "How Far Is Psychotherapy Scientific?" *Psychotherapy* (1909) 2:1:24-25; idem, "Literature of Psychotherapy":24-25.

67. Nathan G. Hale, Jr., *Freud and the Americans: The Beginnings of Psychoanalysis in the United States, 1876–1917* (New York: Oxford University Press, 1971), pp. 92, 99; Meyer, *Positive Thinkers*, p. 70; James J. Putnam, "The Philosophy of Psychotherapy," *Psychotherapy* (1909) 1:1:19-34.

68. Hale, *Freud and the Americans*, p. 299, coined the phrase *somatic style*. See also Beatrice Hinkle, "Methods of Psychotherapy," *Psychotherapy* (1909) 2:1:9; Veith, *Hysteria*, pp. 155-274; W. B. Parker, "Editorial Summary," *Psychotherapy* (1909) 1:2:72.

69. Cabot, "American Type of Psychotherapy":6; idem, "Literature of Psychotherapy":21; Hale, *Freud and the Americans*, pp. 138, 146; Parker, "Editor's Survey," *Psychotherapy* (1909) 1:2:4.

70. Cabot, "Is Psychotherapy Scientific?":18; Paul Dubois, "The Method of Persuasion," *Psychotherapy* (1909) 2:4:22, 3:1:43; James J. Putnam, "The Psychology of Health," *Psychotherapy* (1909) 2:1:41; Hinkle, "Methods of Psychotherapy":14; A. A. Brill, "A Contribution to the Psychopathology of Every-Day Life," *Psychotherapy* (1909) 3:1:5-20.

71. Cabot, "Is Psychotherapy Scientific?":25, 30; Joseph Jastrow, "The Subconscious in Health and Disease," *Psychotherapy* (1909) 2:1:48-58; Cabot, "Literature of Psychotherapy":23; Elwood Worcester, Samuel McComb, and Isador H. Coriat, *Religion and Medicine: The Moral Control of Nervous Disorders* (New York: Moffat, Yard & Co., 1908), pp. 103-4.

72. A. A. Brill, "Freud's Method of Psychoanalysis," *Psychotherapy* (1909) 2:4-37, 42.

73. F. H. Mathews, "The Americanization of Sigmund Freud: Adaptation of Psychoanalysis before 1917," *Journal of American Studies* 1 (1967): 39-62; Elwood Worcester and Samuel McComb, *The Christian Religion as a Healing Power* (New York: Moffat, Yard & Co., 1909), p. 99.
74. Bushnell, *Nature and the Supernatural*, pp. 40-43; Theodore T. Munger, *Horace Bushnell: Preacher and Theologian* (Boston, 1899), pp. 212-31, 382; Clarke, *Outline of Christian Theology*, p. 290.
75. Clarke, *Outline of Christian Theology*, p. 19.
76. A.V.G. Allen, "The Continuity of Christian Thought" (Boston, 1884), in William R. Hutchison, *American Protestant Thought: The Liberal Era* (New York: Harper & Row, 1968), p. 57; cited in William R. Hutchison, *The Modernist Impulse in American Protestantism* (Cambridge, Mass.: Harvard University Press, 1976), p. 127.
77. Hutchison, *Modernist Impulse*, pp. 121-32.
78. Newman Smyth, *The Religious Feeling: A Study for Faith* (New York, 1877), p. 15; King, *Reconstruction in Theology*, p. 232.
79. Edwin D. Starbuck, "A Study of Conversion," *The American Journal of Psychology* 8 (1896-97): 302; James H. Leuba, "A Study in Psychology of Religious Phenomena," *The American Journal of Psychology* 7 (1896): 327; idem, "The Contents of Religious Consciousness," *The Monist* 11 (1901): 571; idem, "On the Psychology of a Group of Christian Mystics," *Mind*, n.s. 14 (1905): 16-17; James B. Pratt, "The Psychology of Religion," *Harvard Theological Review* 1 (1908): 450; Edward L. Schaub, "The Psychology of Religion in America During the Past Quarter-Century," *The Journal of Religion* 6 (1926): 120.
80. G. Stanley Hall, *Life and Confessions of a Psychologist* (New York: D. Appleton & Co., 1923), p. 518; James H. Leuba, "Introduction to a Psychological Study of Religion," *The Monist* 11 (1901): 200.
81. Leuba, "Study in Psychology":311.
82. Edwin D. Starbuck, "Contributions to the Psychology of Religion," *The American Journal of Psychology* 9 (1897–98): 119-24; Arthur H. Daniels, "The New Life: A Study of Regeneration," *The American Journal of Psychology* 6 (1893): 95-98; Starbuck, "Study of Conversion":306.
83. Leuba, "Study of Religious Phenomena":337, 345; Starbuck, "Study of Conversion":303-7; G. Stanley Hall, *Adolescence* (New York, 1911) 2:301-4.
84. Leuba, "Study of Religious Phenomena":309; Hall, *Life and Confessions*, p. 361; James, *Varieties of Religious Experience*, p. 502.
85. James, *Varieties of Religious Experience*, pp. 168, 506.

385

86. Edward Scribner Ames, "Theology from the Standpoint of Functional Psychology," *The American Journal of Theology* 10 (1906): 219-32.

87. W. B. Parker, "Psychotherapy in the Churches," *Psychotherapy* (1908) 1:2:7-8; idem, "Announcement," *Psychotherapy* (1908) 1:1:1; Raymond J. Cunningham, "The Emmanuel Movement: A Variety of American Religious Experience," *American Quarterly* 14 (1962): 57.

88. Worcester and McComb, *Christian Religion as a Healing Power*, pp. 7, 43.

89. Ibid., pp. 12-20. See also Worcester, McComb, and Coriat, *Religion and Medicine*, pp. 150, 170; Lyman P. Powell, *The Emmanuel Movement in a New England Town* (New York: G. P. Putnam's Sons, 1909), p. 53; Cunningham, "Emmanuel Movement":52.

90. Cabot, "Literature of Psychotherapy":24; Hale, *Freud and the Americans*, pp. 233, 377; John Greene, "The Emmanuel Movement, 1906–1929," *New England Quarterly* 7 (1943): 501; Worcester and McComb, *Christian Religion as a Healing Power*, p. 23; Isador Coriat, "The Anatomy of the Central Nervous System," *Psychotherapy* (1908) 1:2:56.

91. Worcester and McComb, *Christian Religion as a Healing Power*, p. 26.

92. Powell, *Emmanuel Movement*, p. 17; Cabot, "Literature of Psychotherapy":24; Hale, *Freud and the Americans*, p. 232.

93. Powell, *Emmanuel Movement*, pp. 77, 146; Worcester, McComb, and Coriat, *Religion and Medicine*, p. 134.

94. Worcester and McComb, *Christian Religion as a Healing Power*, pp. 18, 73.

95. William James, *The Moral Equivalent of War and Other Essays*, ed. John Roth (New York: Harper & Row, 1971), p. 49; Kemp, *Physicians of the Soul*, p. 7; Worcester and McComb, *Christian Religion as a Healing Power*, p. 73; Worcester, McComb, and Coriat, *Religion and Medicine*, pp. 16, 92; Hale, *Freud and the Americans*, p. 241.

96. Worcester and McComb, *Christian Religion as a Healing Power*, pp. 98, 99, 101, 103; Worcester, McComb, and Coriat, *Religion and Medicine*, pp. 16, 92; Hale, *Freud and the Americans*, p. 241.

97. Powell, *Emmanuel Movement*, pp. 68, 71, 92.

98. W. B. Parker, "Editor's Note," *Psychotherapy* (1908): 1:1:73; James J. Putnam, "The Physician and the Minister," *Psychotherapy* (1909) 3:4:15; Richard Cabot, "Whose Business Is Psychotherapy?" *Psychotherapy* (1909) 3:3:11; Parker, "Editor's Survey":4; Worcester and McComb, *Christian Religion as a Healing Power*, p. 23.

99. Cabot, "Whose Business Is Psychotherapy?":12; Greene, "Emmanuel Movement":516.
100. Greene, "Emmanuel Movement":515; Faunce, *Educational Ideal*, pp. 4, 158, 167.
101. Clarke, *Outline of Christian Theology*, p. 238; Hutchison, *American Protestant Thought*, p. 38.
102. Kuklick, *Rise of American Philosophy*, pp. 215-27.
103. Josiah Royce, "The Modern Psychotherapeutic Movement in America," *Psychotherapy* (1909) 3:4:20, 33.

6: From Adjustment to Insight

1. Grace Adams, "The Rise and Fall of Psychology," *Atlantic Monthly* 153 (1934): 82-92; Walter Marshall Horton, *Theism and the Modern Mood* (New York: Harper & Brothers, 1930), p. 14.
2. Walter Marshall Horton, *A Psychological Approach to Theology* (New York: Harper & Brothers, 1931), p. 1; Hale, *Freud and the Americans* (see ch. 5, n. 67), p. 475.
3. William E. Leuchtenberg, *The Perils of Prosperity* (Chicago: University of Chicago Press, 1958), p. 164; Misiak and Sexton, *History of Psychology* (see ch. 5, n. 50), p. 154.
4. Adams, "Rise and Fall of Psychology":82-92; Misiak and Sexton, *History of Psychology*, pp. 178-79; Leuchtenberg, *Perils of Prosperity*, pp. 144-57, 162, 165, 200.
5. Adams, "Rise and Fall of Psychology":82-92; Misiak and Sexton, *History of Psychology*, pp. 178-79; Leuchtenberg, *Perils of Prosperity*, pp. 144-57, 162, 165, 200.
6. Walter Lippmann, "Freud and the Layman," *New Republic Supplement*, 2 (April 17, 1915): 10; Celia Burns Stendler, "New Ideas for Old: How Freudism Was Renewed in the United States from 1900 to 1925," *The Journal of Educational Psychology* 38 (1947): 193-206; Karl Menninger, "Pseudoanalysis: Perils of Freudian Verbalisms," *Outlook* 155 (July 9, 1930): 363-5, 397.
7. Lucille C. Birnbaum, "Behaviorism in the 1920's," *American Quarterly* 7 (1955): 15-30.
8. Clifford Whittingham Beers, *A Mind That Found Itself* (Garden City, N.Y.: Doubleday, Doran & Co., 1944), pp. 275-94; Helen Flanders Dunbar, "The Clinical Training of Theological Students," *Religion in Life* (1935): 383; Harry Elmer Barnes, "Medical Science Versus Religion as a Guide to Life," *New York Times* (December 30, 1928), cited in Horton, *Psychological Approach to Theology*, p. 6.
9. Albert Deutsch, "The History of Mental Hygiene," in *One Hundred Years of American Psychiatry* (New York: Columbia University Press, 1944); Daniel W. LaRue, *Mental Hygiene* (New York: Macmillan Co., 1927), pp. 240-46, 262; "The

Mental Health Movement," *The Encyclopedia of Mental Health* (1963); Edwin Kirkpatrick, *Mental Hygiene for Effective Living* (New York: Appleton-Century Co., 1934), pp. 1-21, 225-58.

10. Robert S. Lynd and Helen Merrell Lynd, *Middletown: A Study in Contemporary American Culture* (New York: Harcourt, Brace & Co., 1929), pp. 21-24; idem, *Middletown in Transition* (New York: Harcourt, Brace & Co., 1937), pp. 70, 425-86.

11. Leuchtenberg, *Perils of Prosperity*, p. 199.

12. Robert T. Handy, "The American Religious Depression, 1925–1935," *Church History* 29 (1960): 3-16; Mark A. May, *The Education of American Ministers*, vol. 2 of *The Profession of the Ministry* (New York: Institute of Social and Religious Research, 1934), pp. 11-19, 103; C. Luther Fry, *The U.S. Looks at Its Churches* (New York: Institute of Social and Religious Research, 1930), pp. 64-68; Lynd and Lynd, *Middletown: A Study*, pp. 348, 351.

13. Lynd and Lynd, *Middletown: A Study*, pp. 344, 349. May, *Education of American Ministers*, pp. 130-37.

14. May, *Education of American Ministers*, p. 141.

15. For examples of advice books, see Ernest Elliott, *How to Advertise a Church* (New York: George H. Doran Co., 1920); Mary Russell, *How to Dramatize Bible Lessons* (New York: George H. Doran Co., 1924); Frank Wade Smith, *How to Improve Your Sunday School* (New York: Abingdon Press, 1924); International Council of Religious Education, *How to Increase Your Sunday School Attendance* (New York, 1932). For laments over effeminacy, see Charles Franklin Thwing, *The Ministry: An Appeal to College Men* (Boston: Pilgrim Press, 1916), p. 41; Cleland Boyd McAfee, *Ministerial Practices: Some Fraternal Suggestions* (New York: Harper & Brothers, 1928), p. 191; Charles Reynolds Brown, *The Making of a Minister* (New York: Century Co., 1927), pp. viii, 130; Hampton Adams, *The Pastoral Ministry* (Nashville: Cokesbury Press, 1932), p. 50; Austen Kennedy de Blois, *Some Problems of the Modern Minister* (Garden City, N.Y.: Doubleday & Co., 1928), pp. 75, 104.

16. May, *Education of American Ministers*, pp. 167, 168, 200; Lynd and Lynd, *Middletown: A Study*, pp. 346-47.

17. May, *Education of American Ministers*, p. 392.

18. Harry Emerson Fosdick, *The Living of These Days* (New York: Harper & Row, 1956), pp. 214-15, 280.

19. Harry Emerson Fosdick, *On Being a Real Person* (New York: Harper & Row, 1943), pp. viii, 42, 210; Donald Meyer, *The Positive Thinkers* (Garden City, N.Y.: Doubleday & Co., 1965), p. 219.

20. Fosdick, *Living of These Days*, pp. 214-15.
21. John McNeill, "Some Historical Aspects of the Cure of Souls," *Crozier Quarterly* (1934), cited in Kemp, *Physicians of the Soul* (see ch. 4, n. 26); Seward Hiltner, *Religion and Health* (New York: Macmillan Co., 1943), p. 11.
22. Kuklick, *Rise of American Philosophy* (see ch. 5, n. 57), p. 215; John Dewey, *Outlines of a Critical Theory of Ethics* (Ann Arbor, Mich., 1891), pp. 95-96; Josiah Royce, *The Philosophy of Loyalty* (New York: Macmillan Co., 1908), pp. 3-48.
23. Kuklick, *Rise of American Philosophy*, pp. 222-23, 244; Royce, *Philosophy*, pp. 101, 146; Dewey, *Outlines*, p. 131.
24. Kuklick, *Rise of American Philosophy*, p. 221; Dewey, *Outlines*, p. 117.
25. John Dewey, *Democracy and Education* (New York: Macmillan Co., 1963; 1st ed., 1916), pp. 46, 76. See Howard Kirschenbaum, *On Becoming Carl Rogers* (New York: Delacorte Press, 1979), pp. 48-49, 95, for Dewey's influence on Rogers.
26. John Dewey, *Human Nature and Conduct: An Introduction to Social Psychology* (New York: Henry Holt & Co., 1922), p. 137; Dewey, *Democracy and Education*, pp. 51, 56; James Gouinlock, ed., *The Moral Writings of John Dewey: A Selection* (New York: Hafner Press, 1976), pp. 98, 99, 119.
27. Dewey, *Democracy and Education*, p. 122; Gouinlock, *Moral Writings of John Dewey*, pp. 51-52; Dewey, *Human Nature and Conduct*, pp. 166, 167.
28. Robert W. Lynn and Elliott Wright, *The Big Little School: Sunday Child of American Protestantism* (New York: Harper & Row, 1971), p. 84; Seward Hiltner, "Pastoral Theology and Psychology," in *Protestant Thought in the Twentieth Century*, ed. Arnold Nash (New York: Macmillan Co., 1951), p. 191.
29. George Albert Coe, *The Psychology of Religion* (Chicago: University of Chicago Press, 1916), p. 20; idem, *A Social Theory of Religious Education* (New York: Charles Scribner's Sons, 1917), p. 55; idem, *The Religion of a Mature Mind* (New York: Fleming H. Revell Co., 1902), p. 31; idem, *Education in Religion and Morals* (New York: Fleming H. Revell Co., 1904), pp. 121, 203; idem, *What Is Christian Education?* (New York: Charles Scribner's Sons, 1929), p. 94.
30. Coe, *Education in Religion and Morals*, p. 25; idem, *Social Theory of Religious Education*, pp. 72-80.
31. George Albert Coe, *The Motives of Men* (New York: Charles Scribner's Sons, 1928), p. 211.
32. George Albert Coe, *The Spiritual Life* (New York: Eaton & Mains, 1900), p. 21.

33. Brown, *Making of a Minister*, p. 144; Seward Hiltner, editorial, *Pastoral Psychology* 2/17 (1951): 9.
34. Kirschenbaum, *On Becoming Carl Rogers*, p. 46; Seward Hiltner, "A Descriptive Appraisal, 1935–1980," *Theology Today* 37 (1980): 216; idem, editorial, *Pastoral Psychology* 3/23 (1952): 9; Harrison S. Elliott and Grace Loucks Elliott, *Solving Personal Problems: A Counseling Manual* (New York: Henry Holt & Co., 1936); Gaines Dobbins, "Theological Education in a Changing Social Order," *Review and Expositor* (1935): 193-94 and "Capturing Psychology for Christ," *Review and Expositor* (1936): 436, both cited in David A. Galloway, "The Beginning of Pastoral Care at Southern Seminary: Capturing Psychology for Christ" (term paper, Emory University, 1979), pp. 14, 20; Francis L. Strickland, "Pastoral Psychology—A Retrospect," *Pastoral Psychology* 4/37 (1953): 9-12.
35. Galloway, "Beginning of Pastoral Care":2-11; Elliott and Elliott, *Solving Personal Problems*, pp. 4, 100, 113, 223, 287.
36. Douglas Clyde Macintosh, *Theology as an Empirical Science* (New York: Macmillan Co., 1919), pp. 90-99, 140-56.
37. Matthew Arnold, *Literature and Dogma* (New York, 1895), pp. 38, 46; Meyer, *Positive Thinkers*, p. 86; Horton, *Psychological Approach to Theology*, p. 8.
38. Charles Harvey Arnold, *Near the Edge of Battle: A Short History of the Divinity School and the Chicago School of Theology: 1866–1966* (Chicago: Divinity School Assn., 1966), p. 60; Henry Nelson Wieman, *The Wrestle of Religion with Truth* (New York: Macmillan Co., 1927), p. 54, ch. 2.
39. Charles T. Holman, *The Cure of Souls: A Socio-Psychological Approach* (Chicago: University of Chicago Press, 1932), pp. 231, 247, 251, 292, 296; Karl Stolz, *Pastoral Psychology* (Nashville: Cokesbury Press, 1932), pp. 94, 207. One can find similar themes in books written in England during the period: See John G. Mackenzie, *Souls in the Making* (New York: Macmillan Co., 1930) and Leslie Weatherhead, *Psychology in the Service of the Soul* (New York: Macmillan Co., 1930).
40. John Sutherland Bonnell, *Pastoral Psychiatry* (New York: Harper & Brothers, 1938), p. 18.
41. Elliott and Elliott, *Solving Personal Problems*, p. 276.
42. Paul E. Johnson, "Clinical Training in Preparation for Classroom Teaching of Pastoral Subjects," in *Clinical Pastoral Training*, ed. Seward Hiltner (n.p., Commission on Religion and Health, Federal Council of the Churches of Christ in America, 1945), p. 68; Richard Cabot and Russell Dicks, *The Art of Ministering to the Sick* (New York:

Macmillan Co., 1936), p. 5; Helen Flanders Dunbar, *A New Opportunity in Theological Education* (New York: Council for the Clinical Training of Theological Students, 1935), p. 4; idem, "Clinical Training":380-81; Edward E. Thornton, *Professional Education for Ministry: A History of Clinical Pastoral Education* (Nashville: Abingdon Press, 1970), p. 49.

43. Roy Lubove, *The Professional Altruist: The Emergence of Social Work as a Career, 1880–1930* (Cambridge, Mass.: Harvard University Press, 1965), p. 35; Richard Cabot, *Adventures on the Borderlands of Ethics* (New York: Harper & Brothers, 1926), pp. 23-55.

44. Robert C. Powell, *CPE: Fifty Years of Learning Through Supervised Encounter with Living Human Documents* (New York: n.p., 1975), pp. 3-5.

45. Cabot, *Adventures*, pp. 1-22; Russell L. Dicks, *Pastoral Work and Personal Counseling* (New York: Macmillan Co., 1944), p. 37.

46. Anton Boisen, *Out of the Depths* (New York: Harper & Row, 1960), p. 196; Richard Cabot, *The Meaning of Right and Wrong* (New York: Macmillan Co., 1933), pp. 5, 15-16, 110.

47. Cabot and Dicks, *Art of Ministering*, pp. 13-14, 16-18, 71, 94, 378.

48. Cabot, *Meaning of Right and Wrong*, pp. 5, 15-16, 110; Richard Cabot, *Honesty* (New York: Macmillan Co., 1938), pp. 281, 293.

49. Cabot, *Meaning of Right and Wrong*, p. 13; idem, *Honesty*, pp. 284-303.

50. Thornton, *Professional Education for Ministry*, p. 52; Dicks, *Pastoral Work and Personal Counseling*, p. 37.

51. Russell Dicks, "The Art of Ministering to the Sick," *Pastoral Psychology* 3/28 (1952): 11; Kenneth Arlyn Nelson, "Richard Clarke Cabot and the Development of Clinical Pastoral Education" (Ph.D. diss., University of Iowa, 1970), p. 131; Seward Hiltner, "Fifty Years of CPE," *Journal of Pastoral Care* 29 (1975): 91-92.

52. Cabot and Dicks, *Art of Ministering*, pp. 16, 74, 96, 117-18, 130.

53. Ibid., pp. 16, 172-78, 190, 197.

54. Ibid., p. 181.

55. Russell Dicks, *And Ye Visited Me* (New York: Harper & Brothers, 1939), pp. 9, 31-36. I have kept the exact wording of the conversation but slightly modified some of the transitional words and phrases.

56. Dicks, *Pastoral Work and Personal Counseling*, pp. 4, 9.

57. Thornton, *Professional Education for Ministry*, pp. 52, 100; A. Philip Guiles, "Clinical Training and Classroom Pastoral Courses," in *Clinical Pastoral Training*, ed. Hiltner, pp. 114-16; idem, "Standards for Clinical Training," in *Clinical*

Pastoral Training, p. 45; Porter French, "Innocents Abroad: Clinical Training in the Early Days," *Journal of Pastoral Care* 29 (1975): 7-10. Guiles also helped form the Cabot Club, a group of pastoral counselors that met to discuss case studies of pastoral conversations.

58. Dicks, "Art of Ministering to the Sick," p. 11; "General Discussion," in *Clinical Pastoral Training,* ed. Hiltner, p. 41; Rollin Fairbanks, "The Appeal of Existentialism," *Journal of Pastoral Care* 11 (1957): 111-12; idem, "Strengthening Theology in Pastoral Theology," *Journal of Pastoral Care* 12 (1958): 2.

59. Rollin Fairbanks, "Standards for Full-Time Clinical Training," in *Clinical Pastoral Training,* ed. Hiltner, p. 37; idem, "On Clinical Pastoral Training," *Journal of Pastoral Care* 17 (1963): 154-55; idem, "Ministering to the Sick," *Journal of Clinical Pastoral Work* 1/2 (1948): 6.

60. Dicks, *Pastoral Work and Personal Counseling,* p. 12.

61. Boisen, *Out of the Depths,* pp. 143, 150; Hugh Sanborn, "An Analysis of Boisen's, Hiltner's and Clinebell's Models of the Nature and Relation of Mental Health and Salvation" (Ph.D. diss., University of Iowa, 1975), p. 34.

62. Boisen, *Out of the Depths,* pp. 9-132.

63. Anton Boisen, *The Exploration of the Inner World* (Philadelphia: University of Pennsylvania Press, 1971; 1st ed., New York: Willett, Clark, & Co., 1936), pp. 3-111.

64. Boisen, *Out of the Depths,* pp. 9-199. The Council extended far beyond New York City, but its headquarters remained there.

65. Boisen, *Exploration of the Inner World,* pp. 178-79.

66. Boisen, *Out of the Depths,* p. 186; Carroll A. Wise, "Annual Report on the Training of Theological Students," cited in Powell, *CPE: Fifty Years of Learning,* p. 14.

67. Thornton, *Professional Education for Ministry,* p. 77.

68. Dunbar, *New Opportunity,* p. 10; Robert Brinkman, "Standards for a Full-Time Program in the Light of the Experience of the Council for Clinical Training," in *Clinical Pastoral Training,* ed. Hiltner, pp. 23-24; Thornton, *Professional Education for Ministry,* pp. 92-93; Boisen, *Out of the Depths,* pp. 185-86.

69. Ernest Bruder, "Clinical Pastoral Training in a Mental Hospital," *Journal of Clinical Pastoral Work* 2 (1949): 24; Brinkman, "Standards," pp. 23-30; Thomas J. Bigham, Jr., "The Development of the Clinical Training Movement through the Council for Clinical Training," in *Clinical Pastoral Training,* ed. Hiltner, p. 10.

70. Bigham, "Clinical Training Movement," p. 10; "General Discussion," p. 43; Ernest Bruder, "Some Considerations on

the Loss of Faith," *Journal of Clinical Pastoral Work* 1 (1947): 8-10.

71. The Chaplains, "American Protestantism and Mental Health," *Journal of Clinical Pastoral Work* 2 (1949): 16.

72. Hale, *Freud and the Americans*, p. 321. My list of leaders was quite small: for the Council, Boisen, Hiltner, Bruder, Rice, Bigham, Hall, Howe, Brinkman, and Kuether; for the Institute, Leslie, Dicks, Johnson, Fletcher, Muelder, Strunk, Cabot, Fairbanks, Burns, and Guiles.

73. H. Richard Niebuhr, "Religious Realism and the Twentieth Century," in *Religious Realism*, ed. D. C. Macintosh (New York: Macmillan Co., 1931), pp. 413-28; Paul Tillich, *The Religious Situation*, trans. H. R. Niebuhr (New York: Meridian Books, 1956; 1st ed., 1932), pp. 116, 219-25.

74. George Richards, *Beyond Fundamentalism and Modernism: The Gospel of God* (New York: Charles Scribner's Sons, 1934), p. 297; H. Richard Niebuhr, "Value-Theory and Theology," in *The Nature of Religious Experience: Essays in Honor of Douglas Clyde Macintosh*, ed. J. S. Bixler, Robert Calhoun, and H. Richard Niebuhr (New York: Harper & Brothers, 1937), p. 97.

75. Rollo May, *The Springs of Creative Living: A Study of Human Nature and God* (Nashville: Abingdon Press, 1940), p. 97.

76. Rollo May, *The Art of Counseling* (Nashville: Abingdon Press, 1978; 1st ed., 1939), foreword; idem, "Religion, Psychotherapy, and the Achievement of Selfhood," *Pastoral Psychology* 2/17 (1951): 29-33.

77. May, *Springs of Creative Living*, pp. 70-97, 200, 208, 232, 257.

78. May, *Art of Counseling*, pp. 220-21, 154-57.

79. Ibid., pp. 131-41.

7: Acceptance and Self-Realization

1. George Gerbner, "Psychology, Psychiatry, and Mental Illness in the Mass Media: A Study of Trends, 1900–1959," *Mental Hygiene* 45 (1961): 92; Kirschenbaum, *On Becoming Carl Rogers* (see ch. 6, n. 25), p. 151; Misiak and Sexton, *History of Psychology* (see ch. 5, n. 50), p. 160; Ernest Havemann, "Age of Psychology in the United States," *Life* 42 (January 7, 1957): 79; *New York Times* (May 6, 1948) 22:1; (April 27, 1946) 17:1; (November 2, 1946) 18:3.

2. Ernest Havemann, "The Psychologists' Service in Solving Daily Problems," *Life* 42 (January 21, 1957): 84, 89; idem, "Age of Psychology":71; *New York Times* (November 17, 1946) 3:1:2; Douglas T. Miller and Marion Nowack, *The Fifties: The Way We Really Were* (New York: Doubleday & Co., 1975), pp. 129, 141.

3. *New York Times* (March 28, 1946) 22:1; (June 24, 1946) 14:6; (May 16, 1946) 23:3; (January 20, 1949) 40:5; (December 12, 1962) 1:2; (September 3, 1957) 27:8; (September 19, 1945) 17:7; (May 6, 1953) 12:1; (August 16, 1946) 36:2; "Wanted: 1000 Psychiatrists," *Fortune* 50 (August 1954): 68.

4. *New York Times* (August 29, 1956) 27:1; (June 25, 1956) 25:3; (May 8, 1955) 1:8; (February 24, 1953) 1:2.

5. *New York Times* (March 16, 1948) 28:8; (October 13, 1958) 31:7; (August 8, 1948) 5:1; (October 9, 1951) 32:6; (August 3, 1956) 22:6; (January 27, 1956) 10:4; (March 16, 1946) 28:8.

6. *New York Times* (July 12, 1954) 19:1; (August 4, 1953) 1:6; (September 18, 1954) 17:6; (November 19, 1959) 1:16.

7. Havemann, "Age of Psychology":71-72; Ernest Havemann, "Unlocking the Mind in Psychoanalysis," *Life* 42 (January 28, 1957): 82, 119; *New York Times* (April 20, 1956), 17:1.

8. Lee R. Steiner, *Where Do People Take Their Troubles?* (Boston: Houghton Mifflin Co., 1945), p. 18; Carl R. Rogers, *Client-Centered Therapy* (Boston: Houghton Mifflin Co., 1951), p. 3; Misiak and Sexton, *History of Psychology*, p. 183.

9. *New York Times* (November 17, 1950) 35:6; (August 28, 1950) 19:8; (November 2, 1950) 37:3; (June 22, 1947) 21:2; (September 3, 1955) 3:6:7; (February 27, 1950) 17:1; (February 6, 1949) 2:7:8; Alfred Kazin, "Freudian Revolution Analyzed," *New York Times Magazine* (May 6, 1956): 47.

10. Franklin Fearing, "The Screen Discovers Psychiatry," *Hollywood Quarterly* 1 (1945-46): 154-58; idem, "Psychology and the Films," *Hollywood Quarterly* 2 (1947): 118-21; Lawrence Kubie, "Psychiatry and the Films," *Hollywood Quarterly* 2 (1947): 113-16; Gerbner, "Psychology . . . in the Mass Media":92; Garth Jowett, *Film: The Democratic Art* (Boston: Little, Brown & Co., 1976), p. 369; Kazin, "Freudian Revolution":37; Robert Coles, "Madness in Films," *Horizon* (January 1978): 18-22; Havemann, "Age of Psychology":72; *New York Times* (October 31, 1946) 48:7; (May 18, 1948) 20:8.

11. Alice Payne Hackett and James Henry Burke, *80 Years of Best Sellers 1895-1975* (New York: R. R. Bowker Co., 1977), p. 143; Havemann, "Age of Psychology":73.

12. Havemann, "Age of Psychology":68, 72; David Riesman, *The Lonely Crowd: A Study of the Changing American Character* (New Haven: Yale University Press, 1970; 1st ed., 1950), p. 161; John R. Seeley, "The Americanization of the Unconscious," *The Atlantic* 208 (July 1961): 72; Joshua Loth Liebman, *Peace of Mind* (New York: Simon & Schuster, 1946), p. 95.

13. Seeley, "Americanization of Unconscious":72; Kazin,

"Freudian Revolution":37; Charles L. Allen, *God's Psychiatry* (Westwood, N.J.: Fleming H. Revell Co., 1953), p. 7; Liebman, *Peace of Mind*, p. 12.

14. Norman Vincent Peale, *The Power of Positive Thinking* (New York: Prentice Hall, 1952), p. ix; Paul Hutchinson, "Have We a New Religion?" *Life* 38 (April 11, 1955): 146-48.

15. Milton J. Rosenberg, "The Social Sources of the Current Religious Revival," *Pastoral Psychology* 8/75 (1957): 35; Wayne Oates, "The Cult of Reassurance," *Religion in Life* 24 (1954-55): 72-82; Seward Hiltner, *Pastoral Counseling* (Nashville: Abingdon Press, 1949), p. 256; see also Crawford Brown, "Review of *The Art of Real Happiness*, by Smiley Blanton and Norman V. Peale," *Pastoral Psychology* 1/6 (1950): 58.

16. C. Wright Mills, *White Collar: The American Middle Classes* (New York: Oxford University Press, 1951), pp. 24, 63-64; Eric F. Goldman, *The Crucial Decade and After: America, 1945–1960* (New York: Random House, 1960), p. 298.

17. Mills, *White Collar*, pp. ix, xii, xv, 112, 182, 230; Frederick Lewis Allen, *The Big Change: America Transforms Itself, 1900–1950* (New York: Harper & Row, 1952), p. 147; Gibson Winter, *The Suburban Captivity of the Churches* (New York: Macmillan Co., 1962), p. 60.

18. Miller and Nowack, *The Fifties*, pp. 127-46, 129, 248-68; Riesman, *The Lonely Crowd*, pp. 22, 97, 133.

19. Seward Hiltner, *Preface to Pastoral Theology* (Nashville: Abingdon Press, 1958), p. 26.

20. A. L. McKnight, "The Evolution of Pastoral Care in the Army Hospitals," *Journal of Pastoral Care* 7 (1953): 170; Sydney Ahlstrom, *A Religious History of the American People* (New York: Doubleday & Co., 1975) 2:144; Gordon W. Allport, *The Individual and His Religion: A Psychological Interpretation* (New York: Macmillan Co., 1950), p. 50; Wayne E. Oates, "The Findings of the Commission on the Ministry," *Pastoral Psychology* 7/62 (1955): 15-24; see also Seward Hiltner, "The Man of the Month: Charles T. Holman," *Pastoral Psychology* 6/52 (1955): 66.

21. Allen, *The Big Change*, pp. 147, 184; Winter, *Suburban Captivity*, p. 60; Benson Y. Landis, "Incomes of Ministers," *Pastoral Psychology* 16/152 (1965): 9-10.

22. Seward Hiltner, "Why Pastoral Psychology?—An Editorial," *Pastoral Psychology* 1/1 (1950): 7; E. Llewellyn Queener, "The Psychological Training of Ministers," *Pastoral Psychology* 7/67 (1956): 29; Wayne E. Oates, "Protestant Principles and Pastoral Care," *Pastoral Psychology* 11/107 (1960): 19; "Notes and News," *Pastoral Psychology* 10/91 (1959): 47; Seward

Hiltner, "Advanced Training in Pastoral Psychology," *Pastoral Psychology* 3/21 (1952): 46-47; "Opportunities for Study, Training, and Experience in Pastoral Psychology," *Pastoral Psychology* 4/40 (1954): 36; "Opportunities for Study—1956," *Pastoral Psychology* 6/56 (1956): 48; Paul E. Johnson, "The Clinical Approach to Religion," *Journal of Pastoral Care* 15 (1961): 11; *New York Times* (February 6, 1956) 25:7; (July 18, 1956) 25:5; (January 11, 1959) 81:1.

23. "Council for Clinical Training, Inc., Clinical Pastoral Training Programs," *Journal of Pastoral Care* 15 (1961): 225-37; "Opportunities for Study," 4/40 (1954): 25-38, 43; Oates, "Findings of Commission":20; Russell Dicks, "The Hospital Chaplain," *Pastoral Psychology* 1/3 (1950): 52.

24. Hiltner, "Fifty Years of CPE" (see ch. 6, n. 51):92; Thornton, *Professional Education for Ministry* (see ch. 6, n. 42), p. 191.

25. "Opportunities for Study," 4/40 (1954): 26; Seward Hiltner, "Freshmen and Seniors," *Pastoral Psychology* 10/93 (1959): 7-10; "Notes and News," *Pastoral Psychology* 7/61 (1956): 55; "Religion and Mental Health Academy Is Launched," *Christian Century* 73 (April 18, 1956): 477; *New York Times* (March 26, 1956) 31:3; Seward Hiltner, "Pastoral Services," *Pastoral Psychology* 7/67 (1956): 7-9.

26. James N. Lapsley, Jr., "Pastoral Counseling Centers: Mid-Century Phenomenon," *Pastoral Psychology* 13/130 (1963): 43-53; Paul E. Johnson, "The Pastor as Counselor," *Pastoral Psychology* 7/62 (1955): 25-28.

27. Russell L. Dicks, "The Hospital Chaplain":50-54; Hiltner, "Pastoral Services":7-9.

28. Seward Hiltner, "Psychotherapy and Counseling in Professions Other than the Ministry," *Pastoral Psychology* 7/62 (1956): 14; "Communications," *Journal of Pastoral Care* 14 (1960): 49; George Kalif, "Pastoral Uses of Community Resources," *Pastoral Psychology* 1/8 (1950): 37; Meyer, *Positive Thinkers* (see ch. 6, n. 64), p. 252; Ernest Bruder, "The Minister and the Psychiatrist: Areas of Mutual Concern," in *Healing: Human and Divine*, ed. Simon Doniger (New York: Association Press, 1957), p. 117; Harry Emerson Fosdick, "The Ministry and Psychotherapy," *Pastoral Psychology* 11/101 (1960): 13; Gibson Winter, "Pastoral Counseling or Pastoral Care," *Pastoral Psychology* 8/71 (1957): 16.

29. Hiltner, "Why Pastoral Psychology?—An Editorial":8, 43; Havemann, "Age of Psychology":80.

30. Paul Johnson, *Psychology of Pastoral Care* (Nashville: Abingdon Press, 1953), p. 45; Hiltner, *Pastoral Counseling*, p. 27.

31. Ahlstrom, *Religious History*, 2:431; Sören Kierkegaard, *The*

Sickness Unto Death, trans. Walter Lowrie (Princeton, N.J.: Princeton University Press, 1961; 1st trans. ed., 1941), p. 167; see also idem, *Fear and Trembling,* trans. Walter Lowrie (Princeton, N.J.: Princeton University Press, 1968; 1st trans. ed., 1941), pp. 64-77, and *The Concept of Dread,* trans. Walter Lowrie (Princeton, N.J.: Princeton University Press, 1944), pp. 45-72; David Roberts, "Either/Or: A Review Article," *Review of Religion* 10 (1946): 167, 171; idem, "Training in Christianity: A Review Article," *Review of Religion* 10 (1946): 307.

32. Seward Hiltner, "Review of *Situation Ethics,* by Joseph Fletcher," in *The Situation Ethics Debate,* ed. Harvey Cox (Philadelphia: Westminster Press, 1968), pp. 51-54, 132-39, reprinted from *Pastoral Psychology* (May 1966); Emil Brunner, *The Divine Imperative: A Study in Christian Ethics* (Philadelphia: Westminster Press, 1947; 1st ed., 1932), pp. 71, 74-75.

33. Rudolf Bultmann, *Jesus and the Word* (New York: Charles Scribner's Sons, 1958; 1st trans. ed., 1934), pp. 82-84, 92; idem, *Jesus Christ and Mythology* (New York: Charles Scribner's Sons, 1958), pp. 29, 31, 56.

34. Dietrich Bonhoeffer, *Letters and Papers from Prison,* ed. Eberhard Bethge, trans. Reginald Fuller (New York: Macmillan Co., 1962; 1st ed., *Prisoner of God,* 1953), pp. 7, 23, 248.

35. Karl Barth, *Church Dogmatics,* trans. Bromiley (Edinburgh: T & T Clark, 1957): 2:2:517, 539.

36. Paul Tillich, *Morality and Beyond* (New York: Harper & Row, 1963), pp. 82-95, 65-81; Paul L. Lehmann, "The Foundation and Pattern of Christian Behavior," *Christian Faith and Social Action,* ed. John A. Hutchison (New York: Charles Scribner's Sons, 1953), pp. 100, 102, 109, 112; Joseph Sittler, *The Structure of Christian Ethics* (Baton Rouge: Louisiana State University Press, 1958), pp. 50, 55; Joseph Fletcher, "Six Propositions: The New Look in Christian Ethics," *Harvard Divinity Bulletin* (October 1959): 7-18.

37. Seward Hiltner, "Religion and Psychoanalysis," *Journal of Pastoral Care* 4 (1950): 35.

38. See, e.g., The Chaplains, "American Protestantism and Mental Health" (see ch. 6, n. 71): 1-9; Bruder, "Clinical Pastoral Training in a Mental Hospital" (see ch. 6, n. 69): 16; Ernest Bruder, "Some Theological Considerations in Clinical Pastoral Education," *Journal of Pastoral Care* 8 (1954): 142.

39. Seward Hiltner, "Toward an Ethical Conscience," *The Journal of Religion* 25 (1945): 1-9.

40. Hiltner, *Pastoral Counseling,* pp. 43, 49, 50.

41. Seward Hiltner, *The Counselor in Counseling* (Nashville: Abingdon Press, 1952; 1st ed., 1950), pp. 134, 145; Wayne E. Oates, *Religious Factors in Mental Illness* (New York: Association Press, 1955), p. 28; idem, *The Christian Pastor* (Philadelphia: Westminster Press, 1951), pp. 30, 32, 130.
42. Carroll A. Wise, *Pastoral Counseling: Its Theory and Practice* (New York: Harper & Brothers, 1951), pp. 45-46; idem, "Pastoral Counseling and Human Values," *The Pastoral Counselor* 6/2 (1968): 3.
43. Johnson, *Psychology of Pastoral Care*, pp. 83, 181.
44. Riesman, *Lonely Crowd*, pp. 22, 97, 133; William H. Whyte, Jr., *The Organization Man* (Garden City, N.Y.: Doubleday & Co., n.d.; 1st ed., 1956), pp. 36-66.
45. Seward Hiltner, "Editorial—Erich Fromm and Pastoral Psychology," *Pastoral Psychology* 5/56 (1955): 11-12.
46. Erich Fromm, *Escape from Freedom* (New York: Holt, Rinehart & Winston, 1941), pp. 13, 18.
47. Ibid., pp. 105, 186-206.
48. Erich Fromm, *Man for Himself: An Inquiry into the Psychology of Ethics* (New York: Rinehart & Co., 1947), p. 78; idem, *The Sane Society* (New York: Holt, Rinehart & Winston, 1955), pp. 78, 208; idem, *Escape from Freedom*, p. 185.
49. Karen Horney, *The Neurotic Personality of Our Time* (New York: W. W. Norton & Co., 1937), p. 15; Seward Hiltner, "Editorial—Karen Horney," *Pastoral Psychology* 1/6 (1950): 11.
50. Horney, *Neurotic Personality*, pp. 50, 59.
51. Oates, *Religious Factors in Mental Illness*, pp. 46, 58, 91, 222; Wayne E. Oates, "Pastoral Psychology and Faith Healing," in *Healing*, ed. Simon Doniger (New York: Association Press, 1957), p. 231; idem, "Editorial: Pastoral Psychology in the South," *Pastoral Psychology* 2/14 (1951): 10.
52. Hiltner, *Pastoral Counseling*, p. 261; Seward Hiltner, *The Christian Shepherd: Some Aspects of Pastoral Care* (Nashville: Abingdon Press, 1959), pp. 98, 110; idem, *Sex Ethics and the Kinsey Report* (New York: Association Press, 1953), p. 110. See also Paul Johnson, *Personality and Religion* (Nashville: Abingdon Press, 1962), pp. 105, 192.
53. Tillich, *Morality and Beyond*, pp. 20-21, 43; Paul Tillich, "The Theology of Pastoral Care," *Pastoral Psychology* 10/97 (1959): 22.
54. Fromm, *Man for Himself*, pp. 3-7, 8-37, 84, 129-41, 156, 197, 198.
55. Ibid., pp. 13, 29, 8-37.
56. Ibid., pp. 159, 197; Erich Fromm, *The Art of Loving* (New York: Harper & Row, 1956), p. 20.

57. Erich Fromm, *Psychoanalysis and Religion* (New York: Bantam Books, 1972; 1st ed., 1950), pp. 19, 22, 82, 115.

58. Fromm, *Psychoanalysis and Religion*, pp. 22, 72, quoted in Seward Hiltner, "Erich Fromm: The Man of the Month," *Pastoral Psychology* 6/56 (1955): 10.

59. Fromm, *The Sane Society*, p. 282; idem, *Escape from Freedom*, pp. 3-12; Paul Tillich, "Erich Fromm's *The Sane Society*," *Pastoral Psychology* 6/56 (1955): 13-14.

60. Karen Horney, *New Ways in Psychoanalysis* (New York: W. W. Norton, 1939), p. 10; idem, *Our Inner Conflicts: A Constructive Theory of Neurosis* (New York: W. W. Norton, 1945), pp. 13-18; idem, *Neurosis and Human Growth: The Struggle Toward Self-Realization* (New York: W. W. Norton, 1950), pp. 23, 24, 64, 111, 113.

61. Horney, *Neurosis and Human Growth*, pp. 15, 38, 129, 158, 300-302, 348, 365.

62. Carroll A. Wise, *Religion in Illness and Health* (New York: Harper & Brothers, 1942), pp. 146, 153; Paul Tillich, "Psychoanalysis, Existentialism, and Theology," *Pastoral Psychology* 9/87 (1958): 15; Carroll A. Wise, "The Ministry to the Physically Ill," *Journal of Clinical Pastoral Work* 1/1 (1947): 33; idem, *Pastoral Counseling*, p. 150.

63. Seward Hiltner, *Religion and Health* (New York: Macmillan Co., 1943), pp. 30-32; idem, *Pastoral Counseling*, pp. 30, 31, 32.

64. Hiltner, *Pastoral Counseling*, pp. 64-65, 73; Seward Hiltner, *Self-Understanding Through Psychology and Religion* (New York: Charles Scribner's Sons, 1951), pp. 118, 170, 211.

65. Johnson, *Psychology of Pastoral Care*, p. 17; Oates, *Christian Pastor*, p. 32.

66. Seward Hiltner, "The Literature of Pastoral Counseling—Past, Present, and Future," *Pastoral Psychology* 2/15 (1951): 25-26; idem, "What We Get and Give in Pastoral Care," *Pastoral Psychology* 5/43 (1954): 31-32.

67. Don Browning, "Images of Man in Contemporary Models of Pastoral Care," *Interpretation* 33 (April 1979): 145; Queener, "Psychological Training of Ministers": 30.

68. Carl R. Rogers, *On Becoming a Person* (Boston: Houghton Mifflin Co., 1961), pp. 5, 7, 8.

69. Kirschenbaum, *On Becoming Carl Rogers*, pp. 75, 93; Rogers, *On Becoming a Person*, p. 11; Carl R. Rogers, *Counseling and Psychotherapy: Newer Concepts in Practice* (New York: Houghton Mifflin Co., 1942), pp. 28, 40.

70. Rogers, *Counseling and Psychotherapy*, pp. 174-216.

71. Rogers, *Client-Centered Therapy*, pp. 12, 27, 29, 32; idem, *On Becoming a Person*, p. 34; Seward Hiltner, "Empathy in

Counseling," *Pastoral Psychology* 1/10 (1950): 25 (Hiltner liked the word *empathy* because it suggested an ability "to feel our way into the feelings of someone else").

72. Rogers, *Client-Centered Therapy*, pp. 489-90; idem, *On Becoming a Person*, p. 532.

73. Rogers, *On Becoming a Person*, pp. 500, 532.

74. Ibid., pp. 481-533.

75. Ibid., pp. 61, 62.

76. Carl Rogers, "The Emerging Person: A New Revolution," in *Carl Rogers: The Man and His Work*, ed. Richard I. Evans (New York: E. P. Dutton & Co., 1975), p. 158; idem, *Client-Centered Therapy*, p. 501; Kirschenbaum, *On Becoming Carl Rogers*, pp. 152, 182, 291-92; Peter Homans, "The Case of Freud and Carl Rogers," in *Psychology in Social Context*, ed. Alan Bass (New York: Irvington Publishers, 1979), pp. 369-90. Homans first suggested the relationship between Rogerian therapy and the theory of mass society.

77. Evans, ed., *Carl Rogers*, p. 73.

78. Reinhold Niebuhr, "The Dialogue Between the Will and Conscience," *Pastoral Psychology* 9/85 (1958): 9-13; Carl R. Rogers, "Reinhold Niebuhr's *The Self and the Dramas of History:* A Criticism," *Pastoral Psychology* 9/85 (1958): 14-17; Seward Hiltner, "Rogers and Niebuhr: Editorial," *Pastoral Psychology* 9/85 (1958): 7-8; Bernard Loomer, "Reinhold Niebuhr and Carl R. Rogers," *Pastoral Psychology* 9/85 (1958): 17-20; Reinhold Niebuhr, "The Christian Moral Witness and Some Disciplines of Modern Culture," *Pastoral Psychology* 11/101 (1960): 45-54; Carl Rogers, "The Nature of Man," *Pastoral Psychology* 11/104 (1960): 23-26.

79. "News and Notes," *Pastoral Psychology* 8/72 (1956): 54; Queener, "Psychological Training of Ministers": 30.

80. Carl Rogers and Russell Becker, "A Basic Orientation for Counseling," *Pastoral Psychology* 1/1 (1950): 26-34; Hiltner, "Rogers and Niebuhr: Editorial": 7-8; Walter M. Horton, "A Psychological Approach to Theology—After 25 Years," in *Healing*, ed. Doniger, p. 112.

81. Wise, *Pastoral Counseling*, pp. 73-75.

82. Browning, "Images of Man": 146; Howard J. Clinebell, "Ego Psychology and Pastoral Counseling," *Pastoral Psychology* 14/131 (1963): 26-37.

83. Dicks, *Pastoral Work and Pastoral Counseling* (see ch. 6, n. 45), pp. 45-47; Hiltner, *Pastoral Counseling*, p. 264.

84. Hiltner, *Pastoral Counseling*, pp. 81, 97, 254-55.

85. Wise, *Pastoral Counseling*, pp. 6, 63, 67, 221.

86. Oates, *Christian Pastor*, pp. 127, 129, 162.

87. Paul E. Johnson, *Person and Counselor* (Nashville: Abingdon Press, 1967), pp. 93-94.

8: Context of Pastoral Care

1. William A. Clebsch, "American Religion and the Cure of Souls," in *Religion in America*, ed. William G. McLoughlin and Robert Bellah (Boston: Houghton Mifflin Co., 1968), pp. 249, 264.
2. Ibid., p. 263; Philip Rieff, *Freud: The Mind of the Moralist* (Garden City, N.Y.: Doubleday & Co., 1961; 1st ed., 1959), p. 390; Joseph Veroff, Richard A. Kulka, and Elizabeth Douvan, *Mental Health in America: Patterns of Help-Seeking from 1957 to 1976* (New York: Basic Books, 1981), pp. 5-7, 23-40.
3. William L. O'Neill, *Coming Apart: An Informal History of America in the 1960s* (New York: Quadrangle Books, 1971), pp. 233-71; Flo Conway and Jim Seigelman, *Snapping: America's Epidemic of Sudden Personality Change* (Philadelphia: Lippincott Books, 1978), pp. 54-55.
4. Kenneth Benne, "History of the T-Group in the Laboratory Setting," in *T-Group Theory and Laboratory Method*, eds. Leland Bradford, Jack R. Gibb, and Kenneth Benne (New York: John Wiley & Sons, 1964), pp. 81-117.
5. Steve M. Tipton, *Getting Saved from the Sixties* (Berkeley: University of California Press, 1982), pp. 2-30.
6. Seward Hiltner, "A Descriptive Appraisal, 1935–1980," *Theology Today* 37 (1980): 220.
7. Clebsch, "American Religion and Cure of Souls," p. 251; Carroll A. Wise, *The Meaning of Pastoral Care* (New York: Harper & Row, 1966), p. 67.
8. Hiltner, *Preface to Pastoral Theology* (see ch. 7, n. 19), p. 36.
9. T. J. Bigham, "Moral Responsibility of the Parishioner or Patient," *Journal of Pastoral Care* 6 (1952): 54; A. T. Mollegen, "A Christian View of Psychoanalysis," *Journal of Pastoral Care* 6 (1952): 1-4.
10. Wayne E. Oates, *The Religious Dimensions of Personality* (New York: Association Press, 1957), pp. 141-70; Hiltner, *Christian Shepherd* (see ch. 7, n. 52), p. 159; Lewis Joseph Sherrill, *The Struggle of the Soul* (New York: Macmillan Co., 1963), p. vii.
11. Seward Hiltner, "Darwin and Religious Development," *Journal of Religion* 40 (1960): 282-95; Wayne E. Oates, *Christ and Selfhood* (New York: Association Press, 1961), pp. 143, 163-69; Thomas W. Klink, *Depth Perspectives in Pastoral Work* (Philadelphia: Fortress Press, 1965), pp. 17-32.
12. Paul E. Johnson, *Personality and Religion* (Nashville: Abingdon Press, 1962), pp. 210, 215, 259, 261.

13. Johnson, *Person and Counselor* (see ch. 7, n. 87), p. 46; Anton Boisen, "The Therapeutic Significance of Anxiety," *Journal of Pastoral Care* 5 (1951): 10.
14. Robert C. Leslie, "Small Groups in the Church," *Pastoral Psychology* 15/145 (1964): 5; Clifton E. Kew and Clinton J. Kew, "Group Psychotherapy in a Church Setting," *Pastoral Psychology* 1/10 (1950): 31-37; Liston O. Mills, "The Relationship of Discipline to Pastoral Care in Frontier Churches, 1800–1850," *Pastoral Psychology* 16/159 (1965): 22-35; Thomas C. Oden, *The Intensive Group Experience: The New Pietism* (Philadelphia: Westminster Press, 1972); Rollin Fairbanks, "Summer Laboratories for Group Dynamics," *Journal of Pastoral Care* 9 (1955): 104.
15. Robert Leslie, "Pastoral Group Psychotherapy," *Journal of Pastoral Care* 6/1 (1952): 56-61; idem, "Growth Through Group Interaction," *Journal of Pastoral Care* 5 (1951): 39; Theodore Wedd, "Group Dynamics and the Church," *Journal of Pastoral Care* 9 (1955): 205.
16. Wedd, "Group Dynamics and the Church": 206; Paul Johnson, editorial, *Pastoral Psychology* 6/53 (1955): 8; Robert W. Leeper, *Lewin's Topological and Vector Psychology* (Eugene, Ore.: University of Oregon Press, 1943), pp. 10-44; Kurt Lewin, *A Dynamic Theory of Personality* (New York: McGraw Hill, 1935), pp. 43-65; idem, *Principles of Topological Psychology*, trans. Fritz Heider and Grace Heider (New York: McGraw Hill, 1936), pp. 18-40.
17. Carroll A. Wise, "The Roots and Resolution of Conflict," *Journal of Pastoral Care* 24 (1970): 11.
18. Seward Hiltner, "Review of *The Contributions of Harry Stack Sullivan*, ed. Patrick Mullahy," *Pastoral Psychology* 3/28 (1952): 65; Sanborn, "Analysis of Boisen's, Hiltner's, and Clinebell's Models" (Ph.D. diss., University of Iowa, 1975), p. 42; Carroll Wise, "Review of *The Psychiatric Interview*," *Pastoral Psychology* 5/46 (1954): 57; Oates, *Religious Factors in Mental Illness* (see ch. 7, n. 41), p. 227.
19. A. H. Chapman, *Harry Stack Sullivan: His Life and Work* (New York: G. P. Putnam's Sons, 1976), pp. 38, 45, 56.
20. Harry Stack Sullivan, *The Interpersonal Theory of Psychiatry*, ed. H. S. Perry and M. L. Gawell (New York: W. W. Norton Co., 1953), p. 111; idem, *The Psychiatric Interview*, ed. H. S. Perry and M. L. Gawell (New York: W. W. Norton Co., 1954), p. 102.
21. Sullivan, *Psychiatric Interview*, pp. 17, 21, 172, 226.
22. Albert Outler, "Christian Faith and Psychotherapy," *Religion in Life* 21 (1952): 506; Oates, *Religious Factors in Mental Illness*, p. 115. See also Johnson, *Personality and Religion*,

pp. 48, 246; Wayne Oates, *Protestant Pastoral Counseling* (Philadelphia: Westminster Press, 1962), p. 190; Edward E. Thornton, *Theology and Pastoral Counseling* (Englewood Cliffs, N.J.: Prentice-Hall, 1964), pp. 73-84; Albert Outler, *Psychotherapy and the Christian Message* (New York: Harper & Brothers, 1954), p. 157.

23. Johnson, *Person and Counselor*, p. 94; Howard J. Clinebell, Jr., *Mental Health through Christian Community* (Nashville: Abingdon Press, 1965), p. 217; idem, *Basic Types of Pastoral Counseling* (Nashville: Abingdon Press, 1966), p. 23.

24. Donald Krill, "Psychoanalysis, Mowrer, and the Existentialists," *Pastoral Psychology* 16/157 (1965): 27-36; O. Hobart Mowrer, *The Crisis in Psychiatry and Religion* (Princeton, N.J.: Van Nostrand, 1961), pp. 56-80.

25. Clinebell, *Basic Types of Pastoral Counseling*, p. 32; Johnson, *Person and Counselor*, p. 122; Seward Hiltner, "Judgment and Appraisal in Pastoral Care," *Pastoral Psychology* 16/159 (1965): 43-46; Samuel Southard, "Pastoral Judgment," *Pastoral Psychology* 16/159 (1965): 11; Seward Hiltner, "Clinical and Theological Notes on Responsibility," *Journal of Religion and Health* 2 (1962): 7-20; Wise, *Meaning of Pastoral Care*, p. 83; Samuel Southard, "Discipline or Die," *Pastoral Psychology* 16/159 (1965): 56-63.

26. Wise, *Meaning of Pastoral Care*, p. 14; Johnson, *Person and Counselor*, p. 23; Seward Hiltner and Lowell Colston, *The Context of Pastoral Counseling* (Nashville: Abingdon Press, 1961), p. 24; Clinebell, *Basic Types of Pastoral Counseling*, pp. 32-33; Oates, *Protestant Pastoral Counseling*, p. 45.

27. Seward Hiltner, "Pastoral Psychology and Pastoral Counseling," *Pastoral Psychology* 3/28 (1952): 23; Sanborn, "Analysis of Boisen's, Hiltner's, and Clinebell's Models," p. 71; Clinebell, *Basic Types of Pastoral Counseling*, pp. 27-29, 270.

28. Seward Hiltner, "The Social Self," *Pastoral Psychology* 8/81 (1958): 7; Outler, *Psychotherapy and the Christian Message*, p. 156; Johnson, *Person and Counselor*, p. 63; idem, *Personality and Religion*, p. 151; Oates, *Religious Factors in Mental Illness*, pp. 115, 114-47, 225; idem, *Christ and Selfhood*, p. 174; Wise, *Meaning of Pastoral Care*, pp. 34-60; Oates, *Protestant Pastoral Counseling*, p. 12. See also Reuel L. Howe, *The Miracle of Dialogue* (New York: Seabury Press, 1963).

29. Thornton, *Theology and Pastoral Counseling*, pp. 19, 67, 70, 94; Wise, *Meaning of Pastoral Care*, p. 111; Seward Hiltner, "Salvation's Message About Health," *International Review of Missions* 57 (1968): 166; and see the discussion in James N. Lapsley, *Salvation and Health: The Interlocking Processes of Life* (Philadelphia: Westminster Press, 1972).

30. Daniel Day Williams, "What Psychiatry Means to Theological Education," *Pastoral Psychology* 16/157 (1965): 49.
31. Johnson, *Person and Counselor*, p. 133; David E. Roberts, *Psychotherapy and a Christian View of Man* (New York: Charles Scribner's Sons, 1950), pp. 75, 116; Seward Hiltner, "The Future of Christian Anthropology," *Theology Today* 20 (1963): 246, 248; Outler, *Psychotherapy and the Christian Message*, p. 139; Oates, *Protestant Pastoral Counseling*, pp. 23-24.
32. Roberts, *Psychotherapy and a Christian View of Man*, p. 153.
33. Ibid., pp. 115, 133, 134, 135, 153.
34. Outler, *Psychotherapy and the Christian Message*, pp. 8, 57-60.
35. Ibid., pp. 21-30, 45, 51.
36. Ibid., pp. 66, 69, 92, 129, 132, 178, 226, 228.
37. Ibid., pp. 140, 141, 143; Albert Outler, *A Christian Context for Counseling* (New York: Hazen Foundation, 1946), p. 10.
38. Carroll Wise, "Review of *Psychotherapy and the Christian Message*," *Pastoral Psychology* 5/41 (1954): 62.
39. Wilhelm Pauck and Marion Pauck, *Paul Tillich: His Life and Thought*, 2 vols. (New York: Harper & Row, 1976) 1:219, 245-85.
40. Seward Hiltner, "Paul Tillich and Pastoral Psychology: An Editorial," *Pastoral Psychology* 16/159 (1965): 10; Pauck and Pauck, *Paul Tillich*, 1:118; Paul Tillich, *Systematic Theology* (Chicago: University of Chicago Press, 1951) 1:64; Wayne Oates, "The Contribution of Paul Tillich to Pastoral Psychology," *Pastoral Psychology* 19/181 (1968): 13.
41. Paul Tillich, *The Shaking of the Foundations* (New York: Charles Scribner's Sons, 1948), p. 162.
42. Pauck and Pauck, *Paul Tillich*, 1:93; Paul Tillich, "The Impact of Pastoral Psychology on Theological Thought," in *The Ministry and Mental Health*, ed. Hans Hofmann (New York: Association Press, 1960), p. 16.
43. Paul Tillich, "Psychoanalysis, Existentialism, and Theology," *Pastoral Psychology* 9/87 (1958): 16; idem, "Impact of Pastoral Psychology," p. 16.
44. Paul Tillich, *The New Being* (New York: Charles Scribner's Sons, 1955), p. 12; idem, *The Courage to Be* (New Haven, Conn.: Yale University Press, 1952), pp. 155, 165, 179-81.
45. Paul Tillich, *On the Boundary: An Autobiographical Sketch* (New York: Charles Scribner's Sons, 1966; 1st ed., 1936), pp. 115-24; idem, *The Courage to Be*, p. 165.
46. "Paul Tillich and Carl Rogers: A Dialogue," transcript of meeting televised at San Diego State College, *Pastoral Psychology* 19/181 (1968): 55-61.

47. Paul Johnson, "The Trend Toward Dynamic Interpersonalism," *Religion in Life* 35 (1966): 756; idem, *Person and Counselor*, pp. 9, 58, 61, 91.
48. Borden Parker Bowne, *Personalism* (Evanston, Ill.: Northwestern University Press, 1908), pp. 115-58; Edgar Sheffield Brightman, *The Finding of God* (Nashville: Abingdon Press, 1931), pp. 94-122.
49. Johnson, *Person and Counselor*, p. 68; Paul Johnson, "Jesus as Psychologist," *Pastoral Psychology* 2/19 (1951): 18-20.
50. Wayne Oates, "The Contribution of Paul Tillich to Pastoral Psychology," *Pastoral Psychology* 19/181 (1968): 12; idem, *Religious Dimensions of Personality*, introduction; idem, *What Psychology Says About Religion* (New York: Association Press, 1958), p. 111.
51. Oates, *Christ and Selfhood*, pp. 18, 186; idem, *Protestant Pastoral Counseling*, p. 12.
52. Oates, *Christ and Selfhood*, pp. 227, 230. See also Wayne E. Oates, *The Bible in Pastoral Care* (Philadelphia: Westminster Press, 1953).
53. See Thomas Oden, *Kerygma and Counseling* (Philadelphia: Westminster Press, 1966) and Edward Thurneysen, *A Theology of Pastoral Care* (Richmond, Va.: John Knox Press, 1962).
54. Don Browning, "Analogy, Symbol, and Pastoral Theology in Tillich's Thought," *Pastoral Psychology* 19/181 (1968): 50; see also Charles Hartshorne, *Man's Vision of God and the Logic of Theism* (Chicago: Willett, Clark & Co., 1941), p. xiii.
55. H. N. Wieman, "A Philosophy of Religion," *Journal of Religion* 10 (1930): 137; see also Charles Harvey Arnold, *Near the Edge of Battle* (see ch. 6, n. 38).
56. Hartshorne, *Man's Vision of God*, p. ix.
57. Ibid., p. 93.
58. Bernard Loomer, "Christian Faith and Process Philosophy," *Journal of Religion* 29 (1949): 181.
59. Charles Hartshorne, *The Divine Relativity: A Social Conception of God* (New Haven, Conn.: Yale University Press, 1948), pp. xv, 25, 55.
60. Daniel Day Williams, *God's Grace and Man's Hope* (New York: Harper & Brothers, 1949), pp. 178, 187; idem, *The Minister and the Care of Souls* (New York: Harper & Brothers, 1961), pp. 71, 83, 86, 90-92.
61. Seward Hiltner, "The Minister and Process Theology," *Theology Today* 31 (1974): 102.
62. Hiltner, *Self-Understanding Through Psychology and Religion* (see ch. 7, n. 64), p. 207; Seward Hiltner, "Christian Faith and

Psychotherapy," *Religion in Life* 21 (1952): 495; idem, letter to the editor, *Pastoral Psychology* 4/32 (1953); 62.

63. Hiltner, "Future of Christian Anthropology": 247, 248, 255; see also John B. Cobb, Jr., *A Christian Natural Theology* (Philadelphia: Westminster Press, 1965), p. 254.
64. Hiltner, *Preface to Pastoral Theology*, p. 51.
65. Ibid., pp. 51, 55, 64.
66. Ibid., pp. 18, 20, 22.
67. Ibid., pp. 112, 115.
68. Joseph Fletcher, "Review of *Preface to Pastoral Theology*," *Pastoral Psychology* 8/80 (1958): 83; Thornton, *Theology and Pastoral Counseling*, p. 19; Hiltner, "Descriptive Appraisal": 220.
69. Oates, "Findings of the Commission" (see ch. 7, n. 20): 16; idem, *Religious Factors in Mental Illness*, p. 213.
70. Gibson Winter, "Pastoral Counseling or Pastoral Care," *Pastoral Psychology* 8/71 (1957): 19; James E. Dittes, "Psychology and a Ministry of Faith," in *Ministry and Mental Health*, ed. Hofmann, p. 149.
71. Hiltner and Colston, *Context of Pastoral Counseling*, pp. 7, 16.
72. Ibid., pp. 21, 29-30.
73. Ibid., p. 16; Oates, *Protestant Pastoral Counseling*, pp. 43, 35-74, 119.
74. Dale Ratliff, letter to the editor, *Pastoral Psychology* 12/113 (1961): 53.
75. Howard Clinebell, "The Challenge of the Speciality of Pastoral Counseling," and Seward Hiltner, "The American Association of Pastoral Counselors: A Critique," *Pastoral Psychology* 15/143 (April 1964): 21, 9.
76. Frederick C. Kuether, "Pastoral Counseling: Community or Chaos," *The Pastoral Counselor* 1 (1963): 3-10.
77. Clinebell, "Challenge of Specialty of Pastoral Counseling": 22.
78. Ibid., pp. 22-23; Clinebell, *Mental Health Through Christian Community*, p. 214; idem, *Basic Types of Pastoral Counseling*, pp. 20, 22.
79. Oates, *Protestant Pastoral Counseling*, pp. 31-32; Hiltner, "Association of Pastoral Counselors: A Critique," 11-14.
80. Orlo Strunk, Jr., ed., *Dynamic Interpersonalism for Ministry* (Nashville: Abingdon Press, 1973), p. 292; Johnson, *Person and Counselor*, p. 42; Seward Hiltner, *Ferment in the Ministry* (Nashville: Abingdon Press, 1969); see also James Dittes, *The Church in the Way* (New York: Charles Scribner's Sons, 1967).

Index

INDEX